Management for Professionals

The Springer series *Management for Professionals* comprises high-level business and management books for executives. The authors are experienced business professionals and renowned professors who combine scientific background, best practice, and entrepreneurial vision to provide powerful insights into how to achieve business excellence.

More information about this series at https://link.springer.com/bookseries/10101

Angel Gavieiro Besteiro

Strategy in Action

A Holistic Management Strategy Framework to Navigate Businesses and Multinational Organizations

Springer

Angel Gavieiro Besteiro
London, UK

ISSN 2192-8096 ISSN 2192-810X (electronic)
Management for Professionals
ISBN 978-3-030-94758-3 ISBN 978-3-030-94759-0 (eBook)
https://doi.org/10.1007/978-3-030-94759-0

This Springer imprint is published by the registered company Springer Nature Switzerland AG
The registered company address is: Gewerbestrasse 11, 6330 Cham, Switzerland

To Isabel, my wife, my lifetime navigator
To Diego, our son, our North Star
To my parents, my departure harbour

Foreword

The 'Art of Management' or the 'Art of the Deal'... the 'Leadership Qualities'... the 'Vision'... All of these lofty concepts and definitions have been and still are identified as the key to corporate success by a large corpus of both formal and 'folk' management science books. A corpus that still constitutes the basis, if any, of the education of many executives. The personal, almost heroic, traits of those at the helm of the institution, with their capacity to read into the future and into others, coupled with the quasi-magnetic attraction that they are able to exert around them, constitute the best explanation of what makes an organization able to survive and to excel in its field. The welcome incorporation to management science of elements stemming from social psychology in recent years, with their emphasis on concepts like empathy, inclusiveness or personal identity recognition, can sometimes be misunderstood as being again innate personal qualities which only those gifted with them can employ as effective leaders.

I will not be the one to deny the value of personal leadership, when it provides an anchor to the organization and creates a positive culture, both important conditions for success. It is also true that in many nascent sectors, especially in those being created by disruptive technologies which may compete amongst each other, having a leadership team with a prescient vision about the future is an essential feature (I will leave open for debate till what extent the same 'blind' processes of natural evolution, and not so much the capacity to anticipate the future, are operating here). But these and other factors linked to the qualities of those at the helm quickly become powerless in the absence of a sound strategy.

I have many times witnessed how the term 'strategy' has been mis-interpreted. Most of the times, those in charge of formulating it end up providing a set of intermediate and final goals, without identifying the clues about how to achieve them. Some other times the planning stops at the enunciation of some more or less vague guiding principles of the strategy, useful no doubt, but short of defining the detailed plans that should explain the modus operandi of the organization. A good strategy never loses sight of the goals, always operates within certain overall hypothesis or principles that enable to maximize the competitive advantages of the business and has built-in mechanisms to challenge and eventually correct itself. But it also defines the concrete steps that the organization needs to take, at all vertical and horizontal dimensions and in a coordinated fashion, to meet the goals of all its stakeholders.

This coordination, that is, the articulation of the many levers of the organization in a coherent way within the strategy, is precisely the focus of this book. Its author, Dr. Angel Gavieiro has a long experience of operational and strategic missions in the corporate world, combined with a sound academic background. This double exposure enables Dr. Gavieiro to filter the classical principles of strategic planning through a lens of concrete experience on the field. While the book is not a manual, the reader will surely feel impelled to action upon reading it, now equipped with the necessary tools for the right holistic planning of the journey ahead of her organization.

UK CEO, Société Générale
London, UK

Demetrio Salorio

Acknowledgements

Management is the most noble of professions if it is practiced well. No other occupation offers as many ways to help others learn and grow, take responsibility and be recognized for achievement, and contribute to the success of a team (Clayton M. Christensen [1]).

A book like this is far from being my own creation, it is a collective effort that cumulatively over time many people have contributed to, in many cases in an unanticipated way and with many years of lapse since they made their mark on the author.

Let me start with the authors of the books explicitly referred in several of the chapters of this book and those of the research papers cited in the Bibliography. As Sir Isaac Newton said, '*If I have seen further, it is by standing on the shoulders of Giants*'. As far as this book is concerned, I can certainly subscribe the latter part of his quote for this book. As such, I am deeply thankful for the permission to refer to their work and contributions and I apologize in advance for any potential misinterpretation from my side of any of their findings and frameworks. Thank you for sharing your research, thinking and legacy.

Turning now to thank another collective of incredibly especial and talented people, for whom I reserve eternal gratitude in my heart, the teams and colleagues that I had the honour to lead and work with during my professional career, both as a strategist and as a banker. There are many to mention but, given the subject matter of the book, at minimum I would like to refer to the strategy-related teams that lived with me through the core of the practice and examples provided in the book. Chronologically, starting from the project teams at McKinsey & Co in the Madrid office; Barclays Bank both Group Strategy & Planning and the Business Development Team at the International Retail & Commercial Banking division; Lloyds Bank including the Financial Institutions Strategy Team, Corporate Banking Strategy & Business Development Team and Wholesale Banking & Markets Decision Support Team; Wells Fargo's Wholesale & International Strategy Team and EMEA Strategy Team; and finishing with the partner companies and clients of AG Strategy & Partners. Thank you for your excellent work, ideas and journey together.

Along with them, it is due a recognition to the CEOs and C-suite executives that entrusted me with the opportunity to either lead some of these teams or to engage our consulting services, so to bring suggested 'best-practices' to improve the process and outcome of strategy development, and to challenge their thinking and/or decisions (sometimes, I must confess, a bit too stubbornly). Thank you for your trust, support and sponsorship.

Getting now closer to the book creation itself, I have a debt of gratitude with the generous and patient reviewers of the book's content. Starting with Peter Newbury, senior officer at the Little Ship Club, who with exquisite detail reviewed the maritime narrative pages that introduce the five parts of the book. In terms of individual chapter review, my profound appreciation goes to Steve Winningham (Introduction, Chaps. 1 and 2), Akhil D. Shah (Chap. 1), Almudena Peña (Chaps. 3 and 6), Neil Allerton (Chaps. 4 and 5), Diana Brightmore-Armour (Chaps. 7 and 8), Demetrio Salorio (Chap. 9), Robert Merrett and Professor Olivier Sibony (Chap. 10), Víctor Matarranz (Chap. 11), Alessandro Hatami (Chap. 12), and last but definitely not least, Rafael Gonzalo, professor at IE Business School, for reviewing the entire book providing very insightful suggestions for its improvement as well as a rigorous peer review; any error or inaccuracy still left in the book is entirely my fault. I had the honour and pleasure to coincide both on a professional and personal basis with most of them during my career, learning tons from their experience. Thank you for dedicating part of your scarce time to provide very insightful feedback and for your fellowship, which I highly cherish.

This book could not possibly be in your hands without the 'buy in' and embracement by the Springer team, an excellent publisher that have made the physical realization of this project a true pleasure. In special, recognition is due to Rocío Torregrosa my editor and amazing guide for this novel author, Parthiban Kannan, Manigandan Jayabalan and their respective teams for the excellent end-to-end project coordination and Dr Prashanth Mahagaonkar for his initial positive hunch on the book that sparked all the rest. Thank you all for believing in this project and bringing this book to life.

Finally, at the end of this page but at the beginning of my heart, my wife, Isabel González Costa for her patience while I was away writing, her grit in supporting me through life's ups & downs and still keeping smiling and, ultimately, for our shared journey with our dear son Diego. Thank you both for your love.

Reference

1. "How Will You Measure Your Life?" by Clayton M. Christensen (Jul-Aug.10; HBR)

Introduction

Twenty years from now you will be more disappointed by the things that you didn't do than by the ones you did do. So, throw off the bowlines. Sail away from the safe harbour. Catch the trade winds in your sails. Explore! Dream! Discover! (Mark Twain)

Strategy, according to the Oxford English dictionary is defined as:

1. *[countable]* a plan that is intended to achieve a particular purpose
2. *[uncountable]* the process of planning something or putting a plan into operation
3. *[uncountable, countable]* the skill of planning the movements of armies in a battle or war

This book is not going to tackle in any depth what strategy is or is not (the 'what'), for which task many other books precede it. Hence, I provide the above dictionary entry as a given, as a starting assumption, so to leave the book free to focus on its actual purpose: the 'how', the action of developing a strategy, in its three definitions, as a plan, as a process and as a skill, within the sphere of the business world (so, leaving outside the book's remit any other areas of human endeavour, like the military, public sector or non-for-profit sector).

The action of developing strategy in business happens within a particular context, within companies. Companies, since first emerged in the late sixteenth century in the coffee shops of London's Exchange Alley [1], as associations of groups of people pooling resources to set up, own and run a business, and its subsequent inheritor, corporations that added the novelty of separating ownership from management. Both have become the undisputable engine of progress and growth in modern capitalist societies.

Having said that, over the more than two decades that I have been in the corporate world, something that has always called my attention is the surprising fact that companies, especially large corporations, which often we refer to as 'organizations', are much less organized than most of us usually imagine or assume.

If you talk to anyone working at these organizations and manage to go pass through the understandable layer of conventional façade to defend the brand for which everyone works, so we talk reality, you will be quite surprised. If you listen carefully to their accounts, about what works well and what does not in their daily jobs, you will quickly conclude that the level of chaos, siloes, wasted effort, misunderstanding and overall noise is quite rampant.

Nevertheless, organizations as live animals, pulling somehow from their own collective will, manage to survive, some even thrive, despite the alleged doze of mayhem. *Why?*

Organizations' Excellence vs Mediocrity

As one reviews management literature from academia, practitioners and management consultants over the last 50 years, attempting to distil the holy grail of excellence in organizations, they find different key traits that apparently seem to correlate well to the data each study used.

After reflecting on my own experience inside the organizations I have worked or consulted for in my career, mostly circumscribed to the Financial Services industry, when I try to identify which of these excellence traits were present in each of them, I struggled to find much correlation. Basically, each organization I knew compared to its competitors was very good at very few things, quite behind on a another few and around average in most other traits, without any of them being close to the 'excellence' pattern described by the literature.

A potential explanation would be that, certainly, the limited sample I was reflecting upon was composed of organizations that would have never been selected by researchers as part of the study group to test for excellence, or at most they would make it into the control group. Fair enough. However, talking over the years with many people in my network across banking, and so covering a large number and variety of financial institutions, their accounts resemble quite often to my own observations in terms of 'distance from excellence', or in other words, we all concurred about the overall 'mediocrity' of the organizations we knew about. *Why?*

Effectively, we could make an extensive list of strategic and operational reasons that could collectively explain perhaps the 80:20 of the observed organizational disfunctions. As we tried to find structure or patterns from that list, not surprisingly in hindsight, it would point to people-related issues in the organization as the common trait, and among them, very saliently, senior executives.

On some occasions, I recall we wondered: *how many of the C-level executives you have worked with in different capacities would you consider to be 'excellent'?* [dear reader, please do take a second to reflect on your own answer before you keep reading]

If we included in the sample not just C-levels, but a wider level of executives across Group, Divisions up to Managing Directors of Business Units, and we expanded the range from 'excellent' to include 'very good', our estimate was in the 10–20% maximum. Only 10–20% of excellence within the executive cadre... it does not sound as much!

Now, *are we talking here about excellence among senior executives in their role as leaders? or as managers? or both?*

Leadership is a very wide term, quite 'hyped' I would say in the recent 10–15 years, but regardless still critical for the teams being led, of course. As such, many books on the subject have been written, with many very interesting angles, from communication, power, team building, coaching, etc..., however, the one that really opened my eyes correlating this topic to the findings and reflections above was 'Management' by Prof. Peter Drucker [2].

A famous quote often attributed to him differentiates the terms: *'Management is doing the things right; Leadership is doing the right things'*. In his book, while Prof. Drucker pays due respect to the criticality of the Leadership role, his acknowledged laser-beam focus was on Management. At a point, he said that Management is a key component of Leadership, and without it this leadership would necessarily become ineffective. This point switched on a light in my mental room.

Given that in today's society the bar for 'excellence' in leadership is generally quite high (i.e. Gandhi, Luther King, Mandela... even in business Andrew Carnegie, Jack Welch, Steve Jobs), the fact that many of the senior executives we observed were or not excellent leaders may be widely argued. However, at least you would expect them to be accomplished Managers, being equipped with the required skillset and practices to manage their areas of responsibility with effectiveness, even most of them were yet developing their leadership profile.

Therefore, the question became, *do senior executives in organizations show excellence in management quality?*

Management Quality

A recent study [3], undertaken over a large sample of 12,000 companies across many industries in 34 countries over 10 years, measured different key dimensions to proxy for management quality. The results were not different from our anecdotical observations: achieving management excellence was a massive challenge for many organizations, with large dispersion in management scores across firms (and within firms), also within the same country. During a decade of study, it was confirmed that the lack of management quality in organizations was long-lasting. Only 6% of firms achieved average scores at or above 4 (out of a maximum score of 5). Not surprisingly, differences of management quality were strongly correlated with large, persistent differences in firm performance in terms of profit growth, profitability, productivity and R&D. So, management quality does matter for achieving excellence in an organization. But, *how?*

The study showed aligned considerations regarding potential causes of management mediocrity: deficient managerial skillsets (i.e. companies from developing vs developed countries), governance structure (i.e. family-owned companies were run with less managerial deliberation), overconfidence by managers (i.e. false perception of own quality) and organizational politics/culture.

As it happens, a large part of my professional career has occurred within the strategy field, either leading this support function in-house for large multinational banks or serving from outside as a management consultant. Also, I have been a senior executive of frontline business units, which has helped to complement the testing of my ideas about strategy from this angle, the decision-maker chair. On both counts, I have been able to bring a formed opinion with regard to the causes identified in the above study.

In my view, in large organizations, the last two factors of the study (overconfidence by managers and organizational politics/culture) become critical because of the number of executives involved, so the negative impact from managerial quality mediocrity is highly amplified. Because of this, I believe the managerial part of the company is the key field where half of the battle in the marketplace is won or lost (the other half is where execution meets the market itself).

But every day we observe that many executives get promoted to managerial positions, starting in a Business Unit and following up to Division or even Group level. *Why is this happening even when their managerial skillset falters?*

Two reasons in my opinion. First, to be promoted in the first place is not necessarily driven by a forward-looking assessment of how managerial capability might be performed, but rather by a backward-looking assessment of results delivered in previous roles. Also, quite crucially, being entirely truthful to the process experienced in many places, promotion also depends on the personal sympathies from and allegiances to other senior executives higher up in the ladder. The promotion/assessment process, by the way, was one of the dimensions analysed in the above referred study in order to proxy managerial quality.

Second, once the executive has been promoted, there are no systematic mechanisms in the organization that support him/her to develop their managerial skillset (let alone the leadership one), other than some formal courses, informal mentoring, or development away day here or there, at all lights insufficient. Thus, as usual, executives learn their managerial (and leadership) cues as they go, with the serendipity and heterogeneity inherent to such a journey. Hence, no surprise the distribution of managerial (and leadership) capability across an organization is so dispersed, as the study demonstrated.

Being strategy one of the key responsibilities of the Management role, I was curious to know, *how excellent are sr. executives and their organizations in developing strategy?*

Management Strategy

Management as a subject is a large universe that only some towering figures, like Prof. Drucker, have the intellect and lifetime dedication to throw a truly discerning light at.

This book will not attempt to look at these heights. Having said that, there was a moment a few years ago when I realized that I had something to contribute to this important topic of management regarding a small but critical part of it, management strategy.

In my years of professional strategy practice, time and again I have found myself arriving at organizations, or parts of them such as Divisions or Business Units, to start building the blocks of management strategy best-practice for their senior executives. Only to find, after a few years, that as the executives moved around many of these best-practices were diluted once new executives arrived and preferred to do things 'their own way', fully disregarding the cumulative existing body of work. Or perhaps large reorganizations, organic or inorganic, suddenly happened and again the best-practice edifice stumbled, so to start rebuilding it yet another time.

Basically, many organizations do not have an established function of management strategy as a key architectural lever of the building, as a perennial element, like, for instance, usually is the case for the Finance function so to control the all-important organization's financial performance, or the Risk function so to effectively monitor risk management.

As I took a business management role in the mid-2010s, this move provided me with some distance from the strategy function role so to learn and reflect, both in terms of leveraging the applied strategy lessons for my new executive role but also harvesting the fruit from the large period (since 2001) dedicated to this attractive but challenging function. From this reflection came the urge to distil, select and combine the key management strategy best-practices (in the form of frameworks) that I found essential to make Business Units, Divisions and Groups effective and performing within organizations. From this gestation period, the Holistic Management Strategy framework (aka HMS, like 'Her Majesty Ship'—analogy which inspiration will shortly resonate in this book—) was born.

HMS brought together ten frameworks at three organizational levels which I concluded were enough to run the bulk of management strategy responsibilities along and across the organization to drive it as a coherent and aligned sum of the parts. Many of the frameworks derived from my own development within organizations, sometimes starting from pre-existing ones in management consulting firms and a few were also borrowed from management literature.

Thus, HMS became the soul and heart of this book that is now in your hands dear reader. I hope it adds some value to you in your role within your business or organization.

Book's Intent

This book will not attempt to replicate yet another effort to distil drivers of success by reviewing and comparing a set of multinational organizations. Instead, it will attempt a bottom-up effort to share the management strategy frameworks and best-practices that are essential for a senior executive to be effective from the very moment he or she starts being responsible for a business, for instance, as a Managing Director of a Business Unit, and continuing his/her journey up through the 'greasy pole', as he/she gains higher level of managerial responsibility at Divisional level, until ultimately conquering the CEO top post at Group level.

Necessarily, being a book based on my own professional experience, it will be tainted and limited by it. Thus, first and foremost this is an empirical, inductive piece of work, so I would be cautious on the generalization of its practices and conclusions, as I am sure there must be key elements that it may have overlooked.

Second, as my experience has occurred in the Financial Services industry, the examples and tales shared are from this industry, and though my intent is for the HMS management strategy best-practices shared to be extendable to other industries, I do not know how well that would work, so caution again.

Third, precisely due to the limitations of my approach, I would encourage other professionals, academia and business authors to build from this limited edifice to keep adding to it so that, in time, perhaps we could arrive at a body of knowledge on this matter that can provide the level of generalization required to produce universal good to senior executives and organizations that opt for taking this subject matter to its full potential.

Book' Structure

The synopsis for the book is depicted below, *how not?*, as a PowerPoint slide of the HMS pyramid (Fig. 1).

The ten frameworks are distributed in three levels, two for Group, two for Division and six for Business Unit.

At Business Unit level, two 'slopes' differentiate frameworks that concern 'Existing Geography/Business' (i.e. Business Model / Strategy Blueprint / Financial Plan) vs 'New Geography/Business' (i.e. Attractiveness vs Opportunities / Inorganic Growth Process), since the questions to answer and approach to adopt are quite different. As well, the five frameworks are shown against Strategy Development phase vs Business Development phase (prior to the Implementation phase). The sixth framework (i.e. Strategy & Execution) brings together the connection among

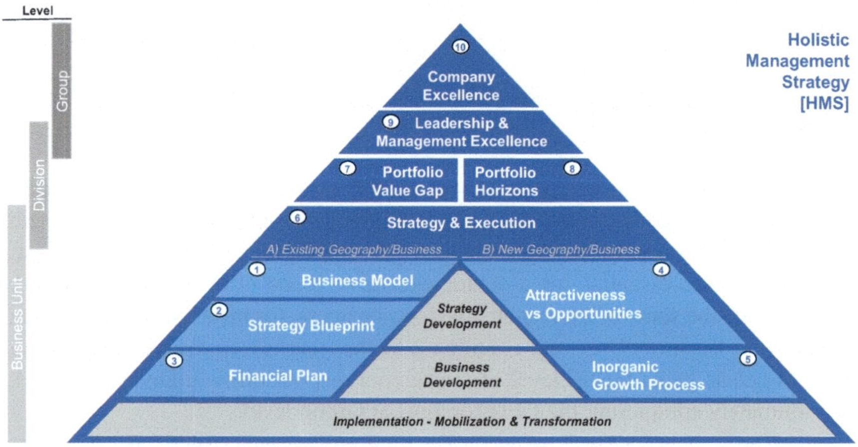

Fig. 1 Holistic Management Strategy framework. Sources: Holistic Management Strategy© framework (Angel Gavieiro; 2015)

the other five and discusses the 'Mobilization & Transformation' necessary to prepare the company for the Implementation phase.

The 'Existing Geography/Business' slope represents the default business-as-usual in management strategy for any organization, big or small. The 'New Geography/Business' slope is obviously relevant only when an organization considers the strategic decision of expanding, either geographically or in terms of business remit to adjacent arenas where it was not present before.

At Divisional level, two frameworks are required (i.e. Portfolio Value Gap / Portfolio Horizons) which analyse its portfolio of Business Units in terms of dynamics of value and time, respectively. At Group level, two frameworks are considered (i.e. Leadership & Management Excellence / Company Excellence) for addressing the critical dimensions that could provide executives, both as individuals and as a collective, with the skillset, balanced design and considered decision-making discipline to achieve and sustain excellence.

In deciding how to tell this story, I had two options: going top-down from the Group level, or bottom-up from the Business Unit level. I decided for the latter for several reasons. First, because I think it will be easier to understand for most readers, since their day-to-day experiences sit within the Business Unit. Also, it is not so difficult to visualize oneself having the first executive responsibility in a Business Unit, and so relate to the challenges it entails and make sense of the basic building blocks of management strategy best-practice.

Second, because it is at Business Unit level where the marketplace battle happens for any organization; any level above is a level of aggregation but not of client-facing and competitor-facing interaction. At the Business Unit is where the crux of strategy and execution gets won or lost, hence where the managerial practices are of life-or-death importance.

Third, because in order to bring these frameworks to life, it was advisable to adopt some form of storytelling format that could make easier for the reader to understand the concepts as well as to gain, hopefully, some entertainment out of the reading (otherwise I would risk the book would become too dull or academic to shallow). Thus, I threaded across the book, at the start of each of its five parts, a metaphor in the way of a maritime based story of a navy officer as he gains successive command and responsibility, bottom-up, starting in a navy ship, Her Majesty Ship (HMS again!), during the eighteenth to nineteenth turn of century... the great Age of Sail!

Following this bottom-up approach, then, I divide the work in five Parts. Part I (Chaps. 1–3), where we review the three frameworks for 'Existing Geography/Business'. First, the Business Model framework that allows you to take snapshots of your business 'as-is', and similarly can be used to project the targeted business model 'as-should-be' in the future. Second, the Strategy Blueprint framework that will help you to chart your path from the current business model to the future one, becoming the bedrock of strategy development for a Business Unit. Third, the Financial Plan framework that will translate the strategy into numbers within the Medium Term Planning process embedded in the organization.

Part II (Chaps. 4–6), where we cover first the two frameworks for 'New Geography/Business'. Starting with the 'Attractiveness vs Opportunities' framework that will help you to prioritize geographies for an eventual organic/inorganic expansion and potential targets for the latter case. Following with the 'Inorganic Growth Process' that provides four-step governance and activity framework for a disciplined execution in the challenging terrain of mergers & acquisitions and alliances. In addition, this part tackles the 'Strategy & Execution' framework, which puts the previous five frameworks in context by: (a) using a clear semantic convention for the phases of Strategy Development, Business Development and Implementation; (b) introducing for the latter phase the processes for Mobilization (of the people) and Transformation (of the general management levers).

Part III (Chaps. 7 and 8) focuses on two frameworks at Division level that necessarily are of portfolio aggregation nature, namely The 'Portfolio Value Gap' and the 'Portfolio Horizons' frameworks. They will be very useful to gain perspective about the drivers of future activity of the BUs and to take decisions of resource reallocation among them. They apply equally at Group level when looking at the portfolio of Divisions.

Part IV (Chaps. 9 and 10), reaches the Group level, with two frameworks focused on achieving Excellence. On the critical topic of 'Leadership & Management Excellence', the THICOSIV framework has been distilled from multiple readings from academia and practitioners (e.g. Kahneman, Ariely, Carnegie, Rumelt, Buffett,...) and, although I have not had yet the opportunity of applying it, I feel it will be likely proven to be very successful.. My recommendation would be to roll it, to start with, across all senior executives at Group level leveraging a 18–24 month programme to ensure the upgrading and homogenization of their leadership and management standards as individuals and as a collective.

Chapter 10, as the capstone of the HMS pyramid, addresses 'Company Excellence', where I tried to summarize in one framework the essence of the enormous work that Jim Collins and Jerry Porras successfully undertook in 'Build to Last' (1994; Harper Business), applying it to two leader banks in the industry. Their master work, given that it precisely derives from the experience over the span of +60 years of 18 'visionary' companies (as compared to a similar number in the control sample), has looked to me over time a compellingly tested approach to achieve a company's balanced design towards excellence. In addition, in an attempt to build upon their work, a Decision-Making framework is suggested (distilled from my own take on best-practices) to avoid as much as possible the threat of bias/noise and politics, so to ensure a considered decision-making that 'lean' the company towards excellence.

Finally, Part V is a closing dual chapter focused on the Future of Strategy. Chapter 11, where I want to share a reflection upon the Strategy Function itself, in my judgement one of the most poorly understood and underleveraged among organizations. I believe there is a substantial potential for value creation in organizing this function towards best-practice, which would contribute in a very powerful way to decision-making for senior executives. Most crucially, preserving the questions, answers, decisions and results obtained via this function would be like creating a long-term memory in the organization that would go beyond of specific people or teams moving in and out over time. I would suggest that this Strategy

Function capability should be demanded by any sensible Board of Directors acting in the best interests of their shareholders and stakeholders at large in the same way as the Finance function is required.

The final Chap. 12 is dedicated to Digital Strategy as the response of this decision science in the context of the twenty-first century's main paradigm shift, digital disruption. Many industries are being transformed globally driven by the innovation impact of digitalization of their business models. From news and taxis to books and music, everything is changing very rapidly. Financial services industry is not an exception, and this phenomenon must affect the way Strategy is conducted in organizations. Even more importantly, Strategy needs to provide an answer about how to undertake a successful digital transformation especially for complex, large, multinational banks. As a McKinsey's report [4] highlights, involving a cross-industry review of the state of digital transformation, two patterns emerge: (a) industries that go through it experiment a significant shrinkage of revenues and profit pools; (b) a concentration of the competitors distribution towards a subset of winners, leaving a long tail of underperforming and failing players. Thus, Digital is not just another change, it is The Change... *is your Strategy ready for this ultimate test?*

Now, the final word, my dear reader, rests with you. My only hope is that even a small part of this book could call your attention and so perhaps inspire you to bring it to life within your business reality, creating value for your executives and their teams... making ***Strategy In Action*** an impactful benefit for you and your organization's success.

References

1. "The Corporation" by Joel Bakan (2004; Free Press)
2. "Management" by Peter Drucker (1973, 2008 revised; Collins)
3. "Why Do We Undervalue Competent Management?" by Raffaella Sadun, Nicholas Bloom, John Van Reenen (Sept.17; HBR)
4. "The Case For Digital Reinvention" by Jacques Bughin, Laura LaBerge and Anette Mellbye (Feb.17; McKinsey & Co)

Contents

Part II About 'Strategy for New Geographies and/or Businesses' and 'Strategy & Execution'

Part III About 'Portfolio Strategy'

Part IV About 'Company & Leadership Excellence'

About the Author

Dr. Angel Gavieiro Besteiro has more than 25 years of international executive experience as a banker and strategist across corporate and investment banking and retail and commercial banking, covering EMEA, North America, and Asia-Pacific markets out of the UK, the UAE, and Spain. As a strategist, he has held senior executive roles as SVP/divisional head of strategy and business development for Barclays Bank's international retail and commercial banking division, Lloyds Bank's wholesale banking and markets division, and Wells Fargo's EMEA region. Before that, he was a management consultant at McKinsey & Co. In addition, he is the founder and managing partner of AG Strategy & Partners, a London-based management consulting and advisory boutique focused on the financial services industry. As a banker, Angel has run business P&L as SVP head of domestic corporate markets for Al Hilal Bank's wholesale banking division and agency treasury services and corporate finance for Lloyds Bank's financial institutions group, starting his career in debt capital markets at Société Générale. He has an MBA from Duke University (USA) and Ph.D. in financial economy from the Universidad Autónoma de Madrid (Spain). Angel is a Fulbright scholar, Fuqua scholar, and Liveryman of the Worshipful Company of International Bankers of the City of London.

List of Figures

Part I

About 'Strategy for Existing Geography and Business'

Without goals, and plans to reach them, you are like a ship that has set sail with no destination (Fitzhugh Dodson).

You, dear successful Team Leader, with top record sales in your business and strong market recognition, you have just been rightly promoted to Managing Director of a full Business Unit, congratulations!

Now, you suddenly face quite different challenges compared to the ones you were used to as a Team Leader: a shock, as your company (like the majority of them) has not prepared you to become a line manager; among the shocks... Strategy... *what is this?* (b/s surely!—you think—).

You fetch a book somebody recommended, sounds nice and easy, in theory.... but, back to reality, is way too messy, so, *where do you really start?*

Well, let me spark our imagination with a maritime story, leveraging navigation, the art of directing a vessel from one place to another, as a metaphor for the development of strategy. Parallelism not better reflected than in the words of Richard Dunn [1], '*done well, it ensures safe, speedy travel; executed poorly, it can lead to disaster*', or in the observations by the seventeenth century diarist and administrator of the English navy Samuel Pepys, '*the best navigator is the best looker-out*'.

* * *

In 1782, Great Britain is fighting the American Revolutionary War. You are a First Lieutenant, second in command on board of a late-eighteenth century, 20-gun, one-deck ship. Today we have rough seas, 15–20 ft waves and strong south-southwest winds off The Bay of Biscay, between French and Spanish waters, returning back home from a long Atlantic crossing.

Suddenly your captain falls terribly ill, so you are given command in a full storm... what do you do?... you start where the action is: what sails are in use? what is the crew labouring with as we speak? (*Action Plans*).

Once you have reached the quarterdeck, having a quick look at the weather, you order to trim here, haul there, so you try to put some sort of initial 'order in the chaos'

(*Strategic Priorities*). With these two you have just taken the steering and the sails in your hands, so you are now really commanding the ship. Aye, aye, captain!

After a few hours the storm calms down, so you take a respite to ask yourself, what is the status of the ship's arrangement (*Business Model framework*)? where are we in our navigation plan (*Strategy Blueprint framework*)? and by the way, where are we with our supplies and crew? (*Financial Plan framework*). So, you check with the Master, who after some reckoning helps you to approximately locate the ship on a nautical chart, estimate how far she has sailed till now and what is the distance to the destination.

At this point it is perhaps wise, using the weather lull, to start with a review of the ship's status (*Business Model framework*): what is the current state of the ship (*Business Model 'as-is'*), and how do you need to change it to ensure arrival? (*Business Model 'as-should-be'*)

First, you need to understand the seas your ship is navigating in (*Marketplace*), which has two main components in constant interaction: the natural elements (*Clients*) and other ships (*Competitors*) (i.e. the 'Three Cs', the third one being your *Company*, your ship!). You try to understand their trends, sudden movements, special features... you find out as much as you can and try to foresee where they are heading (*Market Dynamics*); also, you compare your ship with the natural elements and against other ships (*Diagnosis*), from many different angles and perspectives.

Then, you observe very closely the natural elements (*Client Segmentation*), one by one, separating finely the types of winds, seas, tides, currents (*Client Segments*) that affect the speed and direction of your ship towards the destination, trying to predict what you may encounter in your journey.

At this point, you compare alternative passage plans (*Strategic Alternatives*), estimating the days each will approximately take (*Financial Impact*), so to decide the preferred one (*Core Strategy*). This preferred passage plan determines which wind (*Client Strategy*), sailing tack (*Product Strategy*) and routes (*Geographical Strategy*) to take.

This will serve you then to reorganize the ship's sailing plan accordingly (*Value Proposition Definition*), adapting all the ship's components that affect its interaction with the natural elements to best favour the navigation, such as sail surface, which sails to deploy, angle of sailing, weight distribution, ... (*Product/Services, Pricing, Promotions, and Positioning*).

From there, you reorganize the ship as necessary (*Value Proposition Delivery*) to facilitate the sailing plan, arranging yards and sails, reviewing routines, training manoeuvres, etc.... (*Segmentation, Staff, Structure, Systems, Style, Shared Outlook*).

In parallel to this reorganization, you keep your purser by your side estimating the changes in disposition of crew, supplies and rations needed (*i.e. Financial Plan framework: Financial Drivers Analysis, Baseline Financial Modelling, and Investment/Divestment Cases*).

With all of that it looks like you have an idea of the 'target' ship that you need for your voyage, but unfortunately you do not have the luxury of a dry dock to undertake the works, instead you will have to modify or adjust it as you sail, quite a challenge!

You will need to get a navigation plan (*Strategy Blueprint framework*) that you can communicate again and again to your crew to ensure everybody is 'onboard' and we are on course.

The plan starts with reminding ourselves of our ultimate destination (*Purpose*): why are we in this ship (*Mission*)? what the destination is going to look like (*Vision*)? how we are we going to behave together (*Values*)? and where our destination and intermediate milestones are (*Goals*)?

Then we share the anticipated weather conditions (*Diagnosis*), so everybody understands the reasons for change of tack, the chosen navigation course (*Core Strategy*) and how you intend to reorganize the ship (*Business Model 'as-should-be'*) for optimal navigation. Thus, you order to execute on the new 'order of the chaos' (*Strategic Priorities*) and the crew gets on with changing masts, rigging and sails accordingly (*Action Plans*).

Now, you are on course to the destination, only to find new storms and unexpected changes in the natural elements, or other ships that force us to change course; with a bit of luck, we can anticipate these, and we change again the navigation plan, ship's arrangement and the disposition of supplies and crew as required to stay on track.

You look to the horizon as, deep down, you reflect that, after this terrible storm, if you successfully bring back ship and crew to your destination, the Master & Commander appointment will be waiting for you.

* * *

This, my dear Managing Director, is ***Strategy in Action*** for an ***Existing Geography and Business***.

Reference

1. "Navigational Instruments" by Richard Dunn (2016; National Maritime Museum)

1 Business Model

For an 'Existing Geography and Business', the Business Model framework is designed to provide a snapshot of a Business Unit (BU) 'as-is' at present, as well as to visualize this business model 'as-should-be' at a point in the future. This is the fundamental block upon which a strategy development exercise occurs at Business Unit level (Fig. 1.1).

The framework has 5 components, 2 of them external to the Business Model per se but are critical input and output to the BU Business Model hence the reason for being included in the framework:

- Market Dynamics: Looks outside of the BU at clients and competitors.
- Financial Impact: Looks at the BU's financial performance.

The core components of the BU Business Model are:

- Client Segmentation (i.e. the 'who'): The lenses through which the BU looks at the marketplace to determine which clients to serve, lenses that may logically vary among competitors.
- Value Proposition Definition (i.e. the 'what'): The offering that the BU brings to each client segment.
- Value Proposition Delivery (i.e. the 'how'): The way the BU organizes itself to provide its offering to the clients.

The elements displayed under each component are an illustrative non-exhaustive list, which should be tailored for each BU. The key success factors for the application of this framework are to deep dive into each of these elements to understand their detail and, for each targeted client segment, to elicit a horizontal visualization of the alignment across the components of the Business Model.

Let us analyze each component more carefully.

A. Gavieiro Besteiro, *Strategy in Action*, Management for Professionals,
https://doi.org/10.1007/978-3-030-94759-0_1

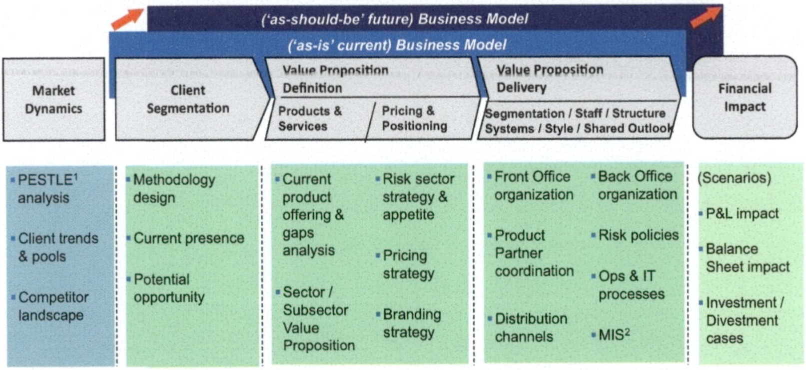

Fig. 1.1 Business Model framework. Note: Elements suggested under the framework are illustrative and non-exhaustive. 1. PESTLE = Political, Economic, Social, Technological, Legal and Environmental; 2. MIS = Management Information Systems. Sources: 'Holistic Management Framework v.5' (Angel Gavieiro; Apr.17; AG Strategy & Partners)

1.1 Market Dynamics

Everything starts and finishes with a market. Ships come and go but the natural elements in the ocean remain, in constant flux, but remain.

Determining what is the marketplace you are in and, as importantly, who are the players you are competing with may seem trivial... until when it ceases to be so.

For instance, the retail banking market might have been defined, in a not-so-distant past, like the provision of current and savings accounts, credit and payments to retail customers by a limited number of authorized deposit-taking entities (e.g. in the UK, banks, credit unions, friendly societies and building societies). Fast-forward just a few years to come to the realization that these activities are currently provided also by many other entities, from grocery retailers like Tesco in the UK, online logistic mammoths like Amazon, to telecom providers or peer-to-peer lenders (i.e. network of individuals lending and borrowing among themselves, without any banking intermediary).

'Well, perhaps' you think, but this does not happen in the more sophisticated corporate banking market, where for centuries bankers have been extending working capital and term lending via the credit underwriting activity funded out retail savings or wholesale funding. Until you realize that many of these corporates long ago started, in parallel, also to secure their equity raisings and bond issuance directly in the capital markets from institutional investors. 'Well, no problem' you reason, banks have been capturing that activity by expanding their services to the provision of investment banking. Only to find that, nowadays, institutional investors have looked for ways to bypass the bank as an intermediary and develop direct lending to corporates of all sizes, or for corporates to extend supply chain finance to their SME suppliers funded with their own excess cash, or for networks of high-net-worth individuals to jointly create funds of private equity and private debt for SMEs. The world is certainly changing!

Who is your client? Who is your competitor?... now it is a bit more confusing.

Identifying your clients and competitors is the first non-trivial step and, as implied by the examples above, the definition of your market changes over time, sometimes quite rapidly as all banks have realized since 2014 with the start of the FinTech revolution (a lot more about this exciting topic in Chap. 12).

Once the market boundary is defined, then you are ready to analyze, *but what exactly? everything?*

Yes and no. You need to be open to all questions and sources of information, but time and resources for analysis are limited (and must be limited, if we are to avoid 'analysis paralysis'), so there is the need to prioritize the areas of focus for the research. *How?*

Not a clear rule here, intuition and experience will guide you, but perhaps useful to look at several dimensions such as client characterization (i.e. revenues and profit pools, segment sizes and growths), dynamics (i.e. PESTLE[1] trends, competitiveness and customer needs changes) and benchmarking (i.e. comparative profitability, market shares and shares of wallet). And for each of these dimensions, *how?*

With a framework, of course. A solid framework is a Mutually Exclusive Comprehensively Exhaustive (MECE) issue tree of the focus areas to analyze. You can do that either by creating the issue tree from scratch in a deductive manner or by leveraging a pre-existing, tested framework out there.

Figure 1.2 shows a real example of a business, part of a bigger banking group, dedicated to the provision of treasury services (let us call it 'TS'), where the main problem to solve was how to grow to the next level. The tree developed for the analysis started to look at clients, competitors and the company's current position. On the client subtree, identified client segments or types, the product/service needs and the trends impacting them; in that subtree, from the preliminary analysis done, it looked like internal clients (from other parts of the banking group) were one of the most promising pools to study. Moving to the competitors' subtree, we reviewed competitor types, customer bases, offering, market shares and margins, finding that the latter were the most interesting hypothesis to investigate further. The bottom subtree looked at the internal position leveraging the 3 core elements of the Business Model framework (as we will discover in the next 3 sections); the analysis identified the most promising client sectors (i.e. public sector / financial institutions/corporates) and the most promising opportunity for efficiency improvement (i.e. current processes). Subsequently to this issue tree analysis, further detailed analysis zeroed only in the identified 4 hypotheses, therefore switching from a deductive to an inductive approach.

By contrast, if the focus area is to understand the competitive dynamics in the industry, perhaps it is easier to draw Porter's Five Forces framework [1] and analyze each of the areas (i.e. bargaining power of buyers, bargaining power of sellers,

[1] Political, Economic, Social, Technological, Legal and Environmental.

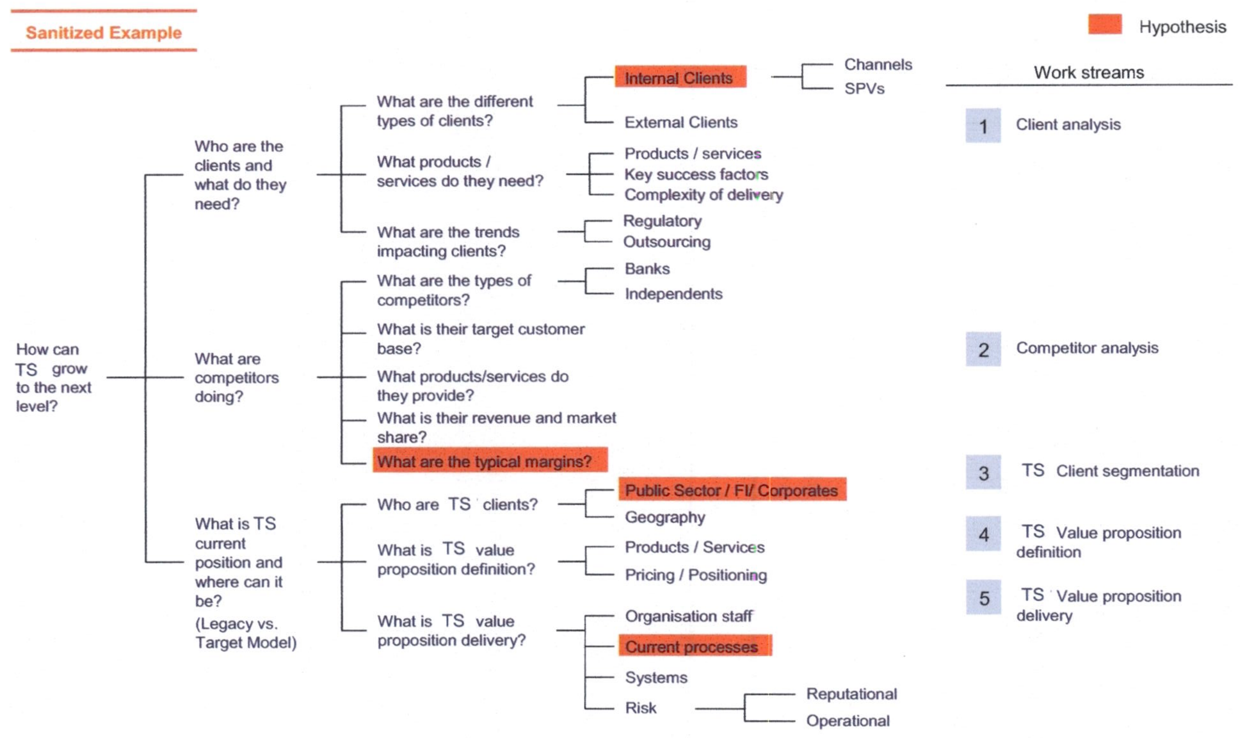

Fig. 1.2 Issue Tree (example). Sources: Sanitized example

substitute products, new entrants and internal rivalry). The example below was developed for a Middle Eastern bank in the competitive context of the Gulf Cooperation Council (GCC[2]) market in 2016 (Fig. 1.3).

Each of the five forces shows trends positive (in blue) or negative (in red) from the viewpoint of the bank. Thus, for instance, Internal Rivalry was a 'mixed trend' force, on the one hand favourable because international banks were exiting the GCC market easing down lending competition, on the other hand unfavourable because of the rapid proliferation of Islamic banks in the market; similarly, Political/Macro external force was 'mixed trend', with the benefit from high oil prices was offset by the risk of QE tapering and Arab Spring. Overall, this bank, having achieved a dominant position in the region, manifested in a competitive advantage in terms of bargaining power with Suppliers and Buyers, it was now facing strong headwinds in particular from New Entrants, Substitute Products and Regulatory pressure. Like with the issue tree analysis reviewed earlier, further detailed analysis zeroed only in some of the identified trends of the Five Forces framework, therefore switching from a deductive to an inductive approach.

Another very interesting exercise is to analyze competitive dynamics with the Strategy Canvas framework [2, 3]. Strategy canvas is a Blue Ocean Strategy methodology that visualizes the value curves of each player or group of players based on key industry factors that determine the industry competitiveness. The example below was developed for the Corporate and Investment Banking industry in 2012, which helped to cluster the competitors into five groups depending on the factors of competitiveness they lever and to identify two areas of high competitive intensity (Fig. 1.4).

The industry factors need to be, ideally, independent without much overlap. In this case, 7 factors were identified as relevant for the analysis: 3 differentiated the Client Orientation (i.e. Institutional Investors vs Corporates vs Retail), 2 their Product Focus (i.e. Liquidity and Price Discovery vs Lending Capability), and the final 2 were Scale & Geographical Scope and Relationship Focus. The competitors were clustered in 5 groups depending on the mix of their respective Business Models (as far as Corporate and Investment Banking business), which were then plotted against the 7 industry factors using a numerical 0–10 scale. The resulting Strategy Canvas told a very interesting narrative about the existence of 2 battles, one for the 'Primary Markets' (i.e. issuance of bonds and equities or extending loans) vs one for the 'Secondary Markets' (i.e. sales and trading towards institutional investors), where only 2 of the competitor groups (i.e. 'Global CIB and Local Universals' and 'CIB Specialists') were playing in both battlegrounds.

At the end of this phase of analysis, surely you will still feel that many areas have been left to be explored... but that is fine, later on as you develop your way through the Business Model framework other questions will pop that will suggest you revisit the Market Dynamics analysis again and complement it with additional focused deep dives.

---

[2] Saudi Arabia, Kuwait, Qatar, Bahrain, UAE and Oman.

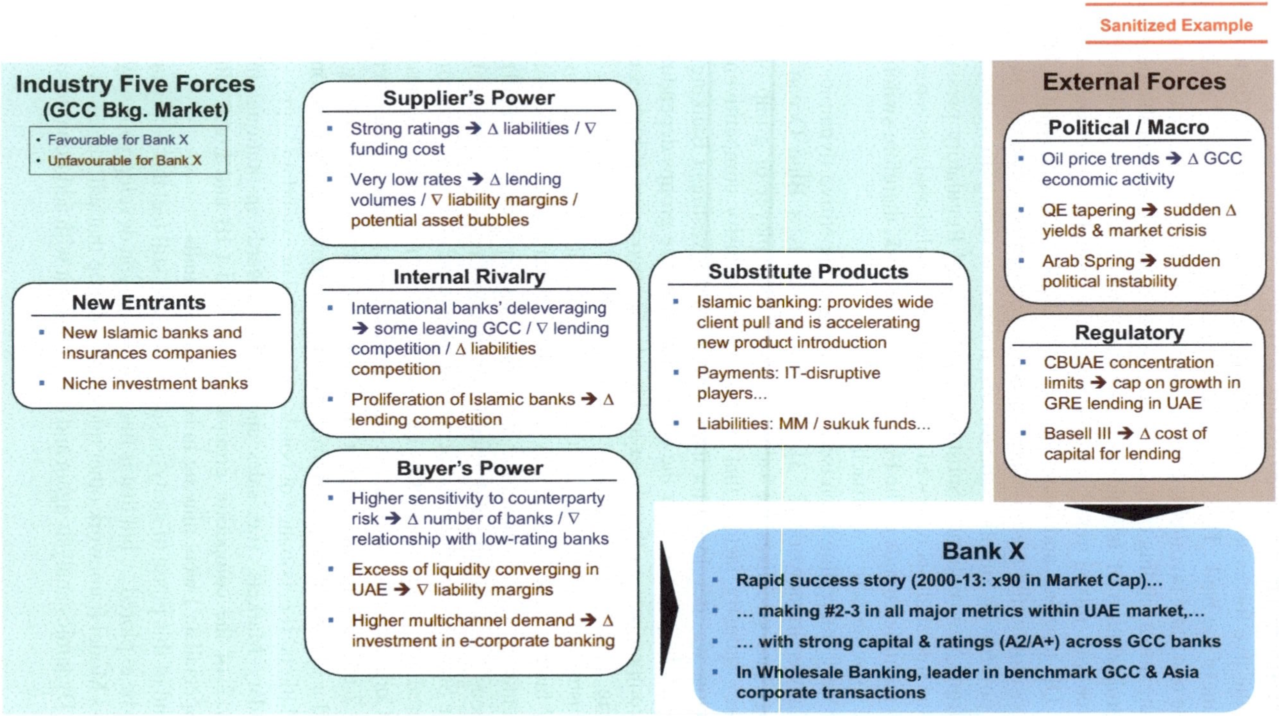

Fig. 1.3 Five Forces framework (example). Sources: Sanitized example; bank website and financials; 'Holistic Management Framework v.5' (Angel Gavieiro; Apr.17; AG Strategy & Partners)

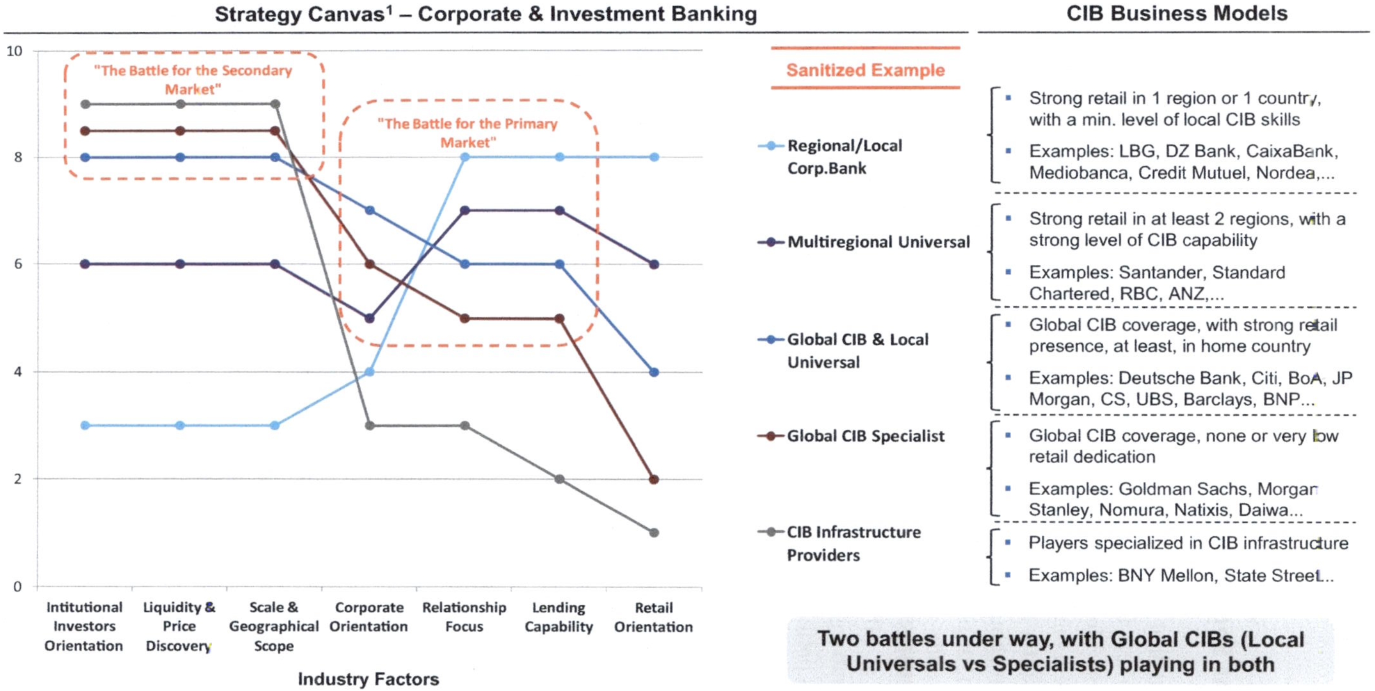

Fig. 1.4 Strategy Canvas framework (example). 1. Strategy canvas is a Blue Ocean Strategy methodology that visualizes the value curves of each competitor or competitor group based on key industry factors that determine the industry competitiveness. Sources: Sanitized example; 'Holistic Management Framework v.5' (Angel Gavieiro; Apr. 17; AG Strategy & Partners) [2, 3]

Hence, no need to fully consume your research capacity in this first step, let us leave some of these resources available for later in the process, we will need them again.

1.2 Client Segmentation

At the moment that you touch Client Segmentation, you pass the frontier from discussing Markets Dynamics (i.e. Clients and Competitors...) to discussing your current Business Model (i.e. . . .Company, as per the 3 C's framework), because segmenting clients necessarily entails wearing certain glasses, which will be different from competitor to competitor.

The decision about what glasses to wear defines a lot 'the way', idiosyncratic to your institution, of positioning itself in the marketplace. This is quite true even for 'competing' brands within the same bank. For instance, at Lloyds Bank after the acquisition of HBOS it was decided to retain the 2 retail brands, Lloyds and Halifax, but addressed at different client segments, hence the 'glasses' used to identify segments and subsegments were very different in each one.

Some banks prefer segmentation approaches based on the characterization of the market's client base, defining cuts based on features such as, for instance, in wealth management, the average income and investable asset sizes to differentiate segments such as Affluent, Upper Affluent, High Net Worth Individuals and Ultra Hight Net Worth Individuals.

Other banks choose behavioural segmentation cuts based on, for instance in retail banking, client's lifecycle where the resulting segments track different stages in people's life, usually marked by key life events: Youth, Young Professionals, Married Couples, Families, Empty Nesters and Retirees.

The whole point of segmenting, which in many banks is not followed consistently throughout, is that you do so because you are genuinely convinced that each of these segments has fundamental different needs to the point that you believe you will create more value for those individuals (and for the bank) if you design a greatly differentiated value proposition for each segment. If you have two segments for which you dedicate the same, or practically the same value proposition, then there is no justification for separating them in the first place.

The act of segmenting will become, therefore, the first 'high stakes' step you will make in the foundation of your strategy and your eventual competitive advantage in the marketplace. 'High stakes' because, if coherently implemented, you will subsequently develop the value proposition offered to each segment (the 'what') accordingly, and you will sink investment building up the organization and processes to deliver that value proposition (the 'how')... so you will be 'locked-in' into those segments for a long while. Hence, please do take your time to define your segments wisely. But, *how?*

The key is to identify differentiated and meaningful clients' needs and pivot them accordingly so that each of the resulting segments is large enough and homogeneous enough. At the same time, you need to keep an eye on your current capabilities (and

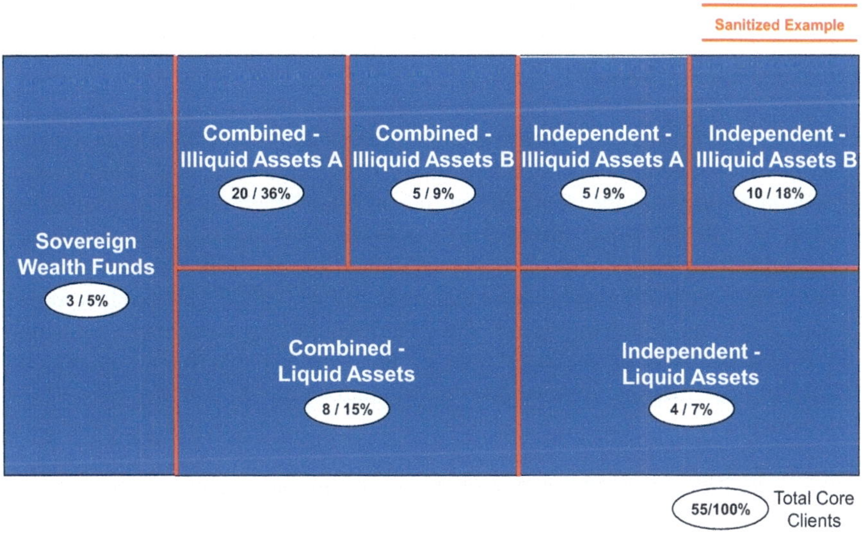

Fig. 1.5 Asset Managers—Client Segmentation (example). Sources: Sanitized example

your expected capacity to build additional ones) so to ensure you will be able to deliver the value propositions that will fulfil the customers' needs. In other words, you should not segment in isolation, you need to move backwards and forwards along the Business Model framework horizontally to ensure the consistency and the feasibility of segment and proposition.

Thus, for instance a bank's Financial Institutions BU, for its participation in the marketplace of Asset Managers, decides to go for a behavioural segmentation articulated along the axis of whether or not the asset manager was part of a 'Combined' group (i.e. belongs to bank or insurance company) vs 'Independent'. Within each, whether or not the fund focused on any combination of 'Illiquid Asset's (e.g. Private Equity, Property or Infrastructure); and within the former case, whether or not they were open to receive from this bank different products/services or only a single product/service ('A' vs 'B'). Thus, quite apparently, despite looking at the client behaviour, this segmentation had a close eye also at the real capabilities the bank had at its disposal, namely in this example: (i) having strong relationship with the parent group that could be eventually leveraged to further penetrate the share of wallet of its asset manager; (ii) having a strong product-line catering for fund management in property, infrastructure and private equity and (iii) having the possibility of cross-selling many products to a given fund management (Fig. 1.5).

Another much more sophisticated example in a corporate bank, was the 'Trusted Relationship' segmentation, designed with the purpose of deepening client relationships and increasing share of wallet penetration. This segmentation was developed post-2008 Credit Crisis, a period where banks were experiencing a continuous push for deleveraging, and so reduced lending year after year, along with the pressure to actively manage clients with non-performing loans.

It was an example of hybrid segmentation, combining both behavioural-based vs characterization-based approaches. In this context, the challenge was that the segmentation required two initial filters:

- First to fully separate the clients with debt problems ('Non-Core') from the rest, usually taking a characterization type filter (not depicted in the illustration below).
- Second, to prioritize the clients to dedicate the banks' increasingly scarce lending capacity; this obviously demanded to estimate very carefully the opportunity potential from each client, in turn, determined by the bank's current product and service capabilities (plus those that could be built with the limited investment available in the following years). This effort would help to identify clients that had real potential vs the ones with no potential but that were important to support for different reasons like having attractive, patient deposits ('Low Potential').

After filtering out the 'Low Potential' clients, now the actual behavioural segmentation could be done based on 2 dimensions and 2 measurements. The dimensions were:

- 'Holistic-client-needs' as per comparison with its sector peers... *do/will we have capability to cover all/most of this client's needs or only partly?* ('Trusted Relation' vs 'Specialist Relation', in short 'TR' vs 'SR').
- 'Time-to-potential' as per comparison with its sector peers... *has our business with this client reached potential or not yet?* ('TR' vs 'potential-TR'; 'SR' vs 'potential-SR').

The measurements were:

- Quantitative, in order to track the expected increased share of wallet penetration in terms of depth (i.e. total revenue per client) and width (i.e. number of products per client).
  This would produce a neat 2×2 matrix, appropriately calibrated per each sector or industry, with 4 quadrants (being the top-right one, high revenue and high number of products, the one generating the most positive impact).
- Qualitative, in order to track the expected deepened relationship penetration in terms of the bank's capability to fulfil all the potential financial needs of the client (Trusted Relation (TR)) or only part of them (Specialist Relation (SR)).
  To determine whether the client fit TR vs SR, and whether it had achieved a complete penetration or was on the way to do so (potential state), a series of 6–7 qualitative parameters would be assessed, during the Key Account Planning sessions between relationship managers, product specialists and top management at the bank. Some of these parameters would be whether the bank was lead/sole provider for the client, involved in its strategic priorities, engaged at CEO level and multiple layers, or was recognized by the client as having deep expertise in its industry.

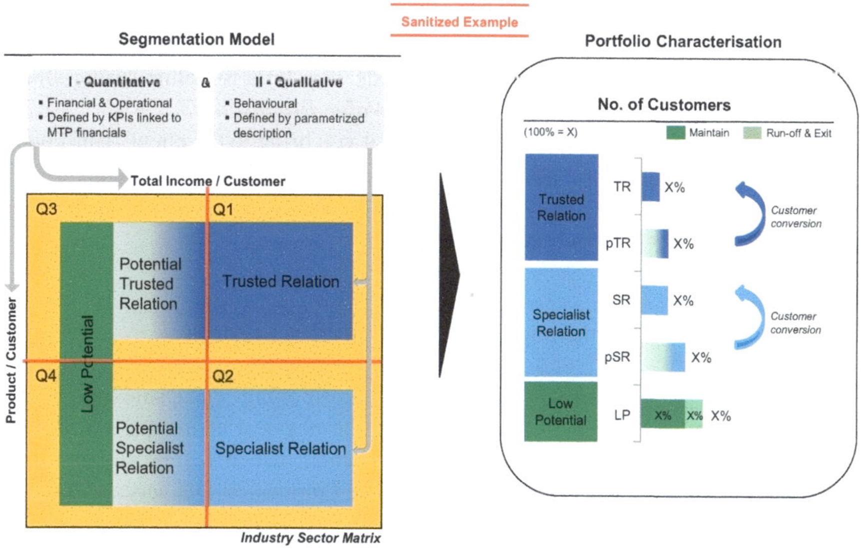

Fig. 1.6 Trusted Relationship—Client Segmentation (example). Note: Applies to 'Core' clients after 'Non-Core' filter (i.e. clients in arrears/default) has been used. Sources: Sanitized example

Thus, when you put it all together, the segmentation ended up being quite simple (see Fig. 1.6). The whole game for the relationship managers was to focus on the clients with potential, bringing the product specialists to satisfy their clients' needs over time. Therefore, progressively we would migrate the relationship, being either of a TR or a SR nature, from a 'potential' state to a 'realized' state. This migration was proven by being the client both in the right quadrants (quantitative test) and with the right ticks across most of the relationship parameters (qualitative test), which automatically would translate in the expected higher revenues.

Designing and, even more importantly, gathering the management information necessary for undertaking this type of more sophisticated segmentation is not a small effort. However, the level of depth reached in understanding how the bank was advancing in the relationship penetration and how this migration did translate into results was definitely worth it. The cherry on the cake for the team was to experience how the apparent complexity of the design was ultimately implemented in a very intuitive and simple framework for the entire organization to use and refer to, as a single compass to guide their client commercial activity. We will review later the impact that the deployment of this methodology had across the portfolio of BUs in which was applied (ref. Sect. 7.2 in Chap. 7).

1.3 Value Proposition Definition

Once the differentiated client segments are clear, it is time to define strong value propositions for each of them. Now, *what is a Value Proposition?*

The simplest way to define it is the 'what' that you bring to the client. This could be associated approximately with the traditional marketing framework of the 4 Ps:

- *Product* (to which I would add 'Services')
- *Pricing*
- *Promotion*
- *Positioning* (instead of the traditional 'Place' in the 4 Ps)

Just to clarify a bit further on the last point, 'Positioning' encapsules the brand connotation element that is left after extracting the physical element from 'Place' (e.g. branch, relationship manager, online and mobile), which will be addressed as the distribution channels element within the Value Proposition Delivery, later on in this chapter.

In the context of the financial services industry, it is more about services (though in the trade we call them products, which may seem a paradox or perhaps speaks more about the lack of customer centricity that has prevailed in the industry in years past): from a loan, a deposit, to a payment or an interest rate derivative. Pricing relates to the interest rates (debited or credited) and fees associated with the product/services. Promotion, though less prevalent than in other industries, often takes part more within retail and commercial banking, although as well is found in price subsidization in the corporate and investment banking space (though much less nowadays because of regulatory pressure). Positioning has its importance specifically to differentiate connotations among segments, not necessarily but sometimes devising entirely dedicated independent brands or sub-brands to make the point, as it is frequent to see with Private Banking brands or Islamic Banking dedicated brands.

The crucial issues in this section are: *what specific product/services do you choose to incorporate into a Value Proposition for a given segment?* and, even more difficult to solve, *what pricing policy do you define?*

Regarding *Product/Services*, if the segmentation exercise has been thoroughly done, its outcome will provide the necessary cues we are after, the different customer needs of each segment. When defining the proposition, it is easy to lose track of the north star in the compass, moreover when we have a look at the annual budget and fear that, as usual, it is way too stretchy. Hence, the temptation to cross-sell as much product as you possibly can to each client... you guess it, tempting but probably wrong. Surely the bankers among you will feel identified with this, so often witnessed, product-push approach.

Thus, the exercise of curating the product/services for your proposition is an exercise of elimination, not of inclusion. You need to identify what is not necessary, or superfluous, so you focus on the signal, of what really will satisfy the customer's need. So, for instance, probably you want to consider carefully how many types of credit cards (if more than 1 is absolutely needed) you want to offer to a student segment, and also that they do not probably require long-term pension savings products, at least for now.

Another critical aspect to think ahead is the value associated with the 'delivery' (as opposed to the 'definition') of the proposition. Although we will cover it in more depth in the next section, let me advance that in financial services, a lot of the value has to do with convenience and speed. These two critical elements are not the product/service per se, but they are vastly associated with it. They are driven by our configuration of processes, systems, procedures, policies etc. that form part of the delivery mechanism for the proposition, but ultimately could sum up a large part of the value added for the client. Thus, they need to be foreseen and reckoned with at this stage. Here again, we will need to go back and forth between the 'definition' and the 'delivery' phases to calibrate optimally the outcome, so to not get clients negatively surprised compared to the expectation created when they subscribed to the product/service. One of the most important drivers of the FinTech revolution that the industry has been experiencing since 2014 is precisely the low (or even negative) perceived value clients receive from banks' propositions in terms of the hassle to deal with slow decision-making and bureaucratic processes.

When it comes to *Pricing*, in financial services it has usually two components: interest rates and fees/commissions. Interest rates, by definition, are formed outside banks, they are formed in the financial markets as a consequence of the laws of offer and demand plus the intervention policy by the Central Bank. Markets every day produce interest rates along all tenors of the time curve, from overnight to 30 years (or even more). Those rates, which logically change every day (and every second) are taken as an input of reference for banks to use in pricing their products: paying interest to their depositors and charging interest to their borrowers, the difference between both becoming an important part of the bank's revenues, the so-called net interest margin.

At this point of our discussion about pricing, we need to enter a part that is quite technical and complex but that for the purposes of this chapter we will greatly simplify. The bank will determine the pricing policy for its deposits by, having an eye on the comparison with their competitors, taking a call on whether they may have excess of deposits (i.e. pay less interest) or deficit of deposits (i.e. pay more interest). This is so because the alternative to deposit shortfalls is to draw funding from wholesale markets, and those funds usually are more expensive for the bank than clients' deposits. Now, in this decision, the bank may differentiate the pricing between depositors depending on its client segmentation, for instance, paying higher pricing to preferably 'sticky' (i.e. contractually or behaviourally expected to stay for a long term), larger size deposits, which often will be correlated with Upper Affluent or High Net Worth segments in retail banking, or to large ticket, more-than-90-day deposits by business clients in corporate banking.

Also, the bank will determine the pricing policy for loans, which effectively will look at its competitors for a benchmarking, but even more importantly will look at its internal economics (i.e. costs) to define a minimum threshold pricing for not losing money and above that a margin for profit. Thus, in terms of internal economics, the bank will reckon 3 costs:

- Cost of funds (as per the above discussion of pricing of deposits and pricing of wholesale funding).
- Costs of operations (of all types for running the bank).
- Cost of risk (the 'pandora box' and 'philosopher stone' of the business of banking).

The cost of risk is associated with the risk taken in underwriting loans, so it will depend on the creditworthiness of the borrowers from the market segments the bank has chosen to compete in, which ultimately will depend on the evolution of macro and microeconomic factors. Thus, the cost of risk is uncertain and only can be estimated with some modelling that has limitations. Therefore, the business of the banker is, at its core, the business of estimating this risk... hence if he/she does it well, the cost of risk will become a 'philosopher stone' (and get golden with its touch), but if he/she does not, it will become a 'pandora box' (like the world witnessed in 2008).

Finally, the bank's loan pricing will add a 'reasonable' margin for profit, usually correlated with the need to provide for a decent return on capital for its equity shareholders, and thus calculated to ensure that the expected return on equity is fulfilled, which should exceed the cost of capital (market standards base this cost of capital at a minimum around 10–12% for banks, and targeted returns of equity 2–4 percentage points above that, depending on the bank and geography).

Now, again in this loan pricing decision, the bank may introduce differences among client segments, depending on its appetite for risk exposure to each one, and sometimes as well on commercial considerations in terms of market share penetration targets. This is particularly important for the SME and Corporate segments because risk appetites are expressed in terms of limits to the exposure that bank wishes for specific sectors, segments and individual borrowers, and that will have a clear and important impact on the value proposition definition for each segment. Once again, these are elements articulated in the 'delivery' of the Value Proposition but that need to be reckoned with in the 'definition' of it.

Figure 1.7 shares a template example used to differentiate Value Propositions among client segments in the Financial Institutions BU of an European bank (the 'select' labels indicate the options to switch on/off for the 3 elements; promotion was included in pricing).

Promotion, in the end, is a cost of sale. Thus, it could be defined like an extra spread offered in the interest rate paid in a saving product, or a period free of interest or fees for a credit card, or just a physical or monetary prize draw randomly among customers who have demonstrated some pre-requisites during a certain period. Whatever the shape or form, it translates into a cost. The key question to answer in order to decide the introduction of a promotion is to reckon what the estimated effect on volume is, and so whether the income associated to that extra volume more than compensates the extra cost incurred.

Many times, decisions about promotions get done in the context of specific product campaigns, which normally are quite agnostic of segment. In a more customer-oriented bank, it would be critical to switch this approach to tailor the

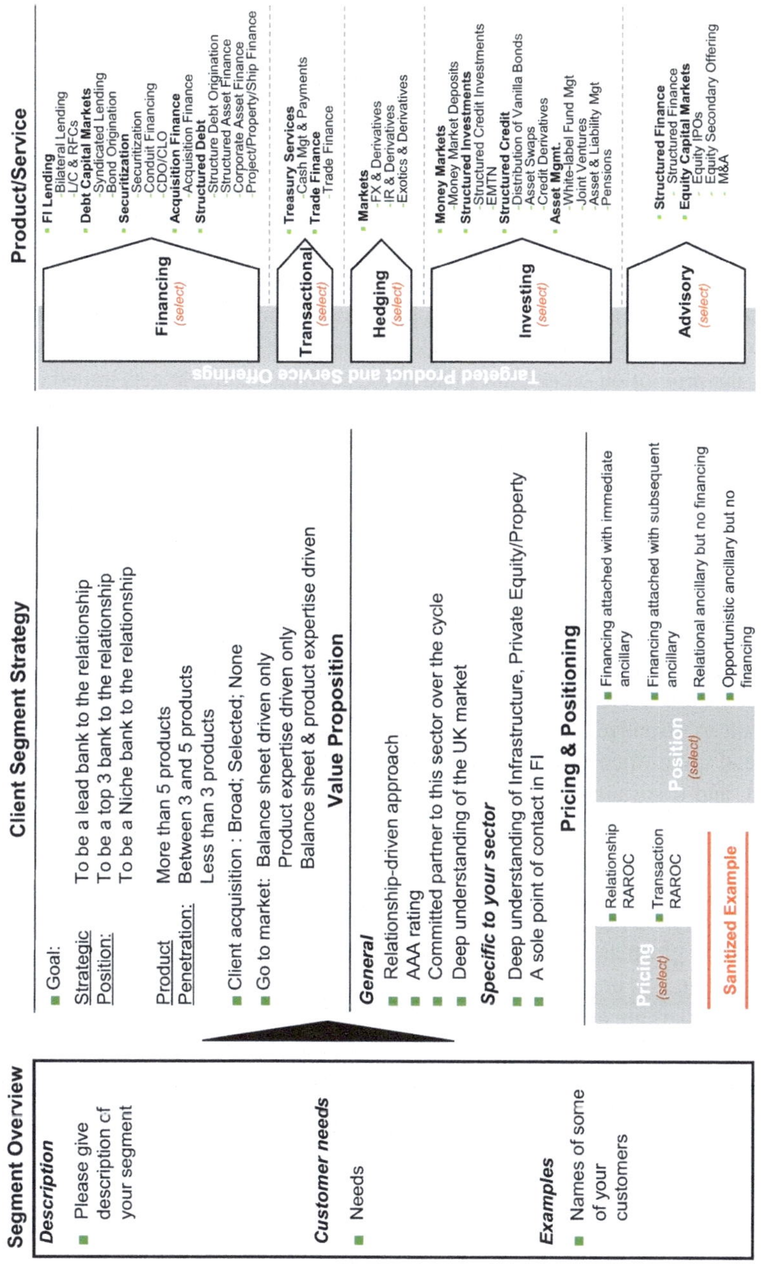

Fig. 1.7 Value Proposition Definition (example). Sources: Sanitized example

promotions for each client segment in a differentiated way (provided the regulation of that jurisdiction allows this practice if done without personal discrimination). To that effect, it is essential to gather the elasticity curves of the segment to the presence or not of specific promotions (some specialized consulting companies gather this type of market information). Thus, for instance, a 3-month fee waiver for a credit card might have large incremental volume impact in a mass-market segment of a retail bank, while only a marginal impact for the HNWI segment.

In corporate banking segments, promotions take the form of special concessions during the negotiation of terms and conditions of some products like loans, where perhaps there is room to concede in the arrangement fees versus the standard ones. More often, the promotion can become embedded in the joint-pricing of a bundle of products, like, for instance, a term loan with an associated fix-floating interest rate swap, where the bank may decide to put a joint-pricing[3] inferior to the separate initial quotes so to ensure to win the deal mandate in presence of fierce competition.

Often, the promotion on revenues like in the previous example gets traded off by a promotion in terms of risk acceptance, by softening some of the risk protection parameters (covenants) usually established by policy to that product. For instance, it may be instrumentalized by flexing some of the quantitative thresholds to some covenants (e.g. accepting a change in the Loan-to-Value ratio from 70% maximum to 80% maximum) or eliminating altogether some of the covenants (i.e. cov-lite loans). This flexibilization of risk acceptance should be compensated as an upward revision of the credit spread added to the interest rate of reference for that credit facility; but, more often than not, this spread is not adjusted, so the bank at its peril assumes a higher risk without asking for additional compensation for it, with permission of the credit risk department of course. Once this is understood, it is not difficult to visualize how periods of high competitive intensity among banking players lead quite often to an overall softening of credit standards in the way just described, and if sustained for a long time only can have an unhappy ending, as it happened in the 2008 Credit Crisis. Corollary: hidden costs have the nasty habitude of biting back, sooner or later.

Positioning is the last piece of the Value Proposition definition. This is an eminently intangible factor but extremely powerful in enabling the proposition itself; it is difficult to grasp and more so to manage effectively.

To start with, it is important to reach for external information (i.e. surveys, focus groups, benchmarking and net promoter score) about what the clients in that specific segment really value, what do they associate your brand with and per comparison to other competitors' brands. Then you can generate several alternatives of positioning and test each with the target market in a controlled environment. The goal is to fine-tune, by trial and error, the positioning well before you are ready for launch. Once selected the appropriate positioning, it is very important to develop the right messaging, across all the different types of distribution channels used, including own

[3] Although some jurisdictions have in recent years enacted regulation that limits or forbids product bundling or tying.

sales force and client interaction teams. Ultimately, you are trying to ensure consistency, homogeneity and focus when projecting the positioning of your Value Proposition.

Thus, for instance, when developing the Trusted Relationship segmentation for customer relationship management analyzed earlier, it was essential to modify all the usual sources for capturing external information about the segment so as to ensure we asked the right questions. Then, equally important was to start an 18-month programme to educate and train all the client-oriented teams in the new Trusted Relationship positioning and to reinforce their skillsets towards penetrating CEO-level relationships. Also, all marketing materials, hospitality events and thought leadership published in the media (part of the marketing strategy in the Value Proposition Delivery, again horizontal alignment is required) was redesigned towards the new Trusted Relationship theme. The impact of this reorientation was specifically measured in the regular customer surveys, and the results were astonishingly positive.

I had the luck to participate in the rebranding of a small payments bank after an acquisition, with the simultaneous launch of a new business platform on it. In special cases such as this, the Positioning becomes much more a critical part of the Value Proposition because it involves, respectively, rebranding or new branding launch. In this situation, the engagement with external brand consulting experts is highly recommended. Starting from the Vision, Mission and Values (refer to Chap. 2) of the new organization, an in-depth exercise based on external information is performed to sculpt the brand identity intended, with an aim to reflect the organization' Purpose and to achieve differentiation. Also, the exercise will look for an ideally unoccupied space within the visual colour palette considering where the competitors are positioned.

In this case study, it was very interesting to notice, after several focus groups, how the management team realized that, having the bank's offering positioned in the B2B2C chain and their new mission focused on enabling the creation of value between their corporate clients and their clients' retail customers, the metaphor of a 'Sherpa' was a very good fit for their brand identity. Similarly, the market study highlighted that the green and magenta colours were empty spaces in the palette compared to their competitors, which in the light of their interest in ESG and community purpose in the Values led to choose green as their main colour theme. Logo, fonts and mottos were step by step emerging following a structured and creative process, which usually started with a dozen or so distinct options, to gradually narrow down to 3 for final choice. Overall, in the space of surprisingly only 6 weeks they were able to distil a fresh, completely new brand ready to be sketched out towards a marketing strategy.

1.4 Value Proposition Delivery

At this point, we have properly identified and defined 'who', the Client Segments, and 'what', the Value Proposition Definition. Now, we arrive at the section where the rubber meets the road, where decisions usually embed the burden of investment and operational cost and, as such, become high stakes decisions due to their, oftentimes, irreversibility. This is about Value Proposition Delivery, the 'how'.

Thus, delivery involves all the rest of components necessary to bring the value proposition to the respective client segment, and that means ALL the components. There are different ways we can slice and dice this chapter. Given the large customer exposure that banking has (it is one of the few industries where both the asset side and the liability side of the balance-sheet is driven by direct sales interaction with customers), I usually prefer to divide delivery between 'front-office' and 'back-office', the former involving all areas related to direct customer interaction and service, while the latter all the remaining functional areas that support the activity of the front. As a counterpoint, we will study in Sect. 9.5, Chap. 9 a very interesting alternative approach based instead on workflows, intangibles and behaviours.

For both areas, it is required to use a framework that tackles the 'static' vs 'dynamic' components. The General Management Framework [4] (which is a derivative of the famous McKinsey's 7S framework [5]) does a great job at this challenge (Fig. 1.8).

Leaving aside the Strategy element (we will tackle it in Chap. 2), the dimensions of Division of Work vs Coordination of Work (worth to reflect on how organizations have a tendency to emphasize a lot the former while neglecting quite often the latter) allow to identify neatly the 6 elements:

- *Segmentation* (usually referred to as well as Organizational Design—I will use this term instead to avoid confusion with Client Segmentation): The organigram of formal, direct and indirect reporting lines among all different roles, which determine the decision-making remits as well.
- *Staff*: The people and the skillset and diversity associated required for filling the Segmentation.
- *Structure*: The network of informal links between individuals and groups in the organization, normally uncorrelated with the Segmentation, and that drive the flows of information and decision-making influence.
- *Systems*: All policies, processes and procedures, plus IT architecture sustaining them, designed to coordinate the flows of work among Staff in the Segmentation, and usually are organized via support functions such as risk, compliance, operations, distribution channels, legal or finance.
- *Style*: This is commonly known as Behaviours, so culturally accepted patterns of interaction at individual and collective levels across the organization.
- *Shared outlook*: This is commonly known as Values (ref. Sect. 2.1 in Chap. 2), so culturally accepted general principles that guide the action and behaviours of individuals and groups within the organization.

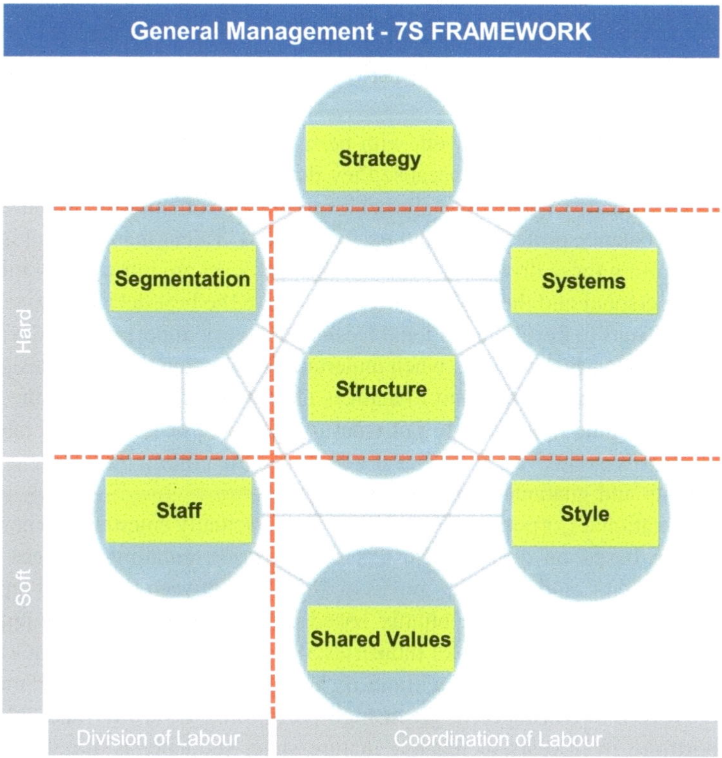

Fig. 1.8 General Management framework. Sources: [4, 5]

Thus, for instance, if we take a BU like Multinational Corporates (so clients with threshold of total revenues or turnover above, for instance, $500 m) within a typical wholesale bank with 15% market share in an average-size developed country. As far as frontline is concern, the *Organizational Design* would include the Managing Director of the BU, with 5–7 MD Team Leaders underneath tackling each a different cluster of industries such as utilities or manufacturing, each with a team of 2–3 Directors taking 1–3 sub-industries, supported each by 2–4 Relationship Managers (with an average individual portfolio of, let us say, 20–25 clients), and then a pool of Associates and Analysts supporting across the sectors.

The *Staff* element would be the description of job requirements and skillsets necessary to perform at minimum everyone of the roles above. Within that, the specific individuals that currently perform those jobs, with their respective backgrounds (i.e. nationality, studies, languages, previous employers and jobs), capabilities (i.e. sales, finance, modelling, credit risk, corporate banking/transaction banking/investment banking product-line knowledge), skillset gaps (i.e. across the previously listed capabilities) and other personal circumstances (i.e. family, travel appetite and work-from-home flexibility). Critical across this analysis is to ensure that the principles of diversity and inclusion, in all their dimensions (i.e. genre, nationality, religion and sexual orientation, disabilities), permeate both in the associated processes (i.e. recruitment, assessment and promotion) and in the culture (i.e. values and beliefs upheld collectively) that support the assignment of Staff to roles.

It is important to understand well, with permission of the individuals of course, the above personal dimensions, because they determine heavily the individual and collective performance, and a lot can be achieved in terms of employee satisfaction if we attempt to balance professional and personal needs. Talent management is about deeply penetrating these drivers, which at individual level are intrinsically mixed in terms of the personal and the professional, so to make the best decisions in terms of assignation of Staff to the Organizational Design and, very importantly to devise any changes in the latter. For instance, when undertaking an organizational redesign, this dimension must matter if you want to address those who are working in the wrong roles but, at the same time, you do not want to upset and/or lose critical talent; so moving the boxes exclusively in an 'ideal world' and then fitting the people is recipe for inflexibility and guarantee for conflict.

The Multinational Corporates BU example above actually entertained a new team reorganization based on different clusters of industries, entailing changes in the individual portfolios, and implying moves of key Staff between teams and reporting lines. If this exercise were done bluntly based on a theoretical redesign approach only considering the new clusters of industries, it might have happened that we were moving clients among portfolios without reckoning its impact on the relationship managers (RMs). For instance, a given high-performing RM, who had cultivated his/her portfolio over years to reach a mature state, suddenly is allocated a new portfolio, and so he/she needs to start near from scratch again or with a very 'green' set of client names. This would be something difficult to swallow by the affected RM, provoking resentment, and so providing a good excuse for departing to the competition after the next bonus round. Thankfully, that potentially negative situation was avoided in this reorganization, because the management took a deep understanding of the personal impact for each individual affected.

Under *Structure* we try to understand who the key players in the organizational network are, as well as the gatekeepers, influencers, detractors, groups of special interests, etc... and what informational or decisional flows they are able to influence, either positively or negatively. Confronting an organizational redesign these informal structures can become a real obstacle to make it work, bypassing the new hierarchy and so creating havoc in the decision-making process. For instance, another Large Corporates BU in a smaller country than the case study above, showed networks of mutual interest among RMs of the same nationality dispersed across the industry segment teams, where they owe strong loyalty to each other. Being the loyalty to their national community much stronger than the one to the reporting hierarchy, that drove an enormous amount of noise and havoc in the communication and decision activities, making the organization very dysfunctional. For instance, in annual assessment reviews the MDs of a given community openly helped the juniors of the same community regardless of meritocratic principles. These informal

Structures had to be reckoned with in order to restore confidence in the assessment process across this BU.

Systems is a wide area that includes any formal coordination mechanisms such as policies, processes and procedures, usually supported by IT systems (but also by paper). Most times these mechanisms are explicit, but sometimes they are not properly gathered so they exist only in the minds of the people with experience in the organization; thus, they need to be captured and clearly identified. A lot about change in organizations involves the continuous improvement of these mechanisms, because, otherwise, you will witness their progressive deterioration by time, obsolescence, lack of discipline or just inertia.

For instance, in another Financial Institutions unit, they had an annual assessment of employee performance supported by a very bureaucratic IT system and complex evaluation framework, with many types of heterogeneous objectives, not clearly defined and tracked, which paved the way for an overall sense of process fatigue and unjust assessment across the troops. On the other side of the spectrum, I found a multinational Wholesale bank with a very fast but very loose approach to the same task, with lot of subjective thinking defining the outcome and significant personal influencing along the way, resulting in a similar negative feeling of injustice. Both extremes, one very formal, the other very informal, actually led to a great level of employee dissatisfaction and ultimately attrition, as shown in the annual employee satisfaction surveys, which ultimately required managerial intervention. Therefore, this area of Systems needs a finetuning of trade-offs considering how these processes and supporting IT are designed, and always keeping a continuous improvement mindset in the knowledge that it will never be a finished job.

Shared Outlook and *Style* are together commonly known as the Culture of the organization. Shared Outlook (this section will tackle it from a BU business model perspective, Chap. 2 will discuss it as Values from a strategy perspective) starts with the top leadership at the strategy level (i.e. Values) and permeates across the entire organization, ideally, in an homogeneous fashion. It takes long time and sustained effort to significantly move the needle of change in this terrain. Style is about behaviours, which is the interpretation of the Shared Outlook in the actual context of each BU, and as such is more malleable. Some organizations try to model style at the BUs by linking it to the annual performance assessment, by identifying and praising role models, and by the visible exemplification from senior leadership so to lead by example. The key is that Style aligns to Shared Outlook, however, this does not always happens.

For instance, in recent years some banks have decided to adopt the quite often repeated mantra of 'customer centricity' as a core value, only to meet the obstinate reality of customer surveys crying out and loud how short they were to achieve this intent. *Why?* Possibly because the much-vaulted change of values ended up on a nice poster hung in a wall, repeated from time to time in top management speeches. Cultural change requires engineering, with a multi-year programme of intervention at all levels and for which an external monitoring (that some specialized consultants offer) is essential, starting from the top and going all the way to the remotest units of the organization (more about this topic in Chap. 12 in the context of digital transformation).

1.5 Financial Impact

With Client Segmentation, Value Proposition Definition and Value Proposition Delivery, the Business Model of the unit is complete. This is the model the organization chooses to compete and, hopefully, win in the marketplace at the light of the Market Dynamics initially analyzed.

Obviously, all this organizational effort is expected to produce a Financial Impact. Resources are going to be mobilized (e.g. capital and people), Investment Cases will be approved and implemented, and so lines of revenues, costs and profits will be expected, forming a Profit & Loss account (or P&L for short), along with the respective cumulative impact in assets and liabilities at the Balance-Sheet. These elements will become the Financial Plan, normally upon a medium-term horizon anything within the 3–5 year range (Investment Cases might have a longer horizon).

Financial Plans have developed from the necessity of the publicly listed organization to use a planning tool that provides some predictability of the performance ahead, so that management can act in anticipation of any deviations towards medium-long term targets on specific key performance indicators (KPIs), such as revenue growth, 'jaws' (revenue growth minus cost growth), cost-to-income (costs over revenues) or return on equity. These KPIs are the key contractual terms between the Board of Directors (representing the interests of shareholders) and the CEO with regard to the quantitative goals of the company and so, usually, they are linked to the overall compensation of the CEO and the top management of the organization (via the LTIP, Long-Term Incentive Plan). This way, the Board determines the expected results over the medium term that the CEO should aim at delivering. These expected results are public in listed companies, so equity market participants discount this performance in the share price of the company, and follow very closely its progress, quarter by quarter, as the company publishes its effective performance against targets.

We will leave for Chap. 3 how to develop a Financial Plan fully linked, in best-practice, with the Strategy Blueprint of the BU, making together the Medium Term Plan (MTP). In this section, let's understand how the combination of the different elements of the Business Model relate to its Financial Impact.

Starting with the clients, the company will have an expectation at different points in time within the Financial Plan period (e.g. 1-year vs 3-year target) for each segment defined in the Client Segmentation with regard to:

(A) How many clients currently has (i.e. Existing Clients) vs how many more expects to capture in the marketplace (i.e. New-to-Bank Clients) by the end of the plan period.
(B) What levels of product penetration has on this segment at this moment (e.g. maybe out of the existing clients, 80% have current accounts; 20% have

consumer loans, 40% have mortgages), versus what target levels expects to have in the future (e.g. from 20% going to 30% in consumer loans, from 40% to 55% in mortgages by year 3).

(C) What average revenue per product and per client currently enjoys in this segment at this moment (e.g. maybe out of the existing clients, $500 of revenue per client annually on average from consumer loans), and where that average could go in the future (e.g. from $500 to $550 in consumer loans by year-3).

Of course, for New-to-Bank Clients, KPIs (B) and (C) would likely have different target levels that for Existing Clients. As we see, the Segmentation and the Value Proposition definition play a critical part in determining the Revenue lines. With these 3 variables, the finance department can build the revenue lines expected from this Business Model over the MTP period; from that baseline, they could simulate scenarios by varying the original assumptions of expected change for each variable or KPI.

Equally, the cost lines, either linked to personnel or linked to non-personnel, could be estimated, leveraging assumptions over expected growth of those costs based on external pricing (e.g. inflation of remuneration and cost of goods or services from providers). The Value Proposition Delivery is what determines all the elements of costs aforementioned; thus, the level of efficiency and automation of the delivery is crucial in terms of cost impact. Very importantly for the Financial Plan development process, this part of cost estimation makes the involvement of the functions in the organization such as HR, Operations or IT fundamental, so to both get an accurate estimation along with their involvement for their own resource planning (i.e. their own Financial Plan as a function or cost centre for the organization).

A critical part of these cost estimates, for banks, is the cost of risk. For that, in close collaboration with the Risk function, estimates of costs related to credit, market and operational risks are generated (there could be several other types depending on the categorization defined by the Risk Management Framework of each bank). The first one, credit risk, depending on the volume of lending assumed during the revenue exercise, and the relative riskiness associated to the respective client segments and products (e.g. a mortgage has a level of security higher than a consumer loan). The second one, market risk, depending on the volume of activity related with banking activities that expose the bank to such a risk, normally associated to the financial markets trading desks (fixed income, equities or foreign exchange open positions) and treasury desks (money markets positions). The third one, operational risk, depending on a qualitative assessment under a robust framework of the losses that could be incurred by all the parts of the organization regarding activities not related to credit or market risk. For all of them, the Basel III regulatory framework along with the IFRS accounting framework define quite precise methodologies about how to estimate the financial impact of all these costs, idiosyncratic to the Financial Services industry.

Thereby, it is critical that the process and procedures within the Value Proposition Delivery include a very good control and feedback process related to these regulatory frameworks, so to ensure the frontline focuses its activity where it plays to the strengths of the organization in the context of regulation. Thus, for instance, in Corporate Banking is essential a mechanism that helps RMs to prioritize their product activity with their clients (considering how the impact of regulation affects risk-adjusted return on capital, liquidity transfer pricing and cross-selling). This mechanism is critical both for productivity purposes and for avoiding client disappointment (e.g. from turning down too late in the process a loan that, given existing regulatory or policy constraints, we knew it would have been very difficult for the bank's credit committee to approve).

From Revenues and Costs (including cost of risk) Profit lines (including taxes) are estimated. Similarly, following IFRS accounting framework, the P&L dynamics have their reflexion in pro forma Balance-Sheets for the Financial Plan period. This will reflect the expected evolution of assets (especially lending), liabilities (especially deposits) and equity capital (including retained earnings). The balance-sheet items will be relevant also for checking whether the bank expects to meet comfortably or not some specific regulatory ratios established by the Basel III framework to ensure the solvency, funding and liquidity of the bank. Thus, the process of elaborating a MTP will bear in mind not only the expected targets set by the Board but as well the compliance of the institution with the required regulatory hurdles for solvency of Basel III, not a small feat (more about that in Chap. 3).

Investment Cases are particular ad hoc, stand-alone revenue and cost lines projected for a planning period or beyond articulated around single strategic initiatives that the business is suggesting to start doing. For instance, a Financial Institutions BU in a corporate bank wanted to expand its business organically in Hong Kong, where they did not have presence before, and so proposed some recruitment, office and licence costs etc... along with expected revenues lines along particular assumptions of activity.

They could be as well framed as Divestment Cases, and so identifying a current activity the business is doing for which is proposing an orderly discontinuation until its final elimination of the portfolio. For instance, out of a change of market conditions that makes a particular business unprofitable and so unsustainable, like it happened with Social Housing lending in some European markets after the 2008 Credit Crisis (in which the higher cost of funds for banks was well above the usual pricing level after cost of risk of these projects, which was very low given the guarantee from the government). In this case, these banks had to halt the extension of loans to these clients, and set the existing lending book in a winddown mode, reducing drastically the workforce assigned to this segment (i.e. Divestment Case); fortunately, the banks reinvented a new way to provide solutions to Social Housing outside the banks' balance-sheets, as it happened, by advising the issuance of bonds by these clients in the capital markets.

Investment/Divestment Cases become then overlays upon the regular Financial Plan exercise of the business-as-usual activities of the BU. The overall exercise is then discussed for approval in the respective MTP forums or committees following the internal process designed to that effect.

As we see, for best-practice, a given Business Model needs to be fully mapped in terms of its Financial Impact at this point and over a Financial Plan horizon (i.e. initial baseline). Only this way we have a holistic control on how the strategic decisions management suggests for a change of its Business Model will affect the change of the Financial Plan. As a consequence, that feedback will be critical in order to define what elements of change create more or less economic value via their respective Financial Impact by comparison with the initial baseline. Needless to say, the Financial Impact (and its change) is based on financial assumptions, and those need to be tweaked as well to simulate future scenarios... but overall, the principle is the same, to effect change in the Business Model we need to reckon its Financial Impact before decisions of change (especially, irreversible ones) get made and execution rolls down the slope to incur expenses.

* * *

This finalizes the discussion about the Business Model framework and its components. The next chapter will study the tool that will articulate the changes from Business Model 'as-is' to 'as-should-be', that will connect the present with the future, that is the Strategy Blueprint framework.

References

1. "How Competitive Forces Shape Strategy" by Michael Porter (1979; Harvard Business Review).
2. "Blue Ocean Strategy" by W. Chan Kim and Renee Mauborgne (2005; HBS Press).
3. "The State of Global Banking—In Search of a Sustainable Model" (Stephano Visalli, Charles Roxburgh, Toos Daruvala, Miklos Dietz, Susan Lund and Anna Marrs; Sep. 11; McKinsey & Co).
4. "General Management Framework" by Chip Heath and Greg Fisher (2000; Duke University).
5. "7 S Framework" (1979; McKinsey & Co).

2 Strategy Blueprint

The next framework in HMS, within the 'Existing Geography and Business' slope, is the Strategy Blueprint with the Core Strategy framework at its centre.

The Strategy Blueprint articulates how the Business Model intents to change from the current 'as-is' state to its future 'as-should-be' state, and also connects the organization's purpose with its current action. The Strategy Blueprint along with its associated Financial Plan make two sides of the same coin, the Medium Term Plan (MTP). We will leave for Chap. 3 the discussion about the Financial Plan along with the best-practice process to put both elements together within the MTP (Fig. 2.1).

The framework is deployed over 4 elements:

- *Purpose*: Defined over the long-term and composed of Mission, Vision, Values and Goals.
- *Diagnosis*: A set of rigorous analyses, using standard or ad hoc frameworks, to depict the state and future outlook of the BU.
- *Core Strategy*: Defines the going forward strategic intent in terms of Client, Product and Geography.
- *Coherent Action*: Identifies over the next 1–2 years the set of Action Plans, aligned to Strategic Priorities, for delivery of the strategy.

After reading Richard Rumelt's great book 'Good Strategy, Bad Strategy' [1] (more about it in Chap. 9), I found that his '*kernel of strategy*' ('*Diagnosis*, *Guiding Policy* and *Coherent Action*') mapped superbly to the last 3 elements of the Strategy Blueprint framework, so I took the freedom to use the 'Diagnosis' and 'Coherent Action' title labels (credit due to Professor Rumelt).

Let us analyze each of the Strategy Blueprint elements more in detail.

A. Gavieiro Besteiro, *Strategy in Action*, Management for Professionals,
https://doi.org/10.1007/978-3-030-94759-0_2

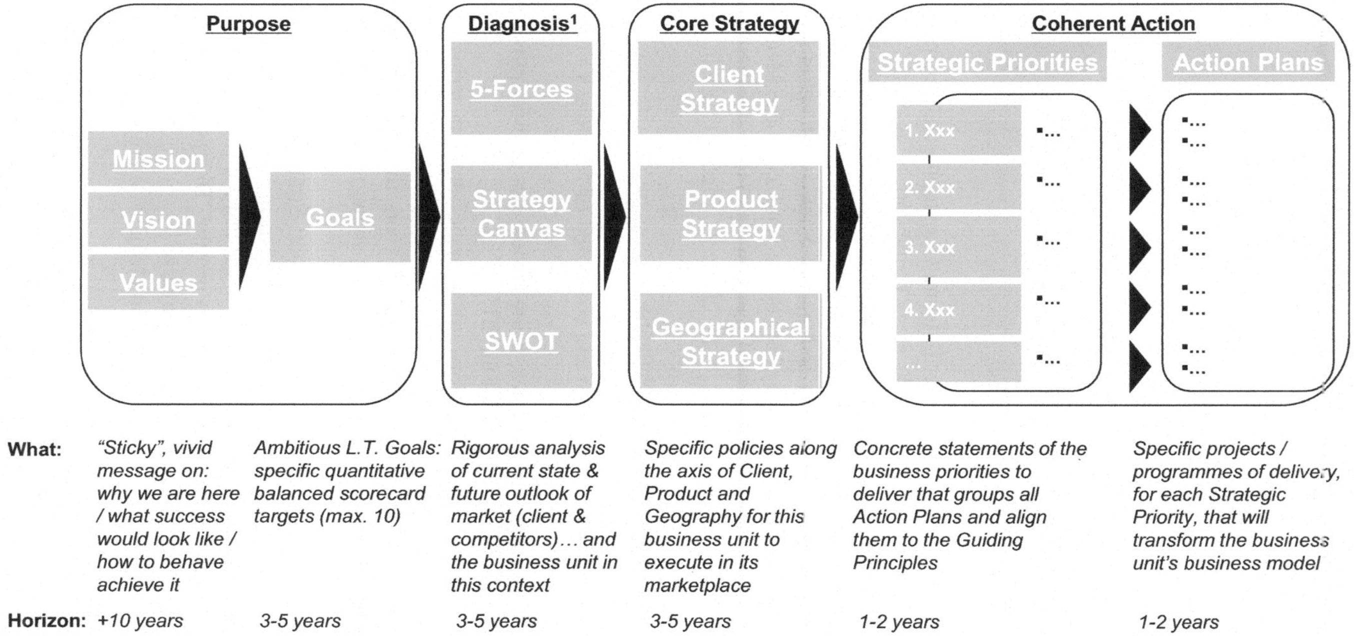

Fig. 2.1 **Strategy Blueprint framework**. 1. Other frameworks or ad hoc analyses could be used. Sources: 'Holistic Management Framework v.5' (Angel Gavieiro; Apr.17; AG Strategy & Partners)

2.1 Purpose

A navigation journey for a crew requires a collective Purpose, which should cover both the very long term and the near term, having elements both of a perennial and a changeable nature.

Let us address first the three elements of a more perennial nature: clear motive, clear destination and clear 'rules of the game' . . . Mission, Vision and Values.

Once the motive/destination/rules are set in your navigation plan, it is necessary to define some intermediate milestones or reference points within the journey, so that it is divided into stages. Then, the skipper will be able to estimate the time required to cover each leg. As opposed to the first three, this fourth element is therefore of a more changeable nature: Goals.

2.1.1 Mission, Vision and Values

Simon Sinek [2] has brought the concept of '*start with Why*' at the centre of the leadership role of a CEO, claiming that while many organizations do manage to articulate very well 'What' they want to be, and reasonably well 'How' they will get there, however, organizations do not articulate as well 'Why' they do it. . . and so fixing this makes a big difference.

A Mission (*why?*), it would be a statement that defines the reason for the people of the organization to form part of it. . . *why are we here?*

A Vision (*what?*), it would be a statement that defines, in a vivid manner, what success looks like for the organization. . . *what do we want to be?*

Mission is different from Vision in that it refers to an inner motivation for individuals in the organization, as opposed to an externally visible destination for the collective. For instance, '*we want to make a difference in our clients' financial lives*' is a Mission, while '*we want to be recognized as the bank of choice for our clients*' is a Vision.

A well-crafted Mission and Vision could very well suffice to provide meaning and destination to everyone in a company. Now, some organizations decide to include as well other complementary or reinforcing concepts of corporate identity, in which case it is helpful to define and differentiate them clearly to avoid confusion. For instance, a Motto, usually refers to a phrase that is used and repeated as a collective identification of what people in that organization stand for. For instance, '*our word is our promise to our clients*'.

Values (*how?*), as introduced in the previous chapter, are culturally accepted general principles that guide the action and behaviours of individuals and groups within the organization. They establish the mutually accepted boundaries for the organization's journey towards its Vision. Given their importance to guide behaviour, we will address these in more depth later on in the book when we talk about implementation and communication (ref. Sects. 6.4 and 9.4 in Chaps. 6 and 9).

Can a company live without an explicitly stated Vision and/or Mission? Of course. Having said that, it is worth referring to the research done by professors

Jim Collins and Jerry Porras [3] that compared a set of 18 companies that were 'visionary' (i.e. premier institution in its industry, widely admired and that made an imprint on the world) with like-for-like comparable companies in the same industry (i.e. that are just good but not 'visionary') in order to distil the critical characteristics that explain their performance difference over a long time period. In all these 18 companies, the Vision played an important role to anchor the culture of the organization across generations of CEOs, which constituted one of the key differentiating factors versus the comparable set.

Is one set of Mission/Vision/Values at Group level enough and valid for all Divisions and Business Units underneath? Though, as a principle, Mission and Values are meant to be universal across the organization, there are instances of large, complex, multinational banks that benefited from creating a cascade of Visions at Divisional level. The rationale stems from the fact that in a large universal bank, they may coexist very different sub-industries: retail banking, commercial banking, corporate banking, investment banking, insurance, asset management and/or wealth management. Thus, it is understandable that each Division could craft its own Vision statement, but it is essential to ensure its alignment with Group's Vision. At BU level, and even team level, sometimes I found the exercise could be occasionally beneficial, but in general I discourage it so to avoid the risk of message dilution.

How do we write high-quality great Mission, Vision and Values? Following professor Chip Heath [4], there are 6 best-practice principles to follow in order to craft statements that are sticky, and I think that ideally we want them reflected in our Mission, Vision and Values: '*simple, unexpected, concrete, credible, emotional and story-type*'. Each statement would be conveyed in one single line or short paragraph and remain valid for a long time period. A famous example of a vision that embeds these principles is: '*to put a man in the moon*', by J.F. Kennedy's speech at the inception of the Apollo programme in May 1961.

Finally, *who would be best placed to craft these statements?* If we are tempted to save time the CEO could go and write his/her own statement, however, this shortcut could end up defeating the intention. The intention here is to involve the top management, and even in some cases somehow the entire organization, so that the resulting Mission/Vision/Values are a product of the collective, which ensures their self-identification. At the same time, it is sensible to avoid creating a time consuming, expensive process for doing so. As importantly, it is not advisable either to engage in a consensus making mashup, accommodating all views without challenge, that results in a Vision far from the 6 best-practice principles mentioned above. I guess it is a question of balance. Normally, a half-a-day workshop would do, or even better, divided into 2–3 sessions on different days, so people can go, reflect on it and come back with some refinements.

2.1.2 Goals

We define a set of Goals for a given time horizon, perhaps 3 or 5 years (usually the MTP horizon), with specific targets for the immediate milepost at 1-year horizon, which become the annual Budget. The Goals form part, along with the Mission, Vision and Values, of the Purpose for the organization.

Now, *what metrics are we using to define the Goals?* That is a crucially strategic question that requires in-depth reflection by the CEO and his/her top management, as well as by the Board supervising the overall performance of the organization. These metrics are often referred to as well as Key Performance Indicators (KPIs).

I recommend a small set of not more than 10 metrics. A majority will necessarily be quantitative, but there could be room for some qualitative metrics as well. A higher number would create too much confusion and little focus across the organization. We have witnessed extremely cumbersome KPI exercises that ended up with balanced scorecards with +30 or +40 metrics... pointless.

Another best-practice for KPIs is to avoid overlaps. Thus, for instance, if we take Revenue growth and 'Jaws' ratio (i.e. Revenue growth minus Cost growth), then it is redundant to include Cost growth as well, because it is a mathematical consequence of the first two metrics.

To have a balanced mix of KPIs is as well recommendable. There are institutions where, having a Finance function with very strong weight, might end up with a Goal set entirely made of P&L and Balance-sheet metrics. Financial metrics are critical but a balanced dashboard of KPIs requires also metrics related to, for instance, customers and employees.

It is very important to monitor closely the cascade down of the Goal set across the Divisions and BUs. Sometimes, the work is carefully crafted at Group level and then the cascade is left on its own devices, only to see how the KPIs begin to derive and multiply as the cascade progresses, arriving at the frontline teams with a set far away from best-practice principles. At each level of the cascade, each KPI should become 'relevant' for that level of the organization. 'Relevant' means that the KPI is actionable by the team subject to its delivery (it is absurd to have a KPI in your balanced scorecard that you cannot do much about driving it with your activity), and that can be measured either quantitatively or qualitatively. Qualitative measurement can be accomplished by using some sort of parametrization, identifying characteristics that capture well the metric, along with a definition of best-practice for each of these characteristics. Again, at each level, there should not be more than 10 KPIs, as it is very common that they increase as the cascade descends.

For instance, about KPI cascading, a metric of Cost measured at Group level, can end up being Direct Costs when you arrive at Business Unit level; while the remainder, the Indirect Costs, would cascade to the respective Functions such as Operations or IT. Another instance, regarding qualitative metrics, a metric tracking compliance to corrective actions by the audit function (e.g. the KPI being 'Audit Corrective Actions') may be parametrized with a qualitative RAG scale (i.e. Red/Amber/Green, with clear criteria associated with each one), and then a target established accordingly (e.g. 'no Reds').

Functions receive some financial metrics, such as Indirect Costs or Cost of Risk, however, they use also other quantitative metrics related to activity, such as efficiency, %errors, output units, or time-related KPIs stemming from service level agreements (SLAs). Also, Functions are prone to receive qualitative metrics, often informed from vetted feedback from their internal clients, the Business Units.

2.2 Diagnosis

Having destination and scales identified, the whole planning exercise for your voyage will depend on your navigation plan, so your strategy. Now, strategy starts from a deep, fact-based understanding of the current situation as well as the challenges and opportunities you face, the Diagnosis.

Where ought the diagnosis to look at? The ocean is an infinite of water…

Let us start with the simple 3 Cs: Clients, Competitors and Company.

In Chap. 1 about the Business Model framework, when reviewing Market Dynamics we covered Clients and Competitors, so I refer to that part and the tools such as the Five Forces or the Strategy Canvas frameworks to distil rich insights on these 2 topics. Market Dynamics analysis, therefore, is the first part of the Diagnosis.

The second part of the Diagnosis is to analyze the Company per se in the context of the Market Dynamics' insights. To that purpose, the typical SWOT (Strengths, Weaknesses, Opportunities and Threats) framework serves as a good starting point.

Often you find renderings of the SWOT analysis that look just like a long laundry list of, sometimes overlapping, bullet points. To avoid this, a methodology and process (ref. Fig. 2.2) are suggested to arrive at a meaningful and succinct SWOT. Never forget that creating a SWOT for a BU is an art more than a science, the suggested 5 best-practice principles are:

1. SWOT approach: With the lenses of the BU's main 'themes of change', generating an initial list of bullets for each quadrant as per the next 2 principles.
2. Strengths and Weaknesses: Focused on the company itself, with statements referring to internal and current factors, usually articulated in the present tense (e.g. '*strong values based culture creates employee loyalty, retention and drives client trust*'; '*transfer pricing makes our product pricing uncompetitive*').
3. Opportunities and Threats: Focused on the competitive environment, with statements that refer to external and future factors, usually articulated in the future or conditional tense (e.g. '*industry restructuring and consolidation would uplift overall returns*'; '*double-dip recession would hit impairments*').
4. 'Big fish vs small fish': For each quadrant, reduce the list of bullets by throwing a 'fishing net' on them in order to catch the 'big fish' and let go of the 'small fish', for which a simple test of impact vs likelihood will help (as per the illustration).
5. Refinement via iterative process: Bouncing it with sr. executives and other stakeholders to gather their feedback (i.e. create > use > refresh > re-create).

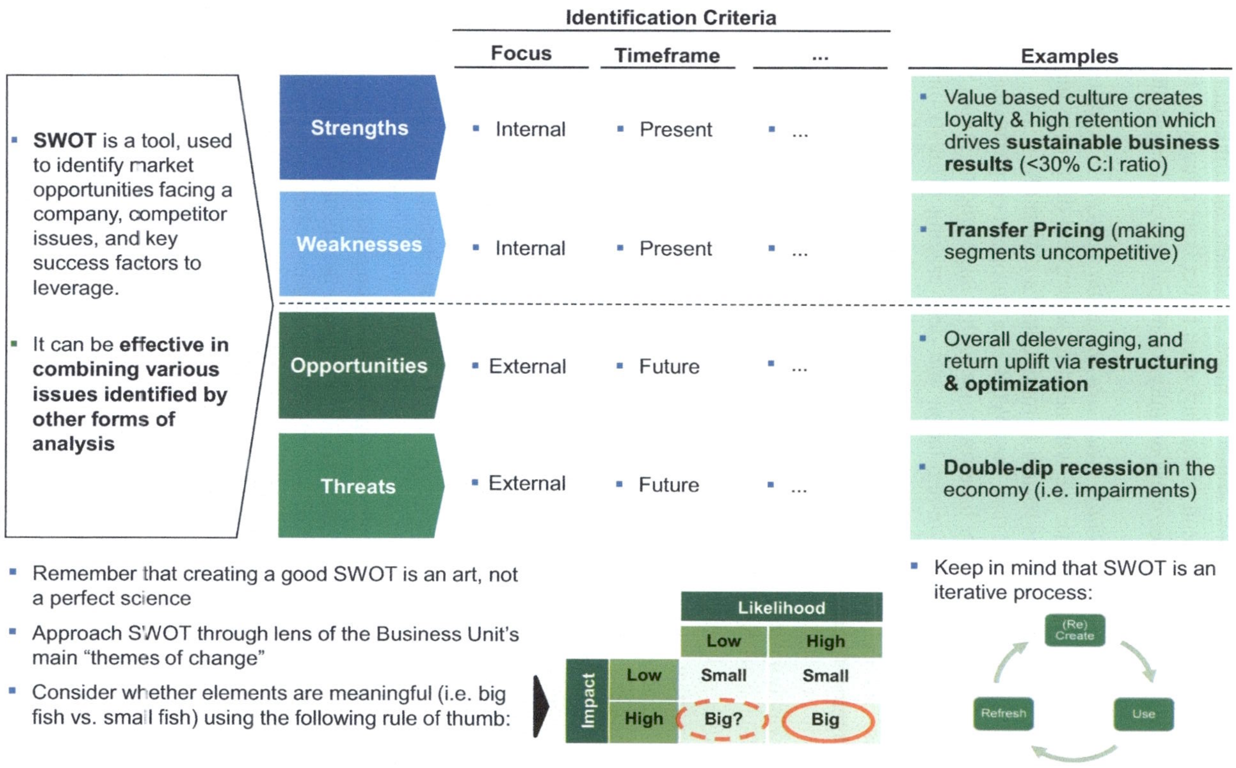

Fig. 2.2 SWOT framework and process. Sources: 'Holistic Management Framework v.5' (Angel Gavieiro; Apr.17; AG Strategy & Partners)

Once you got a robust SWOT, a common mistake in formulating strategy is to try to exhaustively tackle all the points of the SWOT in your next step, defining the Core Strategy. It is not advisable because prioritization is a key success factor, and not all bullets in the SWOT are equal, some are more important and impactful for your company than others. At the end of the day, each bullet is an issue to tackle (either positive to lever strength or seize opportunity, or negative to address weakness and mitigate threats).

Therefore, *how do we identify what are the main issues?* It comes down to problem definition and for that we will need to selectively deep dive further into some of them. To do so, let us review in more detail a case study.

Just after the 2008 Credit Crisis, the SWOT of a European corporate bank told us that enjoyed a strong customer base franchise with a large lending book (Strength), but it was facing a wave of re-regulation and deleveraging (Threat) on top of a complicated situation of managing an increasing book of non-performing loans (Weakness). At the same time, the transaction banking activity (e.g. payments, cash management, trade finance and cards) was losing many requests-for-proposal (RFP) from existing clients and winning very few from new clients, because the platform was quite obsolete vis-à-vis competitors (Weakness). Finally, the cross-selling of what is called ancillary products and services (i.e. treasury and capital markets) over existing clients was relatively low vs competitors, because the bank did not enjoy at that time a large platform with these capabilities (Weakness), however, great market talent was available because of industry redundancies (Opportunity).

Thus, among all these issues, *which ones were the main ones to solve here? … how to allocate decreasing lending across the existing client base? how to manage the underperforming book and its clients? how to mitigate the transaction banking RFP outflow? how to build the required investment banking capabilities to improve cross-selling?*

To see the forest for the trees is not easy. The way to prioritize the right issues is to take a distance from the SWOT, by simplifying and going to basics. In simple terms, a corporate banking business at its basic provides lending and payment services to its clients ('bread and butter'). If that is done effectively the client can then reward the relationship with its trust by increasing the bank share of wallet on its cash management and buying ancillary products (so the 'meat and vegies' on top of the 'bread and butter'). However, without lending and/or payments, forget it… you do not have a strong corporate banking business anymore.

With this simplified description of the basics in mind, the question at hand now was much simpler: *how do we tackle the lending and payments issues?*

The performance at that time in these two areas was not great, but *what was driving it?* It was time then for the team to roll out the sleeves and start crunching numbers, interviewing clients to better understand their needs vs our capability gaps, interviewing relationship managers and product specialists to understand their perspective to the same question, benchmarking competitors offering and investment plans, reviewing macro and micro trends etc. … you are guessing right, effectively

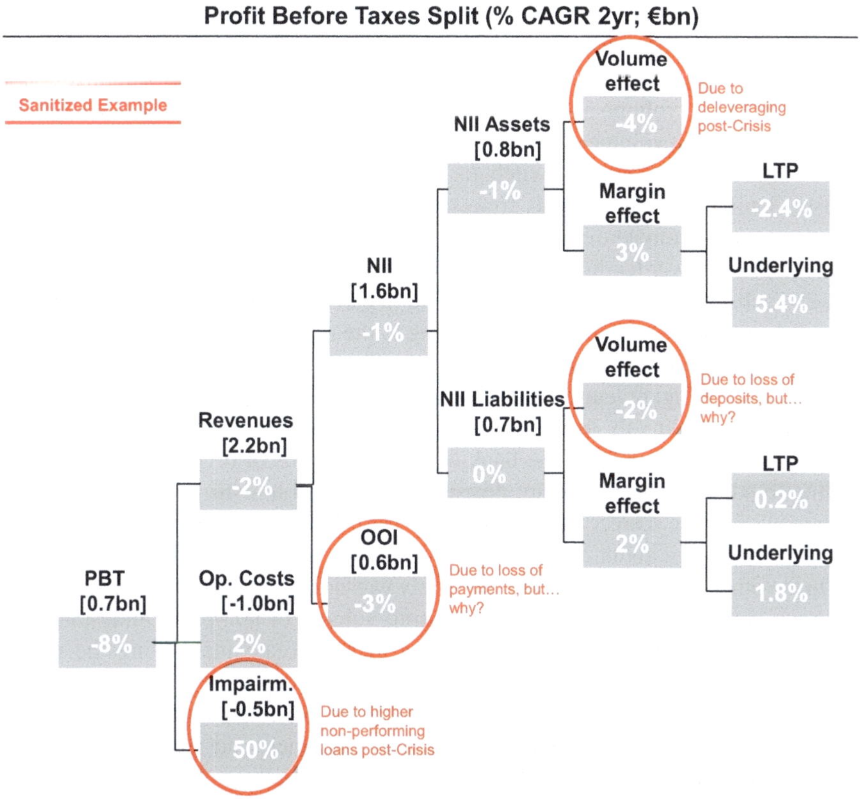

Fig. 2.3 Issue Tree—Corporate Banking activity (example). Sources: Sanitized example

so, we could be literally 'boiling the ocean' if we were not careful in this analysis phase. What I call the trap of the 'carpet bombing' analysis.

Thus, to avoid this trap it is important to adopt the right mix of inductive vs deductive approaches.

In this case study, we started deductive developing an issue tree for corporate banking P&L, showing lending, deposits and payments activity to identify drivers and evolution of its profits. As discussed in Chap. 1, the issue tree is an analysis that enumerates the different drivers in logical and sequential order until arriving at the low order ones.

Therefore, looking at Fig. 2.3 in detail: for the lending activity, net interest income from assets (NII Assets) stems from volume times margins; margins are a function of liquidity transfer pricing (LTP or cost of funds) combined with the 'underlying' interest rate received from clients. Similarly, Fig. 2.3 shows the deposits activity (NII Liabilities), while the fees of payments activity are the driver of 'other operating income' (OOI). These 3 components make the Revenues, out of which the tree finishes by subtracting operating costs and impairments, to arrive at profit before tax (PBT).

In the case above, the tree was pointing to 4 issues, 2 of them clearly understood in the aftermath of the Credit Crisis: reduction of lending volume due to deleveraging (that more than compensated increased margin from repricing efforts), and the increasing volume of impairments (due to higher non-performing loans). The other 2, decreasing volume of liabilities and payments, were a bit unclear.

This was the moment to switch to an inductive-based approach. Leveraging industry knowledge and insights from talking to clients and staff, the team could hypothesize the ultimate drivers of the observed underperformance.

The issue of lower lending activity was driven by macro and re-regulatory factors post-2008. From both perspectives, it would negatively impact the lending activity going forward, so everybody was awakening to the ugly truth that the lending book, in net terms, would decrease over the next 3–5 years, perhaps more. That would mean only one thing: revenue would drop substantially for the division, since 75% of revenues derived directly from the lending activity. Therefore, the team concluded that there was very little that the bank could do in terms of reversing the negative lending trend; the only remaining decision was instead how to prioritize clients in order to allocate the scarcer lending going forward, and for this type of issue the bank could do something about it.

On the other hand, what the bank definitely was doing, and had still much more to do about, was tackling the issue of increasing volume of non-performing loans; it was urgent and also in the bank's hand to manage (e.g. intensifying the client conversations to renegotiate their facilities and to restructure).

But what about the other 2 issues? Looking at the faltering payments activity and deposits volume, after some conversations with customers and teams, it transpired these issues were driven more from the banks' own failings in investing in the transaction banking platform over the years, by comparison to competitors that had kept upgrading their offerings... therefore, the loss of requests-for-proposal was only a logical consequence.

Therefore, among the 4 issues, the logical conclusion based on the facts above was to focus on prioritizing dwindling lending capacity among existing clients (1st priority), restructuring of non-performing loans (2nd priority), and investing in the transaction banking platform (3rd priority); also, while waiting till the macro situation improved and lending grew again, gradually build the investment banking capabilities to earn future ancillary business over that new lending (4th priority). The main issues identified in the SWOT were now finally diagnosed and prioritized.

2.3 Core Strategy

Only from that base of solid insight provided by the Diagnosis, your team will be able to craft potential strategic alternatives to tackle the weaknesses and threats, as well as to seize the opportunities. It is advisable to define several alternatives, as opposed to just one course of action, so that trade-offs can be identified in terms of outcomes and risks expected from each one. This will result in a decision about a preferred strategic alternative, which becomes part of the Core Strategy.

But, *what are the Core Strategy's components?* Any business at its essence needs to take a line in the sand to define (1) which client segments will target, (2) with which products/services and (3) in which geographical location/s.

The Core Strategy should articulate the policy decisions made about what evolution or change to make across Clients, Products and Geography based on the prioritization of main issues from the Diagnosis. It should aim to cover the MTP time horizon (3–5 years typically).

The discussion about Business Model in Chap. 1, addresses in-depth Client Segmentation and Products/Services (one element of the Value Proposition Definition—to simplify I will refer to it just as Product). Regarding Geography, when discussing Business Model 'as-is', geography refers to the existing market for that BU at that point in time. However, when discussing Business Model 'as-should-be', a decision could be made about potentially expanding the model to new geographies, and so the geographical aspect does matter when we are talking about the evolution or change of the Business Model. The Strategy Blueprint precisely is meant to focus on articulating these changes, hence Geography becomes a key element that requires explicit articulation in this Core Strategy framework in parallel with the targeted evolution for Clients and Products.

My suggestion for developing a Core Strategy is to craft an ad hoc, bespoken 1-page framework that gathers visually the 3 elements, along with any twists that might deserve a place to emphasize the relative importance of the elements. Supporting that 1 page, subsequently you can add all the required qualitative and quantitative detail that substantiate the intended change in each of the elements (e.g. for Client: expected evolution of product penetration by segments, or average revenue per product, or new-to-bank client acquisition per segment). However, the 1-page Core Strategy framework would ideally be the single one that the MD of the BU would always take with him/her to explain 'at 10k-feet' what the strategy for that BU is. Figure 2.4 shows the one used for the corporate bank case.

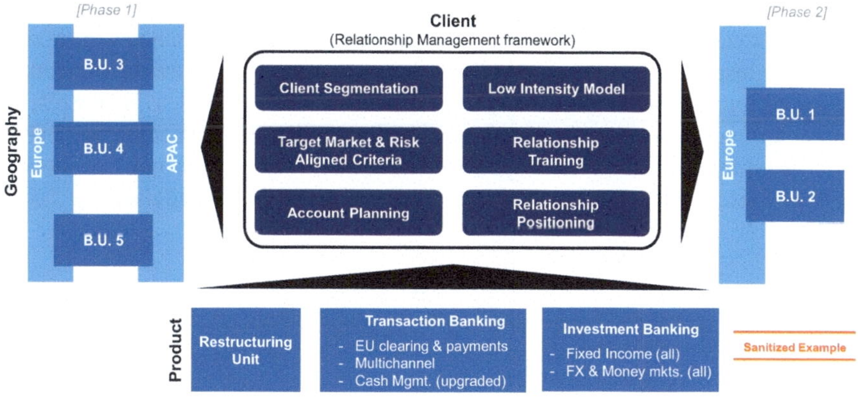

Fig. 2.4 Core strategy framework (example). Sources: Sanitized example

Now, there is an implicit intermediate step from the Diagnosis outcome (i.e. the prioritized main issues) to the Core Strategy 1-page: the production of strategic alternatives for each main issue and the selection of the preferred one. The judgement to make that choice should be based on a profound understanding of the sources of strategic power for the BU in its marketplace (ref. Sect. 9.6 in Chap. 9). This is the act of making decisions for guiding policy, and it is one of the (if not THE) main responsibilities of the executive.

From the above case study's Diagnosis, issue #1 was prioritizing dwindling lending capacity (i.e. scarcer risk-weighting assets[1]) among existing clients. Given the importance of this issue, an entirely separate project spun off that focused on developing a holistic customer relationship management framework that was based on: client segmentation (the 'brains' of the CRM, 'Trusted Relationship' in Sect. 1.2 in Chap. 1 was a good example), target market & risk aligned criteria (to align with credit appetite), relationship training (for upskilling), account planning (to coordinate action), low-intensity model (to reduce cost-to-serve) and relationship positioning (to change positioning, as described in Sect. 1.2, Chap. 1).

The Geography element was simpler, as no geographical expansion or exit was considered for that corporate bank, it was reduced only to the policy of applying the new CRM across all the 5 existing BUs in Europe, as well as to the 3 BUs based in the Asia-Pacific region. The roll-out was planned in 2 phases, first with the BUs with dual-region presence, then the rest.

The Product element also involved choices among several strategic alternatives. For issue #2, restructuring of non-performing loans, several models were studied: a separate portfolio within each segment (i.e. several 'bad book sub-segments'), or a transfer to a separate team fully dedicated to restructuring (i.e. a 'restructuring unit'), or a transfer outside the bank to an SPV with own balance-sheet created for that purpose (i.e. a 'bad bank'). The bank decided to form a Restructuring Unit, which would require dedicated investment.

Issues #3 and #4 demanded product investment as well, respectively, in Transaction Banking and Investment Banking capabilities. Both became spun-off complex projects that articulated bottom-up the requirements to upgrade the platform and its investment case. Each of them eventually presented strategic alternatives to choose from. For instance, the Transaction Banking case contemplated several alternative ambitions for core clearing, selecting one that focused on the Euro leaving the rest of currencies under corresponding banking. The Investment Banking case choice was to focus on reinforcing all offerings in fixed income, foreign exchange and money markets, therefore leaving out of its ambition equities and M&A advisory.

[1]Concept derived from Basel Accord for Regulatory Capital, by which a bank needs to maintain a minimum amount of capital in proportionality to the lending book (i.e. assets) it holds; the book value of those assets is categorized and weighted depending on their riskiness, hence the resulting concept of Risk Weighted Assets (or RWAs in short).

In sum, based on a thorough fact-based Diagnosis, the Core Strategy 1-page framework becomes the main compass at the heart of the Strategy Blueprint, which will guide all the subsequent Strategic Priorities and Actions for execution.

2.4 Coherent Action

Finally, this Core Strategy will be materialized in a cascade of actions, in a logical and orderly way. First defining some Strategic Priorities that allow us to determine where the focus should be now vs later during the MTP time horizon. Then, within each Strategic Priority, clearly articulated Action Plans, usually several per Priority would be devised. The keyword about this set of Priorities and Plans is coherence; coherence with the Core Strategy and expectation that their outcomes will deliver the Goals the whole plan aims to achieve. That is Coherent Action.

Strategy execution will be delivered by a portfolio of Action Plans. Specific projects or programmes (i.e. several interconnected projects) of delivery that aim, in effect, transforms the BU Business Model from 'as-is' to 'as-should-be' over the MTP horizon. Normally, these projects might range in duration from several months to 1–2 years, and easily amount from +50 to +200 depending on the size of the organization.

We use Strategic Priorities to put some 'order in the galaxy' and to ensure 'coherence'. These are concrete statements of the business priorities to deliver via a cluster of Action Plans and are aligned to the Core Strategy.

For the corporate bank case study, the portfolio of Action Plans resulted in a large number of projects (perhaps 40–50), grouped in terms of Strategic Priorities (not many, 5–12) distributed along 3 horizons of time (more about this in Chap. 8). Each Action Plan had an Executive Sponsor from the top management, and a team for delivery, with clear expectations in terms of timing.

To ensure the consistency and alignment of Strategic Priorities and Action Plans, 2 tests are suggested:

(1) *Is there any Action Plan that is not facing a concrete Strategic Priority in the portfolio?* If an Action Plan does not belong to a Strategic Priority, and assuming that these have been thoroughly formulated from the Core Strategy, then it probably needs to be shut down and resources tied to it liberated for other uses.
(2) If any Strategic Priority does not have Action Plans attached, either in current or planned for future execution, it begs the question: *is this Strategic Priority valid according to the Core Strategy? If yes, then what Action Plans do we need to formulate for making it happen?*

Another best-practice is to ensure that all Action Plans follow a similar discipline of execution. To start with, an Action Plan requires a Terms of Reference (ToR), which details some essential description of goals and workstreams, owners and governance, core team and virtual team and delivery plan and milestones. This document serves as well to frame expectations of all teams and stakeholders

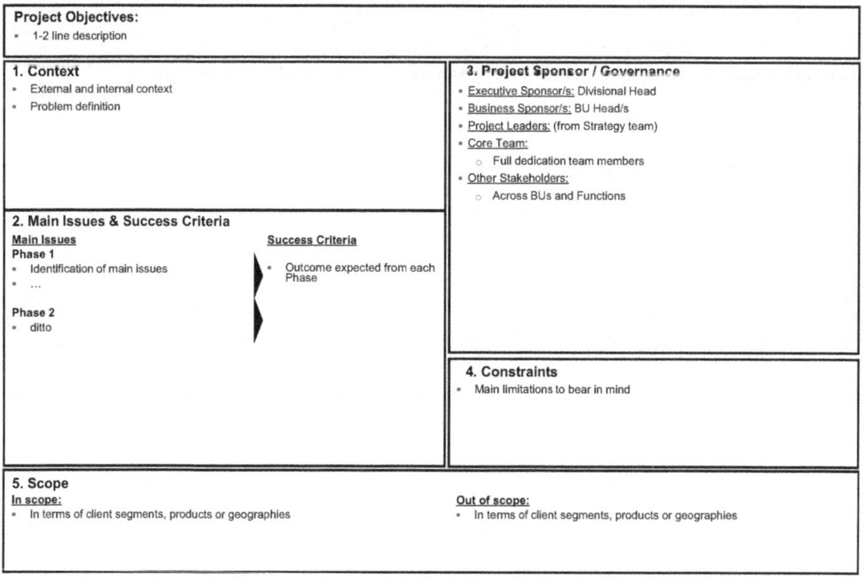

Fig. 2.5 Action Plan—Terms of Reference (example). Sources: Sanitized example

involved, since they will need to liberate and reallocate time for dedication to the project and will need the commitment to ensure their contribution is positive and recognized (Fig. 2.5).

Finally, it is key to ensure a Governance mechanism for decision-making of the Action Plans is in place, with clear rules of the game and communicated to all actors involved. Depending on the organizations, there could be a general Execution Gateway Committee or Operating Committee (OpCo) that supervises the pipeline of execution of all Action Plans, with specific milestones for the team driving each Action Plan to report progress and ask for decisions in terms of go-ahead to next milestone and/or approve expenditure of resources.

Those OpCos sit at BU-level, Division-level or even Group-level depending on the remit of the Action Plans. Each OpCo has to have clear charters themselves that define who sits at the decision table, who has voting power and who does not, their remit of decision-making, quorums and frequency of meetings along with logistics (e.g. agenda, secretary, virtual vs presential settings and prep documentation distribution).

At first sight, especially for readers coming from a more entrepreneurial background, it can sound like an utterly bureaucratic process, and effectively on many occasions becomes so, even to a degree of reaching full stagnation. However, it is important not to throw the baby with the bathwater. A large organization is a complex place, where mechanisms of coordination are essential to get things done. The Governance suggested above, like everything in life, can be designed and executed superbly and so that organization will be able to run execution smoothly and efficiently (without anything to envy to a more entrepreneurial and nimble setting), or can per contrary be designed and executed in a patchy, negligent way, in which case the negative connotations of the term ‘bureaucracy’ gain all its meaning.

If Action Plans are aligned to Strategic Priorities and consistent with the Core Strategy, have best-practice Terms of Reference and are supported by the efficient, rigorous, fit-for-purpose Governance... then you got all the ‘hard’ ingredients for success in rolling out your strategy.

* * *

Many business disasters derived from poor execution, but many as well from deficiently crafted strategies. To ensure a strategy is robust it needs to ensure that Purpose, Diagnosis, Core Strategy and Coherent Action are properly designed and performed with methodological rigour. Neglect of any of these elements will ensure a doomed strategy and, with high likelihood, execution failure.

Now, quite often some business practitioners, particularly among entrepreneurs and SME owners, believe that investing time and effort in this rigorous approach to strategy development is a waste. This viewpoint is probably justifiable given their experience of past execution successes where such a planning effort was not performed. Interestingly, when you dig deeper on how they went about succeeding in those example of success, what you find is that these business actors and their teams did, indeed, go informally through and ticked many of the Strategy Blueprint’s elements, but without explicitly articulating them as such. Their small size and close communication allowed them to do so easily.

The development of Purpose, Diagnosis, Core Strategy and Coherent Action does not necessarily require engaging an external management consulting firm, nor an internal team focused for a limited time to strategy formulation. It quite simply may happen in the head of an entrepreneur of a start-up by thinking around the opportunity he got at hand, what he/she would like to aspire to create (an embryo of Purpose), then checking out with potential clients, suppliers, equity sponsors, partners to test his/her hunch vs the facts (which could amount to a serious Diagnosis, particularly when there is a focus on disproving his/her idea, and still it passes the test). The entrepreneur could be pivoting with his/her soon-to-be co-founders different alternatives of client segment focus, proposition, business model, go-to-market approach, even to virtually display several fundamental alternative ways to go about it, to naturally discard those they believe less powerful or riskier, and so conclude on a preferred way (this could amount to a solid Core Strategy). Finally, they will get busy on an array of execution initiatives along the way, which necessarily, a savvy entrepreneur knows he/she will need to prioritize in order to get the most out of the execution from its limited resources (this could amount to a full set of Coherent Action). Now, perhaps not a single document holds all this activity together, it may perfectly all be in the mind of one or several people, but nonetheless, that does not preclude it from constituting ‘Good Strategy’ as per Prof. Rumelt.

References

1. "Good Strategy, Bad Strategy" by Richard Rumelt (Profile Books; 2011).
2. "Start With Why: How Great Leaders Inspire Everyone To Take Action" by Simon Sinek (2009; Portfolio).
3. "Build To Last" by Jim Collins and Jerry Porras (1994; Harper Business).
4. "Made To Stick" by Chip Heath and Dan Heath (2007; Penguin Random House).

3 Financial Plan

Completing the MTP's other side of the coin, the Financial Plan will translate into numbers what the Strategy Blueprint has articulated.

There is no good strategy without an estimation of its financial impact on the organization. Equally, preparing financial plans without prior articulation of a strategy is merely an isolated number crunching exercise.

This chapter suggests a 3-phase best-practice process to develop in tandem the Strategy Blueprint and the Financial Plan, with a core of client and product related KPIs as the hinge that links both together, in order to arrive at a coherent MTP.

3.1 Financial Plan

MTPs and Financial Plans are traditionally owned by the Finance department in organizations. Its existence obeys the necessity by management, and ultimately the Board and shareholders, of having a financial forecast of where performance is heading and a target of what should be expected, over a reasonable timeframe into the future, 3 or 5 years usually.

The best-practice for developing the content of MTPs has gone through a historical evolution, very finely captured by McKinsey & Co. in its classic paper [1]. They started like simple 'Financial Planning' exercises with 1-year horizon, which basically corresponds to what currently we denominate the yearly Budget, lacking any sort of strategy articulation, as it was 'assumed' to be known. Then, they evolved into a second phase of 'Forecast-based Planning', which involved a longer time horizon, 3–5 years, along with a strategic internal diagnosis in the form of, for instance, a SWOT analysis (refer to Sect. 2.2 in Chap. 2). In a third phase, the process muted into an 'Externally-oriented Planning', which in addition to the internal diagnosis included now a proper external market analysis, involving both clients and competitors, and continued with a definition of core strategy articulated via participation choices in terms of geography, client and product. Finally, the MTP arrives at its current 'Strategic Management' form, by adding Goals or KPIs for

A. Gavieiro Besteiro, *Strategy in Action*, Management for Professionals,
https://doi.org/10.1007/978-3-030-94759-0_3

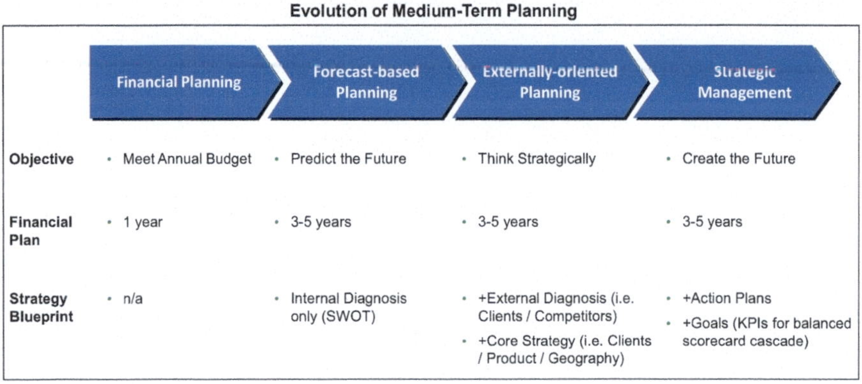

Fig. 3.1 Evolution of Medium-Term Planning. Note: The graphic depiction of this framework has been created for this book, so it is not original from the authors referred to in the source. Sources: Own analysis [1]

cascading balanced scorecard and Action Plans, thereby linking the strategic agenda with the operational agenda. Figure 3.1 shows the correspondence of this historical evolution to different components of the Strategy Blueprint and Financial Plan.

Despite many MTPs having evolved to best-practice, we still find, as mentioned at the beginning of this chapter, many organizations where the MTP is just a Financial Plan exercise, without articulated strategy. *Why?*

Over time, as organizations became publicly listed and institutional investors won a say in the Boards, the MTP became the preferred tool for corporate governance. Given the critical focus of equity markets on quarterly performance, the MTP mimics this prioritization and so becomes an instrument to capture and reflect the consensus expectations in terms of results, its quarterly Budget vs Forecast updates and key milestones for the CEO, the CFO and, indeed, the entire organization. This prioritization of the finance component of the MTP gradually led to a relegation of the strategy component to a secondary role (sometimes referred to as 'the wording' or 'the story'). Consequently, the 2 elements ended up being almost independent of each other within the whole exercise. In sum, there was no linkage anymore between the 'words' and the 'numbers'.

The trouble with this approach is that, given that strategy and finance are like 2 sides of the same coin, they need to match and link very clearly, otherwise the MTP exercise becomes a senseless numbers game. As a result, the organization gets easily lost in an effort of number-making, with the Group high-bowling overarching targets, while the Business Units low-bowling as much as they can in order to make the yearly Budget achievable (and so the related bonus awards). Despite the absurd dynamics, this planning approach is a reality in many large banks (sometimes the larger, the worse it gets).

The only solution to this futile game is to link back the Financial Plan to the Strategy Blueprint at the very root of it. *How?*

If we look at the revenue line in a P&L, we can break it down into its component drivers (as per the example in Fig. 2.2 earlier): volume times margins (in banking, simplifying: 'loan advances' times 'average interest income margin', minus 'customer deposits' times 'average interest expense margin'). This revenue drivers' analysis, as far as the Finance function is concerned, usually stopped there because then you could build the revenues simply by eliciting growth of volumes (i.e. of loan advances and customer deposits) and the associated changes in margins. There is nothing wrong with this approach, however, it does not allow us to look at the revenues line from a 'client perspective', which usually is recommended for strategy purposes.

To allow for the full linkage with strategy, it is necessary to break down revenues into 3 fundamental KPIs at client segment level (which links to the discussion earlier in Sect. 1.5, Chap. 1):

1. Average (existing) client penetration per product.
2. Average revenue per (existing) client per product.
3. New-to-bank clients (expected to be acquired over MTP time horizon).

To tally back to the traditional Finance approach, KPI #2 above could be broken down by volume and margins for that given client segment and product (e.g. lending and deposits).

For any business (at least as far as I have seen within the financial services industry), its revenue lines can be derived from this mutually exclusive, comprehensively exhaustive classification of ultimate revenue drivers. Eureka! it is precisely at this level that Strategy meets Finance.

Strategy works at understanding what is the current position of the company in the marketplace, which in quantitative terms equates, for a given geography, to market shares by client segment and product; in addition, what is outside of the company's current market share is the potential ocean of new-to-bank clients, to attempt to capture in the future. Hence, it is only natural that the Core Strategy formulation focuses on the dimensions of Client, Product and Geography, and tries to articulate the guiding policies to achieve higher market share across these 3 dimensions.

Therefore, only by articulating over the Financial Plan time horizon the targets across the 3 KPIs above we can sensibly justify the revenue lines at the top of our P&L with a narrative univocally linked to the Core Strategy.

Logically, the growth expected for each client segment over the MTP period will be a result of the estimates of new-to-bank clients for each year; and the MTP's revenue growth will result from a combination of the product penetration and revenue per product estimates upon both the existing and the new client base (these estimates could be similar or, more often than not, different between existing vs new clients).

Moreover, only at this KPI level we are able as well to make sensitivity analysis that links to our business intuition of whether the assumed increases in productivity are feasible, considering the nature of each geography, client segment and product line. Thus, for instance, in a large corporate bank's home country it is logical to expect high levels of client penetration, however, while its estimates for current account penetration on existing clients could be as high as 90–95%, the penetration for debt capital markets origination will not clearly reach any near those numbers, where a level of 20–30% could be considered high.

Another great advantage of working out the revenues at KPI level is that it allows for other critical implementation-related functions like Risk, Operations, IT or HR to participate in the KPI discussion and so to derive Financial Planning implications for their respective capabilities, considering their limitations and bottlenecks. This input is essential if we are to elaborate Cost lines (with their respective KPIs as well) that correlate with the efforts required out of the Revenue lines projected, otherwise we would be underestimating the investment effort needed and overestimating Profits. As importantly, this collaboration would pave the way for more robust Action Plan development and so would ensure a kick-off of the implementation cascade with more certainty, improving the chances of success in the execution of the projects and programmes across the organization.

Therefore, the formulation of the Financial Plan requires to open a dialog among the Business Unit, Finance, Strategy and Management in order to derive revenue lines based on KPIs' assumptions informed by proper business acumen. This can only be done in the space where Strategy meets Finance.

As a result, it looks like elaborating a best-in-class MTP entails an arduous undertaking that involves a high level of energy and participation across the entire company. Effectively it does... though with proper frameworks, coordination and experience it can be made to work like a Swiss clock. *How exactly?*

To describe how we suggest a process of 3 phases for the MTP development:

1. Strategy Blueprint Refresh: Aimed at creating or updating the Strategy Blueprint of the BU, led by the Strategy team and with critical participation of Finance and, of course, the business executive team.
2. Financial Plan Modelling: Led by the Finance team instead, and with additional participation of the main support functions.
3. Innovation Strategy and Finance Loop: Conceived as a frequent, within-the-year periodic exercise for updating the previous 2 phases with innovation cases coming bottom-up from the BUs across the organization.

This new, latter phase is important in the context of high level of digital innovation and transformation that an industry like Financial Services is currently experiencing (as we will discuss in Chap. 12).

3.2 Phase I—Strategy Blueprint Refresh

The goal of this phase is to update the Strategy Blueprint (as per Chap. 2) or, if it does not exist yet, to create it for the first time (which will obviously require an ad hoc exercise with time in its own right).

Now, the effort must focus on a Business Unit level, as the MTP's basic unit of account, since it is at this level where the organization meets a particular marketplace. Thereafter, we can elevate the exercise at Divisional and Group level, but there we will be working on an aggregated basis, which I refer to as 'Portfolio Strategy' (more on this topic in Chaps. 7 and 8). This will be altogether a different type of exercise, because it will focus on resource reallocation as opposed to the interaction of company, clients and competitors in each of the marketplaces where that Division or Group participates via the respective BUs.

We could subdivide this Phase I of the process for a given BU into 2 steps: Diagnosis and Strategy Development (Fig. 3.2).

3.2.1 Step-1: Diagnosis

The Strategy team would normally lead this exercise, with the participation of Finance, BU Business Management, Marketing and Risk.

We start looking outside, to the external world and its Market Dynamics, identifying Macro trends using, for instance, the PESTLE framework, and Clients / Competitors trends leveraging Five Forces or Strategy Canvas frameworks (refer to Sect. 1.1 in Chap. 1).

Then we look inside, to the state of our Company's BU using a SWOT framework (Sect. 2.3.1 in Chap. 2) considering both the insights from Market Dynamics analysis and the internal key parameters or constraints that could set limits to our MTP exercise. For instance, perhaps Group Finance has defined some guidance of the high-level Goals sought after by the end of the 3 or 5-year MTP horizon; or perhaps there are some overriding constraints in terms of balance-sheet (i.e. loan book size and deposits), cost of funds, portfolio (i.e. core vs non-core loan book) or risk appetite. The point is to ensure that the resulting SWOT is informed by these insights, limits or guidance.

I would like to highlight the importance, at this juncture of the process, of preparing very rigorously the quantitative and qualitative underlying information in order to generate these frameworks. It is important because once the frameworks are filled, the business team and BU stakeholders may use them without questioning too much the underlying information, assumed as 'a given' (i.e. anchoring bias). Therefore, we rather ensure it is prepared thoroughly, otherwise, a strategy formulation based on biased or inaccurate assumptions could backfire later on.

3.2.2 Step-2: Strategy Development

This exercise would be ideally performed during an Away Day Workshop with the BU's top management, and its purpose is to refresh the 4 elements of the Strategy Blueprint as required (ref. Chap. 2), based on a reflection about the changes in the Business Model (ref. Chap. 1).

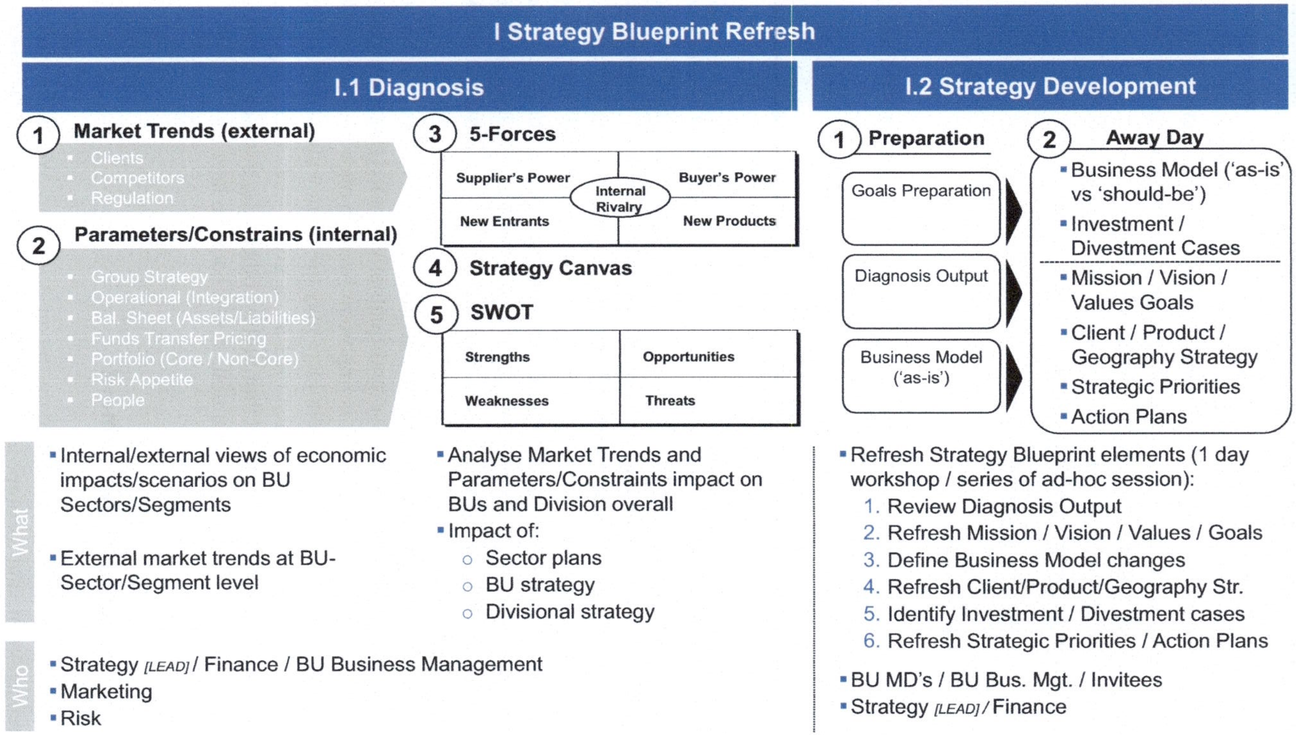

Fig. 3.2 **MTP process—Strategy Blueprint Refresh** (1/3). Sources: 'Holistic Management Framework v.5' (Angel Gavieiro; Apr.17; AG Strategy & Partners)

Like any workshop, its success will depend on having a solid preparation that serves to inform the meeting, and a well-thought structure for its execution during the day. In terms of preparation, 3 key inputs: (a) a pre-definition of Goals from the Head of the BU (goals inspired by the guidance from Group Finance); (b) the outputs from the Diagnosis step and (c) the 'as-is' Business Model (either existing from prior year, or newly minted if done for first time).

The Strategy team would normally lead this workshop, with the support of Finance, BU Business Management, and the participation of the BU Top Management and guests, perhaps for some of the sessions, from specific functions that have a strong involvement with this BU: for instance, for a Corporate Banking BU, the main Product-line partners and the Risk department.

The centrepiece of the Away Day involves the discussion of the Core Strategy itself, and so the comparison of the current position in terms of Client, Product and Geography, vs the targeted position towards the end of the MTP horizon. The conversation becomes concrete by discussing the KPIs for each of these 3 dimensions, and so reaching consensus of what should be the target KPI values each year within the 3 or 5-year horizon is critical. For instance, in a corporate bank's large multinationals client segment, the current client share is 20%, and the discussion arrives at a consensus to target 25% (so implying an estimate for customer acquisition target); and within it perhaps the transaction banking's current account penetration is 80%, and they may agree to raise it to 90% as a final target.

All of that dialog would include a recurrent testing of the feasibility of the targets at the face of client trends and competitor reactions. This KPI triangulation will become a critical input for the next phase of the process.

By the end of these Steps 1 (Diagnosis) and 2 (Strategy Development), the Strategy Blueprint of the BU would be refreshed, its future Business Model ('as should be') defined, and all key parties in the organization closely related to the BU fully aware of and aligned as they participated in its update. So, now, we are ready to translate it all into financials.

3.3 Phase II—Financial Plan Modelling

At this point, the Finance function takes the baton from the Strategy team to lead the process. The time for the number crunching has arrived.

We could subdivide this Phase II of the process into 3 steps: Financial Drivers Analysis, Baseline Financial Modelling and Investment/Divestment Cases (Fig. 3.3).

3.3.1 Step-1: Financial Drivers Analysis

This step focuses on estimating the revenues and costs for the 'Business As Usual' (BAU) operations, not for any new investment cases or divestment cases of that BU, which will be done separately on a standalone basis later.

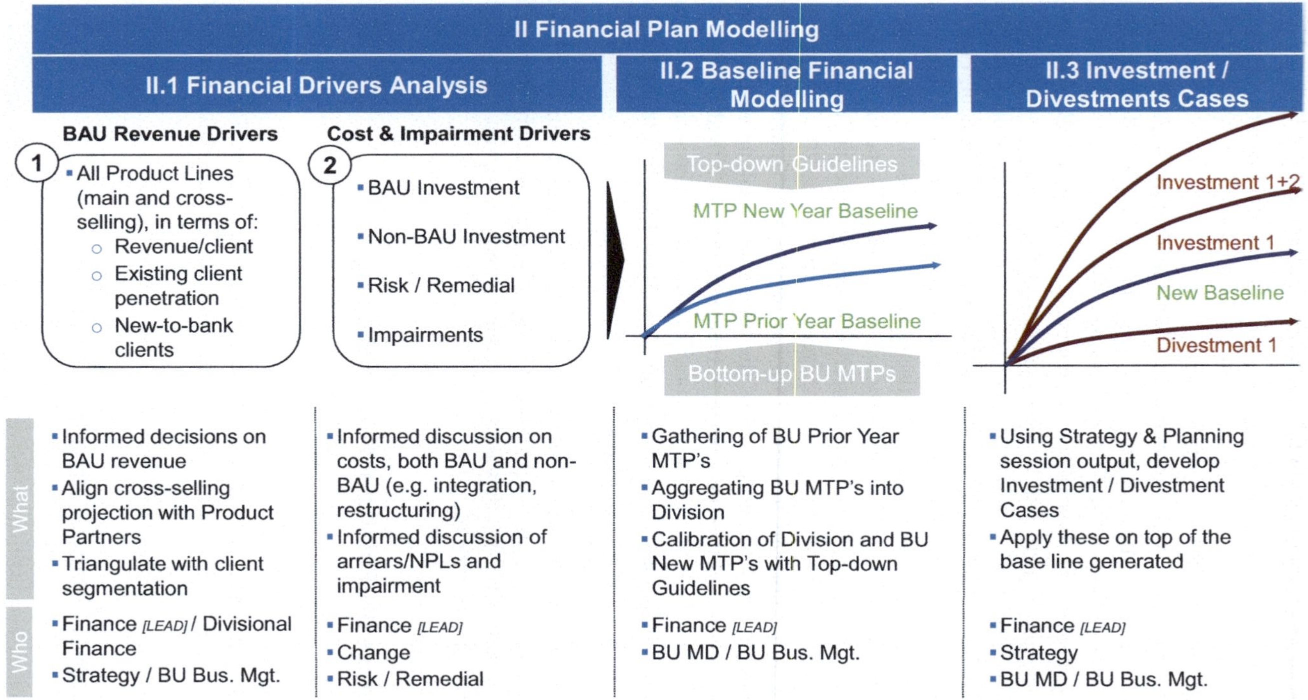

Fig. 3.3 **MTP Process—Financial Plan Modelling** (2/3). Sources: 'Holistic Management Framework v.5' (Angel Gavieiro; Apr.17; AG Strategy & Fartners)

Regarding revenues, the estimation over the Financial Plan horizon (for instance, 3 years) would stem from the KPI targets discussed, during the Phase I, in the Strategy Blueprint for each Geography, Client and Product (as described in Sect. 1.5 in Chap. 1 and Sect. 3.1).

Thus, for a given Geography (e.g. the EU), Client segment (e.g. Major Corporates) and Product line (e.g. transaction banking's current accounts), there would be a clear initial point (year 0) and final point (year 3) in terms of (A) existing-client penetration per product, (B) revenue per existing-client per product and (C) new-to-bank clients. From this information, each revenue line is created, presenting a year-on-year growth (y-o-y) and compounded annual growth rate (CAGR) vs. the initial point. The same goes for all the remaining product lines for that Geography and Client segment; repeating the process subsequently for each Client segment, and ultimately aggregating them for each Geography.

This would provide the revenue lines for this BU over the 3-year horizon. At that point, we can check whether the implied CAGR is aligned with the top guidance received (if any), and if it falls short, we can adjust back the estimates using judgement and guidance from the Strategy Blueprint discussion.

The cross-selling revenue lines and targets between Client segments and Product lines become dilucidated and agreed at this juncture as well, with the appropriate escalation process in place to elevate disagreements to higher levels of authority as required.

Also, a triangulation with the Client Segmentation framework used in the organization is important at this moment, just to ensure the resulting 'snapshots' of existing plus new-to-bank clients and share of wallet product penetrations by the end of the 3-year horizon are sensible and reasonably achievable. Triangulating these estimates with external information as much as possible is highly recommendable.

Regarding costs, in light of the client and product ramp up derived from the revenue lines, the functional experts (i.e. operations, IT and HR) would provide advice of what does the planned business growth implies in terms of increase of operational cost and capital expenditure.

It is a very common flaw in Financial Planning exercises to skip this last step and basically extrapolate the growth of cost lines at par with revenue lines or, even worse, below these (and so creating a 'positive jaw', i.e. revenue growth minus cost growth, which improves the Cost-to-Income ratio). This provides a 'nice outcome' but at the expense of ignoring the reality of the facts. It is a wrong approach because usually it leads to an underestimation of costs, that can lead to underperformance in subsequent years… and a spiral of urgent cost cuts ('does not matter what and where') to make the targets… all because the planning phase was deficient on the cost side.

Therefore, the engagement of the cost-related functions is critical during this step of the Financial Planning process to make sensible estimations of the next 3–5 years of expected opex and capex.

Regarding impairments, here it is where the contribution of the Risk department is paramount. Risk understood in all its modalities (i.e. credit, market, operational, liquidity,... with an eye put on the resulting capital adequacy ratios) and in alignment with the relevant regulatory and accounting criteria and models.

As an illustration, taking credit risk as an example (not wanting to get in too much depth on a very technical and complex subject), the exercise starts by having accurate visibility of the breakdown of activity volume expected for each relevant product line (not all products bear these type of risks) and client segment (which we have from the revenue estimation exercise above); then, the risk models for the respective combinations would yield the expected losses estimated for credit risk (i.e. as a result of estimating probabilities of default, loss given default and exposure at default), and so we have the associated estimates for non-performing loans and impairments. Quite often, the resulting impairment profile is modelled again under stressed scenarios (e.g. worsening economic conditions, financial crises and geopolitical crisis) to arrive at alternative worse/worst case scenarios (stressed modelling these days is used in banks as well for regulatory purposes[1]).

With all the above, the Finance team will have all the inputs required to undertake the next step in the process.

3.3.2 Step-2: Baseline Financial Modelling

This step normally happens at Divisional Finance level leveraging the inputs collected from the Finance teams supporting each BU.

Here, for the BAU business (let us recall we leave aside the Investment/Divestment Cases discussion until the last step), starting from the initial (from prior-year exercise) 3-year MTP curves, we overlay the new 3-year MTP curves of Revenues, Costs and Impairments. Also, P&L statements are now constructed and so the PBT lines can be calculated and compared between the old and the new Financial Plans.

Equally, the team can now create the Balance-Sheets (B/S) starting from last year's and compare the evolution of the main lines (e.g. client loans and advances, client deposits, short-term assets, short-term liabilities and equity) as well as the related regulatory magnitudes and ratios (e.g. risk-weighted assets, leverage ratio, common equity Tier1 ratio, total capital adequacy ratio, liquidity coverage ratio and net stable financing ratio).

These P&L and B/S curves are then benchmarked against the guidance received from Group, to identify and address potential shortfalls. This would require a feedback loop between Division and the respective BUs (usually channelled via bilateral discussions at a MTP Steering Committee). This is an exercise of building up the numbers over the 3-year horizon and comparing them with prior-year MTP, as well as distilling what story the CAGR percentages and the regulatory ratios say about the business. From there, we compare the estimates with Group guidance and, with management judgement, undertake changes, keeping a strong foot on the

[1]ICAAP (Internal Capital Adequacy Assessment Process) and ILAAP (Internal Liquidity Adequacy Assessment Process), reporting required under Basel III regulatory framework.

reality: the basic KPIs about Client, Product and Geography, that always will prompt us to be honest and realistic of what is feasible vs what is wishful thinking.

After this feedback loop, the BUs could either have their BAU Financial Plan approved 'in-principle' (as it is still subject to the subsequent MTP discussion between Division and Group), or alternatively be given a 'Financial Challenge' to some particular lines or metrics of the P&L and/or B/S, and therefore they would need to go back to their BUs to discuss internally and provide modifications to their plan that fit the required challenge.

Once all the 'Financial Challenges' have been smoothed out, and the Investment / Divestment Cases (addressed in the next step) agreed the Financial Plan is ready for going 'upstairs'.

3.3.3 Step-3: Investment / Divestment Cases

Starting at BU, and coming directly from the Strategy Refresh Phase, the BU Management team surely has identified several Opportunities, Threats or Weaknesses that they would like to prioritize for execution within their next 3-year horizon. The MTP will be the main formal process they usually have to make their cases for investment (or divestment), so normally only one window per year (phase 3 below addresses a more frequent process in this regard).

The Strategy team in collaboration with the Finance team and the specific people in the BU sponsoring the respective Case, will articulate the rationale from a business perspective and estimate the financial impact (for both P&L and B/S).

So, for instance, the Financial Institutions BU of a European bank is thinking of expanding their presence in Asia and selected the Hong Kong hub for setting up a locally based team leveraging the existing premises of the bank there. Thus, they would present an Investment Case with a strategy part that discusses the market trends (clients vs competitors), the client segments they will focus on and why, the value proposition of product/services they will offer there, along with any consideration of pricing and positioning in that market, and a discussion on how they will build up the front, middle and back-office along with all the processes of risk, operations, IT, etc... necessary to have the platform ready for delivery. In parallel, the Case will include a finance section that, starting from the basic KPIs (i.e. new-to-bank clients to acquire in each segment, product penetration for each and revenues per product per segment) will develop the revenue curves. Leveraging the information on the value proposition build-up, the costs could be estimated, along with the cost allocation from the premises and support of the existing bank branch. Finally, some estimations of impairments based on risk would be included. At that point, the Financial Institutions BU would have a full Investment Case ready for discussion at the MTP Steering Committee (usually, it is all done in the same conversation or in parallel Case sessions of the same Committee as referred above).

In the same way as a BU may present Investment Cases, it might as well present Divestment Cases. Actually, these add a lot to the credibility of a BU Managing Director constantly thinking what 'dead wood' in the current business model should be 'pruned'. It is not uncommon that BU leaders fail to grasp this part of their duties as managers of a business, simply because usually it is painful to clean up, restructure or shut down, it is much more attractive to have just a 'growth mindset'. However, resources by definition are limited, at BU, at Division and, indeed, at Group level. Therefore, the best MTP Case discussions I have participated in were those when a BU leader brought 2–3 Investment Cases to the table accompanied with 1–2 Divestment Cases, which actually were able to liberate via divestment over time perhaps 40–60% of the resources required to finance their investment in the first place... beautiful!

3.4 Phase III—Innovation Strategy and Finance Loop

I will leave to Chap. 12 the discussion about the market context of digital disruption and its impact in the Financial Services industry. One of the main effects of this trend has been that banks have started to redefine their strategy to include digital transformation, in different degrees and ambitions.

Now, the process of design and execution of that strategy is affected by the very nature of how digital transformation 'behaves'. Many other industries such as media, music or advertising have already gone through that journey, and the behaviour of such a disruption could be characterized as bumpy, fast, twisting and turning, full of optionality forks, where fail fast is welcomed, where self-cannibalization sometimes is unavoidable and, of course, where substantial investment will be required.

For many banks, the MTP process is the main resource allocation mechanism for investment. As described in the previous 2 phases, it is a slow process, meant for reflection and planning, with some feedback iterations and following a top-down guidance along with a bottom-up submission in 2 stages, Division and Group. Depending on the bank size, it could perfectly take 2 or even 3 months, at minimum. Therefore, MTP is often an annual exercise, in some banks even it is done once every 2–3 years.

The MTP process as originally conceived works well for its intended purpose of providing clear alignment along the organization on medium and long-term targets and a clear way of how to achieve them, as well as informing the Board and shareholders about these decisions and furnishing the markets with benchmarks against which to keep the bank top management accountable for delivery.

However, this MTP process is far from adequate to provide the agility and flexible approach required to tackle with nimbleness the opportunities and threats that digital disruption generates, and the demands driven by the internal digital transformation of the organization.

In order to enable organizations to embrace digital transformation in earnest, there is the urge to redesign several key 'Meta-architectural Levers' (as we will discuss in depth in Chap. 12), one among them is the MTP process. And the right verb is 'redesign' as opposed to 'substitute', because the original purpose the MTP was meant to fulfil (i.e. strategic and financial planning towards Board and external markets) must still be properly performed.

My suggestion is to maintain the MTP process like a yearly exercise, however, it would ideally be complemented by a continuum of 'Innovation Strategy & Finance Loops': monthly or maximum bimonthly sessions throughout the entire year where different BUs (for instance 2–8 each time) show up in the MTP Steering Committee to discuss Investment/Divestment Cases focused on digital transformation (or other relevant drivers of change). Thus, it means basically to open a set of windows along the year to repeat a similar exercise to Step-3 of Phase II (i.e. Investment/Divestment Cases), having a modification impact (a 'pivot') on the official MTP of the respective BU (and also for the respective Division's and Group's). Crucially, this would be done in a gradual way across the entire organization, flexibly to accommodate the pace of the digital transformation problem solving and experimentation happening in each BU.

For instance, a single BU might decide to experiment with 2–3 alliances with FinTech start-ups. Perhaps at a point, it decides to buy one of them and integrate it within the business model and thereafter dispose of or shutdown some legacy systems. The BU would be making use of these Loops by tapping this window 3–4 times in the space of 2 years to gain approval for each of these moves.

From a Group perspective, over a 3–5 year span most of the BUs in the company would have had the chance to undertake a full or partial digital transformation at their own pace. Obviously, the resulting MTP would continuously be updated, however, the resource reallocation would be much more active and, over time, cumulatively more impactful in terms of redistribution to where the business needs are.

This redesigned MTP process, which empowers quite considerably the BU in order to 'own' its innovation investment and transformation, would also require some discipline. Therefore, I suggest embedding within the Loops proper Dynamic Strategic Planning practices [2] to ensure there is a good ex ante control of the effort at BU level and to avoid unintended large MTP deviations vs target at aggregate Group level. The Dynamic Strategic Planning within Strategy and Finance Loops would involve 3 steps (ref. illustration below):

1. Strategic Analysis: Starting from the Strategy Blueprint from Phase I as a base, the BU assesses how innovation is impacting Clients' behaviour, articulates what impact is intended at their journey and experience, and determines how that impact will occur by changing different elements of the Value Proposition definition and delivery (usually incorporating elements of technological innovation to the Business Model, even radically transforming it in its entirety if that were the case).
2. Dynamic Planning: It might happen that there could be different scenarios of potential innovation paths, perhaps because the technology is still being explored under different variants (for instance, as currently happens with blockchain); so, these scenarios need to be identfied, as well as any real options for collaboration with third parties at different milestones and any knots for negotiation expected in the decision trees.
3. Investment/Divestment Cases: Similarly to Step-3 in Phase II in a regular MTP, the previous 2 steps translate themselves in numbers for P&L and B/S impact,

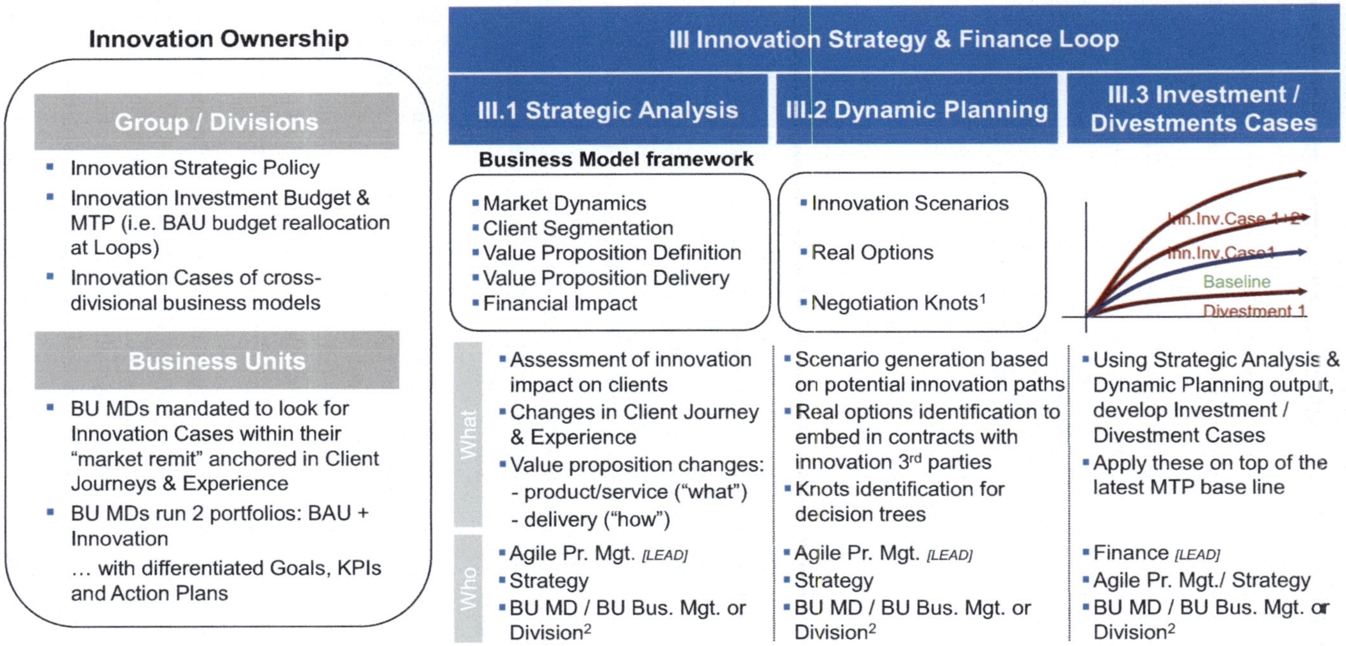

Fig. 3.4 **MTP Process—Innovation Strategy & Finance Loop** (3/3). (1) Point in time where outcomes from negotiations among industry stakeholders involved in an innovation are expected; (2) Depending on ownership. Sources: 'Holistic Management Framework v.5' (Angel Gavieiro; Apr.17; AG Strategy & Partners) [2]

including all the capex and opex required (plus potential JVs/acquisitions of FinTech start-ups) (Fig. 3.4).

The first step will help to visualize how the innovation will change the BU Business Model and the intended benefit to clients. The second step will help to understand the complexity and uncertainty embedded in the path to materialize the innovation and surely it will be subject to changes as the execution progresses. The third step generates the financial impact and should be acceptable if some of the estimates are given in bracket ranges due to the uncertainty involved in the dynamic planning.

* * *

The MTP will tell the story, both in 'words' and in 'numbers', of how the BU's Business Model will evolve from 'as is' to 'as should be' over the MTP time horizon.

The evolution of MTP as an art and science for developing a joint Strategy Blueprint and Financial Plan, united at their root by the 3 basic core KPIs, has reached a high level of proficiency when best-practice is considered both in terms of rigorous frameworks and disciplined process.

A key success factor will continue to be thorough preparation, in terms of the market dynamics and diagnosis, ensuring that facts, insights are properly distilled, and strategic alternatives carefully crafted for decision-making by the relevant stakeholders.

Finally, driven by the impact of the 4th revolution (digital) across industries, times have changed, and speed is now of the essence. Similarly, the MTP development has to change to gain agility and flexibility. Innovation Strategy and Finance Loops, scheduled monthly or bimonthly, will open the door to a bottom-up flow of investment/divestment cases that help BUs to adapt their business models to their dynamic marketplaces.

References

1. "Thinking Strategically" by Frederick W. Gluck, Stephen P. Kaufman, and A. Stephen Walleck (2000; McKinsey Quarterly; McKinsey & Co).
2. "Dynamic Strategic Planning for Technology Policy" by Richard de Neufville (2000; MIT).

Part II

About 'Strategy for New Geographies and/or Businesses' and 'Strategy & Execution'

It is not the ship so much as the skilful sailing that assures the prosperous voyage (George William Curtis)

You, dear successful Managing Director of a Business Unit, following the lessons from Part I you have been able to grow your unit, make or in some cases exceed your MTP targets, and achieved a leading market share position in the geography and business marketplace where you compete, well done!

Now, the senior leadership team looks at you as the next promising star for management career and promotion; however, these fruits will come in due time, and at a price... the price of the effort to deliver something well beyond usual duty, a true opportunity to make a distinctive mark in the history of the organization. You are given the golden chance to spearhead the international expansion and/or the lateral expansion of your business remit to entirely new marketplaces, congratulations!

In this new endeavour, you will surely face quite different challenges compared to the ones you were used to as a MD of a BU in an existing market: a shock, as your company (like the majority of them) has not prepared you to become an explorer; among the new stuff... Mergers & Acquisitions & Alliances... *how to do this?* ('whatever, sounds cool!'—you think—).

You fetch a book somebody recommended, as you happen to have some good corporate finance background it sounds to you nice and easy, in theory.... but, in practice, again outcomes are way too messy, so, *where do you really start?*

Well, like in the previous part, let us entice our imagination by reverting back to our maritime story...

* * *

You are satisfied, smoking your fine tobacco leaf in your preferred white pipe sitting on Greenwich hill watching the busy docks in London. Since your promotion to Post-Captain, now 7 years ago, you have been commanding frigates and some sixth to fourth rate ships. You are expecting now to be given command of your first 74-gun ship-of-the-line.

You briefly peek up at the sun, it seems a bit past noon (the red ball at Greenwich Observatory was yet to be installed about 40 years later to help clock synchronization across ships). Time to head back to London to receive new orders; the outbreak of war is imminent again with the Continent, so you expect you will be thrown into the eye of the hurricane once again, though this time will be quite different, as it will not be just about managing the natural elements (*Clients*), it will be about directly engaging other ships (*Competitors*).

You arrive just in time as the session which the Admiralty gathers for strategic discussions, including the main ship-of-the-line captains of the Blue Squadron, where your ship belongs.

In December 1792, war with France is nearly there. There has been a dispute about colonies in the Caribbean and the Indian Ocean; more worryingly, close to home there have been movements of troops in Western and Central Europe. Thus, the variety of potential geographic scenarios for action is staggering, and the enemy forces are dispersed across them. We just do not have enough ships to simultaneously juggle so much. It is necessary to devise a plan that prioritizes our action across regions and potential enemy fleets (*Attractiveness vs Opportunities framework*).

First, we need to strategically identify which areas are more important for our political interests (*Geography/Business Attractiveness*) by understanding the diplomatic and economic dynamics (*Environment*) and the confronted interests of the parties (*Industry*) for each of these regions. The politicians at Whitehall and our Admiralty have been working hard on this part.

At the same time, taking a region at a time, our intelligence service points to different concentrations of enemy ships (*Target Identification*); in some cases, we have a reliable picture of their strength, in other cases our estimates are vastly speculative. We review the arrangement of our logistics, crew and ships (*Company Legacy*); also, we need to analyse how best they can combine to face each of the enemy forces in the different regions, so we can finely reckon the chances, and so select the most favourable in which to focus on (*Organic/Inorganic Opportunities*).

It is a game of prioritization, where two types of outputs are required. On the one hand, we need to prioritize the regions we are going to sail to (*Portfolio View*). On the other hand, we need to prioritize what would be our targets (*Entry/Expansion Cases*), on sea or land, based on a proper judgement of chances to win in case of a battle.

The first prioritization output, already worked out for us by the 'higher-ups', shows a list of the regions we will focus on in the first year of war, and scenarios for the second and third years for other regions (*Priority Geography/Market Horizons*) as well. They have for each one a high-level script of the way to approach each region in terms of combination of sea and land forces, journeys and timings (*Geography/Market Strategy*).

The second prioritization output is precisely the object of discussion at our meeting today, where they need bottom-out input from the latest intelligence and ship Captains views, so to determine how to prioritize the specific targets and battlegrounds, on land or sea (*Priority Organic/Inorganic Pipeline*), at least for this first year of war.

The session, not surprisingly, lasted longer than anticipated, but now you are fully informed. You are aware of the wider geopolitical map, the priorities in terms of regions and targets. Time to sail on the high seas and execute.

A couple of weeks later you are well on your course to your assigned region; the war is now official, and you are actively trying to find where the enemy fleet might be hiding so to be able to engage at close quarters (*Inorganic Growth Process framework*).

Therefore, your ship, along with other ships in the squadron assigned to the same area, is looking for targets (*Deal Origination*). As you stop by neutral ports, your informants update you about the whereabouts of some enemy ships (*Deal Suggestion*), you quickly compare both ships and respective positions vis-à-vis the overall goal for this first year of war in your area of action (*Strategic Fit*) to decide whether to start an approach. As you gather more information about different targets you report back to the Admiral in charge of the squadron, so to contribute to the update of the overall picture (*Portfolio Prioritization*); then you receive a 'green light' to find and proceed towards a specific enemy ship.

Time to get the crew ready for a potential engagement. As you approach the patch of sea where the target was last seen, you get to study, at a very high level so far because the information is scant and dated, what is its potential strength [*Base Case Valuation (high level)*] and reckon the offensive effort it will entail to win and the rewards and benefits (*Synergies*) towards the overall goal in terms of command of the seas.

Your lookout cries 'enemy ship in sight'. We are getting closer, now we deploy full sail, and our enemy does the same, so we both know we are engaged in a chase (*Information Memorandum & Confidentiality Agreement*). You prepare gunnery, defining the ship areas to target, calculating the type of shot, getting the marine sharpshooters ready (*Due Diligence Team Design*), properly calibrated to deal with the expected defence from the enemy. The mutual engagement starts, logically under our initiative, the initiative of the attacker (*Due Diligence Execution*). Now we are closer, so you can get a much more accurate appraisal of the value of this target towards the war goals [*Valuation (detailed)*]; however, you are not yet close enough for starting broadside firing, still you are on time to change course and disengage if you judge the target was not as worthy as thought, or perhaps you underestimated its strength. You will need to take the call (*Non-Binding Pricing*), perhaps in the next hour or two.

The call is made, you go ahead, close the distance, and enter into an exchange of broadsides and your bow catches up with your enemy's (*Contract Negotiation*), then you make a final broadside (*Final Binding Pricing*), which hits the ship's rudder and main mast. The target slows down and your ship manoeuvres for boarding, the marines and crew jump to the fighting (*Execution of Deal Documentation*), your sailors get to the rigging, wheel (*Confirmatory Due Diligence & Regulatory Approval*) and take control of the cannons (*Integration Planning*), the enemy Commander surrenders the ship (*Completion*), the battle is over.

Now, you are the new captain, you have two ships, surely both quite shattered, your crew exhilarated and high in morale, just the opposite for the enemy's. However, they are all now your responsibility, so a new challenge at sea starts for you (*Implementation*), for which you will need to pull from your best skillset repertoire to unite the crew (*Mobilization framework*) and to reorganize both shattered ships (*Transformation framework*) for a successful sailing back to base.

* * *

This, my dear Managing Director, is **Strategy in Action** for ***New Geographies and/or Businesses***, and for ***Strategy & Execution***.

4 Attractiveness and Opportunities

The decision towards a strategy for international expansion to new geographies or for lateral expansion to entirely new businesses within the same geography is not a small matter. It is a complex decision that requires knowledge and insight beyond what the company is used to, as well as new frameworks for decision-making beyond those used for existing markets. Having said that, this decision will require a reflection about the company's current market and business model.

In this regard, a highly recommendable first reflection stems from asking, *what is the opportunity cost of an expansion beyond the current market?* Because a decision to go ahead will distract both financial and human resources as well as management attention from the core franchise.

As a second reflection, *are there any alternative strategies for growth in the current market?* Perhaps there are opportunities for acquisitions and consolidation of competitors in the local marketplace, which may create more value and de-risk the growth strategy vis-à-vis the uncertainty inherent to new geographies or business areas.

A third and final reflection, *what is the source of strength of the current business model?* The organization's starting point could be that of a situation of strength or of weakness. A bank might feel has cracked a strong business model at home that enjoys great scalability and has the potential to disrupt other new markets. However, in time it might surface that this belief was based on assumptions that, under some testing circumstances, might weaken the entire model.

For instance, ING Direct in the 1990s enjoyed a breakthrough business model based on being one of the highest payers for deposits supported on a lean cost online model, and investing them in long-term investment-grade bonds and mortgages. At the time of their European expansion in the mid-90s, ING Direct was able to replicate its business model successfully across many geographies (as per comparison with other players that internationalized their business models only to find them failing when facing competition from local players). On this basis, some may argue that ING's was an expansion based out of strength. Having said that, with the 2008 Global Financial Crisis (GFC) hindsight, someone could also argue that

A. Gavieiro Besteiro, *Strategy in Action*, Management for Professionals,
https://doi.org/10.1007/978-3-030-94759-0_4

this model, after all, had embedded some hidden weaknesses from underestimating the negative impact of liquidity risk (i.e. a part of their investment-grade bonds were downgraded and were difficult to sell when credit markets froze and liquidity was required).

Conversely, a bank might feel that its home market is stagnant, its market share close to the feasible limit for most products and segments, and so decides to look for new pastures of growth to spice up its languishing share price (usually reflected in a flat growth rate embedded in the terminal value of its share price).

This bank would be looking for high-growth, vibrant emerging markets where to export its 'apparent' competitive advantages and gain a strong foothold market share to nurture over time. This was exactly the case for many large banks from Western markets during the between-crisis period 2002–2007. They followed a breaking neck pace of acquisitions and organic build-ups in many emerging markets in Eastern Europe, Middle East & North Africa, India, China and South-East Asia. These were expansions, for many of the banks, based out of weakness as they realized over time that the initially assumed competitive advantages fell short to tackle the reaction from local competition, making many of these market entries loss-making for much longer than expected, in some cases ending up in full retreats.

Nevertheless, the fact that these expansionary efforts stem from strength does not always correlate with outcomes of success. Starting from a position of strength is a necessary but not a sufficient condition. The key root of success or failure stems from how the expansion strategy is designed and, even more importantly, how it is executed. We will tackle the execution theme in the next chapter. Thus, the question for this chapter would be: *how to design an expansion strategy paved for success?*

The answer lies in following a dual-approach process, the Attractiveness & Opportunities framework as per the illustration below: a vertical effort (Environment vs Financial Services Industry) versus a horizontal effort (Legacy vs Targets) both intendedly overlapping at identifying the specific Opportunities for expansion.

The vertical approach is the 'Geography/Business Attractiveness' mapping and focuses on analyzing the dynamics of the Environment and the Financial Services Industry considered, so to arrive at a first assessment of the Opportunities in terms of client segments and product offering to target. The resulting list still will need subsequently further refinement.

The horizontal approach is the 'Organic/Inorganic Opportunities' mapping and starts with an analysis of the bank's strengths and weaknesses, which have a crucial bearing on the design of an expansion strategy. This is accomplished by comparing the identified client segment/product Opportunities with the bank's Legacy (i.e. competitive advantages and disadvantages), in other words, what the bank brings to each of the new geographies/businesses vis-à-vis local or incumbent competitors in that market (some of them potential Targets from an inorganic perspective). The calibration of these factors would yield a refined set of Organic or Inorganic Opportunities (i.e. acquisitions or alliances) for the future build-up.

The rest of the chapter will provide more detail about the process and steps involved (using geographical expansions as an example) (Figs. 4.1 and 4.2).

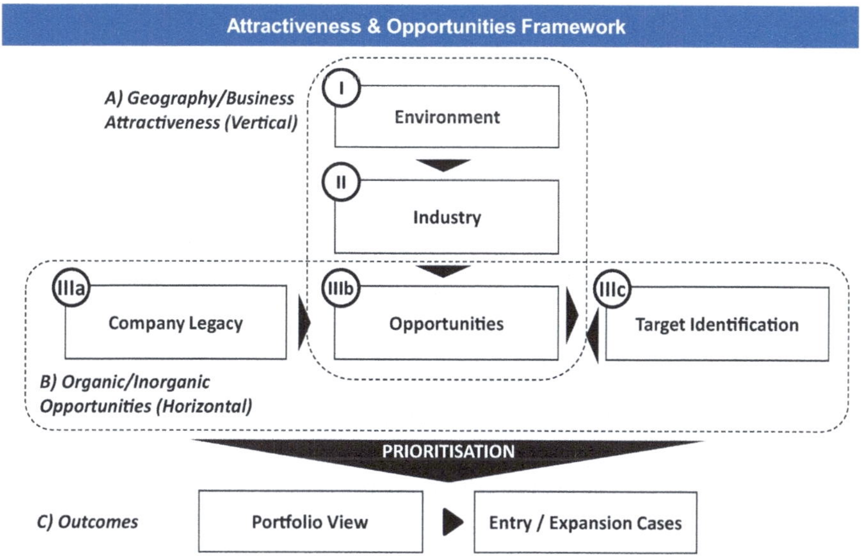

Fig. 4.1 **Attractiveness & Opportunities framework** (1/2). Note: SD = Strategy Development. Sources: 'Holistic Management Framework v.5' (Angel Gavieiro; Apr.17; AG Strategy & Partners)

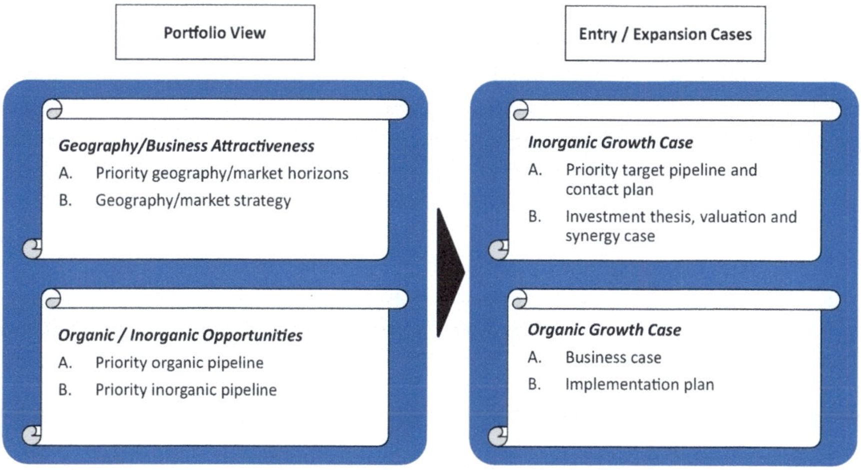

Fig. 4.2 **Attractiveness & Opportunities framework** (2/2). Sources: 'Holistic Management Framework v.5' (Angel Gavieiro; Apr.17; AG Strategy & Partners)

As a result of this dual-approach process, two outcomes are expected. First, a Portfolio View with a prioritization of geography/businesses, perhaps over 2–3 horizons in a 5–10 year period. Taking a geographical expansion example, the Portfolio View would detail the prioritization of countries, the type of business banking presence (e.g. retail, commercial, private, corporate or investment banking), the targeted goals in terms of market share presence over time, and the respective expected financial impact (top-down, high-level) in terms of capital investment and profit contribution (e.g. equity and profit before taxes, respectively).

Second, a defined set of Entry/Expansion Cases that specify for each of the geography/businesses a clear organic/inorganic strategy for the expansion. Thus, taking again the geographical expansion example, the Cases would identify the alternative build-up routes: for Organic Growth Cases, the business case with implementation plan of expected team resources to build up over time and the targeted branches and locations; for Inorganic Growth Cases, the potential players in pipeline targeted for acquisition or/and alliance, and an indication (top-down, high-level) of investment requirements.

4.1 Geography/Business Attractiveness

The sections below discuss the vertical approach, which final output is the Portfolio View. Its third step, Opportunities, intentionally overlaps with the horizontal approach analysis, so it will be discussed in the following section.

4.1.1 Environment

There are different frameworks that can be leveraged for this purpose, PESTLE (ref. Chap. 1) is probably the most complete. Nevertheless, many times it would be more suitable to develop an ad-hoc issue tree or framework given the circumstances of the geographies considered or the limitations in terms of access to reliable information.

For instance, a Western European bank considering its expansion into China used the following ad-hoc framework for Environment assessment:

- Macroeconomic environment: economic growth analysis differentiating by major regions of the country, evolution of government political stance to private business and foreign enterprises, demographic analysis, sector/industry characterization, etc.
- Banking and financial markets regulation: regulatory framework of stated-owned banks versus private banks versus foreign banks, policies limiting expansion, policies on foreign presence, infrastructure development (i.e. payments, cards, credit bureau)

4.1.2 Industry

It is common that the aimed level of detail is larger than the information available in particular if you are dealing with emerging markets, and that the time and budget limitations for the work at hand make a consistent analytical approach prohibiting. In this case, instead of a prescriptive framework like Five Forces (ref. Chap. 1) is more recommendable to be inductive and so to focus on the key areas that might have a higher influence in the decision-making for a market entry. In the expansion to China example above, where the priority was given to the retail and commercial banking division for the entry, these were the dimensions studied:

- Banking market size and profitability: trends in revenue and profit pools, as well as in assets, liabilities and bad debts, cost structure evolution, profitability analysis, drivers of revenue growth, etc.
- Banking market competitiveness: structure of banks by size and ownership, market share distributions and evolution, established presence of foreign banks, etc.
- Client segments: analysis of households by size, income average and growth by segment in retail; analysis of companies by size, turnover and growth by segment, etc.
- Product lines: product breakdown of revenues, profits and growth across all products in retail and commercial banking, product penetration benchmarking with similar countries, service quality and trends, deep dives in particular products (i.e. mortgages, deposits, cards and trade finance), etc.

The resulting fact-base can be very extensive so it demands a systematic process of synthesis to bring it to a succinct format for easy comparison among countries, so that the decision-making committee can more easily discuss and deep dive as necessary.

* * *

The first output out of this vertical approach will be a cross-country comparison of the summary of attractiveness, which would contribute towards the Portfolio View, and so, towards the prioritization of country entry over 3-time horizons. For instance, the example below shows the 'attractiveness map' for GCC and MENA banking markets performed for a retail banking expansion; the key metrics used were GDP per capita, population size and pre-tax profit pools of the financial services industry (Fig. 4.3).

From this analysis, several country clusters were identified: 'Wealthy Hubs', 'Developing-Too Large to Ignore', 'Developing Hubs', 'Emerging-Too Large to Ignore' and 'Emerging Mid-size'. This grouping helps to prioritize the clusters in the first instance from a high-level perspective, and then the countries within like-for-like clusters.

Anticipating what we will discuss later in more detail, assessing the competitiveness of the bank's business lines in each of these clusters will help, along with other key variables (like resources) to prioritize which clusters to enter. Hence, the metrics selected for creating the clusters need to be relevant from the perspective of the alternative business lines the bank is considering bringing into the international expansion (in this case, the metrics are useful to assess expansions for retail banking and wealth management, not so much for commercial banking).

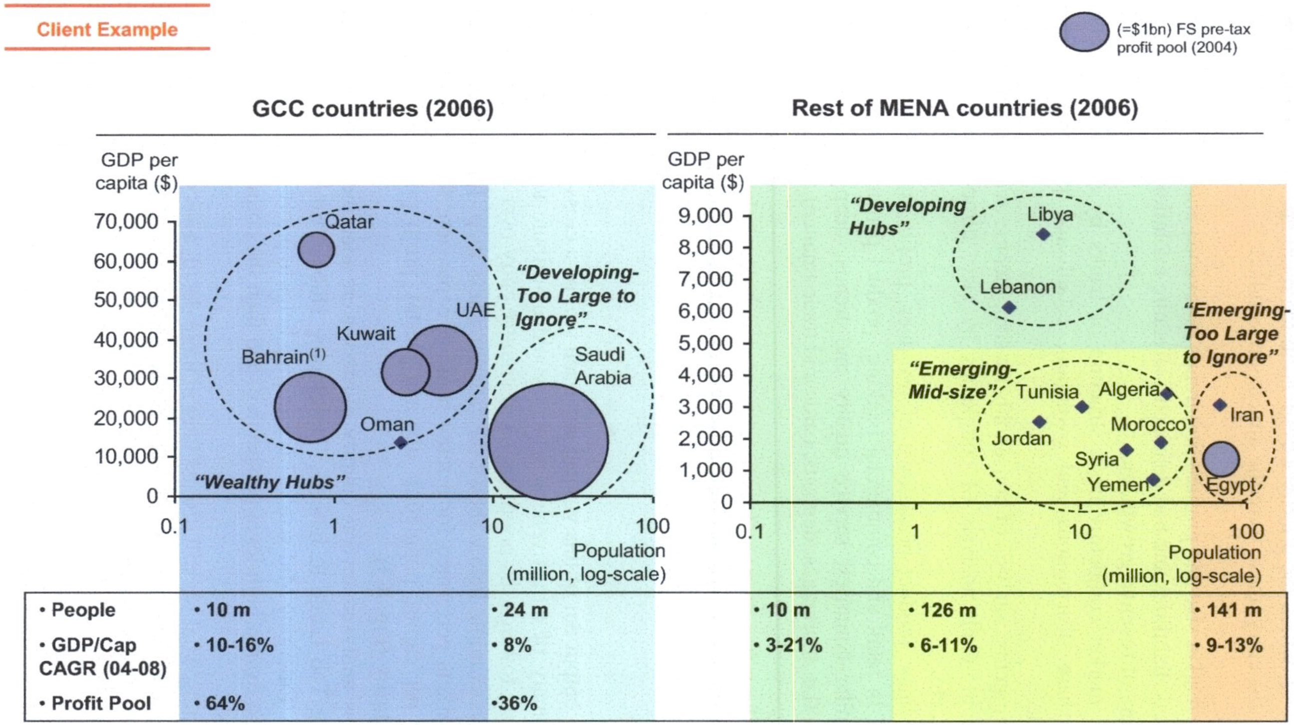

Fig. 4.3 GCC and MENA Markets—Attractiveness Map (example). Note: 2006 GCP per capita are estimates. (1) Includes offshore banking. Sources: IMF; own client experience

The second output from the effort would be, for each country, a first list of specific Organic/Inorganic Opportunities that, given the facts unearthed, look attractive 'per se', before we wear the lenses of our bank's competitive advantages or, for that sake, the lenses from other competitors. These opportunities will need to subsequently be refined in the light of our Legacy as a bank (next section).

4.2 Organic/Inorganic Opportunities

The illustration below shows the horizontal approach, pivoting now to refine the first list of Opportunities identified in the previous vertical approach analysis.

4.2.1 Legacy

In this first step, we begin with the bank's Legacy. The bank's competitive advantages should be apparent if it has in place a solid Strategy Blueprint and Business Model frameworks (as per Chaps. 1 and 2) for each of the Business Units involved in the expansion strategy. If not, then this is the place to start since you cannot embark on such a complex effort without knowing your organization very well in terms of strengths and weaknesses.

This principle apparently seems common sense; however, we have observed during international expansions of Western banks in the 2000s that in many instances there was not a clear understanding of what differential value exactly these banks were bringing to their targeted markets. Perhaps there was a shallow assessment of the competitive advantages that they really enjoyed in the home market, or how exportable these were. As a result, when the tide ebbed, many found themselves in foreign countries without 'armour and weapons' compared to local competitors, so they had to rapidly retreat, as witnessed post-2008 (though, of course, in some cases that retreat was a consequence of the urgent need to consolidate resources at home, rather than a lack of competitiveness of their foreign subsidiaries).

Thus, let us retake the example of the Western bank expanding to China. The above Attractiveness ('per se') analysis confirmed that, at that time, the Chinese market was very attractive:

(a) In retail banking across mass-affluent and affluent segments, and for mortgages, auto-loans, credit cards, personal lending and deposits
(b) In commercial banking, for SME clients, where lending and trade finance were the attractive areas

This bank was quite aware of its competitive strengths at home (i.e. Legacy), so for instance they were very good at mortgages, cards and affluent segments, as well as SME banking and trade finance. Thus, overlaying this Legacy over the Attractiveness analysis, they concluded their focus would be:

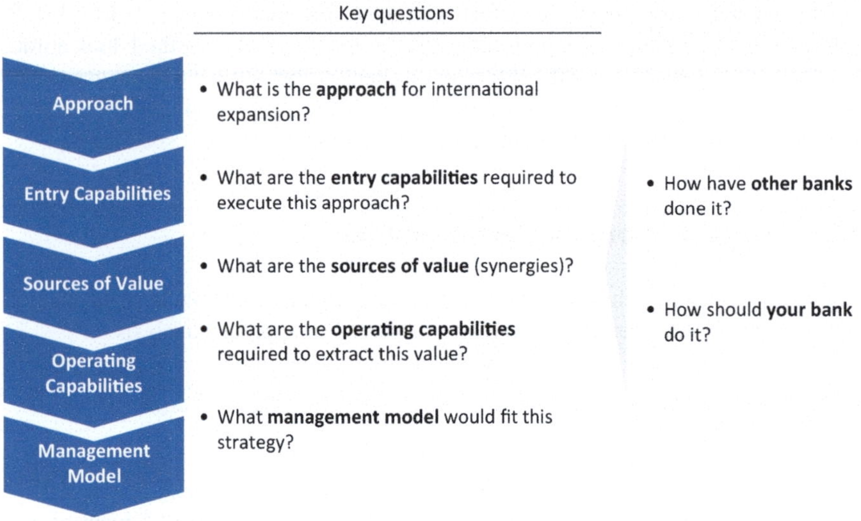

Fig. 4.4 International Business Model framework (1/2). Sources: Sanitized experience

(a) Affluent banking with emphasis on mortgages
(b) SME banking with emphasis on trade

In addition, there was another key consideration for a potential organic approach, the geographical dimension: their focus would be on a selection of coastal cities for both retail and commercial banking.

Another key reflection for the organization to have at this point is to review what approaches have followed other foreign banks that have internationalized. This forensic analysis can reveal interesting lessons about what has worked and what has not. The International Business Model framework is a tool very powerful to undertake this type of benchmarking (illustrations below) (Fig. 4.4).

The tool asks 5 questions to a sample of competitors regarding the way they have internationalized during a past period, perhaps 10 years. The questioning focuses on distilling the most common practices followed along 5 dimensions:

1. Approach: organic only, inorganic only, hybrid
2. Entry capabilities: market selection, corporate finance, M&A execution, portfolio management, integration
3. Sources of value: revenue vs cost synergies, capital synergies, tax synergies, asset diversification synergies and speed of synergy realization
4. Operating capabilities: customer relationship model, cross-selling, IT, operations, reengineering
5. Management model: centralized versus decentralized versus matrix, local versus expat executives (Fig. 4.5)

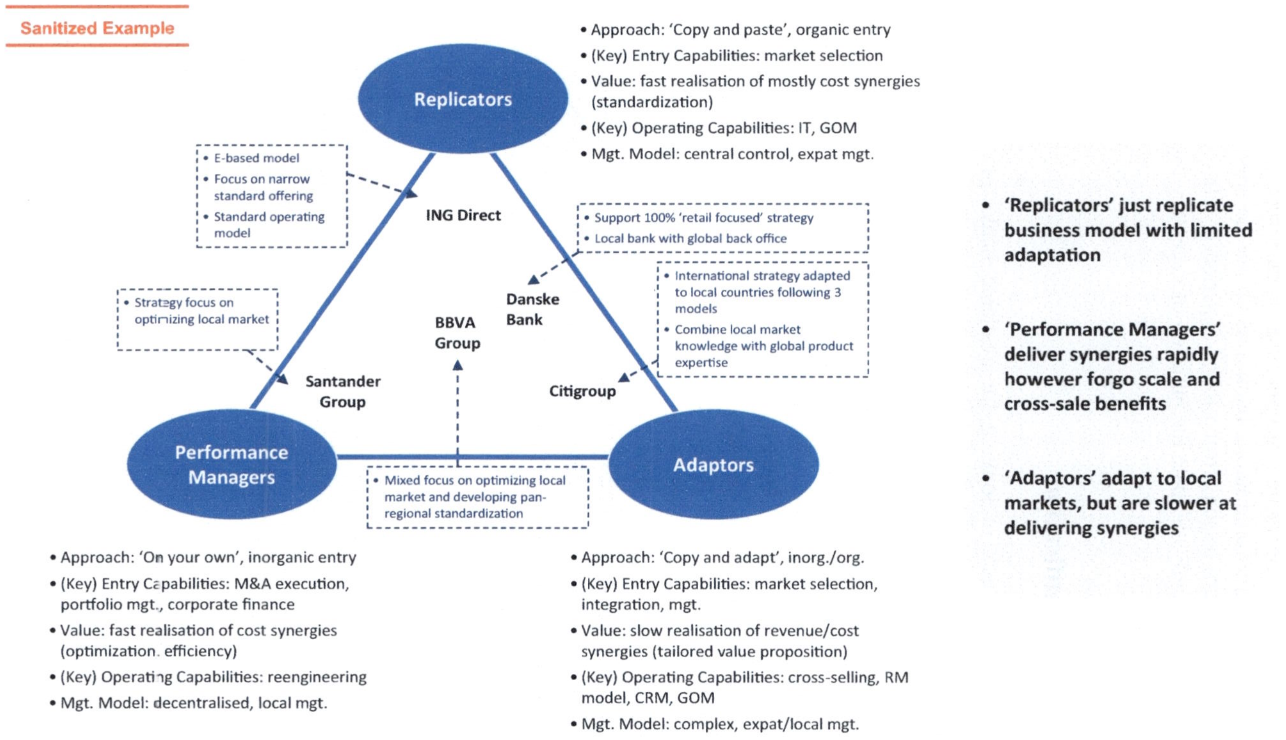

Fig. 4.5 International Business Model framework (Example) (2/2). Sources: McKinsey Quarterly; Sanitized example

The illustration above shows the summary from a study performed in the mid-00s, which leveraged this framework over 5 large international banks and mapped it to 3 categorizations: 'Replicators', 'Performance Managers' and 'Adaptors'. This analysis could help a bank to calibrate the approach it intents for internationalization, learn lessons from others' experience, reflect about the drivers of value of the effort, and anticipate the build-up of necessary capabilities to cover any gaps.

4.2.2 Target Identification

This second step consists in looking for available banks or financial services companies (not necessarily with deposit-taking license by the respective regulatory authority), with whom to consider acquisitions or alliances with the aim of accelerating the build-up of presence in the country.

Normally the corporate development department of the bank would be engaged, usually with the support of some external investment banks in advisory capacity so to procure intelligence from the ground to determine potential target availability.

The International Business Model framework referred to in the previous section should be as well helpful to reveal which banks in each local market are already owned or tied to foreign competitors, so we can focus on the remaining available candidates (except for any potential market exits from foreign competitors that could be in the offing).

It may happen that some Targets could have presence in several of the countries been analyzed, so that the successful acquisition of one of them could become a great leap forward in the overall expansion strategy. More often though, the targets available are small or medium size institutions operating only in one country.

For the available Targets, external advisors usually provide a good description of the footprint, strategy and business model, particularly in terms of client and product coverage, as well as financials and valuations. Now, it cannot be emphasized enough how important it is to have a good picture of the business model and client/product franchise of the Targets, essential for both identifying best-fit as Targets and for estimating with confidence potential synergies. These insights can help justify, eventually, the acquisition control premium in the bidding price (more about this topic will be discussed in Chap. 5).

4.2.3 Opportunities

The outcome from this horizontal approach, for each country, is a second refinement of the Organic/Inorganic Opportunities list from the vertical analysis, now at the light of the Legacy of the bank and the potential Targets available to accelerate the entry.

Subsequently, 2 additional outputs from this horizontal effort emerge: the entry approach via specific Inorganic Growth Cases and/or Organic Growth Cases. For the former, with the identification of a prioritized Target pipeline (plus contact plan for execution), with a high-level investment thesis, valuation and synergy case (fruit of how their client/segment franchise fits the overlay of Legacy vs Attractiveness analysis done by the bank). For the latter, a typical organic business case and implementation plan, as we have seen with the incremental business cases in the MTP (Chap. 3).

The illustration shares a summary from the Attractiveness & Opportunity framework application by a GCC bank studying its entry into the Turkish market in the mid-2010s (Fig. 4.6).

In this example, the bank had initially discarded an organic approach, and within inorganic the preference was for an alliance route with a local bank: (1st priority) with acquisition of a stake; (2nd priority) without stake at first, but with option for future stake or acquisition; (3rd priority) opportunistic acquisition of small size local bank, ideally combined with the alliance.

* * *

As a summary, expansion to a new geography or business line sounds exciting but entails substantially more risk than considering alternative strategies for growth in the core market, therefore, it requires careful reflection before going ahead. Among these reflections, a deep understanding of your business model strengths and weaknesses will be crucial.

When expanding, first we look at the new markets' Attractiveness, by assessing its Environment and Industry so to identify the Opportunities, organic and inorganic. Then, we look at our Company Legacy (i.e. its strengths and weaknesses vis-à-vis those of the local competitors of the target markets), along with the potential Target Identification (i.e. to check the alternative avenues to make the move inorganically, rather than organically), so to revisit the initial list of Opportunities now with this more refined lenses.

As an outcome, we will produce a Portfolio View, mapping the relative attractiveness of the markets studied, along with a set of Entry/Expansion Cases that include a defined plan for potential organic and/or inorganic moves.

Finally, the International Business Model framework can help us to prioritize the alternative pathways of market expansion derived from the two outcomes above, by looking at entry approach, entry capabilities, sources of value, operating capabilities, and management model.

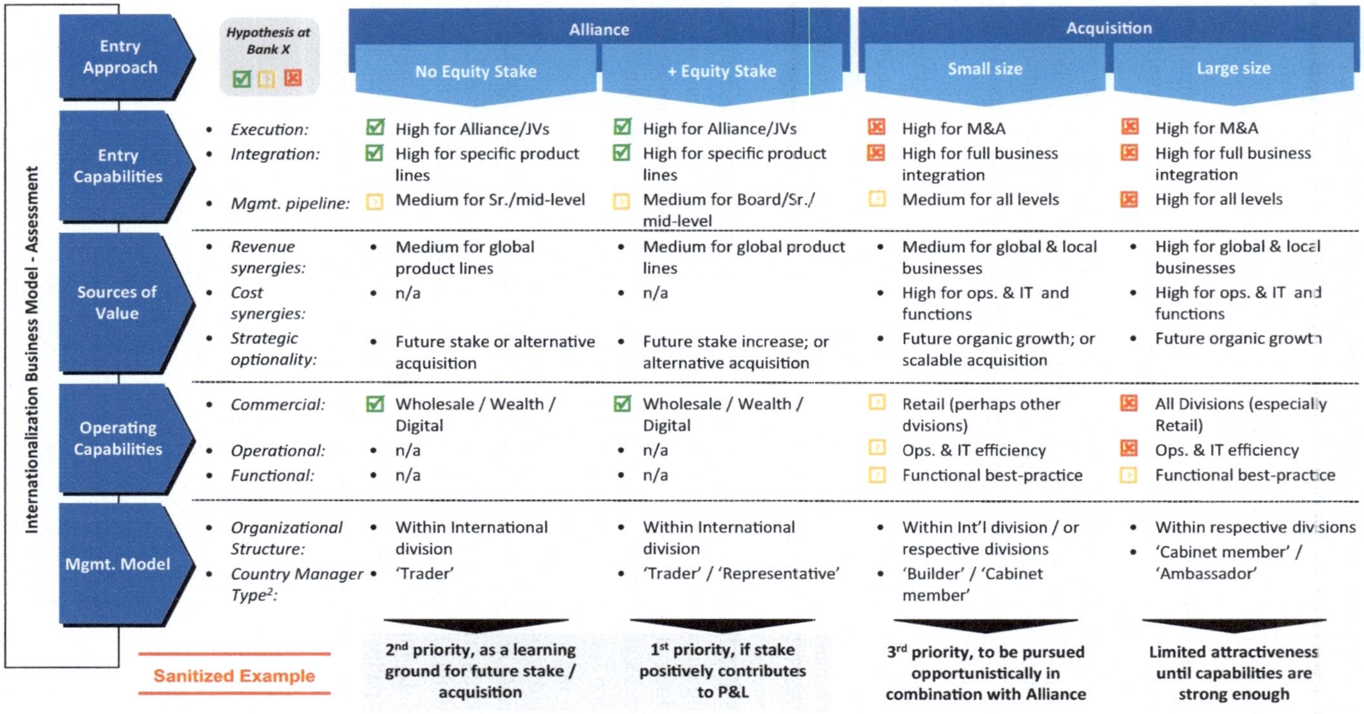

Fig. 4.6 Attractiveness & Opportunities—GCC bank entry into Turkey (Example). Sources: Sanitized example

Inorganic Growth Process

5

At the Strategy Development phase, one of the outputs from the Attractiveness & Opportunities framework is the Entry/Expansion Cases for each new geography/ business. At the Business Development phase, some of these will be Organic Growth cases that require the MTP process, while other will be Inorganic Growth cases (i.e. M&A, JV/Alliances) that require a separately dedicated best-practice Inorganic Growth process.

The methodology to develop Organic Growth cases, either from scratch ('green-field') or from a starting base already existing in that geography ('build up'), would ideally follow the best-practice MTP process explained earlier with the Business Model, Strategy Blueprint and Financial Plan frameworks (Chaps. 1–3).

For the Inorganic Growth cases, either via merger/acquisition or alliance/partnership, the Entry / Expansion Cases output will normally provide concrete targets already identified for this purpose. The question now is: *how to go about executing them at the Business Development phase?*

There are important differences between these 2 types of inorganic growth, and within each one a myriad of possibilities. Mergers and Acquisitions is a whole world, where countless books and academic studies have thrown light and evidence, especially in the last few decades. Thus, best-practice in M&A is easily accessible for practitioners. Alliances and Partnerships is not an area as well researched, perhaps due to the difficulty to obtain empirical evidence because they mostly happen in the private space, unlike M&A, so they do not normally involve stock transactions in the public equity markets and lower regulatory and public scrutiny is involved. Also, the variety of collaboration agreements that two or more parties can undertake for business purposes is probably limitless. Having said that, there are some valuable lessons-learned published, based on deep research of wide samples of alliances and partnerships usually from consultants having assisted these transactions.

It is not the object of this chapter (nor the book) to tackle the world of best-practice in the content of how to go about Inorganic Growth in its different modalities. However, from a managerial viewpoint, it helps to have a common

A. Gavieiro Besteiro, *Strategy in Action*, Management for Professionals,
https://doi.org/10.1007/978-3-030-94759-0_5

process for governing both activities, on a systematic and methodological basis, all the way to the deal closure point. This process is the object of this chapter.

The Implementation phase, after deal closure, is quite different for both, where the process of M&A integration follows a different path than that of implementation of alliances or partnerships, which is more akin to that of Organic Growth build-ups (more about implementation in Chap. 6).

Inorganic Growth opportunities can be managed through a 4-stage process: Deal Origination, Valuation, Due Diligence and Deal Negotiation. Each stage is marked by a specific point of decision governance, which determines a 'go' or 'no-go' call to continue with the following stage. Figure 5.1 illustrates both dimensions.

There is a sound rationale for all this trouble. First, because Inorganic Growth could involve decisions on large investment amounts in one shot, so it becomes a 'high stakes' irreversible move (as opposed to Organic Growth, that is more nuanced and modular, which execution pace can be reasonably accelerated/decelerated as we progress). Second, because the managerial process itself requires important research and due diligence effort, which are not cheap and are time consuming, thereby it demands a wise decision-making process. And third, because inorganic moves come often associated with Board and/or shareholder approval as could entail capital/debt raisings, heavy involvement with regulators and high-stakes reputational impact.

Thus, from a governance perspective, decisions are made at the permanent, periodical (e.g. quarterly) decision committee at Division or Group level, chaired by the Divisional CEO or the Group CFO, or quite often in ad hoc sessions of this committee called following the tempo of the transaction. This meeting often entails a proper representation of the involved business heads and functions (i.e. strategy, corporate development, COO/operations, finance and legal).

5.1 Deal Origination

This first stage is more of a circular loop process as opposed to a linear one. There is a continuous flow back and forth among its 3 steps: Deal Suggestion, Strategic Fit and Portfolio Prioritization.

Step-1 Deal Suggestion: Where, starting from the initial prioritized set of potential inorganic deals from the Entry / Expansion Cases output, the list gets updated by dropping those that get confirmed as 'without legs' and by adding newly identified targets by the corporate development team or the appointed investment banker, testing the waters with the targets to confirm or disconfirm their interest.

Aside from these 2 sources of targets, other different stakeholders or teams in the organization could be mandated to come up with deal ideas, like for instance country managers, regional CEOs and/or the strategy team.

There is an obvious trade-off between having many parties looking for transactions vis-à-vis the market 'noise' the organization is willing to accept to generate by undertaking this activity. Thus, inorganic moves of large scale, being a merger of equals (e.g. BNP and Paribas in the late 1990s), a transformational acquisition (e.g. Lloyds and HBOS in the 2008 aftermath), or a '2nd home country'

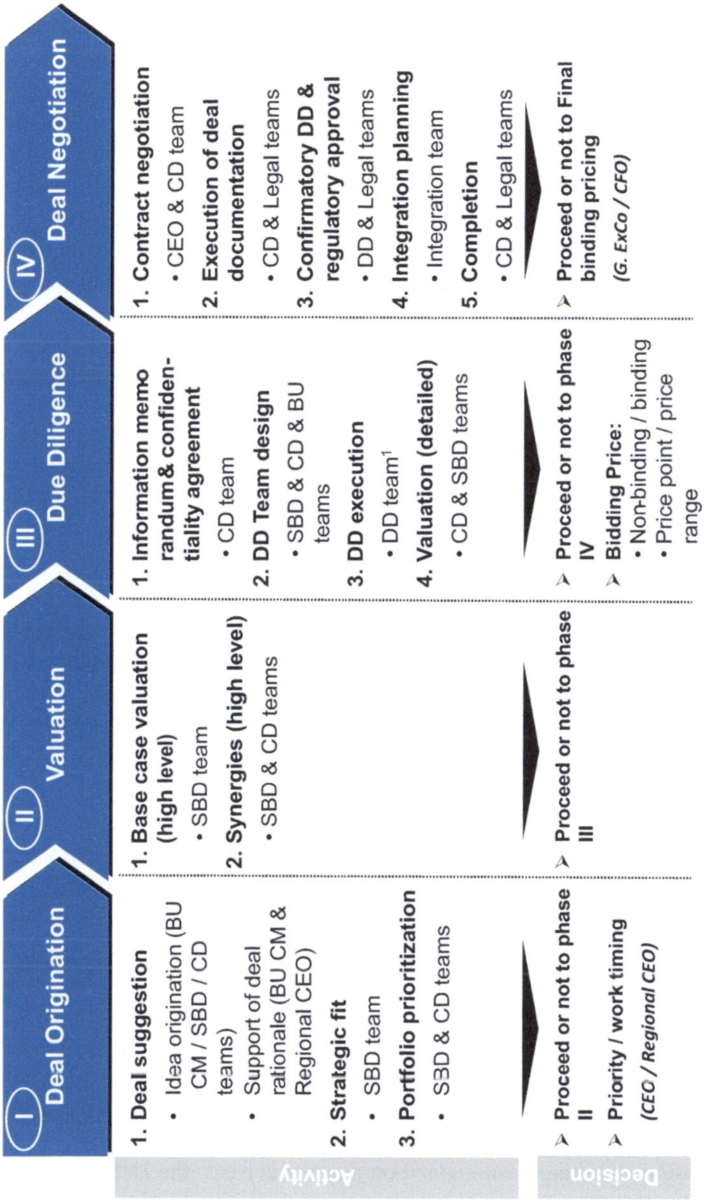

Fig. 5.1 **Inorganic Growth Process**. Note: BU = Business Unit; CM = Country Manager; SBD = Strategy & Business Development; CD = Corporate Development; DD = Due Diligence; 1. Ad hoc. Sources: 'Holistic Management Framework v.5' (Angel Gavieiro; Apr.17; AG Strategy & Partners)

acquisition (e.g. Barclays and Banco Zaragozano in Spain in the early 2000s), required a very silent and careful approach in the months before the announcement. On the other hand, large international expansions targeting many geographies simultaneously (e.g. Citigroup or HSBC expansion in the 1990–2000s) will require a sizeable, diverse and continued target origination effort, which by necessity will be noisier.

Also, it is important to consider at this stage that some of the deals will emerge out of bilateral conversations with the potential seller, while others will be prompted by the seller via an auction process. In the latter, usually with a mandated advisor reaching out to prospective buyers and handing an Information Memorandum (IM) after signing of the appropriate Confidentiality or Non-Disclosure Agreement (CA or NDA). In recent years, there has been a trend in the market to see more deals via an auction process, driven by pressures on management teams to prove they are delivering in their fiduciary duty to maximize value to shareholders.

Step-2 Strategic Fit: Activity is normally led by the strategy team to check the potential targets proposed against the strategic requirements determined in the Portfolio View output from the Attractiveness & Opportunities framework.

Specifically, unearthing at this point a solid high-level view of the target's business franchise in terms of geography, client segments and product offering is important so to compare it with the organization's Legacy and the banking segments/ products of focus prioritized in the expansion strategy. Also, worth to have a look at the market valuation and multiples of the target, just in case they currently are too far from the 'green' or 'yellow' comfortability zone for the acquirer; otherwise, we would risk starting quite a cumbersome process with targets that, under current market conditions, would be uneconomical for the long-term shareholder value creation objectives of the organization.

Step-3 Portfolio Prioritization: The two previous steps inform a review of the Portfolio View prioritization, where necessarily some initially selected targets are dropped (as per above), and others are added.

Importantly, the prioritization is decided combining the initial strategic priorities for the market entry/build-up along with the intelligence we know at this point about the willingness of the targets to start a conversation (e.g. the acquirer normally aims for an amicable acquisition instead of a hostile takeover, which usually is more expensive and higher risk because it can attract other buyers). Sometimes, just due to the fact that current market valuations situate the target in 'red' zone, it is better to wait for more benign market conditions for a particular deal (e.g. the target having a substantial advantage in terms of valuation multiples vs the acquirer, like Price-to-Book x2.5 vs x1.0 respectively, while showing a lower profitability, which could make the acquisition very dilutive in terms of Earnings-per-Share to the acquirer' shareholders).

At the decision committee, summoned on a periodic basis, the Deal Origination activity gets discussed, clarifications sought after and target prioritization officially confirmed. At each meeting, one or several targets gain approval to pass into the next stage, Valuation.

5.2 Valuation

This stage is led by the strategy and/or corporate development teams. It entails a strategic and financial appraisal exercise, where estimations at high-level need to be set. Normally, 2 steps are involved.

Step-1 Base Case Valuation (high level): Where the team values the target 'as-is'. For that purpose, a variety of approaches can be used, but typically Multiples Valuation and Fundamental Analysis Valuation are the most common.

In the Multiples Valuation, the team looks for comparable companies to our target, and distils a range of quantitative metrics for the comparison, such as Price-to-Earnings, Price-to-Book Value ratios, current and forward looking. For wealth or asset management businesses, other ratios are relevant such as Price-to-Assets Under Management.

In the Fundamental Analysis Valuation, the team looks at the most recent financial statements from the target and projects them into the future leveraging some hypothesis of growth, based on reasonable comparison and macro/microeconomic scenarios, across their P&L's revenue, cost, impairment lines and balance-sheet's lending and deposit balances. Then, the team translates the accounting numbers into cashflows. Given we are talking about financial institutions, whose liabilities side of the balance-sheet (contrary to most non-financial services companies) is customer-oriented (i.e. clients' deposits and current accounts), the team needs to arrive at shareholders' cashflow instead of enterprise's cashflows (i.e. from equity and debt). For doing so, they use an Equity-based Discounted Cashflows Model or a Dividend Discount Model[1] (as opposed to a Company Value-based DCF, where cashflows for both debt and equity are the basis for discounting). In the end, the aim is to arrive at a Net Present Value of the equity of the bank to compare with the current market price.

For large banks, sometimes both approaches are undertaken as a 'Sum-of-the-Parts' Valuation (SOTP), where each division (i.e. retail bkg., commercial bkg., corporate bkg., investment bkg., wealth management, asset management and insurance) is valued (with Multiples and/or Equity DCF) on its own, and then aggregated together for the entire group.

Now, it is important to notice that at this point the valuation is entirely done externally to the target, so the target has not been engaged at all with valuation-related questions, and at a relatively high-level focusing on the main drivers of growth for the fundamentals. Later on, there will be the need to update this exercise with much more detail provided by the target.

Step-2 Synergies (high level): This is one of the most critical parts of the entire process. The synergies will translate the competitive advantages that result from the combination of capabilities of the target and the acquirer, typically over the targeted

[1] Both focused on assessing the value of the equity, where the DDM focuses strictly on the expected dividend flow, while the Equity-based DCF focuses on the residual cash flow after meeting all the financial obligations and investment needs.

marketplace; however, there could be synergies also for the acquirer in its home market or in other marketplaces (i.e. reverse Synergies).

Synergies are the additional value that reasonably we can add to the 'as-is' valuation in order to determine how much this particular target is really worth for that given acquirer. Hence, different acquirers will have quite a different view regarding Synergies. Nevertheless, for any acquirer, achieving consensus regarding what constitutes a Synergy and the estimation of the same could be quite a controversial matter.

Let us remember that at this point we are still at a high-level exercise and using only external information about the target. Thus, such a difficult measurement of Synergies will necessarily entail important differences between a first approximation at this phase vis-à-vis a more detailed estimation once we are in due diligence with the target.

It follows that Synergies will become a critical battle horse during the process, starting with the Steering Committee and, eventually, all the way to the Group's and Board's final approvals for eventually submitting a binding bid price for the acquisition.

Synergies are typically classified as Revenue or Costs, although some deals involve other more specific Synergy types (e.g. capital, tax or asset diversification Synergies). Revenue Synergies can stem from bringing existing products or entire value propositions from the acquirer to the target, generating new revenue lines from the acquirer's existing (and perhaps also new) client base.

For instance, when Barclays expanded its international retail and commercial banking franchise by acquiring Banco Zaragozano in Spain in 2003, there was an important Revenue Synergy from extending the successful Affluent Banking value proposition of Barclays to the target's clients, which respective proposition was less developed. Interestingly, this was a transaction where there were as well reverse-Synergies of revenues to account for in deploying Banco Zaragozano's value proposition for SME banking across the pre-existing Barclays network in Spain, which counted with a smaller part of the joint client base in this segment.

Similarly, Costs Synergies stem from the combination of the operational capabilities of delivery for the 2 banks, and come from 3 main sources:

- Costs savings from operations and IT systems: For instance, they amounted to 40% of the total synergy from the acquisition by Banco Santander of Abbey in the UK in 2004, substituting Abbey's old legacy platform with Santander's state-of-the-art Parthenon system.
- Cost savings from staff redundancies: Present in a majority of acquisitions, like Lloyds acquiring HBOS in the aftermath of the September 2008 crisis, where the combined workforce of 126,000 was gradually cut to 65,000 by 2019 (arguably I would reckon only a part of the 61,000 difference would have been initially computed in their Synergy case, the rest being the result of subsequent organic cost rationalization exercises and so outside from the acquisition business case). These Synergies usually generate a per annum cost saving but logically offset by a one-off, upfront, redundancy cost (negative Synergy).

- Cost of funding: For example, this was an important synergy from the acquisition by Barclays of Absa in South Africa in 2005, improving substantially the latter's wholesale markets financing costs given Barclays' higher credit ratings.

Other more ad hoc, specific synergies may occur related to:

- Capital: When the combined entity saves regulatory capital requirements vs the sum of the initial position of the 2 entities, which often happens in some corporate banking books when they could be moved from Foundational to Advanced Internal Rating Based methodology for Risk-Weighted Asset (RWA) calculation,[2] generating, as a result a, lower RWA and so less regulatory capital consumption from those portfolios.
- Tax: In a similar way, the resulting tax position of the combined entity is more favourable than the sum of initial positions, which can be due to multiple tax considerations (e.g. tax allowances from losses and goodwill acquisition tax relief).
- Asset diversification: That could be derived from the combination of portfolios in the combined entity that ends up reducing the overall idiosyncratic risk, and this may lead to a benefit recognition, for instance, in the insurance business (derived from the Solvency II regulatory capital adequacy regime of this industry).

Synergy estimations are usually weighted in terms of probability of materialization, which makes Revenue Synergies less attainable given its dependence on client behaviour and market competition reaction. Cost Synergies depend more on the capability of integration execution of the combined entity, which is a more controllable factor. Hence, the usual rule of thumb used by investment bankers to benchmark banking synergies is 5% for Revenues and 20% for Costs out of the total acquisition price.

At the decision committee, this high-level Valuation is discussed, normally generating a lot of questions regarding assumptions across all cases used and the basis underpinning the Synergies. These assumptions will become key input factors to the eventual Due Diligence phase.

In the end, a decision is made for each target regarding whether or not to pass into the next stage, Due Diligence, which necessarily will involve engaging in close interaction, for first time, with the target.

---

[2] Capital adequacy regulation establishes the methodologies allowed for estimation of RWAs, the most common the Foundation vs Advanced Internal Ratings Based approaches, where on the former banks are allowed to use their own modelling to estimate the Probability of Default factor, while on the latter also are allowed to use their own modelling to estimate the Loss Given Default factor and Exposure at Default factor.

5.3 Due Diligence

The acquirer gives instructions to its appointed investment bank advisor to formally engage with the target regarding the acquisition intent. From that moment on, a sequence of 4 steps starts rolling.

Step-1 Information Memorandum and Confidentiality Agreement: In an auction process, normally the target appointed its own advisor and together prepared a document, the IM, that provides a first layer of depth of information about the strategy, market franchise, business models and financial performance of the target, along with some comparable valuations.

One or several potential acquirers get access to the IM by signing the NDA, which basically establishes the non-sharing conditions of all the information provided during the process of engagement and negotiation, starting with and including the IM and followed by the Due Diligence all the way to, eventually, closure and public announcement.

By contrast, in bilateral acquisitions quite often the IM step is skipped, and the NDA is signed to open a data room (or virtual data room if performed remotely) to provide access to the relevant information.

The acquirer' strategy and/or corporate development teams will quickly update its high-level Valuation with any relevant information from the IM and other available public/private information, which surely will help to cover some of the questions previously raised and, inevitably, will raise further questions to find answers for in the next phases.

Step-2 Due Diligence Team Design: In parallel, the acquirer as well puts together a task-force team of experts from the different departments of the bank, both business-lines and functions, so to undertake the Due Diligence. This will occur either in the data room at the premises of the target or facilitated by its advisor, or virtually via an online data room accessible within a high-security environment by the parties.

The challenge in designing the DD Team is both in terms of breadth and depth, since the time for DD is limited (typically 3–4 weeks) and the potential areas to analyze are many, so you could perfectly boil the ocean if you are not careful. Thus, prioritization will be of the essence, hence the importance of thoroughness in the high-level Valuation phase. In the DD the key questions to answer are clearly identified and classified in terms of their criticality to refine the Valuation exercise and other key points the Steering Committee wanted to gain an answer for. For this purpose, leveraging a MECE hypothesis tree (ref. Chap. 1) would be very handy.

The organization of the team will depend a lot on the type of target, size and nature of businesses, so it will be ad hoc case by case. All functions of the bank will be typically represented and only the business-lines with significant impact on the Valuation for this target.

Another challenge is how to convince and incentivize the involved departments in order to let some key people go for DD purposes for so many weeks. Hence, having a good HR programme backing up the BAU activities with temporary or dedicated personnel could be a key success factor.

A longer term but important consideration, that can disincentivize BAU departments to assign their best people to the DD, would be the fear or risk of losing them 'forever' in the Integration team if the deal successfully completes. Again, this could be addressed by having another well-thought HR programme with clearly appointed succession and contingency plans and with access to talent to cover BAU departments.

Also, it is essential to have a proper incentivization plan in place in terms of a balanced scorecard to recognize their efforts for contributing to the M&A objective of the bank, both for the talent eventually departing the BAU department for a DD (and also for its associated Integration programme), and for the BAU department heads for their contribution. Chapter 5 will address in more detail incentivization in the wider context of Transformation in the execution of both organic and inorganic efforts.

These extra HR programmes are critical for very active acquirers, otherwise, they risk getting short of talent for the DD and Integration efforts or depleting the BAU of critical capability. This conclusion goes as well, quite importantly, for senior management capacity. One of the biggest constraints some of the Western Banks faced during the 2000s decade in their expansion quest was to count with enough management pipeline, and of the right experience, to send to manage the acquired operations in foreign countries, in particular for Asia-Pacific, Africa and Middle East.

Step-3 Due Diligence Execution: DD stems after a non-binding pricing round of discussions between buyer and seller in a bilateral deal, or after the result of the auction process for which non-binding pricing has been submitted (these days sent along with marked-up Selling and Purchase Agreement (SPA) contracts, so to compare across bidders and avoid surprises) and a buyer is selected. In both cases, an exclusivity period is agreed to perform the DD.

The DD, undertaken either in situ or virtually, becomes the critical counterpart to the Synergy section of the Valuation. This exercise is the opportunity for the acquirer to check the facts and fill in its key questions to gain a more founded understanding of the target and the value it brings to its franchise.

As mentioned, time and resources will be limited, so strict prioritization will be the key success factor. In this regard, a circular process of Valuation-Question-Fact-Update is recommendable so to ensure an agile and prioritized approach. However, it will be still critical that the legal team (and often also the commercial team) comb carefully all the available documentation in the data room, so to avoid inadvertently leaving any important facts that might translate in a downside risk for the acquirer. This is so because it has been a prevalent practice in recent years to include clauses in the SPA contract that exonerate the seller from responsibility in the event of any of these risks eventually materializing, so it is deemed the buyer has checked and reviewed all documentation in the data room during the DD.

The business-line and functional teams will have a set of prioritized questions to search for, then go digging into the available data and questioning with the target's representatives in the room. After that, they go back to the central DD coordination team to update Valuation and questions, so to receive another round of points to search for. This iterative process goes back and forth for 3–4 weeks, till the central DD team thinks they got most of what is needed to revert to the Steering Committee.

On occasion, the allotted DD time is not quite enough, so it is down to negotiation between acquirer and target to agree on an extension. Let us not forget that for the acquirer this step becomes quite onerous as it may be employing, depending on the target's size and complexity, like a month value of up to 30–40 people in undertaking this process.

Step-4 Valuation (detailed): The iterative process described in the previous step would be taking care, under the direction of the central DD team, of the continuous update of all the major lines of P&L and balance-sheet of the Valuation 'as-is' and of the Revenue and Cost Synergies.

The Valuation 'as-is' may encounter important changes in the structure of the revenue or cost lines, as the details provided by the target may be more granular than those in the high-level Valuation. More importantly, the assumptions would be changing with the discovery of more granular historic data series from the target and their own views regarding year-end Forecasting and current MTP. It is up to the DD team to validate and confirm these assumptions, in particular looking forward ones, since obviously the target (the eventual seller), and its advisor, are 'conflicted' in their views.

The Synergies will require a very special attention. Here, the most critical aspect is to test the quality of the target's operational capabilities where key Revenue or Costs assumptions rest on. Thus, for instance, for Barclays-B.Zaragozano deal in Spain referred above, the Affluent Banking team representative in the DD would need to understand very well the retail sub-segments of the client franchise, current levels of product penetration and, from there and their experience, extrapolate the effective and reasonable revenue lines that could be expected; even they may create several alternative scenarios depending on the market and/or proposition conditions.

At this moment, we are beginning to visualize also a key learning from M&A and Integration practitioners: the best possible situation for an acquisition, as far as talent is a concern, is to involve in the DD process the individuals that will eventually become the business-line and functional leaders in the combined company, particularly during the subsequent 2–3 year Integration period and, ideally, beyond that.

Why? Because these leaders would be the ones to make the estimations in DD of the Revenues and Costs of a baseline that would become an expectation for the combined entity to deliver. Thus, if they subsequently are the ones responsible for performance delivery, and they are fully aware of that possibility while at DD, chances are those estimates will be sounder and more realistic than if the DD team were composed of leaders who would not participate in the Integration. Basically, leaders should ideally have 'skin in the game', even if reputational, for these estimates.

In any case, the central DD team has the ultimate responsibility of counterchecking those estimates and ensuring balance the temptation between lowballing and highballing the numbers. Once the DD period closes, back to the boardroom for decisions.

At this point, the decision committee is probably a higher instance at the Group level, versus the previous 2 phases that could have been done at the Divisional level. The new detailed Valuation from the DD gets discussed, and all the initial questions are addressed. Valuation 'as is' forward assumptions and Synergies usually get scrutinized to death. Given the importance of the outcome of the decision at this phase (i.e. Bidding Price), it is not unusual the committee meets several times in the same week to discuss, send the team away to re-do numbers and summon again.

In the end, a decision must be made at this stage regarding whether or not to go ahead for this target acquisition with a Bidding Price. There could be 2 possibilities depending on how the selling process has been organized by the target and its advisor:

- Submit a binding single price point or a price range, to be submitted to an auction across several potential acquirers.
- Two-step process where it is required, first, a non-binding price, out of which the seller will form the basis to select one acquirer for exclusive negotiations, while the rest remain 'on hold'.

Whatever the selling process, what the decision committee will focus is on the dichotomy or gap between the final range of Valuation (i.e. 'as-is' + Synergies) from the different methods used, and what could constitute a 'winning' Bidding Price (or price range). Two special considerations enter to play in this dichotomy.

One is the fact that the financial Valuation is based on DCF financial mathematics, and that this method does not necessarily may account for Optionality Value the target may enjoy in the future in the eyes of the acquirer. If that is the case this Optionality Value has to be assessed by the decision committee members, usually the C-levels of the organization, probably with the CEO involved. More often than not this assessment will be qualitative, but in some occasions there could be room for 'real options' analysis like, for instance, when the buyer can exercise a decision about whether or not to expand, defer, wait or abandon a project underway by the target (thus, cash flows of this project can be brought to net present value using option theory if there is a clear 'spot price' that can trigger the future decision and a proxy for 'implied volatility', both key ingredients for option valuation).

The other is that, quite commonly, the target's Board expects what is called a 'control premium', an excess price over their estimated 'own Valuation' to justify, given their fiduciary duty towards their shareholders, relinquishing control of its business. This 'control premium' reflects their views of future prospects out of their current Forecast and MTP, plus their reckoning of what the acquirer estimates as a Synergy. *How much should the 'control premium' be?* ... nobody knows.

This is the game. The acquirer decision committee will need to, starting from the Valuation, add a quite hunch-based, intangible Optionality Value and reckon whether the resulting sum provides a reasonable 'control premium' over current market price (if the target is listed) or the target's 'own Valuation' (if the target is not listed, and we may have any guess about the target's thoughts in this respect!). This excess price over market price is what eventually becomes, in accounting terms the

Goodwill (i.e. reflecting the concept of Optionality Value). Obviously, you do not want to arrive at a Bidding Price that pays too little and ends up losing the bid, nor too much and ends up grossly overpaying.

Hence, foresight becomes extremely valuable at this stage, and so the importance of the Synergies, as remarked earlier. The more robust and founded the decision makers' faith is on the Synergies, the closer they can bridge the 'gap' towards offering a 'winning' Bidding Price and the smaller the need to 'fill in' via hunch-based Optionality Value.

Then, decision is made and a Bidding Price (single point or range, either binding or non-binding, depending on the type of process) is submitted to the target's advisor, or alternatively . . . the acquirer 'walks away'. The latter is as well a strategic choice at this stage, normally because there is a realization that the 'gap' is too wide at current market terms, and/or perhaps the impact on the acquirer shareholders will be quite punitive in the short and medium term (i.e. too heavy Earnings-per-Share dilution for their expectations or appetite), and/or other critical constraints (i.e. funding for the transaction or management pipeline for the integration).

5.4 Deal Negotiation

After the DD execution and detailed Valuation by the buyer, 2 main outcomes are possible, either to go ahead and propose to extend the exclusivity period to start Deal Negotiation, or 'walk away', in which case the seller will be free to retake its auction process (if that was the method used). If we are 'in', then a process of 5 steps begins.

Step-1 Contract Negotiation: Usually headed by the CEO of division or the Group CEO or CFO and supported by the corporate development and legal teams.

All numbers and preparation have been done, so now is down to 2 human beings and their supporting teams to negotiate the 'value gap' between what both organizations consider is the right price as well as the right covenants to cover for the identified risks by both parties.

Both chief negotiators certainly will have clear negotiation protocols from their respective supervisory bodies (i.e. Board of Directors or Group Executive Committee depending); so, they may need from time to time during the negotiations to check back for authorization on specific covenants and price discussions.

From the acquirer's perspective, the risks identified during the DD need to be decided and negotiated upon with the seller. Each of them could be accepted (so the acquirer agrees to bear that specific risk), or agreed upon the seller acceptance of a downward adjustment in the price, or mitigated via the agreed inclusion of protective covenants in the contract. For the latter case, the buyer will assess whether the seller is a company with 'enough means' out of which to provide compensation in case the risk protected is materialized (i.e. counterparty risk).

Of course, each negotiation is unique, so not much generalization is possible at this point. Many things can go wrong during these conversations, and external factors like sudden market events or news can derail the negotiations.

The process will be iterative, and can extend for several weeks, though usually, there would be a limit set by both parties in the MoU that defines the terms of the negotiations' exclusivity. Also, there could be set some agreed penalty associated with dropping out of the negotiations, which incentivizes the parties to focus on reaching an agreement and prevents them from 'bluffing' their way out of them.

Thus, if the stars align, the parties may reach an agreement on a Final Closing Price and conditions, which would be subject to respective approvals by both parties' Boards of Directors.

Step-2 Execution of Deal Documentation: With price and covenants agreement in place, time for the respective legal departments, with support of the appointed lawyers, advisors and corporate development teams, to proceed into the final drafting of the SPA contract and associated documentation.

In this step, the agreed conditions get specified in full detail, which will surely require some iterations with the senior executives that were present in the negotiations and, sometimes, specific conversations between both parties required to clarify intentions of these terms.

Step-3 Confirmatory Due Diligence and Regulatory Approval: Certainly, the buyer will send a team as well to verify the financial and operational assumptions taken in their Valuation based on the detailed information shared in the data room during Due Diligence phase.

It will involve some visits to the seller's premises, meetings with teams across businesses and functions as well as auditors. The agreement is usually conditioned as well to positive pass of this step.

In case any of the involved entities are under supervision (which is always the case with banks), in parallel to the Confirmatory DD, the legal team (usually along with the commercial team) will engage the respective Regulators. Ideally, Regulators have been already given the 'heads up' of the transaction from the moment the parties enter in the exclusivity period, and hopefully they have been kept informed all the way through. This approval will take time (minimum 2–4 months but could extend much longer) and the content it involves depends on each jurisdiction. Nowadays, for banking acquisitions in Western developed markets, it involves at minimum a Regulatory Business Plan (RBP) along with pro forma 5-year financials and respective capital and liquidity reports.[3]

The satisfactory fulfilment of these two activities is usually part of the condition precedents clause in the SPA contract of the transaction.

Step-4 Integration Planning: In parallel to Step 3, the Integration team, ideally already made of many veterans from the Due Diligence team, reinforced by many new additions for the Integration Programme, has surely started to warm up engines during these 2–3 months before completion, preparing a high-level 2–3 year Integration Plan, with special emphasis on D+1 and the first 100 days. The plan would include a comprehensive set of workstreams, key milestones and dependencies,

[3] Internal Capital Adequacy Assessment Process report (ICAAP) and Internal Liquidity Adequacy Assessment Process report (ILAAP).

along with the leaders and sub-teams composition. We will review in more depth key considerations about integration within the Transformation part of execution in Chap. 6.

Because, if the deal was challenging to come about, the Integration will be an actual 'proof of the pudding', and its execution will determine the delivery or not of the value envisaged for this acquisition in the first place. The plan then becomes a reality.

Step-5 Completion: Finalized the above steps, time for signing and execution of clearing and settlement of the transaction by the respective legal and treasury departments (D-Day).

Deal done and dusted.

* * *

In sum, the Inorganic Growth Process is a tool to coordinate systematically the execution of a portfolio of potential acquisitions and alliances across markets.

It starts with Deal Origination, devised like a continuous loop of deal suggestion, strategic fit assessment and portfolio prioritization, which should lead to a decision of whether or not a particular target merits a closer look.

If it does so, then an effort of Valuation kicks off, for both base case and synergies, at a high level. Should the valuation stack up, the decision then follows to proceed with the Due Diligence stage, a more expensive process in terms of time and resources.

We would sign the confidentiality agreement to receive the information memorandum, design our DD team, execute the DD in the assigned data room and, while doing so, update the valuation, now grounded in much more detail to test the original high-level base case and synergies.

After this third step, a decision must be made regarding whether or not to proceed with a bidding price and, if accepted, get engaged in Deal Negotiation, the fourth and last stage. It will involve contract negotiation, execution of deal documentation, confirmatory DD plus (if required) regulatory approval, integration planning and, finally, completion.

Strategy and Execution

6

Up to this point, we have reviewed how to develop best-practice Strategy Development (SD) and Business Development (BD) for 'Existing' vs 'New Geography/Businesses', distinguishing between Organic vs Inorganic growth approaches. Now it is time to review how strategy links with execution by understanding best-practices for implementation.

Quite often these processes get a little bit confused within organizations not having a clear definition of where stages start and finish nor where the handovers take place between the respective leading teams. Across banks, quite often I have witnessed that there are no systematic conventions on these definitions which, in addition to the variety of businesses and functions involved, does not help effective coordination. *Where does Strategy finish and Execution start?*

So far in the book we have described two stages, Strategy Development and Business Development. However, *how do they really connect? What are the dynamics between the frameworks used to describe them?*

Finally, something that we have not really addressed, after SD and BD stages comes Implementation, *what do we have to say about this all-important stage? Are there some best practices or frameworks we could lever?*

The next four sections will attempt to provide some answers. The first section will deal with Strategy vs Execution, the second with SD vs BD dynamics, and the last two sections will cover Implementation management, from a dual viewpoint, Mobilizing the people and Transforming the organization.

6.1 Strategy Versus Execution

To address the semantic confusion involving these concepts, which very frequently permeates organizations, in my teams' practice we have distilled the definitions and boundaries suggested in the Strategy & Execution framework below. It has proven to be clarifying for everyone in the banks where it was applied (Fig. 6.1).

A. Gavieiro Besteiro, *Strategy in Action*, Management for Professionals,
https://doi.org/10.1007/978-3-030-94759-0_6

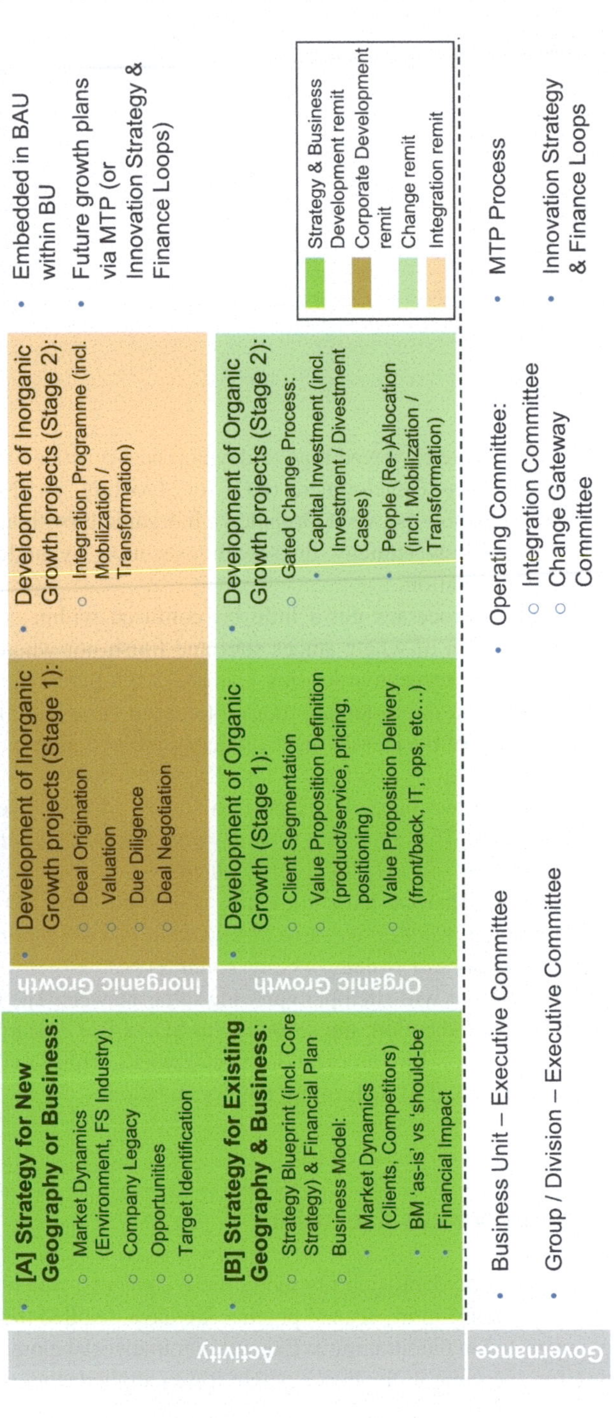

Fig. 6.1 **Strategy & Execution framework**. Note: BU = Business Unit; MTP = Medium Term Planning; M&A = Mergers & Acquisitions; JV = Joint Venture. Sources: 'Holistic Management Framework v.5' (Angel Gavieiro; Apr.17; AG Strategy & Partners)

Important to caveat, in this framework, its definitions and its structure are conventions, as there could be other alternatives out there that might be suggested. The important point is not so much whether this one is better than any other alternative, but rather that everyone in an organization would benefit from following the same one and from making the effort to use its definitions accordingly. *Why?* Because communication is the critical factor for a successful coordination, and the process of Strategy and Execution in any organization is essentially a process of coordination of the interaction of the work done separately by businesses and functions. If the communication is poor, both in terms of active practice and in terms of concepts, then confusion and failure are practically guaranteed.

Starting from the top, the chart introduces the concepts of Strategy and Execution. I often refer to a metaphor from back when we were children at school facing our first serious exams or tests. Teachers often suggested us to dedicate the first 5 min of the exam to get a quick reading of it, think a little bit and plan how you were going to deploy your effort within the time given, and therefore not to start until you had this planning done (as opposed to immediately jumping into writing like mad to make the most of the scarce time available). Well, for me, Strategy is those 5 min, and the rest of the exam is Execution… so everything!

You may think of examples of companies that skip Strategy development or, more accurately, they do not dedicate time to think and design Strategy, preferring to be fully focused on Execution. Having said that, investing those '5 minutes' of Strategy, if performed with good quality, can make the whole difference in the outcome from that Execution; therefore, not surprisingly at this point dear reader, I am of the camp of believers that strategy is really valuable.

Now, *which would be the activities typically associated with Strategy vis-a-vis Execution?*

Here is where the three stages described in this book come in handy, as they perfectly provide a logical convention for grouping all activities involved in a clear way.

Strategy corresponds to the stage of Strategy Development (SD) for both Existing and New Geographies/Businesses. Execution includes the remaining two stages of Business Development (BD) and Implementation just until the resulting operations are considered to be in BAU, and so perfectly embedded in the respective BUs.

A. *SD stage:* is different for Existing vs New Geography/Business:
   - *Existing Geography/Business*: involves the Strategy Blueprint (including Core Strategy) and Financial Plan along with the Business Model at high level (i.e. Market Dynamics, Business Model current vs future, and Financial Impact). (ref. Chaps. 1–3)
   - *New Geography/Business*: involves the Attractiveness and Opportunities framework (i.e. Environment, Industry, Company Legacy, Target Identification, and Opportunities) with its associated outputs of Portfolio View and Entry/Expansion Cases. (ref. Chaps. 4–5)

B. *BD stage (for both Existing and New Geography/Business)*: is different for Inorganic versus Organic growth:
   - *Inorganic Growth*: with its four-step process (i.e. Deal Origination, Valuation, Due Diligence and Deal Negotiation).
   - *Organic Growth*: involves the development of the three core elements of the Business Model framework to their next level (i.e. Client Segmentation, Value Proposition Definition and Value Proposition Delivery).

   Regarding Business Model, let's notice that there is a clear distinction when we are working at SD versus BD stage: at the SD stage we would be identifying the elements of the Business Model in current initial state ('as-is') versus future targeted state ('should-be'); at BD stage we would be working on the details of each of those elements all the way up to (but excluding) the deployment of resources (i.e. people and capital), which would be part of the Implementation stage.

C. *Implementation stage*: is different for Inorganic versus Organic growth.
   - *Inorganic Growth*: starts with the Integration Programme just after deal closure, and results in the combination of both organizations' capabilities.
   - *Organic Growth*: starts with the Gated Change Process for releasing Capital Investment or People (Re-)Allocation to execute the changes in each of the elements of the current Business Model towards the target model; it results in the gated release of funds for the Investment/Divestment Cases approved.

For both types of growth, the Implementation stage involves Mobilization and/or Transformation of resources (i.e. people and capital).

In addition, it is important to understand the Governance of Strategy and Execution, so who has the responsibility for decision-making on the activity that happens at each stage. At SD and BD stages, the respective Executive Committee at Business Unit, Division, or Group level is the right governing body. At the Implementation stage, Integration Committee or the Change Gateway Committee (both usually reporting into an Operating Committee) would make the respective decisions. Once the operations arrive at the BAU stage, then like the rest of existing operations within the BU, decisions of change would follow the usual Medium Term Planning process (and, if it does exist, its Innovation Strategy & Finance Loops), which is the vertical dialogue mechanism among BU, Division and Group for purposes of resource allocation (i.e. people and capital).

Finally, in terms of functional support, the legend box in the chart above shows with colour code which team would be supporting which stage. Given that the organization of these teams could vary among banks (more on this topic in Chap. 11), it is difficult to generalize. With that caveat in mind, the chart suggests that the team of Strategy & Business Development would normally take care of the SD stage for Existing or New Geographies/Businesses and the BD stage for Organic growth, leading to a handover to the Change team at Implementation stage; while the Corporate Development team would take care of the BD stage for Inorganic growth, leading to a handover to the Integration team at the Implementation stage.

6.2 Strategy and Business Development Dynamics

The dynamics of SD versus BD stages are quite different when we are considering Existing versus New Geographies/Businesses.

For New Geographies/Businesses, the illustration in Fig. 6.2 shows that while during the SD stage the Attractiveness & Opportunities framework is a one-off exercise (though live and open to change), in the BD stage the results from this effort cascade, over time, into a portfolio of many Inorganic and Organic Growth processes.

Depending on the bank it could be quite a large portfolio. For instance, a large Western Bank during a 4-year internationalization programme originated a portfolio north of 45 inorganic opportunities (only closing on a few of them) for both New and Existing geographies across EMEA and APAC.

For Existing Geographies/Businesses, the illustration below shows that the SD stage involves a yearly Strategy Blueprint and Financial Plan (within the MTP process) that provides a refresh of the Core Strategy (normally within a 3–5 year horizon). This effort continues with a BD stage focused on transforming the different elements of the Business Model from 'as-is' towards 'should-be', following a myriad of change programmes within short, medium and long-term horizons for delivery. The process is recurrent in the sense that each yearly refresh of the SD work (or intra-year if an Innovation Strategy and Finance Loop process exists) will result in changes to the BD programme of change, which provides more execution flexibility. For instance, the above Western Bank's internationalization strategy put together a coordinated process of 5-year MTP organic growth for all existing +20 countries, in tandem with parallel inorganic growth plans for at least 7–10 geographies (3 within countries where the bank already had an existing presence) (Fig. 6.3).

The illustration above also shows what are the roles that each business and function usually perform in terms of delivering the change in the Business Model. Functions such as Change, Operations, IT or HR, in coordination with the Business Management team of the BUs, have a key responsibility to undertake the change of the Value Proposition itself. Business areas dedicated to Client or Product, therefore, lead the change of market position, including both Client Segmentation and Market Dynamics. Finally, Finance will track, monitor and feedback the change of Performance stemming from the interventions by the rest of businesses and functions.

Therefore, all parts of the orchestra would perform the symphony during the BD and Implementation stages following the music composition defined at the SD stage.

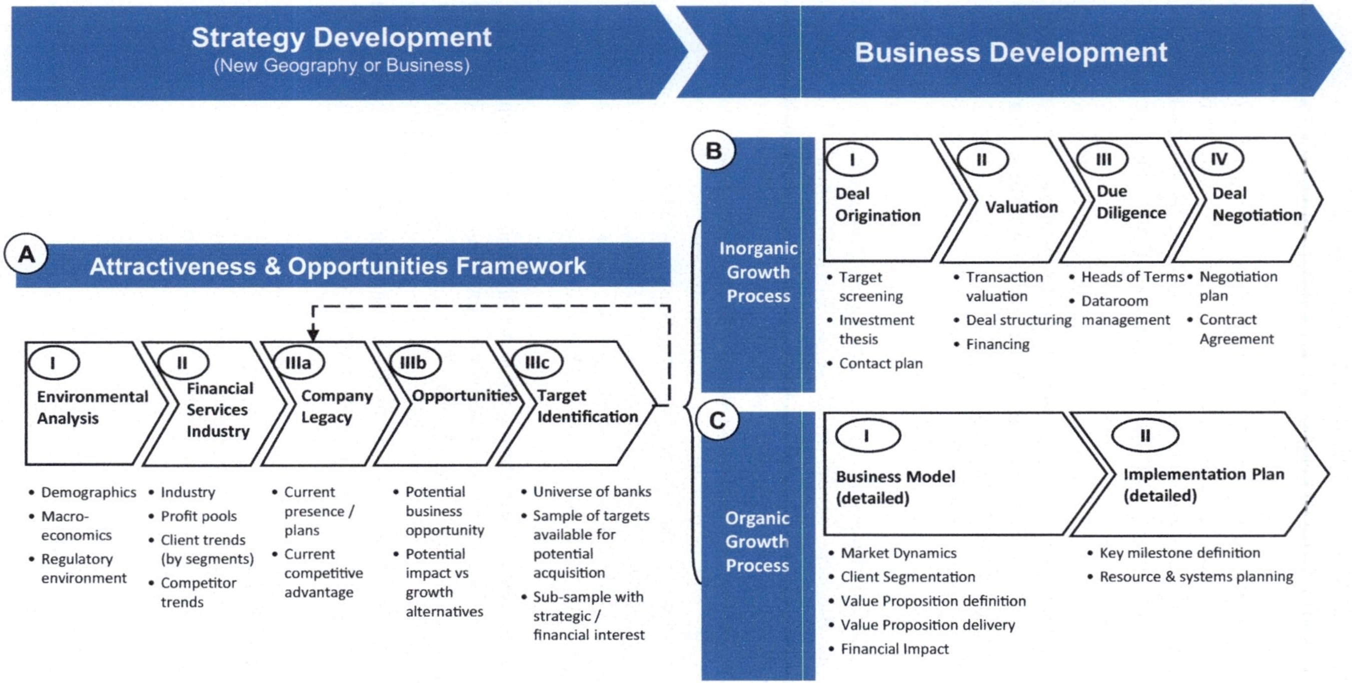

Fig. 6.2 Strategy & Execution—SD and BD: New Geography or Business. Sources: 'Holistic Management Framework v.5' (Angel Gavieiro; Apr.17; AG Strategy & Partners)

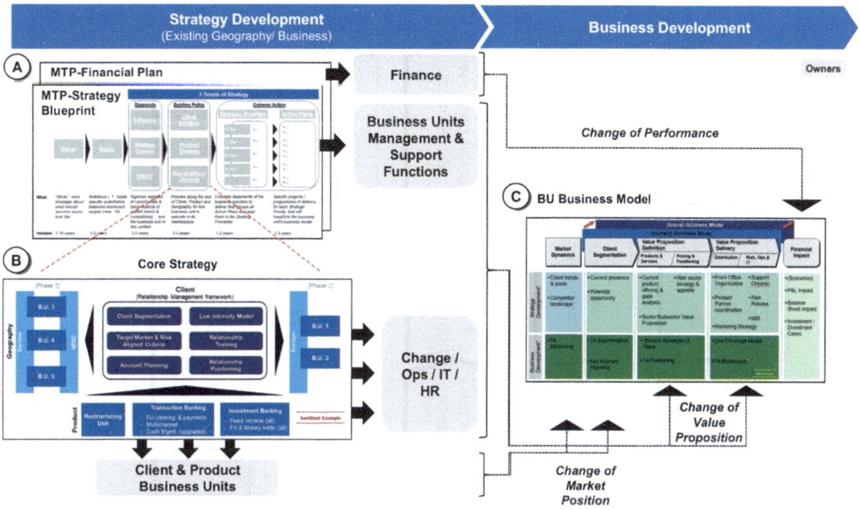

Fig. 6.3 Strategy & Execution—SD & BD: Existing Geography and Business. Sources: 'Holistic Management Framework v.5' (Angel Gavieiro; Apr.17; AG Strategy & Partners)

6.3 Implementation—Mobilization

When it comes to the Implementation stage, being that organic or inorganic, activities suddenly expand to a vast amount of people within the organization (or organizations in the case of M&A integration). Thus, it is essential to get teams ready for what will be a very extraordinary period of change. Actually, the effort starts much in advance to the moment where Implementation really kicks off, involving the top management and subsequently the remaining layers of the organization.

There is some in-depth study work done on this topic. Perhaps the best book in recent years is 'The Strategy of Execution' by Liz Mellon and Simon Carter [1]. It presents a 5-step framework (illustration below), which I will summarize in this section in order to show with examples how it was done in particular instances at banks where I was part of the action. Interestingly, in this specific sample of experience, I have not found a single instance that illustrates quite perfectly all of the 5 steps below. On the one hand, it is a sign that these steps are not systematically followed in practice, which tend to be less organized when it comes to people-related processes. On the other hand, if these efforts were more systematically followed perhaps they would result in a more positive execution impact, given that, as research shows, a large percentage of implementation projects fail (Fig. 6.4).

Step-1 Mobilize the Village: the goal is to ensure that the top-100 (or so) executives effectively internalize and communicate the strategy so as to be able to bring it with passion to their teams.

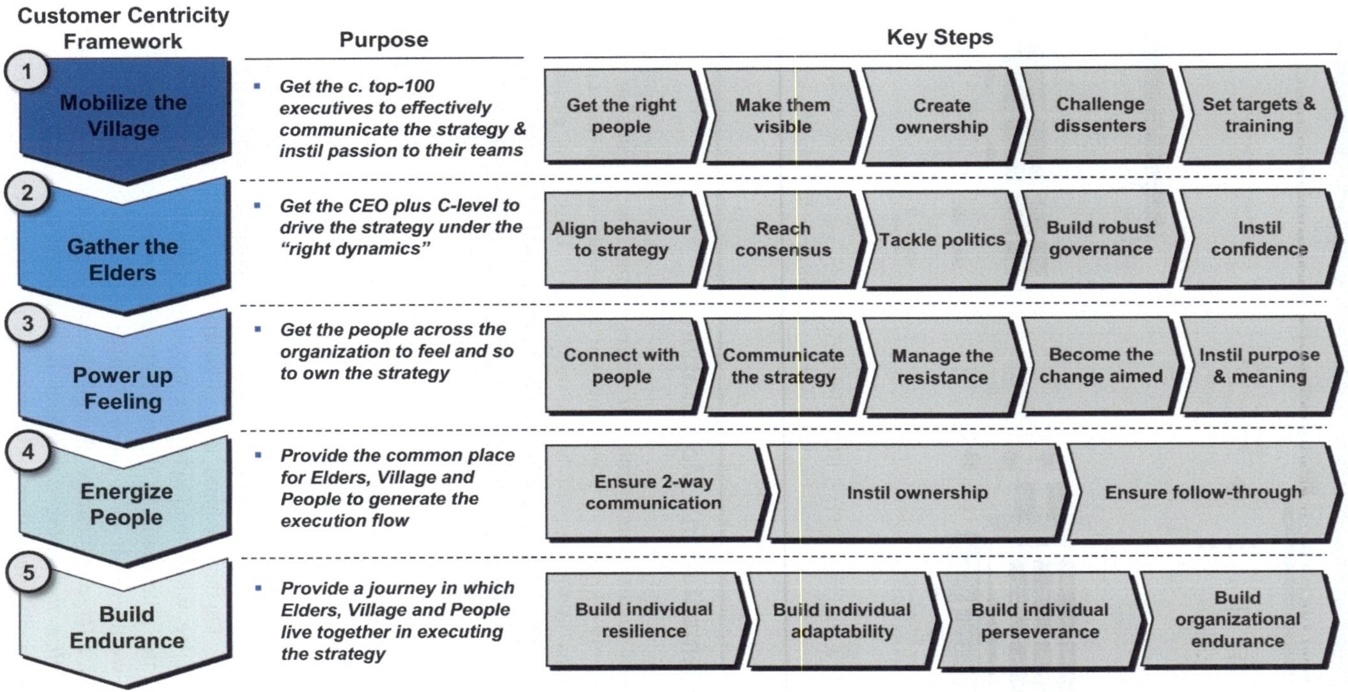

Fig. 6.4 Strategy & Execution—Implementation: Mobilization. Note: the graphic depiction of this framework has been created for this book, so it is not original from the authors referred to in the source. Sources: [1]

The authors point to several necessary considerations to succeed in this goal. First, you need to get the right people in the room, not too many, not too few, but more importantly, those that really move the needle across the entire organization must be there. Then, it is important to make them visible; first among themselves, so that it translates in a 'esprit de corps' and mutual commitment because they are the chosen ones to lead and transmit the new gospel; and second vis-à-vis their teams, so to ensure they have the media support and budget for their respective cascade-down communication efforts.

Within the gathering of the top-100, which can happen all together or in sections, in one or several sessions, there is a subtle but not renounceable objective to achieve: to create ownership. Each of the chosen top-100 must personally own the new strategy, know perfectly what his/her role on it is and fully stand behind it. Of course, there could be dissenter voices, which will need to be properly addressed and hopefully convinced. Subsequently, after the mobilization sessions are done, there cannot be room for dissenters, and if some have not been converted yet, then they could not be part of the top-100, and decisions in this regard will need to be made.

Finally, ownership does not get accomplished without accountability, so targets must be clearly established for each of the top-100, for both business and function leaders, along the different horizons of the new strategy. Any requirements and budget for training for themselves and respective areas would also be considered.

In 2003 a large European bank, with an established base in a foreign market, made a large acquisition to double up its presence, within the context of a '2nd Home Market' strategy. The transaction involved the organization of a joint Integration team, and for that purpose, a multidisciplinary team of business and functional leaders was selected. From the start, the sessions of communication, involving top leaders of both organizations along with the Integration team, under the leadership of the local CEO and the Head of the Integration Programme, were essential to ensure mobilization was a success. As the executives were coming out of the sessions their enthusiasm was quite palpable, and the subsequent cascade to the teams kept the positive spiral across the whole effort. The teams that were not directly involved in the Integration, were always addressed in the communications, which was quite effective for reducing substantially the risk of attrition from the BAU businesses and functions. Also, there was a member in each of the integration workstreams that defended the 'voice of the client', which transmitted a strong signal to the teams outside the integration ensuring that their views and feedback from the existing client base were a crucial input in the decisions. The Village was very effectively mobilized, and this step certainly had an important bearing in the success of that integration programme (which in fact overdelivered in most KPIs, including delivery time and synergies, more than 12 months ahead of the plan).

Step-2 Gather the Elders: the goal is to ensure the CEO and his/her C-level executive team drive the strategy under the 'right dynamics'.

This is often a step 'skipped or overlooked' in many implementation efforts because of the assumption that given the new strategy has been discussed and approved by the Group Executive Committee (ExCo), where all the C-levels had the chance to participate in the discussion, it follows that they are all 'in' for the subsequent execution. As it often happens, the level of political posturing is usually higher at ExCo than anywhere else in organizations; which means that what apparently could be understood like support could hide behind a high level of doubt or even outright opposition, not necessarily visible.

Therefore, what the CEO is looking to achieve out of each ExCo member is an alignment between his/her behaviour and the new strategy. This point can only be reached if there is a search for consensus among the ExCo participants regarding the 3 main axes of the Core Strategy (i.e. client, product and geography), but as well of the specific Strategic Priorities (what goes first and what goes later) and accordingly the Action Plans respectively associated. This latter point is what usually creates ExCo disagreements in the execution phase, because affects the prioritization of resource allocation (i.e. capital and people) dedicated to their respective areas of responsibility, resulting in a perception of winners vs losers, which might provoke in some executives the 'political animal' to react (i.e. flight or fight). Resource reallocation is one of the most common sources of political infighting within ExCos. The CEO will need to foresee, well ahead gathering the Elders, the potential resulting scenarios of political conflict, and so have at hand tactical tacks ready to address the unavoidable issues.

One of the ways to reduce the effect of these politics, which usually filter down through the cracks to the next layers in the organization, is to establish a robust, coherent but at the same time not overdone governance around the execution of the new strategy. The Strategic and Operating agendas of the Divisions and BUs across the organization embed the Strategic Priorities and Action Plans in full coordination with the Group level plan. Quite often, either the Strategy team or an ad-hoc PMO office will take care of ensuring the cascade is well executed and, subsequently followed up with a recurrent frequency, ensuring a log of actions is properly maintained to keep the momentum and facilitate ex-post performance auditing.

Last but not least, fruit of this gathering of the Elders the ExCo needs to gain confidence in the new strategy so that they are able to instil confidence across the organization. This should be quite apparent to their respective teams as soon as the first sessions happen; otherwise, people will see through it and start holding negative perceptions about what is coming. Some organizations hire external coaching teams for the ExCos at Group and Divisional levels to ensure these dynamics are right and the elements above are successfully embedded.

In the 2000s, a European retail bank launched an internationalization programme. The divisional CEO for international, brought together his ExCo members representing the existing footprint across +20 countries in EMEA, and supported by his COO, achieved a solid commitment from all the Regional CEOs and Functional MDs to embrace the strategy. This optimism and enthusiasm for the internationalization effort permeated quickly across the Country Heads and other Functional Heads.

Having said that, there were moments where politics played against the main tune. For instance, when one of the regional Chiefs wanted to prioritize some inorganic moves in their territory which were outside of the Strategic Priorities prevalent at that point; or when the Group Corporate Development team was pushing for selling the existing operations in Egypt when, in fact, contradicted one of the Strategic Priorities focused on developing a strong presence in the Middle-East via an organic growth development across selected GCC countries. In both instances, the CEO acted quickly and swiftly to bring back those tangent priorities to the fold, so to stick to the Strategic and Operating agenda being rolled out at the time.

This successful 'Gathering of the Elders' at the launch of the internationalization effort, and the timely interventions by its CEO to correct tangential moves attempted by some of the ExCo members, were both decisive factors in the effective execution of this divisional strategy that involved both organic and inorganic moves. A large acquisition in Africa made the bank, as a result, leader in many of the Sub-Sahara African countries of the combined footprint. This was complemented with JV/Alliances in Western Europe with life insurance companies, both for bancassurance and 'assurbanking', as well as with a real estate developer in the GCC for mortgages, plus the organic growth plans for the respective existing geographies. Finally, for new geographies organic greenfield growth in counties such as India, both in commercial banking and mortgages, was another success from the Elders' consensus and discipline of alignment with the strategy.

Now, *how do we know that 'Gathering of the Elders' was a key driver of the success in the internationalization effort above?* In this case, coincidentally, we have a very good counterpoint by comparing with a new CEO and ExCo team that took over this retail bank a few years later. The incoming CEO very quickly removed most of the Chiefs, Country Heads and Function MDs at his international ExCo, bringing new executives of his confidence from his prior bank. Subsequently, he also altered quite fundamentally the tenets of the internationalization strategy, like for instance including new prioritized markets that had been previously studied and discarded in emerging markets with high country risk. The change of Elders and strategy was swift, without much time for any gathering, and the signals that permeated down the countries quickly drained confidence, kicking a diaspora of key personnel and the plummeting of morale during 2007–2008. Albeit undoubtedly there were comingling additional negative effects during 2009–2010 from the Credit Crisis, by the end of 2010 the international franchise was in utter disrepair. Post-2007, the lack of 'Gathering of the Elders' and alignment in their dynamics had a very negative impact after all.

Step-3 Power up Feeling: the goal is to get people across the organization to feel the strategy and, so, to own it.

As per the authors, once the Village is mobilized and the Elders gathered, the right feelings about the strategy need to be spread across everyone in the organization. This effort starts with connecting with the people and communicating the strategy.

Over time I have witnessed a variety of ways of empowering feeling, but choosing them wisely is the key, which will depend entirely on the type of organization and circumstances at the time. Examples: 1–2 h Town Halls by the Regional CEOs and Functional Heads repeated every 4 or 6 weeks during the internationalization strategy described earlier; full-day Big Gathering of top 5000 executives that the new CEO of a British bank preferred to use to transmit the main tenets from his first Group Strategy Review in 2011; meticulously timed and messaged email cascades and Head-to-Team meetings orchestrated by the CEO and his C-suite team of another large UK bank for the communication of new management and strategy after the acquisition of rival; big stage presentation of the new management and strategy to the entire team by the CEO of a European corporate bank to reinforce this purpose. A large array of alternatives... but, *which one is the most effective for a given situation?*

The key is to realize that actions do not come without the respective reactions. Thus, anticipating the potential reactions from the audience will guide the selection of communication strategy. Now, among reactions, necessarily, you will find resistance, hidden or outright opposition to the strategy intended. For instance, the cascade down of the new strategy 6 months after the arrival of a new CEO to a European bank in late 2010, and communicated by some of his new ExCo members, did face a large resistance from many upper echelons across one of the divisions. This underlying fight became quite evident during a turbulent period among top management dynamics the following year, so the CEO had no other choice than to actively manage this resistance... by the end of 2012, the large majority of the Divisional Heads and direct reports in that division were gone. Only after that, the CEO was able to fully trust the effective roll-out of the strategy in that division.

Leader's behaviour is another key aspect to consider, hence the importance of the indoctrination at the ExCo and top-100 in the previous 2 steps. Leaders need to become the change that they aspire the team to achieve. This preaching from example is one of the most powerful influencers of behaviour you can find, often more powerful than incentivization. The 'Trusted Relationship' segmentation case study (ref. Sect. 1.2 in Chap. 1) became the key driver of performance for an European corporate bank. The brains of this strategy was a Client Segmentation model, both quantitative and qualitative in nature, that resulted in 5 client categories (Trusted Relation, Specialist Relation, potential TR, potential SR and Low Potential). The usage of this new terminology was critical in the Account Planning sessions, where both client coverage teams and product line teams met up, discussed and agreed clients' categorization status and planned commercial actions in front of top executives in the division. Therefore, the CEO of the division made sure to be present in most of these sessions and, as importantly, did the effort from the very start to use and encourage the usage of the terminology from the Client Segmentation, reinforcing the discipline behind it. As a consequence, very quickly the great majority of the teams were talking in the same terms when discussing if a client was already a 'TR' or still a 'potential-TR' and why. The leaders became the 'Trusted Relationship' segmentation champions, and everyone joined.

Finally, it is all about purpose and meaning. This is probably the most important 'north star' in the compass of instilling feeling across the teams, so they own the new strategy. You cannot feel it, and so own it, if you do not have a clear purpose and meaning about it. This purpose and meaning stems from:

(a) The strategy itself, if it is well constructed and resource supported
(b) From its communication, if it is clear and frequent
(c) More importantly, from the CEO and ExCo, reinforced by the top-100, and followed by each of the team leaders and peer team members

People-driven purpose and meaning is a spiral, either positive or negative, and as such starts with the small few, but following the 'golden ratio', very quickly amplifies as it hits the wider population, at which point it is unstoppable.

A last point, it is worth reflecting on how people instil that purpose and meaning. Referring to Chap. 2, and specifically to the Mission element of the Strategy Blueprint. The Mission addresses the 'why', the reason for people to go to the company every day; ultimately, the adoption of the new strategy should align to the Mission for them 'to buy' into it.

In the 'Trusted Relationship' case referred earlier, both executives and teams knew why they wanted to execute this strategy, simply put: to deepen customer relationships. Customer centricity had been for some time then a key mantra in the approach this bank adopted for client interaction. Therefore, the new strategy reinforced this ultimate reason by adding structure and science to the practice, but still aiming to achieve what had been all along the teams' Mission, i.e. deepening customer relationships... and it worked! The new strategy's alignment with the Mission resonated highly with the teams, which helped to quickly drive adoption of the new practices; this itself led to further results, contributing to reinforcing a positive spiral around the ultimate purpose of the effort, and so underpinning the success of the strategy. Ultimately, everyone was aligned towards the 'why'.

Step-4 Energize People: the goal is to provide a common space among CEO and C-levels, Top-100 and Employees to generate the execution flow.

This process starts with the effective realization of the existence of truly, real, 2-way communication. In Step-3 we addressed the importance of top-down communication of the new strategy at all levels, along with the need to anticipate action-reaction chains to choose wisely the most appropriate means or forums for communication. In this step, the focus is to ensure that these means of communication include bottom-up mechanisms that guarantee the wider organization is heard and that top management is listening, actively and attentively. But *how do we know (do the employees know) that the latter two are happening?*

By the actions, not just words. For instance, during the first months of the integration between 2 UK banks during the late-00s, there were a large number of problems within the integration workstreams, with mixed directions, quarrels among people, difficult progress on the weekly monitoring sessions, etc… The bottom-up noise and complaints soon started to contrast with the greenish flashing 'Xmas tree' for monitoring the integration programme reported by the divisional top management. The divisional CEO, suspecting a disconnect, did not waste time reaching out to the teams directly to verify the reality on the ground. Realizing what was going on, she quickly ensured not only to switch on red and amber lights where was due in the reporting 'Xmas tree' but also, more importantly, to substitute the Integration

Director and part of the PMO (Project Management Office) directors and to appoint fresh hands to steer the boat in the right direction. Mechanisms such as employee satisfaction surveys, customer surveys, open town halls, anonymous feedback or just directly 'walking-the-floors' go a long way to ensure the top team triangulates back to reality. However, insight is necessary but not sufficient to demonstrate active and attentive listening, action needs to follow, which often speaks louder than words to people… and that is in the hands of the leaders to demonstrate.

A second crucial aspect of energizing people is to instil ownership. In the previous step, we have addressed how feeling was 'the way to ownership', in this step we look at how to sustain ownership over time, so that people keep energized. Across my career I have witnessed several effective mechanisms in this regard, top among them, recognition programmes. This tool, organized on a periodic basis (quarterly or semi-annually) and preferably with high participation of the employees in awarding the prizes, allows to make visible the work of specific individuals and teams for their contribution to both the results and the spirit of the execution of the new strategy. In fact, recent neuroscience research confirms that 'excellence recognition' is one of the most powerful management tools to positively affect trust among people in organizations, induced by the production of oxytocin in the human body [2].

Two different instances, first a European large corporate bank institutionalized a prize recognition scheme for the best front-line teamwork by celebrating deals that examplify large cross-collaboration and customer impact, both critical objectives of their strategy. Second, a small-size, GCC-based Islamic bank set a specific budget pot aside for prizes that recognized not only the best deals in terms of coverage-product collaboration but as well the best behaviours in terms of demonstration of the values of the institution; the awards were voted by the team colleagues themselves. In both instances, despite their cultural and organizational differences, the comparative results (before vs after these recognition programmes were implemented) in terms of people motivation, energy level and ultimately, ownership of the execution of the strategy were short of spectacular.

Finally, a key element that ensures that people keep energized is to realize that the efforts undertaken effectively conduce to the intended results. Thus, ensuring an efficient follow-through of all the action plans under the strategy is paramount. This is a core role of the PMO for the execution of any strategy. As discussed in Chap. 2, one of the Strategy Blueprint outcomes is an array of Action Plans with clear timings, milestones and executives responsible for delivery, properly aligned towards specific Strategic Priorities within a 12–24 month timeframe. The PMO will continuously monitor and assess (Red-Ambar-Green status) this delivery, reporting to the top management in the relevant Steering Committees. The delivery of specific milestones or the successful closure of an Action should ideally be properly recognized and publicly celebrated across the organization. At a UK retail bank, its CEO and COO would frequently celebrate in their weekly communiqués or in live town halls the main achievements in the execution of the internationalization strategy at the Action Plan level. This meant a lot for the teams involved and helped to re-commit everyone to follow through their workstreams so as to not let the wider team down... they were all on the same ship!

In the same way, the PMO needs to identify when any Action Plan falls behind and their leaders would be encouraged to flag these problems early on to ask for help as needed, so that corrective action can be devised on time. In the prior example, the PMO detected a substantial deviation vs plan in some of the central African countries, in particular Kenya and Botswana. During the monthly conference call, their country managers highlighted their problems and did not hesitate to ask for diagnosis support to the central teams. The CFO and the Head of Strategy devised couples of Finance+Strategy members to 'parachute' in the respective countries in short time to undertake deep dives in full collaboration with the local management. They identified the causes, at the time, a mix of competitive pressures, wrongly aligned pricing and internal team misalignments, and suggested remedial short and medium-term actions. This is the power of follow-through, to detect problems early on, so you can correct the sooner the better... I have never heard of a problem that corrects itself by procrastination.

Step-5 Build Endurance: the goal is to provide a journey in which CEO and C-levels, Top-100 and Employees live together in executing the strategy.

While step 4 is about the common space, deploying mechanisms that ensure 2-way communication, sustain ownership and ensure follow-through, step 5 is about the common spirit that unites them all to live the same journey. Because it is from that shared position where individuals can really endure the hardships that a long-term journey requires.

Now, following the authors of this framework, endurance starts within the individual and subsequently, within the right settings, grows within the collective. At the individual level requires the building of resilience, adaptability and perseverance. At the collective level, when individuals feel fully sharing the same journey, living the same reality together, then those individual characteristics manifest themselves collectively in the form of endurance.

Behavioural economics has only started to play a significant role among banking practitioners after the 2008 Credit Crisis. However, the acknowledgement of the power of behaviour is something not alien to most leaders in organizations. It is by leveraging the latest insight of how individuals and collectives react to diverse stimuli within different circumstances, that we can make a great difference to create endurance within teams and companies. Within each team in a large organization everything comes down to leaders, and their dynamics with team members and among themselves.

I have had the experience of engaging external coaching to several of my teams with remarkable positive results in this regard. These interventions usually lever a type of behavioural framework, like Insights framework,[1] driven by experienced coaches who apply them both at individual and team level within a programme of

[1] www.insights.com.

several sessions. The insights team members reach about themselves and each other are very helpful and make the teams catalyze their formation process, saving more than 6 months. Compared to before the intervention, these teams end up in a much better position to take ownership of their place and role in the organization and their contribution to its strategy. As importantly, the bonds created out of this realization make the team extremely resilient to adversities, adaptable to continuous changes and perseverant to follow through highly challenging projects... in short, the team endurance multiplies several fold.

For instance, the Corporate Banking Strategy & Business Development team, that I had the honour to create and lead during 2009–2012, undertook during their first 18 months several sessions with an external coaching firm. As new members joined the team, we reiterated versions of the coaching for the newcomers, even at a point integrating an existing team of Client & Markets Insight with 6 members. The way these 20 people came together was amazing, the speed with which they developed trust, shared insights, knowledge, best-practice, as well impressive... and the results spoke by themselves, to the point that many stakeholders referred them as a 'dream team'.

This team bonding demonstrated its worth by showing resilience in several 'moments of truth': for instance, when a project of Commercial Real Estate strategy underway came under heavy criticism from a C-level and, within a short turnaround, the team was able of gathering his re-steering while keeping the essence of the good work done and winning his green-light without morale faltering. The team also demonstrated great adaptability when integrating with another counterpart team as a result of the merger of 2 divisions; the project productivity and quality did not fall at any point during the integration. That team epitomized endurance, which I believe was seeded by the initial coaching programme.

6.4 Implementation—Transformation

In Strategy Implementation mode, the Mobilization of people comes hand-in-hand with the Transformation of the organization's Business Model, which will move from current picture ('as-is') to the new Target Operating Model ('should-be').

Chapter 1 addressed the components of a Business Model, which constitute 'what' will change in the path from A to B. Now, the Transformation effort requires a framework of best practices and tools that helps to focus the action on 'how' to change the Business Model. For that purpose, I have leveraged again the General Management Framework that we used to describe the Value Proposition Delivery (ref. Sect. 1.4 in Chap. 1) to collect, from my transformation experience and the cumulative thought leadership of firms like Bain & Co [3] and McKinsey & Co [4], a variety of best-practices and tools that have been proven again and again to reliably and successfully deliver transformation (Fig. 6.5).

1—Strategy: the 'key ask' transformation requires from strategy is to show ambition in terms of value creation potential. I would identify this point with the Goals element, part of the four that make the Strategy Blueprint's Purpose discussed

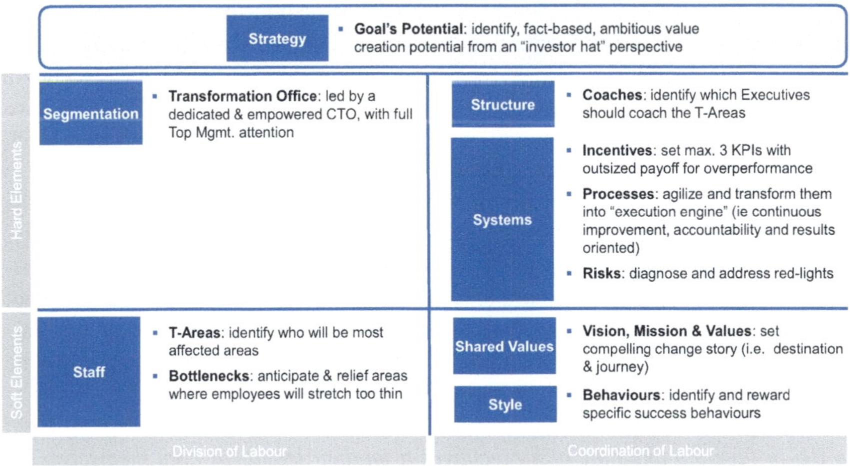

Fig. 6.5 Strategy & Execution—Implementation: Transformation. Sources: own analysis; [3–6]

in Chap. 2. Now, it is not ambition for its own sake, since it must be 'bought in' by the audience of doers; thus, it must be fact-based and reasoned, prepared from the 'investor hat' in terms of expected returns and reachable within the means present and future of the organization. Having said that, still it must be stretchy.

One of the best examples in which I learned how this worked in practice was the internationalization strategy of a European retail and commercial bank in the mid-00s. The arrival of a new CEO prompted the development of a 10-year strategy for the Group. At that point, the bank was mostly centred in its local European market and the stock performance was languishing as per comparison with peers, with a higher presence in emerging markets. On a closer analytical look, the difference in stock performance stemmed from the low growth expectations embedded in the terminal value of the bank's equity valuation at the time, reflecting the lack of exposure to high-growth emerging markets.

Thus, the new CEO concluded that to change that situation we needed to convince the Board and shareholders to substantially uplift the ambition of the Group, and eventually, a goal was set to achieve 50% PBT outside of the home market, 25% of which within emerging markets, with a wider objective of reaching a Top-5 market capitalization vs a selection of the largest Western banks in the next 10 years. Now, as I write in 2021, it might sound like a bit of a far-fetched objective, but back then it was possible, stretchy, ambitious, but within reach according to our facts and expected trends. Once the strategy was approved and management mobilized the people, leveraging many of the practices discussed in the prior section, the whole organization got enthused with the 'Top-5' goal, they did believe in it!

2—Segmentation: this element of the framework refers to any changes or additions to the organizational design configuration required for the Transformation effort. The best practice here is to set up a Transformation Office, led by a CTO fully empowered by the CEO and Top Management. The level of the CTO and the reporting of the Office would depend on the scale of the transformation. For instance, the integration office for specific bolt-on acquisitions like Barclays-Zaragozano in Spain in 2003 would have a local reporting to the local Country Manager, while a more transformative acquisition like Lloyds-HBOS in the UK in 2009 would have the integration office reporting to the Group ExCo; similarly, the CTO level, experience and reporting follows through.

A subtler element is the quality of leadership that is involved in the Office. The usual mistake is to take the transformation effort as a 2nd priority vs BAU activity, and so the businesses and functions send Tier-2 or Tier-3 executives to the Transformation Office. This practice not only would result in lower quality leadership but will signal to the whole organization the poor interest and recognition that this posting entails. Thus, it is important to devise the right mechanisms supporting the staffing of the office, which we will review in the next point.

3—Staff: the first question to understand here is, *what is the incentive of any head of BU or function to let the best executives from their teams (or even themselves) to join a Transformation Office as a 'career visibility opportunity'?* In general, very little. Chapter 5, when discussing the creation of the Due Diligence team within the context of Inorganic Growth, suggested several HR best practices in this regard. Chief among them, the need to devise the right incentivization mechanism that helps to 'pull-in' the right talent, and simultaneously to define a re-balancing mechanism that supports the businesses or functions most affected by the staff moves, what is usually called the 'T-Areas'.

On the incentivization side, a combination of remuneration packages (i.e. assignment allowances, ad-hoc bonuses and retention bonuses) will need to grease the staff moves. As importantly, people expect to have some degree of certainty regarding what will happen once the transformation is delivered (e.g. 2–3 years down the line). Thus, having career path options associated with the delivery post-transformation and/or 'preferred status' for post-delivery internal applications could go a long way. On the re-balancing side, this exercise will demand to identify the potential Bottlenecks of workload that will be generated from the staff assignments to the Transformation Office, and so to have ready both internal and external talent pools from where to recruit to cover the shortfalls.

Also, fundamental to this staffing effort is for the HR department to have a very up-to-date database with the past and present skillset and experiences of personnel across the organization, with predesigned indexes to look for specific requirements depending on the type of transformation effort planned (e.g. organic growth, alliance, JV, acquisition), geographical change involved (e.g. language skills, cultural affinity, relocation availability, family, etc.) and behavioural attitudes (e.g. career focus, compensation sensitivity, teamwork ability, etc.).

For instance, the internationalization strategy prompted a European Bank to prepare such a database for the first time, facing the realization that many of the geographies considered for the expansion (i.e. Africa, Middle East and Asia-Pacific) required previous international experience that many Tier-1 and 2 executives in the organization did not have. Therefore, this created the need to develop a bigger external recruiting pipeline to complement the internal staff relocation efforts as the execution went underway.

4—Structure: the framework uses this term to refer to the formal or informal mechanisms among individuals and teams that help to coordinate the results from the division of work (i.e. Segmentation), such as committees, task forces, cross-functional agile teams as well as external-driven coordination efforts like leveraging the services of team Coaches.

In this regard, I found quite powerful the intervention of Coaches in the context of Transformation Offices, since they are able to galvanize in a very short period of time many people that have not worked ever before together. People, regardless of their position within the Transformation Office, need to 'learn' to work together as a team (i.e. forming, storming, norming and performing). However, the Transformation Office set-up usually does not have a lot of spare time during preparation for allowing naturally the teams to form, especially for inorganic growth-driven transformations.

Hence, it is extremely valuable to engage an external coach firm to accelerate the team formation process, which at the same time can serve to build the 'esprit-de-corps' of the entire Transformation Office. Also, it is important not to forget to lever this type of interventions with the BAU part of the organization, in particular the T-Areas, given the stretch and stress under which they surely are going through, in addition to the need to onboard the new backup members within their teams to cover for the staff moved to the Transformation Office. The value of coaching into a new forming team was well illustrated in Step-5 of the previous section.

5—Systems: the framework uses this term on a wide basis to refer to any formal process for work coordination in HR, Operations, Legal, Risk... not just IT systems. In this area 3 main elements to watch for, especially in transformations.

First, the Incentivization system related to the Transformation Office itself and all the areas involved in the delivery of its workstreams. It is best practice to focus on as few KPIs as possible, ideally not more than 3; otherwise, efforts tend to dissipate as different people and teams steer towards different, diverse KPIs. Also, it is best practice to associate an outsized payoff for overperformance in the delivery of transformation workstreams... *why?* Because the odds are more likely against their success compared to BAU workstreams since many more unforeseen complications can derail the efforts, and because we are working against usually tight deadlines (i.e. with the added difficulty that human biases tend to overestimate timing in the planning phase, creating havoc in the delivery phase... even after adding 25% cushion, which is a customary practice). Therefore, if some workstreams are able to overperform, you need to signal it very vividly to the rest of the Office and to overpay for this success.

Second, the Processes involved at the core of the Business Model must become the 'execution engine' of the transformation. This means an early focus on achieving a continuous improvement of the core machinery, while having a scrutiny on the accountability for the results achieved, is a big signal for the rest of the workstreams across the Office. In terms of the Business Model framework (Chap. 1), these are the core processes that underpin the Value Proposition Delivery. For instance, in the transaction banking strategy and investment case of a wholesale bank in EMEA, out of the 5 major workstreams of the transformation, there were 2 core processes involved, the core accounting system (which recorded all transactions in the ledger and that we aimed to transform to 'real-time' performance) and the payments engine (which processed all payments across the bank, requiring up to that point heavily manual interventions, so we aimed at fully automating it). Ensuring a strong focus on the delivery of these 2 workstreams was essential not just for the entire programme success, but as well to signal the level of high standards demanded for the benefit of all the rest of peripheral workstreams.

And third, having a continuous monitoring for risks is equally paramount. As mentioned, a transformation usually faces higher level of uncertainty and surprises than BAU activities. Thus, the risks involved, operational but also of many other sorts like client attrition, regulatory remediation, competitive leakage, etc. demand a holistic risk assessment framework and constant diagnosis against RAG metrics. Rapid response, as the 'amber' or 'red' light flash, is essential to avoid multiple complications down the line. An international bank having found weaknesses in its regulatory practices across several geographies, embarked on a holistic remediation work in a constant review and iteration with the respective regulatory authorities. Their internal practices tended to whitewash underperformance, and often projects were baselined with an optimistic RAG outlook, only to be caught later with delays and other delivery deficiencies. This only led to a deterioration of its trust with regulators, who redoubled their scrutiny and imposed penalties, eventually leading to the departure of its Group CEO. RAG metrics need to flash reality as soon as the facts emerge.

6—Shared Values: this element comes back to the Purpose set forth in the Strategy Blueprint framework (ref. Sect. 2.1. in Chap. 2). It must involve a compelling change story as well as the rationale, the Mission, Vision and Values, or why, what and how we are doing it. This complements the point of ambition in the Goals mentioned earlier. Starting with the CTO but continuing with all leaders at the Transformation Office, their commitment and communication of the Mission and Vision needs to gradually translate into the Values of the team.

For instance, the '2nd home market' strategy pursued by that European retail bank in its acquisition of a smaller size bank, it conveyed the vision of the bank commitment at that time to make the target market as an important base for its future. The integration office did a great job on instilling this belief in the values of the teams, first within the office itself, and then gradually across the rest of the local bank. This prompted the interest of the local teams to liaise with their counterparts in the home market to bridge best practices across areas. For example, in commercial banking the acquirer subsidiary did not originally have a strong franchise in the local market, however, the acquired franchise brought a sizeable number of SME clients; on the other hand, the bank had a very mature SME presence with large market share at home, so the potential for best-practice cross-fertilization was huge and rightly exploited, among other reasons because the teams believed in the vision (i.e. becoming a 2nd home market) and acted on it.

7—Style: this is about behaviours and so translating the Values (the 'how') of the Strategy Blueprint into the day-to-day activity of the individuals. Transformation leaders need to celebrate success when the Transformation Office behaviours demonstrate the commitment to the Values of the organization, either formally (i.e. 'Leader of the Week') or informally (i.e. CTO stopping by to especially thank a team member for his/her example of demonstration of values).

Overall, transforming a Business Model from A to B (or a portfolio of them if we are talking of organizational transformation) requires both the snapshots of 'what' and the toolkit of 'how', where special attention to the specific elements described along these 7 levers will go a long way to ensure execution success.

A last point before leaving this chapter is the introduction to a theme that we will address in more depth later in this book, and which is quite topical in the banking industry as I write: Digital Transformation (DX, as sometimes it is referred).

DX is often perceived just as a type of transformation like the ones originated from organic or inorganic growth or even restructuring. In my opinion, this is wrongly 'perceived', because DX really involves transforming the whole enterprise to move from a traditional way of understanding and undertaking business in a given marketplace, to heavily leverage technology to reinvent the understanding and the undertaking of that business in that marketplace.

Drawing from other industries currently heavily advanced in their DX path, the music industry for instance surely had the experience of all the types of transformation mentioned above well before the dot.com era. However, once the twenty-first century started, DX took this industry through a path of complete reinvention (and pain), which made the traditional business model fully obsolete, substituted by a succession of disruptive business models, to ultimately satisfy the same customer need but now via totally unrecognizable new business models: for instance, from EMI's CDs selling via stores or mail orders, to Napster's peer-to-peer exchange, to iTunes/iPod's downloading, to Spotify' streaming on a subscription basis.

As I write, the global financial services industry is on the verge of DX, with the FinTech disruption being a clear symptom of a much bigger reshaping happening underneath. Thus, DX cannot be treated just like any other transformation, it requires a much deeper consideration at different levels across the bank's strategy, to which I will dedicate deserved time in Chap. 12.

* * *

Overall, for experiencing a seamless Strategy-to-Execution transition it helps, first, to agree on a common language across the organization so as to understand exactly in which stage a project is, from Strategy Development to Business Development, to Implementation, till reaching BAU. Once arrived at Implementation, two critical tasks to ensure a successful execution: Mobilization of people and Transformation of the business model.

Success in Mobilization comes from a conscious series of interventions with the top-100 executives (Mobilize the Village), the CEO plus C-suite (Gather the Elders) and the wider population (Power up Feeling); all the 3 groups united in a common place to sustain the execution flow (Energize People) and following a common journey together (Build Endurance).

Success in Transformation comes from ensuring best practice is followed across all the 7 levels of the General Management framework. It stems, in the first place, from ensuring ambitious Goals (at Strategy level), and it follows through by creating a Transformation Office to lead the effort (at Segmentation level), identifying the T-Areas and Bottlenecks (at Staff level), including Coaches (at Structure level), carefully modifying Incentives, Processes and Risk procedures (at Systems level), ensuring alignment with Vision, Mission and Values (at Shared Values level), and highlighting the right Behaviours (at Style level).

References

1. "The Strategy of Execution" by Liz Mellon and Simon Carter (2013; McGraw Hill).
2. "The Neuroscience of Trust" by Paul J. Zak (Jan.-Feb. 2017; Harvard Business Review).
3. "The What, Who and How of Delivering Results" by Alan Bird, Torsten Lichtenau and David Michels (2016; Bain & Co).
4. "Transformation with Big T" by Michael Bucy, Stephen Hall and Doug Yakola (2016; McKinsey & Co).
5. "7 S Framework" (McKinsey; 1979).
6. "General Management Framework" (Chip Heath and Greg Fisher; 2000; Duke University).

Part III

About 'Portfolio Strategy'

The good seaman weathers the storm he cannot avoid, and avoids the storm he cannot weather (anonymous).

You, dear successful Chief Executive of a Division, after years internalizing the lessons from Parts I and II you are now in charge of a set of Business Units, and even you got a ticket for a future shot at the top job, the Group CEO, so well done!

Now, running a Division looks like an entire new job; you are not competing in a marketplace anymore, you participate in many marketplaces, serving many different client segments with a wide arrange of product offerings. Moreover, you are not doing so directly as you deal now with several layers of middle management between you and the frontline troops that are in contact with the client base.

In addition, quite possibly you have grown within some of the BUs in your division, so you know them well. However, you are also responsible for many others, some familiar and some perhaps quite alien to you. Equally, each of these BUs likely transits through different phases of its business cycle, some perhaps in start-up or early-stage mode, others in high-growth, probably others are in a more mature or 'milking' stage, and perhaps even some need restructuring or wind-down.

Thus, what you are managing at this point is a rainbow portfolio, and this surely demands quite a different skillset compared with when you were running your BU. Therefore, the management challenge at this stage steps up considerably. The concept of Strategy itself changes dramatically. It is not anymore about the components of the Business Models across the BUs in the portfolio, given that the aggregation of these across BUs does not end up making much sense (i.e. complex amalgamation of very different client segments, products and geographies). It is about Portfolio Strategy, and so about wisely reallocating scarce resources among the different colours of the rainbow in your portfolio, following criteria which hopefully align the division towards the delivery of its financial and non-financial targets.

Like in the previous Parts, let us turn to the narrative of our maritime story...

* * *

Summer of 1805. You are at Chatham undertaking an inspection of the state of your naval squadron. As a newly promoted Admiral of the Royal Navy (congratulations!), you are making sure the repairs on the damaged men of war are progressing to plan, and that the rest of the fleet is being properly refitted. Press gangs have been sent out to nearby coastal towns and villages across Kent and Sussex to cover the gaps among crews after the last battering with French and Spanish navies.

The ship Captains and Commanders are gathered around you, reporting on major issues and covertly lowballing their estimates so to have room to deliver as per targeted schedule. As usual, you hate these dynamics of haggling top-down and bottom-up, but it is the name of the game. Each Captain wants the best gunners, most experienced sailors, newest cannons, you name it... and so the lobbying in public and private becomes a continuous noise in your ears. That's life, an Admiral's life.

As an escape from it all, you are glad to get in your carriage heading to the Admiralty Building in Whitehall, as a meeting has been called at the highest level to discuss the strategy of the fleets towards the next phase, hopefully the last, of the Napoleonic wars.

As you enter the long corridors of the building you begin to salute familiar faces, old comrades from past ships that now, like you, became Commodores, Rear and Vice Admirals commanding their own squadrons. Competitors in some sense towards the most senior role in the navy, First Naval Lord of the Admiralty (*Group CEO*); a competitive race, unlike the very top role, First Lord of the Admiralty (*Group Chairman*), which is a government (*Shareholders*) appointment. In this league, everyone is courteous but at the same time everyone attends ruthlessly to his own game, in a quite siloed way, as they focus on very different geographies or functional roles for this war and, of course, they all expect promotion.

The Boardroom of the Admiralty falls silent as the top brass, followed by their aides, enter. The first order of the day is to discuss the targets for the new campaign season and determine the right composition of units for each squadron so that are battle-ready for their respective goals. In some way, it is effectively a reallocation and optimization of the existing naval power across the fleet (*Portfolio Value Gap framework*).

For each squadron, several aimed target zones are discussed, in your case, the Gibraltar strait, and so the critical strategic connexion between the Atlantic Ocean and the Mediterranean Sea. Your objective is to maintain naval superiority in the area, blockading enemy ports and engaging openly enemy ships whenever they attempt to enter or exit these ports.

However, you realize that the current state of your squadron (*Share Price*) does not tally with where it should be to tackle the task at hand (*Sum-of-the-Parts Valuation*), so the situation calls for some changes (the *Value Gap*): first, you must refit some of the ships both in terms of rigging and guns before they are fit-for-purpose for battle (*Business Performance Improvement*); second, a good bunch of units might be perfectly ready for immediate enemy engagement and so the discussion there will be more on timing approach to battle (*Business Growth, Organic or Inorganic*); and third, surely you should get rid of several transport units you had in the last campaign (*Business Restructurings & Disposals*). Finally, after all the rejuggling, there could be yet some resource gap to fill at fleet level, so still a final lever to use by the First Lord to secure the required resources: playing his political cards with the politicians at Whitehall or even Parliament (*Financial Structuring*). Good luck with that boss!

Back with your squadron, now you need to provide instructions for executing the agreed changes across the ships, and to share the order for the campaign. Thus, you gather your ship Captains and Commanders and work out with them how this will be done over time (*Portfolio Horizons framework*) in alignment with the orders received regarding the Gibraltar strait area you have been entrusted with.

Usually, you divide the time in three sections of short, middle and long term (*Three Horizons*), over months or years depending on the theatre of operations. In this case, you are reckoning a 3-year campaign in the Strait, so you allocate the first 6 months to establish the blockade (*Horizon I*), the next 12 months to engage traffic in the area (*Horizon II*) and the final 18 months to entice the enemy in a trap for a full-blown engagement (*Horizon III*).

For each time horizon, each ship will focus on specific changes to accomplish, aligned to one or more of the three lines of action above. For instance, you call for those ships requiring immediate reallocation to other squadrons or to the arsenal (*Business Restructurings & Disposals*) to be finished within Horizon I. As well, regarding ships that demand specific refitting (*Business Performance Improvement*), you ask some of them to get started in Horizon I, while for the rest to help during a few months in blockading ports for in Horizon II to return to Chatham for the refitting towards the needs of Horizon III. Finally, with the ships that are ready for engagement (*Business Growth, Organic or Inorganic*), you will strategize the best approach in time, perhaps dispatching some directly to the blockade in Horizon I while others should make a wider detour to neutral ports in the area to gather information about shipping flow, so to make time and get ready towards Horizon II to proactively engage traffic once the blockade is successful.

As an Admiral, the past few weeks have been as frantic as you remember. Now you are ready, you have your battle mission, you have the green light for the changes in your squadron (*Portfolio Value Gap framework*) and your Captains and Commanders know their orders orchestrated along a timed masterplan (*Portfolio Horizons framework*). Ready to sail!

* * *

This, my dear Divisional Chief Executive, is **Strategy in Action** for a ***Portfolio Strategy***.

7 Portfolio Value Gap

Used at Division or Group level and inspired by the capital market diagnosis exercises popularized by McKinsey in the early 2000s, the Portfolio Value Gap framework evolved across some publicly listed corporations as a methodology to close the valuation gap from comparing the current share price with internal Sum-Of-The-Parts (SOTP) valuation, using either discounted cash flows or multiples benchmarking.

Quite often these valuations pointed that corporations were quite undervalued, among other factors due to the repricing post-2002 dot-com equity markets crisis. So, listed companies were looking for a set of portfolio actions that would convey to investors what they were missing to account for, hoping the valuation gap would consequently close or even disappear.

For the purposes of this book, it is less relevant the financial valuation method considerations and how different alternative methodologies would lead to wider/narrower valuation gaps; instead, we will be more interested in discussing, in an applied manner, the alternative management actions the framework offers to address the Portfolio Value Gap and how each subsequently aligns with the Portfolio Horizons framework (Chap. 8) (Fig. 7.1).

If we review the illustration above, after comparing stock prices vs SOTP valuation, a sequence of 4 steps is suggested to address this gap:

1. *Business Performance Improvements*: Identify opportunities in this regard across the portfolio of BUs.
2. *Business Growth*: Determine what Organic vs Inorganic growth opportunity can be generated among the BUs.
3. *Business Restructuring & Disposals*: Identify value creation opportunities derived from exits from the existing portfolio.
4. *Financial Structuring*: To review any possibility of changes in the balance-sheet structure. This would be undertaken by Group Finance or Treasury function once the impact from the previous steps has been reckoned and depending on the

A. Gavieiro Besteiro, *Strategy in Action*, Management for Professionals,
https://doi.org/10.1007/978-3-030-94759-0_7

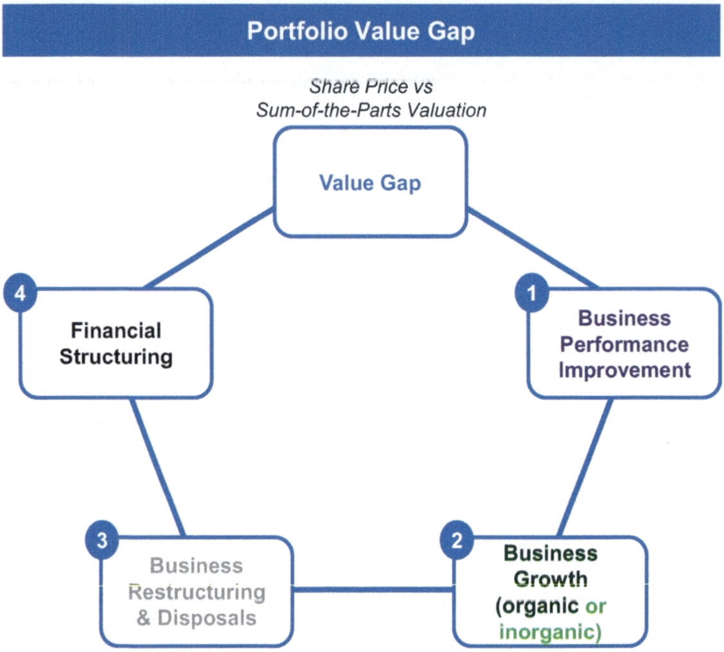

Fig. 7.1 Portfolio Strategy—Portfolio Value Gap framework. Sources: Sanitized example

prevalent equity and debt capital markets conditions (this step is out of the scope for the purpose of this chapter[1]).

As referred to at the start of Part III, the important gist that clearly differentiates the approach to Strategy at this level (i.e. Group/Division vs Business Unit), is that this is a game of resource reallocation. Of course, the drivers of that allocation will stem, ultimately from the value potential identified in each BU and its strategy in the marketplace; however, at Portfolio level this is now an input for decision-making, and the job instead is to calibrate the optimal resource reallocation considering the 3 types of value creation (as per above), the resource requirements from each BU and the expected financial impact estimated from these respective resource investments towards Division and Group Goals. The alignment of timing among these flows, of course, does matter, and it will be considered in more depth in the next chapter.

Let us bring the framework alive with an example related to a wholesale banking division of a European bank after the 2008 Credit Crisis. As a result of the crisis, this

[1]Changes in the capital structure mix (i.e. Tier1 vs Tier2 equity, subordinated/senior debt and related hedging derivatives, plus dividend/share buyback policies) can provide shareholder value depending on their impact in tax profile for the organization; having said that, they are usually outside of the scope of the Division/BU's managerial action. Also, there is controversy about the value recognition some of these practices (ref. Sect. 9.8 in Chap. 9).

bank acquired another one of similar characteristics but with a substantially impaired corporate banking portfolio. Thus, the resulting combination brought together a portfolio of BUs that touched all the potential drivers of value creation at once: Business Improvement, Business Growth and Restructuring/Disposal.

Overall, the combined division[2] on its first year reported €4.3 bn loss before tax, driven by the painful recognition of the bulk of impairments and defaults. By the end of year 3 post-acquisition, the division was able to report €0.7 bn PBT. A very successful turnaround guided by sound strategic management of its portfolio of BUs. But *how did each of the drivers of value creation contribute to the turnaround?*

On the one hand, there was the mid-markets banking BU, which involved a large network of offices and resources serving medium-size businesses in their local markets, with the inevitable geographical overlaps from the acquisition. This unit would need to go through a difficult process of integration and business improvement, shedding overlaps and redundancies, preserving and extending best-practice. At the same time, given the limitations of lending capability in a deleveraging environment, there was the need to select which customers warranted retention, considering their individual value added and fit to the wider customer strategy in the bank. Altogether, this Business Improvement effort contributed around 26% of the value increase.

On the other hand, there were some other BUs, the multinational corporate banking and financial institutions businesses, where the integration impact was smaller and the exposure to troubled loans limited. Therefore, they were in a better condition to become the main engines of growth, mostly organically driven, for the division while navigating this turbulent period. They focused on enhancing customer relationships and building up additional product and service offering, more from the capital markets side, so to increase the return on the established back-book of lending deployed. Overall, this Business Growth effort provided 54% of the value uplift.

Finally, there was a couple of BUs whose post-merger lending books would show an important amount of impaired or defaulted positions (up to about 50% of the outstanding). They were quite concentrated in real estate as well as in the entrepreneurs' sector. These units required a deep Disposal & Restructuring effort. In total this turnaround provided 20% of the value uplift for the division.

The following subsections analyze in detail the 3 steps for this case study.

7.1 Business Performance Improvement

Within the Portfolio Value Gap framework, this is the first lever that management has at their disposal to generate immediate value without looking for deployment of any additional resources (generally). In fact, best-practice organizations make this

[2]Numbers are disguised but follow the proportionality of the real case.

discipline part of their BAU becoming a 'continuous improvement' approach (one of the key traits of excellent companies, as we will see in Chap. 10).

Like in gardening, all businesses have room for pruning, watering, soil reinforcement, cleaning and tidying up. As activity develops, processes become old often patched up from several partial fixings, reporting keeps accumulating sometimes with no clear purpose, client portfolios become skewed with very heterogeneous workloads and misalignments with coverage quality, manual interventions become the rule rather than the exception etc. you name it, ad infinitum. Now, *where to start?*

For this purpose, the Business Model framework (ref. Chap. 1) will become invaluable. It will serve as a diagnostic tool to understand all the elements from Client Segmentation to Value Proposition, from definition (i.e. product/services, pricing, promotion and positioning) to delivery (i.e. front-line coverage, back-office, processes, policies, etc...). Now, the diagnosis requires feedback from the users, both clients and employees, in order to identify not only every element that has potential for improvement, but also which improvements will be more impactful. Because prioritization of business improvement interventions is essential.

Here, reality confirms that the Pareto law applies: specific improvements around 20% of the elements identified drive 80% of the impact perceived by clients and employees. This does not mean that the remaining elements could be forgotten, but not at the expense of relegating the fixing of the most impactful ones.

For instance, the mid-markets BU referred earlier undertook an integration effort of 2 networks that embedded several workstreams dedicated to business improvement. The unit mostly covered a large European country, inherited 2 overlapped sets of relationship managers in an overextended commercial banking branch network, many serving the same clients. Also, as you could expect, there were double processes across all the major activities such as business development, client onboarding, credit risk process, transaction booking and reporting. Thus, several workstreams in the integration programme looked at these specific processes, normally taking one of the 2 legacy ones as 'target', but identifying those elements from the discarded process that could have an impactful value-add and were feasible to be integrated at reasonable effort/cost. In the end, the majority of the incumbent bank's processes were kept as 'target', but the modifications that were included (from the other bank's legacy), representing less than 20% of the potential spectrum, had a very large positive impact for clients and employees (e.g. MS-Dynamics as CRM system for business development).

Let us not forget that for the BU, there is a timing trade-off, because time and resources dedicated to business improvement are usually time not dedicated to BAU activity, and in the short term the effort required to make fixings might lead to some additional underperformance. Thus, you do not want to drive normal activity to a halt because of the need to fix things.

At the European subsidiary of an international bank that was under heavy regulatory scrutiny, the regulatory remediation intensity over the broker–dealer unit imposed by the respective local authorities made performance to really plummet (c.−20% year-on-year). The legal entities and BUs affected had to put 'all hands on deck' to accelerate remediation and get out of the woods. This example was special in the sense that the business improvement was 'obliged' by the regulator, however, it illustrates how much time business improvement activity could suck out of your team and how it can negatively affect BAU performance.

7.2 Business Growth (Organic/Inorganic)

Once all BUs in the portfolio have been analyzed from a business performance improvement perspective, then further investment of resources could be considered in order to generate growth. In fact, sometimes it happens that cost savings identified from business improvement were intended, in the first place, to precisely finance some or all of the investments allocated to business growth. Having said that, timing is usually an issue as you need the investment quicker than the cost savings can be materialized; hence, the subsequent round of portfolio strategy between Divisions and Group centre, who ultimately will support (or not) the financing decision to bridge these investment timing gaps.

Now, it is important here to remember that there is a crucial consideration when thinking about investing for growth, . . . that growth must be profitable. Thus, a usual test for Return on Equity of each of the BUs is advisable in comparison to the Cost of Equity of the bank to ensure each meets or exceeds this threshold, otherwise, any further investment for growth in the unit would destroy shareholder value.[3] Now, this assumes that Return on Equity at BU level is available, which often is a quite generous assumption as the managerial information in many banks is quite poor at these levels of granularity. Usually, there is not a good procedure for equity allocation to the units and, what is worse, a very arbitrary indirect cost allocation, usually disputed by BU leaders. These inaccuracies might easily throw RoE underwater and so potentially jeopardize the BU's chances to secure resources for growth. Hence, you need to be prepared for quite difficult conversations with these leaders on this controversial topic.

At this point, for BUs with RoE > CoE, it is a question of identifying the business cases for growth, either organic or inorganic, following the process described in Chaps. 4 and 5.

Referring to the case study of the European wholesale banking division above, the financial institutions' BU resulting from the acquisition of the bank did not require much integration work, so it was ready to focus on growth. One of the most relevant opportunities for them was in developing one business case for product penetration, increasing substantially the cross-selling of products beyond their core ones (i.e. lending, deposits and payments), particularly in the space of investment banking (i.e. M&A, debt capital markets, equity capital markets and risk management).

[3]For a discussion about why growth only adds shareholder value when RoE > CoE refer to Chapter 2 of 'Value—The Four Cornerstones of Corporate Finance' by Tim Koller, Richard Dobbs and Bill Huyett (2011; McKinsey & Co—Wiley); more on this in Chap. 9.

Similarly, the multinational corporates BU enjoyed a healthy post-integration asset portfolio, perhaps with an excess of RWAs concentrated in some sectors, and with overall levels of product cross-selling that could be improved. This presented the BU with a business case for portfolio optimization: to seize the double opportunity for RWAs reallocation among sectors, driven precisely from the expected relative returns once considered the potential cross-selling that could be gained from the additional RWA investment.

In this context, the 2 business cases together would make these BUs the immediate engines of growth for the division. The question was how to develop a systematic organic growth strategy that would focus on the client segments of these two BUs but that, eventually, could be extended to the remaining units in the division as soon as they come out of their respective integration and restructuring challenges. Hence, the development of the 'Trusted Relationship' segmentation (ref. to Sect. 1.2 in Chap. 1) as a holistic customer relationship management (CRM) best-practice to ensure both customer-centricity and disciplined approach to deepening client relationships via further cross-selling fruit of the additional RWAs investment.

The deployment of 'Trusted Relationship' segmentation on financial institutions and multinational corporates was a great success, with revenues year-on-year growing at high single digits driven by higher margins from the additional lending to the right sectors in terms of overall returns, and also benefiting from post-2008 repriced margins. In addition, the cross-selling increase from the coordinated approach between relationship managers and product specialists in their interaction with each client, brought relationship RoEs above thresholds (at that time defined above 10% CoE). Therefore, a single methodological solution became the enabler of the business growth cases for the 2 BUs initially, and subsequently the 3 remaining ones.

7.3 Business Restructuring and Disposals

This pruning part of the Portfolio Value Gap discipline requires management to ask a very simple, but often overlooked, question referring to a given BU: *is there a better owner for this asset?*

This should ideally be a question to ask out of a portfolio every year, not just when tough years arrive, and we feel obliged to offload some BUs to generate sorely needed cash flow. In fact, by doing so chances are you will get a much better price and even gain out of an undesired BU, vis-à-vis doing so in the bottom or aftermath of a crisis.

In this regard, the first clue to look at in each BU, as indicated in previous sections, is to check if RoE < CoE and understand why it has turned this way. For instance, the re-regulatory environment post-2008 made the social housing BU of a bank, leader by market share, from being a strong RoE business on the basis of very long-term lending facilities with government guarantee to a below-CoE business due to the increase of regulatory capital consumption and the increase of the cost of funding of the bank (driven by post-2008 tough market conditions). In this case, the team was able to fundamentally modify the business model, so to stop the financing via loans starting instead to issue long-term bonds to institutional investors, and so switching revenues from net interest margin to debt capital markets fees and reducing dramatically the capital and funding required by the BU. In the absence of this turnaround, only a disposal or a closure would have been the leftover options.

Nevertheless, even BUs with RoE > CoE might be considered during the annual portfolio review for an exit due to different reasons: lack of fit of this BU to a new strategy for the institution, marketplace disruptions that could substantially threaten the competitive positioning of this BU in the medium or long-term horizon, small market share without prospects for growth, or consolidation movements in the marketplace that drive other competitors to overpay for bolt-on acquisitions. Any of these scenarios could perfectly result in situations where a third party is a better owner of this asset rather than the current owner. Therefore, putting on the 'investor hat' (more about this on Chap. 9), management has to consider a potential disposal of the BU.

Turning now to the troubled part of the business portfolio of the case study above. For corporate real estate BU, at the peak of the acquisition the aggregated balance-sheets held close to 25% of the outstanding real estate lending in that country, which post-2008 was highly defaulted or in arrears. Thus, the challenge at hand was restructuring.

Now, this was a bank that just before the acquisition took pride on disciplined lending underwriting, so it was not used to anything close these levels of impairments; as such, the function with responsibility for the client negotiation for impaired assets, was too small in scale and breadth of experience to tackle the challenge. Therefore, a new business restructuring unit with more than 400 employees was designed and built up to take care systematically of the impaired books. The implementation complexity was necessarily large, beyond the logistics of organizing and recruiting such a large amount of talent in limited time. The plane was in flight so there was the need in parallel to undertake detailed due diligence of every loan to ensure full command of documentation and client situation details to define the right potential courses of action in each case (i.e. extension/renegotiation of terms, client's equity infusion, collateral execution, loan selling, or just non-renewal of loan facilities).

In the entrepreneurs portfolio, not being as heavily impaired as the previous one, the troubled loans were concentrated in a few client counterparts, and they were complex positions (i.e. collateralized across several assets of the entrepreneur patrimony, with several loans in each case and many banks sometimes involved). Therefore, these were not transferred to the new restructuring unit, and instead the current business put 'all hands on deck' to deal with each of these situations individually and within tight timeframes (i.e. defaulted positions only tend to erode recovery value as time passes, which in complex restructurings it can take not months but even years). The discipline of the team and their intimate knowledge of their clients proved this decision right, so in 18 months they were able to renegotiate all the situations and started to turnaround the portfolio towards profitability.

Finally, as another example for the disposals (i.e. loan selling) in the context of this case study, we need to look back at the real estate portfolio handled by the restructuring unit. Loan selling was one of the strategies at hand as the unit was reviewing each of the positions, but the theoretical simple consideration of this decision becomes really painful and complex when facing the reality of starting negotiations with potential buyer counterparts. In a down market, like post-2008, the bank with defaulted or impaired positions was 'caught' on a paper loss, so it is clear will have to swallow a 'hit', the question is how much appetite the top management would have to take these 'hits'. In addition, the potential buyers were the reduced community of hedge and debt funds specialized in troubled assets (i.e. sometimes referred to as vulture funds), for which a buying price with enough headroom for the unforeseen (i.e. 'haircuts') becomes paramount. Thus, the loan disposal process can easily become a multi-year, complicated programme, which will take long to produce its fruits, therefore top management will need to be very aware of this timing reality as well as of the heavy 'haircuts' to be expected.

Surely enough, top management in this particular bank at that time was unable to accept any offers with haircuts beyond the single-digit range. Thus, none were executed until a new management replaced the old one 3 years into the crisis, and subsequently started the loan selling between 2012 and 2015, apparently accepting higher market haircuts of 40–50%.

Overall, during a period of 5 years after the Credit Crisis, to turnaround the situation and make the acquisition work, this bank had to act simultaneously and vigorously on all of the 3 management levers of the Portfolio Value Gap framework: Performance Improvement, Business Growth, and Restructuring & Disposals.

* * *

Eventually, it succeeded, and the operational performance moved from −€4.3 bn of PBT to +€0.7 bn within the first 3 years, substantially contributing to this bank' share price recovery by approximately 100% within 5 years from their bottom marks (though, as of the time of writing it still has not fully recovered pre-2008 levels, but not unexpectedly since the loss realization from the defaulted portfolio and the subsequent re-regulatory effort had made a large drift in bank valuations for the whole banking industry).

Portfolio Horizons

8

The Portfolio Horizons framework is an evolution that tries to combine the outputs from the Portfolio Value Gap framework with McKinsey's 3-Horizons framework. It visualizes over time how each of the 3 types of outputs drive the Strategic Plan of each BU in the Division's portfolio (or each Division in the Group's portfolio) and whether the curves from their Financial Plans are coherently aligned, as well as it suggests a best-practice methodology for resource reallocation across the portfolio.

It can be applied at any level of portfolio aggregation, being that Division or Group (or for that matter other aggregation levels like Region or Continent). For simplicity, across this chapter I will refer again to the Division case study used in the previous chapter.

8.1 3-Horizons Framework

The 3-Horizons framework was originally created by 3 McKinsey consultants back in 1999 [1, 2]. The idea was developed from the observation of the typical S-curve life cycle of products and businesses (i.e. slow start-up adoption, then exponential growth to arrive at mature growth towards a plateau), and the realization that large organizations, juggling a substantial portfolio of these products and business concurrently, would actually be having, at a given moment of time, businesses in each of the 3 phases of the S-curve.

Thus, plotting in time the mature-to-plateau phases for each business they could organize the entire portfolio along 3 time horizons (e.g. 1–2 years, 3–5 years and >5 years). This would allow to understand whether the company had a balanced portfolio that would ensure continuity of revenue growth as time passes (i.e. as some businesses enter their plateau, others take over with exponential growth phase); or alternatively, whether they would be facing some glaring gaps in horizon 2 or 3 due to a lack of current investment in start-up projects and/or potentially high growth businesses that could sustain and drive profits in the medium and long term (Fig. 8.1).

A. Gavieiro Besteiro, *Strategy in Action*, Management for Professionals,
https://doi.org/10.1007/978-3-030-94759-0_8

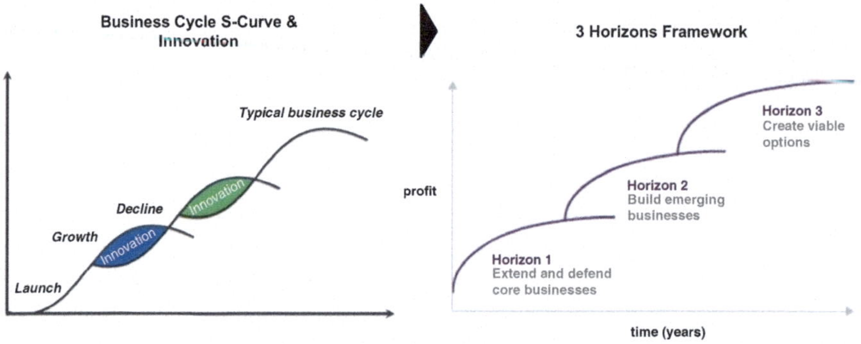

Fig. 8.1 3-Horizons framework. Sources: Exhibit from 'Enduring Ideas: The three horizons of growth', December 2009, McKinsey Quarterly, www.mckinsey.com. Copyright (c) 2021 McKinsey & Company. All rights reserved. Reprinted by permission

To understand well the usage of this framework it is key to recognize that some businesses or products would yield their growth only in horizon 2 or 3, but this does not mean that the current focus of execution must concentrate primarily on businesses of horizon 1. Rather the opposite conclusion applies, management attention needs to focus here and now on investing also in businesses of horizons 2 and 3. Quite often this requires paying significant attention to these nascent businesses, especially in rapidly changing marketplace environments like what currently happens to many industries heavily impacted by digital transformation.

8.2 Portfolio Horizons Framework

In my practice, I pushed a bit further the development of the 3-Horizons framework by combining it with the 3 main outputs from the Portfolio Value Gap framework: Business Performance Improvement, Business Growth (Organic / Inorganic) and Business Restructuring & Disposals. Becoming the Portfolio Horizons framework as illustrated below.

Simply, by visualizing each of these three elements as vectors in time and defining which of them will be the main activity driver for each BU within the 3 Portfolio Horizons, then we gain a further insight about not only which phase of the S-curve each BU experiences over time, but also what are the main activity drivers of the BU at each horizon.

The content of the Portfolio Horizons framework below illustrates an example of a real case for a Division with 5 Business Units. It identifies the 3 drivers of growth as codified in the legend, and applies them to each BU consistently but differentiating the terminology in order to distinguish sub-drivers within each main driver:

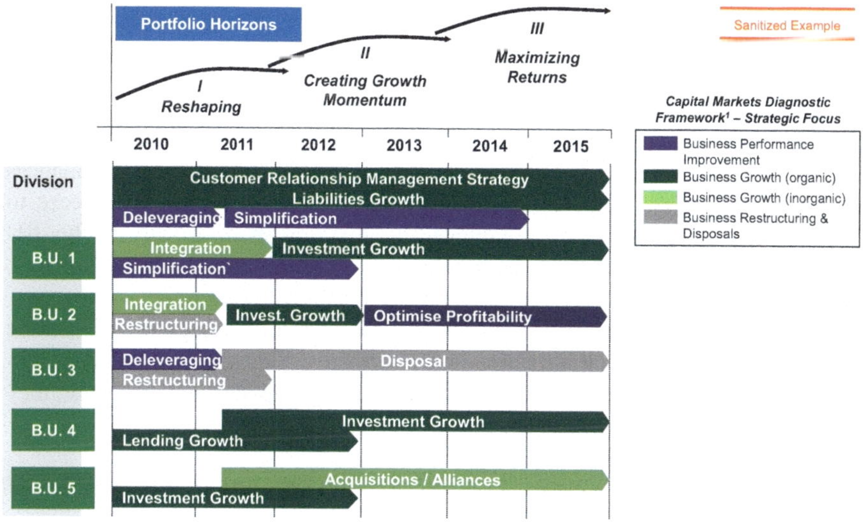

Fig. 8.2 **Portfolio Strategy—Portfolio Horizons framework** (example) (1/2). Sources: Own sanitized example

- *Business Performance Improvement* (magenta): Deleveraging; Simplification
- *Business Growth* (Inorganic—light green / Organic—dark green): Integration; Acquisitions/Alliances; Lending Growth; Investment Growth
- *Business Restructuring & Disposals* (grey)

In addition, in this example, some 'summary' drivers were assigned at the Division level (at the top) as 'overarching' drivers (Fig. 8.2).

First thing to observe is that, in some instances, particularly but not exclusively within the horizon 1, there are 2 drivers simultaneously at work for a given business. This is logical as some businesses might be covering a wide number of client segments and a large portfolio of products, so it could perfectly coexist a situation of Business Growth and Performance Improvement across subsets of them.

Second observation is to notice how horizon 1 presents a very diverse array of current drivers across the businesses, as per comparison to horizons 2 and 3. Thus, for instance, 'B.U. 1' focuses on Improvement and Growth, 'B.U. 3' focuses on Improvement and Restructuring, while 'B.U. 5' just focuses on Growth. This institution had just come out of the Credit Crisis of 2008 and had made a transformational acquisition, so definitely it had quite a lot on the plate.

Third consideration, behind the Growth drivers in horizons 2 and 3 there would be a series of projects of investment, which would be funded and executed during horizon 1 and subsequently as required. Thus, emphasizing the prior point that these horizons cannot be neglected in the current moment, otherwise, the institution would be myopically risking the future for the present.

As with the application of any portfolio framework, it is meant to be alive and changing as time passes, since at portfolio level the chef has the fingers in many pies, so chances are that from one year to the next the drivers need to be adjusted as the marketplace changes or some opportunistic moves present themselves.

Thus, for instance, in the example above, 'B.U. 1' delivered their business case for integration in just 18 months instead of the 24 months originally envisaged, so they accelerated the Investment Growth phase vs initial plan. More drastically though for 'B.U. 5', which was visualizing starting an Acquisitions / Alliances phase 18 months down the line, a top management change brought a freeze to inorganic moves, which totally fulminated the main driver of growth for this BU especially towards horizon 3; so, there was the need to revisit the plan and come up with an alternative organic growth response to sustain its future.

Now, at this point in the chapter, the reader must be wondering: well, these horizon visualizations look very fine and informative but, *what type of decision-making could they possibly help me with?* Leveraging back the chef metaphor, they can help to allocate the ingredients among the pies.

8.3 Resource Reallocation

Ultimately, the end game of portfolio-level decision-making is about allocating scarce resources among the BUs. That is it.

As mentioned in earlier chapters, a Division (or a Group for that matter) is not directly playing in the marketplace, it is just only indirectly via the BUs and throughout a whole variety of marketplaces. Thus, its strategic role is not to define strategy at the marketplace level, which is for each BU to do; its strategic role is to define the most optimal allocation of resources across their BUs to generate the performance required to reach the Goals established in the first place.

What resources? Capital and people. Capital in terms of operating expenditure (Opex) and capital expenditure (Capex), but also in the case of the banking industry equity capital to sustain lending growth (banking industry regulation on capital adequacy, i.e. Basel III, defines the rules for calculating the amount and type of equity a bank needs to retain for a given amount and credit quality of loans in its balance-sheet).

In terms of people, which yes would be an element of cost within the Opex, the process involves a high-level assessment of intangible value in terms of qualification and experience required, as well as managerial and leadership skill set for those with line management roles. Talent resource is usually in scarce supply and not always available, either internally (talent reallocation) or externally (hiring), within the timeframes required. So, these are critical decisions that require planning. For instance, a large retail bank in its expansion efforts towards Eastern markets realized only too late how narrow was its internal pipeline of managerial talent for the type of geographies they were embarking to expand into. This was one of the two major reasons, being the other the dilutive effect on share price, why some critical acquisitions well underway during that expansion were finally halted.

Resource reallocation is at the core of the MTP exercise (ref. Chap. 3), both from Strategy and from Finance perspective. Ultimately, as we have seen in earlier chapters, BUs present their strategic plans with baseline financials over the planned horizon and business cases of investment or divestment that alter the shape (hopefully upwards) of that baseline. What usually happens, and I have never found a case on the contrary, is that the sum of the investment required for the business cases is quite superior to the available resources for investment, hence the need to prioritize in order to reallocate. *But, how?*

There are 2 schools of thought about how to reallocate resources. The most revolutionary one is known as Zero-Based Budgeting (ZBB). Some prominent management consulting firms have been recently advocating it to tackle the insufficiency of investment required to address bold digital transformation. This method starts from 'zero base' every year, so regardless of how large or small your budget was last year, each BU has to justify the expenditure required for next year bottom-up. Theoretically, it sounds like the right recipe for when you need to drastically change tack in your business mix; having said that, it must be quite a challenge to get it done in a large organization... I have not ever experienced ZBB yet in banking (and I have been doing MTPs since 2001 nearly every year for 5 different banks!).

The alternative school is the traditional one: take last year performance as a base and build a baseline of growth leveraging the existing resources, then overlap business cases on top as previously described (so, if you are a large BU, surely you will remain large; if you are smaller, you might have your fighting chance to become bigger gradually over time). Up to that point all well, since all banks show a remarkably similar practice, but then it comes to the 'negotiation' process; here is where we experience the differences among organizations. On the one hand, I have seen banks that barely undertake any formal yearly resource reallocation, they extrapolate or extend last year's budget with minimal tweaks and let us see how the year goes, only to arrive at the 3rd or 4th quarter to start the 'freezings' (i.e. travelling freeze, recruiting freeze and Xmas party freeze; I reckon most of you have been there before). On the other hand, I have seen banks where a heavy competition across divisions happened at Group level to allocate resources. One of them set its divisions to compete for funding among 18 initiatives; having contracted an external management consulting firm to bring rigour and equanimity to the process, the competition necessarily resulted in some winners (some with 100% allocation of their ask) and a few losers (some of the initiatives shelved sine die).

In the cases where serious resource allocation really happens, what normally becomes a challenge, and a pattern, is how do you unearth the resources required for the reallocation. Here the usual practice is the launch of drastic cost challenges across the Group, usually resulting in redundancies and anything but non-discretionary projects paralyzation, which helps to liberate the cash flow required to fund the new investments. An alternative or complementary approach is to ask BUs to produce Divestment Cases (so, the opposite to Investment Cases, which sounds reasonable but is much less frequently done), by which the BU critically analyses its current business model and unilaterally suggests chopping 'dead wood', liberating resources for reinvestment. One of the reasons why this approach is not so popular is the lack of incentivization to do so. This could be sorted by adding a dedicated target to BU Heads' balanced scorecards and providing some guaranteed automatic reinvestment percentage on the BU out of the Divestment Cases effectively approved.

Whatever the case, the Portfolio Horizons allows the divisional management team not only to visualize the strategic drivers of each BU over time, but also to map over the 3 horizons the Financial Baseline + Investment / Divestment Cases (ref. Sect. 3.2 in Chap. 3) to check for consistency with the drivers for each horizon. For instance, if horizons 2 and 3 show the main driver is business growth, the respective financial baseline would speak to that growth. Also, when the investment limit is reached, Portfolio Horizons can be used to compare the effect of different combinations of investment across the BUs in the overall portfolio over time. Basically, the same framework can be used to visualize strategy and financial impact (Fig. 8.3).

Finally, regardless of the school chosen, the allocation has to follow some fact-based criteria that guide decision-making, otherwise becomes a non-substantiated discussion, based only on the ability of the negotiators to get away with their arguments, which could very easily depart from facts and objective comparison.

To develop the criteria, usually you can set up some qualitative filters which allow to make some 'no brainer' decisions that help to reduce the pool of initiatives among which to focus the allocation. For instance, a quite often used qualitative filter is to allocate 100% of the 'non-discretionary' initiatives, which usually are led by regulatory requirements and so must be implemented if we are to avoid regulators' scrutiny and/or sanction. This could produce a big initial dent in the resource pool left over for the rest, but it is usually non-negotiable. There could be other qualitative filter criteria of this type, for instance, around topics that have been adopted like a quasi-dictate by the Board of Directors either as long-term goal (e.g. net-zero carbon emissions by year 5) or as recurrent year-on-year (e.g. ESG budget to ensure the continued bank's contribution impact into environmental, social and governance priorities).

A second point to consider is that not all initiatives need to be prioritized. Not all initiatives need additional resource allocation, since quite often many of them can be delivered within the respective Divisions (if allocating at Group level) or BUs (if allocating at Divisional level) either with BAU resources or with the fruits of Divestment Cases (which would be decided before the Investment cases, precisely to liberate resources for the investment pool). As a result, a subset of the initiatives, those of the Investment Cases (after prior 'netting' of BAU and Divestment Cases) would be the ones where the allocation happens.

Once the qualitative filters and the 'netting' of Investment Cases are applied, the remaining resources and pool of initiatives need to go through a prioritization for allocation. The question is, *which ones?*

To answer that, it is important to go back to the 'north star' of the Strategy Blueprint (ref. Chap. 2); first, reminding the 'Vision' statement (e.g. 'the best mid-market highly profitable bank') and testing how each Investment Case contributes to it; second, looking at Goals, here is where quantitative criteria become essential for comparing across Investment Cases. Still, out of those max. 10 Goals,

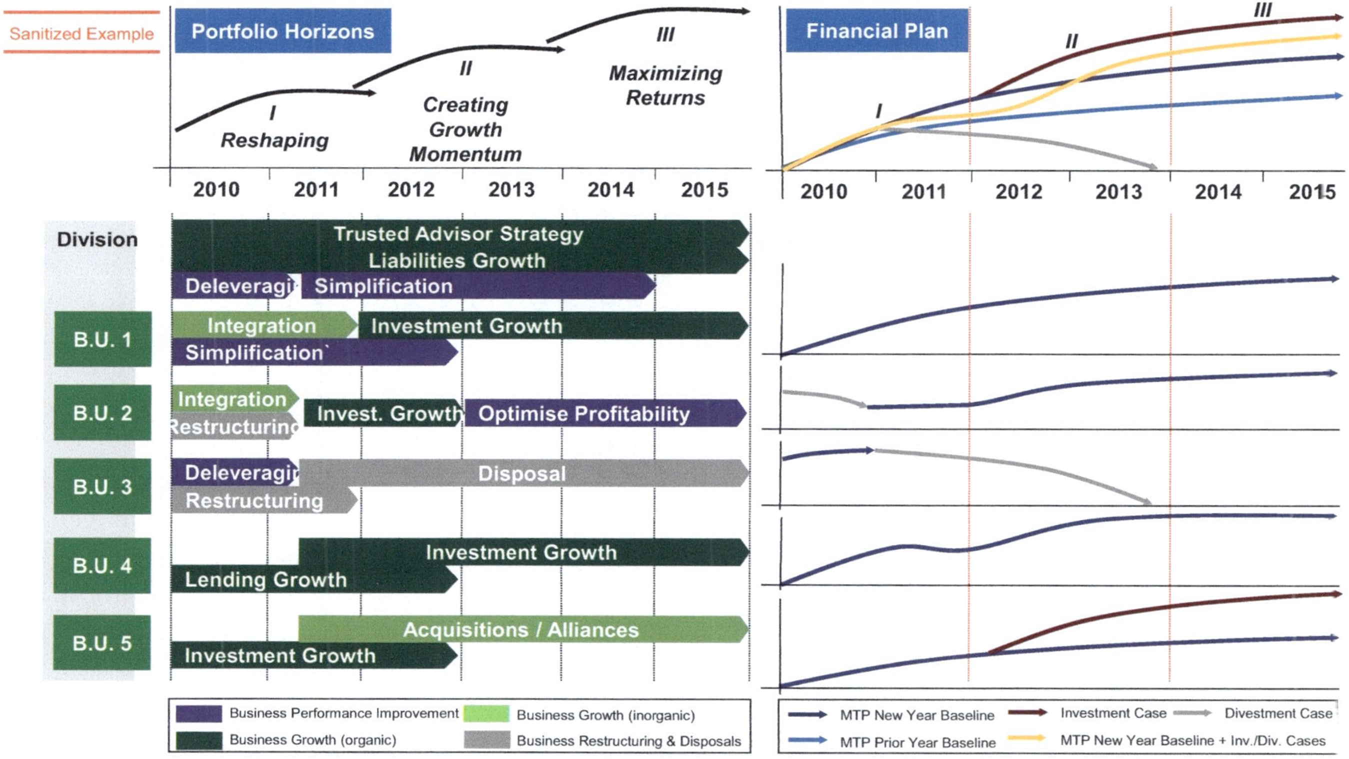

Fig. 8.3 **Portfolio Strategy—Portfolio Horizons framework** (example) (2/2). Sources: Sanitized example

perhaps 5–6 are quantitative in nature (e.g. Revenue growth, Jaws,[1] Cost-to-Income, NPL,[2] PAT, PBT and Lending growth), and possibly only a few would have a potentially universal application to a horizontal pool of initiatives (e.g. not all banking businesses are lending oriented, so NPLs and Lending growth would not apply to them. . .). Besides, human mind can optimize with 2 variables, perhaps 3 at most, beyond that it is near impossible to compare initiatives. The alternative would be to compose Indexes of several metrics, however, then there is the difficult point of attributing weights to these, which again can become very subjective and requires negotiation among the decision makers.

Thus, my recommendation is to select just 2 key quantitative Goals, universally applicable which the Board normally would use to judge the CEO and management team performance at financial level: Profitability (e.g. RoE, RoA, RoRWA,[3] EVA[4] or Economic Profit) and Efficiency (e.g. Cost-to-Income, Jaws or Cost(net of Risk)-to-Income).

Figure 8.4 visualizes the Investment Case portfolio impact by plotting each initiative (A to D) in a 2 × 2 Prioritization Matrix (of the selected 2 KPIs: RoE and Cost-to-Income). Each Investment Case is shown against the 3 horizons (i.e. 3 points by the end of horizon 1, 2 and 3, like a 'horizon journey': A1, A2 and A3).

The current ('Today') vs future ('Goal') levels for the 2 KPIs are displayed for this Division, along with the Cost of Capital of the bank (red line). Finally, isolines or isocurves can be calibrated to divide sections in the 2 × 2 matrix which would englobe initiatives of equivalent impact. Thus, the resource allocation would proceed following the order of isolines or isocurves until depleting the existing resource budget, being the remaining initiatives discarded for this MTP exercise (some of them, if still relevant and properly refreshed, could be revisited in the next MTP period).

Investment Case A starts in horizon 1 (A1) with above 60% Cost-to-Income and RoE borderline with Cost of Capital, but it is expected to improve gradually to exceed divisional target profitability and slightly short of divisional target efficiency of 40% in horizon 3 (A3), ending up within the 2nd isocurve (orange)

Investment Case B starts in a stronger position for both KPIs (B1) and delivers in horizon 3 on both divisional targets (B3). Therefore, under tough investment constraints, Case B would be prioritized vs Case A, as it sits comfortably within the 1st isocurve (orange).

As a contrast, Investment Cases C and D (for simplification displayed only in horizon 3) could not make the thresholds; Case C because its RoE does not make Cost of Capital, despite a brilliant Cost-to-Income; Case D generates better RoE than the division but at a large efficiency sacrifice.

* * *

[1] Income growth minus cost growth.

[2] Non-performing loans.

[3] Return on risk-weighted assets.

[4] Economic value added.

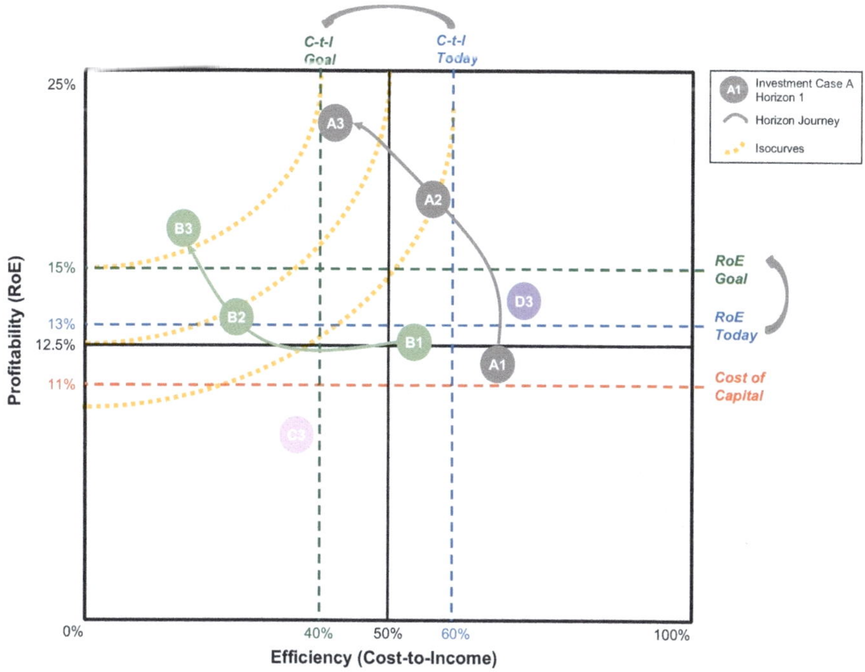

Fig. 8.4 Portfolio Strategy—Prioritization Matrix (example). Sources: Own analysis

In summary, Portfolio Horizons working in tandem with Portfolio Value Gap provide a superb visualization over the short, medium and long term of how the main drivers of management action act upon each BU in the divisional portfolio.

In addition, by aligning the respective Financial Plans, then we can distil the strategy story in terms of the dynamics of financial impact for the Division.

Finally, we can smartly use all this information to take decisions in terms of capital and talent, across the Investment Cases from the BUs following a disciplined, fact-based resource reallocation methodology.

These 2 chapters have been illustrated at Divisional level with its portfolio of BUs, but they would work similarly at Group level with its portfolio of Divisions.

References

1. "The Alchemy of Growth" by Mehrad Baghai, Stephen Coley and David White (1999; McKinsey & Co—Perseus Publishing).
2. "Enduring Ideas: The Three Horizons of Growth" by Steve Coley (Dec. 09; McKinsey Quarterly).

Part IV

About 'Company & Leadership Excellence'

England expects that every man will do his duty (Horatio Nelson[1])

Rivers and seas are rulers of the streams of hundreds of valleys because of the power of their low position. The best leaders become servants of their people (Lao Tzu [1])

You, dear successful Chief Executive of a Division, after years commanding several Divisions across the organization, demonstrating masterly best-practice in portfolio strategy management, and of course overdelivering performance, the Board of Directors has decided to offer you the top executive seat, the Chief Executive Officer of the Group... you humbly and excitedly accept the role, my best congratulations!

Now, you are running the whole show. Definitely, this is a job that, regardless of all the potential internal nurturing and grooming, nobody will ever be fully prepared for when arriving at it. You are the ultimate decision maker.

Having said that, it is important to acknowledge that being at the top of the pyramid becomes a perfect vantage point to realize that, if we invert the pyramid for a second, you are a servant to sustain others, to empower the entire organization, pretty much like Atlas holding the planet. Everybody in the organization will be looking at you for direction and guidance. Suddenly, what you thought was said as a statement, they will listen to it as an order. It will be an entirely new quantum of magnitude in power and responsibility versus any of your prior professional experiences. A place where you are alone, where what you do will affect everyone and where you will need of others across the chain of command, the leaders of the organization, to achieve the ultimately intended results.

Here it raises the first key factor for success, Leadership & Management. Provided mainly through others across several layers, this will be the conduit by which you will be able to have an effect; this team will become crucial in your job. If you manage to nurture a best-in-class executive team in the organization you will have, at least, half of the battle gained. If you fail to do so, your chances of success

[1] Last message to his fleet heading to the Battle of Trafalgar.

will be substantially diminished. Thus, what you will strive for is Leadership & Management Excellence.

The second key factor for success is realizing that the organization has a 'live of its own' that continues regardless the people that pass by it. It is like a mechanism that evolves over time, which complex dynamics can result in a machine pretty well fine-tuned, or conversely a very patchily functioning one. Realizing that as the CEO you are the ultimate 'clockmaker' of this mechanism, it rests on your shoulders the job of thinking how best to effect changes necessary to ensure the organization is fine-tuned, over the long term, into a balanced design towards excellence.

In addition, the organization's leaders are necessarily a diverse, eclectic group with many different personalities and interests. These combine in difficult to anticipate dynamics, which will have a strong bearing when they get together to take decisions. The myriad of these decisions will determine, over time, the performance of the organization. Thus, you also realize that, as the CEO, you must ensure these dynamics result in considered decision-making towards excellence.

This double realization is something that not many CEOs have necessarily come to fully understand during their professional lifetime until they arrive at the job. That is, they are the ultimate stewards of Company Excellence.

You fetch a book, or many books, or you look for external management consultants ... but, reality again is way too messy, so, *where do you really start?*

Once more, let us return to the narrative of our maritime story...

* * *

December 1811. Whitehall, you have just come out of a ceremony that you never dreamed would happen. Prince George (on behalf of King George III) has appointed you his First Naval Lord of the Admiralty (*Group CEO*) . . . Hip, Hip, Hooray!

The mix of emotions is staggering, enormously satisfied and proud, with some flavours of anxiety and perhaps fear (of failure, let us be honest). Though you have led several battle wins during this decade of Napoleonic wars, the scenario does not look yet close to final victory. On the one hand, Napoleon commands vast expanses of Continental Europe from Portugal to Russia, harnessing armies of a million soldiers and combining the fleets of the occupied countries. On the other hand, since Trafalgar was won in 1805, Britain has been the only power standing able to challenge him at sea.

But you are now the one in charge. These thoughts and many others populate your mind as you return to the Admiralty Building to your new office. Sitting at your very comfortable chair looking at the vast dossier piles waiting in the mahogany desk, you wonder, what next?

You start from the basics. Why are we at war? To ensure peace and freedom in Europe—and to keep the concept of monarchy alive vs the populist revolutionary threat—(*Mission*). What do you see the Navy's delivery towards winning the war? Winning a decisive, defining sea victory against the enemy (*Vision*). How is the Navy going to deliver? Through the beliefs and behaviours of its crews (*Values*).

As you reflect on these basics, it starts to get complicated. Yes, it is about people, but the war's weight rests on the shoulders of the officers. How can the Navy build towards excellence? Two dimensions to that: the utmost quality of character of its commanders and captains (*Leadership & Management Excellence*), and the brilliant combination of aligned organization of its ships, squadrons and fleet with sound decision-making (*Company Excellence*).

Sunlight comes through the stained-glass windows to bump straight into your forehead, you feel the warming heat on the skin. The illumination comes literally like an eureka moment for you. Can it be so simple?... clearly it is not.

How can you influence and change this complex people dynamic into a best-in-class fighting force? Again, you deem it helpful to start from basics, from inside to outside the individual... what if your officers were able to understand what drives them as individuals? (*Thinking and Honesty*); what if your officers were able to improve the way they interact with others? (*Influencing and Communications*); what if your officers were able to command best-in-class art and science of running their units? (*Organization and Strategy*); what if your officers were able to master the principles of winning at war? (*Investing and Value*).

Yes, our current Naval College in Portsmouth is intended to do this job. Only that you, and everyone else, knows that their focus is really on navigation and seamanship, not on core individual and collective traits and achieving excellence. Therefore, perhaps, you could entrust the Naval College to design a programme for officers across the entire Navy to ensure a continuous improvement of the above traits, to ensure the quality of Navy commanders does not have rival (*Leadership & Management Excellence—THICOSIV framework*).

The sunshine goes away, darkened by clouds pushed by winds coming from Southend at the tip of the Thames. This helps to turn your mind to the second topic, the fleet's organization and decision-making.

That is another mess. Admittedly, the Navy has improved over time in terms of standardizing the rate of ships, homogenizing the canonry calibres, setting a voluntary and enforced enlistment process to man the ships, and arranging a complex procurement train for all required commodities. Still, the machine was far from well-tuned, you knew that at the core. Proof of it was the constant array of ships stranded in the dockyards waiting weeks or months for repairs, key components, guns or crews. Just not good enough.

A bigger problem was securing the crews, though it was not a big hassle at the start of the Napoleonic war, with recruitment offices full of young lads eager to get into action. The spirit quickly languished as maimed veterans and funerals spread across the country. Now, press gangs must do the job, preying on coastal or country pubs to snatch drunken youngsters and even middle-aged men, as the numbers keep dwindling.

How can you change this chaotic machinery to become a best-in-class organized force? Necessarily you need to look for relevant examples out there in history, in Britain or abroad... even if there are not many, there must be some. You recall having read some books in this regard and so you go to fetch them in your personal library, recently organized at your office.

Yes, you recall, there was a clockmaker from the eighteenth century, John Harrison... yes, the inventor of the marine chronometer which sorted out the problem of longitude in navigation. Somebody wrote about his meticulous focus on clock fine-tuning and how there was an analogy for organizing the different component parts of government or even private enterprises (*Clockbuilder*). Also, a German philosopher from the same century, Friedrich Hegel, came with his dialectic of opposites, which suggested the idea of embracing contradictory concepts (*Genius of the 'And'*); another author brought application of this idea to organizations of different types to advance the level of best practice.

Checking the shelf of history and ancient cultures, you recall another work that emphasized the strength of values and purpose as a cornerstone of all major world religions (*Core Ideology*). Also, on the far right of the shelf just below, you find some new books related to the developments in coal and iron that are driving technological changes across England. You recall one, not its author's, related to invention, and the embracement of self-confidence and self-criticism to arrive at new solutions (*Drive for Progress*).

That sounds like a solid start for the topic of organization towards excellence (*Company Excellence—Balanced Design framework*).

What about the sister matter of excellence in decision-making? Your mind brings the names and faces of the Admirals, Vice Admirals, Rear Admirals, Commodores and many Post-Captains and Commanders of ships that you have dealt with over decades. You know they are a very heterogeneous bunch of characters. When you think of them individually, each one displays a different personality, and their characters change as they grow in power, sometimes for the worse (*Biases*). When you think of them collectively, the picture gets blurred, they develop surprising dynamics (*Noise*), some of camaraderie, even friendship, others of rivalry, even hate, and over time power makes collective decision-making quite frequently a nightmare (*Politics*). Herding cats (at least we got Navy disciplinary rules to keep them at bay!). How do you ensure that when they meet to take decisions their dynamics drive to good quality decision-making?

Then you remember your doctor's comment about an author, a philosopher I believe, called Jeremy Bentham, who wrote some 30 years or so ago about the principle of utility. You reach back to your library shelves, and yes, there it is 'An Introduction to the Principles of Morals and Legislation'. It defines the principle of utility as 'it is the greatest happiness of the greatest number that is the measure of right and wrong'.

Well, that sounds as well like a reasonable start, but in the business of 'making war at sea', you wonder how to bring this principle to homogenous and applied practice (*Company Excellence—Considered Decision-Making framework*).

You put all these volumes on your desk and start frantically collecting the ideas into a cohesive picture. Now, you got a second mandate for the Naval College: to distil from these and other similar treaties a coherent set of basic principles that ensure that organization and decision-making in the Royal Navy can achieve and sustain excellence (*Company Excellence*).

* * *

This, my dear CEO, is **Strategy in Action** for a ***Company & Leadership Excellence***.

Reference

1. Passage 66 and 68 – "Tao Te Ching" by Lao Tzu (IV-III century BC) -translated by John H. McDonald- (2019; Arcturus)

Leadership and Management Excellence 9

Leadership has become a 'hot' topic amongst twenty-first-century business-literature authors, consulting firms and C-level suites. In particular, the concept of leadership has become a mantra for success. Companies spend a tremendous amount of effort each year, supported by mushrooming human resource specialist boutiques and talent consultants, in developing their executives across all ranks in the attitudes and aptitudes required to be recognized as solid leaders.

It is not the purpose of this chapter to make a review of the many approaches that surely can be followed to distil a definition of leadership. Instead, what could be more valuable, as a counterpoint, is to reflect on a comparative basis about another concept that certainly was 'hotter' in twentieth-century literature, nowadays a little bit forgotten, the concept of management.

I find this counterpoint particularly interesting because quite often both concepts are portrayed through lenses of 'relationship of opposites'. I believe this is fundamentally wrong and especially dangerous given the importance of appointing the 'right' individuals to occupy the roles of highest responsibility in organizations at each level.

Peter Drucker somehow anticipated, back in the 1970s, the trend that eventually would lead to this confusion, and so provided the theoretical rationale to avoid such a misunderstanding. Professor Drucker dedicated a vast amount of his effort to the study of management and the traits that this role involves. He distilled from observation and research what would become the best-practices expected across these traits and advocated the need for organizations to ensure that each individual entrusted with management responsibility of others was, first and foremost, at least, a best-in-class manager.

He recognized though the positive impact that an individual, being already an accomplished manager, would achieve by displaying the traits of being considered also to be a great leader. However, he made the point that the organization would be making a mistake by emphasizing the latter facet at the expense of the former one. In other words, it would be foolish to recognize leadership in a person without

A. Gavieiro Besteiro, *Strategy in Action*, Management for Professionals,
https://doi.org/10.1007/978-3-030-94759-0_9

acknowledging first his capability as a manager. Leadership without management is hollow, management with leadership is greatness.

Pulling now from the definitions to illustrate and exemplify the point. As per Drucker [1], '*management is a multi-purpose organ that manages business and manages managers and manages works and work*', and the essence of management, he posited, involved 5 key traits:

1. Making people's strengths effective and their weaknesses irrelevant
2. Enhancing the ability of people to contribute
3. Integrating people in a common venture by thinking through, setting and exemplifying the organizational objectives, values and goals
4. Enabling the enterprise and its members to grow and develop through training, development and teaching
5. Ensuring everyone knows what needs to be accomplished, what they can expect of you and what is expected of them

About leadership, Drucker said, '*leadership is to bring an individual perspective to the next level, to help the others to break through limits of oneself, in order to attain higher achievement*'. Bradberry and Kruse [2], probably one of the most cited authors for a definition of leadership, concluded that '*leadership is a process of social influence which maximizes the efforts of others toward the achievement of a greater good*'. They also identify 5 key traits:

1. Empathy: one of the most valuable traits a human being can possess is the ability to understand people.
2. Awareness: insight about yourself and about the actions and feelings of others is always key to making the best decisions.
3. Honesty: maintain a level of transparency, regardless of how difficult it may seem.
4. Decisiveness: ability to choose from a multitude of options.
5. Optimism: capacity to keep up positive energy, particularly when things go sour.

In comparing both concepts, John Kotter and Holger Rathgeber [3] remark '*Management and leadership are not two ways to achieve the same end. They serve different ends, both of which are essential in complex organizations that operate in changing environments . . ./. . . It is not a matter of having one "or" the other. . . In an organization of some size, in a world that is moving with speed and disruptions, does success not demand "and also"?*'. Therefore, if we consider both sets of traits together and complementary, the obvious conclusion is best expressed by Professor Drucker words: '*management is doing things right; leadership is doing the right things*'.

Thus, when it comes to an organization, as individuals take team responsibility, it is essential to ensure they are equipped with the proper management capability to do so, because the achievement of results is the ultimate purpose the organization expects out of that appointment. Now, as the individual, either because of his/her natural personal endowment or because of his/her development and learning over time, brings traits of leadership to the role, it only will result in enhancing and amplifying his/her achievement in the managerial role.

Conversely, an individual well-endowed with leadership traits but without good core managerial capabilities could survive for a time in his management role, but eventually his/her inability to bring team and resources to results will catch up with him/her. He/she could rely for a time on influencing the team on getting things done, but the team will see through the lack of substance in managerial matters, and that will eventually undermine his/her leadership pull.

Thus, in practice, I would suggest to re-write the formula in our minds when talking about organizations: leader = management + leadership traits

All above established as a context, based on academic literature relating to both areas and on observation of the real world of business, this chapter discusses some principles of what apparently works vs what does not work in this subject.

Also, I have designed a framework that, from both a theoretical and a practical perspective, attempts to distil the essence of the disciplines that must be commanded to arrive at Leadership & Management Excellence, I call it THICOSIV (pronounced '*ticosif*'). An acronym for its 8 dimensions, which I usually present in 'pairs' as each goes hand in hand, starting from the inner individual level (1 & 2 below) towards the outer collective level (3 and 4 below):

1. Thinking and Honesty
2. Influencing and Communication
3. Organization and Strategy
4. Investing and Value

Each dimension is based on the leading work from one or several authors, which learnings are compiled in the illustration below and explained in detail through the sections of this chapter (Figs. 9.1 and 9.2).

Now, it is important to discuss the application of THICOSIV in practice. The framework is designed to be rolled out as a 18/24-month 'experiential' programme, starting with CEO and C-levels, and subsequently involving the next layers of leaders across the company. Ideally, the programme would be carefully crafted with the support of specialized firms in the respective areas coordinated by the Head of Human Resources.

It would be an ambitious, holistic, talent management programme. The word 'experiential' means that it needs to be developed at the practitioners' core activity, acting both at individual level (especially for the first 4 dimensions, 'THIC') and collective level (especially for the last 4 dimensions, 'OSIV'), with a continuous cycle of concept learning, application, feedback and correction, looping again and again for each topic.

The roll-out would happen within the real work agenda of each individual or team, so real impact in decision-making would be occurring as the programme progresses, making it core at the level of learning and internalization for the people involved. That is the key.

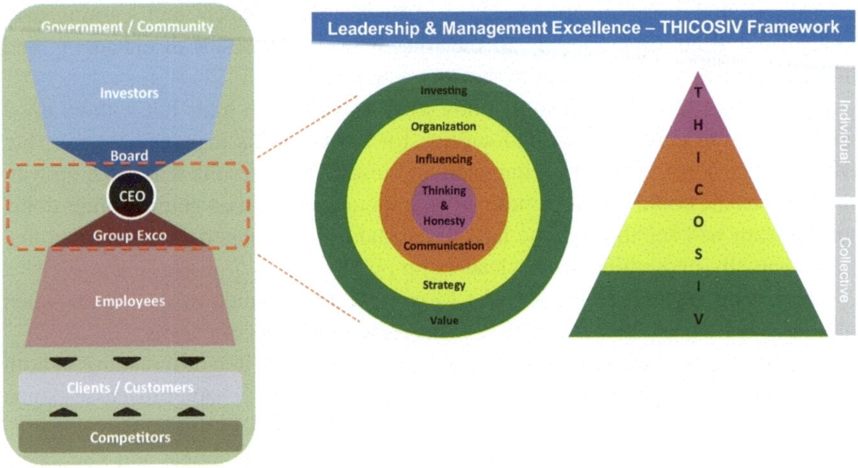

Fig. 9.1 Leadership & Management Excellence—THICOSIV framework (1/2). Sources: THICOSIV© framework (Angel Gavieiro; 2013)

This could not be a programme to be imparted exclusively via lessons, executive masters, or ad-hoc periodic away-days. It needs to be embedded in the day-to-day of the individuals during the entire programme duration. Individuals and collectives need to be assessed on their degree of internalization and practice of the concepts, and both incentives and promotions would align accordingly to recognize and reward progress.

In other terms, a THICOSIV Programme could become the most important catalyst of individual change and collective transformation for the managerial layers of an organization. If that happens, these changes will permeate over time across all employees significantly impacting the organization's performance for the better.

The following eight sections will address each of these dimensions. As they are based on specific books of reference, each section starts with a summary of the key insights from the respective book to then illustrate it drawing from my sample of experience. This format of combining the theoretical analysis with the practical experience in leadership and management excellence makes this chapter suitable for the reader's self-reflection; as you read, I invite you to take a pause after each chapter and ask: *what does it come to your mind about this topic from your professional experience thus far?*

9.1 Thinking

Thinking is the first of 4 dimensions ('THIC') that reside at the core of the individual, i.e. each of us as a person.

Thinking's goal is to enable the executive to command his/her thoughts for better decision-making. Its underlying framework is mostly based on the masterpiece by

THICOSIV Dimension	Goal	Key Learnings	Reference
Thinking	▪ Command your thoughts to better decision making	▪ 2 Systems framework: System 1 vs System 2 ▪ 3 Thought Drivers: Heuristics; Illusions; Choices ▪ 2 Selves: Experiencing Self vs Remembering Self	▪ "Thinking, Fast & Slow" - D. Kahneman (2011; Allen Lane)
Honesty	▪ Lever the factors to increase honesty and behave with integrity	▪ Dishonesty Forces: Increase (8); Decrease (4); Neutral (2)	▪ "The (Honest) Truth About Dishonesty" - D. Ariely (2012; Harper Collins)
Influencing	▪ Master your behaviour to lead effectively	▪ Best-practices to be: Likable; Influential; Leader ▪ 9 Leader best-practices: 5 'Frequent', 4 'Infrequent'	▪ "How to win Friends and Influence People" - D. Carnegie (1936; Vermillion)
Communications	▪ Master your comms. to lead effectively	▪ Circle of Communication Framework: Yourself; Mission/Values/Future; Outside/Engage In	▪ "The Language of Leaders" - K. Murray (2012; Kogan Page)
Organization	▪ Design and implement best-in-class organization	▪ 3 levels: Workflows; Intangibles; Behaviour	▪ "Mobilizing Minds" - L. Bryan C. Joyce (2007; McGrawHill)
Strategy	▪ Design and implement best-in-class strategy	▪ Kernel of Good Strategy: Diagnostic; Policy; Action. 10 Sources of Strategic Power	▪ "Good Strategy, Bad Strategy" - R. Rumelt (2011; Profile Books)
Investing	▪ Take financial decisions with the "investor hat"	▪ Rethink Economics, Markets and Investors ▪ 2 Schools of Investment Methodology ▪ 4 Tenets: Business; Mgmt.; Financial; Market	▪ "The Warren Buffett Way" -R. Hagstrom (1994; Wiley)
Value	▪ Take business decisions that create value	▪ 4 Principles of Value: Core of Value; Conservation of Value; Expectations Treadmill; Best Owner	▪ "Value" - T. Koller, R. Dobbs, B. Huyett (2011; Wiley)

Fig. 9.2 **Leadership & Management Excellence—THICOSIV framework** (2/2). Sources: THICOSIV© framework (Angel Gavieiro; 2013)

Daniel Kahneman, 'Thinking, Fast and Slow' (2011; Allen Lane). There are three key elements to be aware of to improve thinking for decision-making.

The first element is the recognition of our '2-Systems' while thinking (as Prof. Kahneman refers, '*System 1*' and '*System 2*'): a Fast System, automatic, not effortful and not controlled; a Slow System, purposeful, effortful and controlled. The dynamics between these Systems are characterized as an efficient arrangement that minimizes effort and optimizes performance. The Fast System continuously generates impressions, intuitions, intentions and feelings, which the Slow System usually accepts, becoming beliefs and actions. But sometimes the Fast System runs into difficulty and calls for the help of the Slow System, which promptly activates itself to tackle the problem.

Now, these dynamics entail two risks for the individual. First, under specific circumstances the Fast System tends to fall into biases or systematic errors and unfortunately, it cannot be turned off. Second, the Slow System tends to be 'lazy' and may not turn on when needed, its capacity is limited depleting quickly and, when active, tends to be too focused on the topic at hand, easily becoming blind to anything else. These risks can lead the individual to wrong decision-making.

The second element is, therefore, that the individual needs to become aware of the different Biases resulting from the dynamics between the '2-Systems'. Professor Kahneman groups them in 3 buckets, which I refer to as Thought Drivers:

- *Heuristics*: these are biases that happen in situations when in order to address the problem instead of thinking statistically (i.e. probability of an event happening) we fall into thinking causally (i.e. cause and effect). Well-known examples are anchoring or availability bias.
- *Illusions*: these are biases provoked by our excessive confidence on what we believe we know, and our apparent inability to acknowledge our ignorance and world uncertainty. Well-known example is overconfident optimism, hubris being an extreme of it.
- *Choices*: these are biases that stem from the wrong assumption that humans always adopt a rational decision-making process in their actions (e.g. the rational expectations assumption accepted in traditional economics by which humans maximize advantage and utility and minimize risk and costs). In reality, this is heavily affected by System 1. Well-known examples are endowment effect or loss aversion.

The third element is a consequence of the two previous elements. We can differentiate in a human two selves: '*Experiencing Self*' versus '*Remembering Self*'. The former describes the experience in present tense, while the latter describes the experience in past tense from memory. The issue is that the 'Remembering Self' suffers from duration neglect (of the past experience) and peak-end rule (assesses the pleasure/pain of the experience at its peak and at its end), therefore its recollection tends to be quite inaccurate. The problem gets worse because the 'Remembering Self' is who controls the decision-making, hence there is an embedded mechanism for wrong decision-making.

What does this towering edifice of insight about human thinking tells us about executives?

In simple terms, two insights:

1. When taking decisions, both individually and collectively, we need to actively watch for biases in our Thought Drivers, engaging System 2 proactively when the moment for decision arrives and kindly calling each other for any observed biases to correct thinking. This practice would contribute to a higher quality of decision-making.
   I have come to believe that Executive and Operating Committees would benefit from having a specialized psychologist acting as a 'referee' in the conversation. He/she would raise the flag when spotting biases (i.e. 'System 1' in wrecking action across the Thought Drivers) helping the Chair to reconduct the discussion to a more balanced, fact-based path. Even if this intervention would only improve, conservatively, the quality of decisions by 5 or 10%, this, in itself, would create or save enormous value. As a reference of potential impact, based on 20 years of past work analyzing hundreds of business decisions, Professor Paul Nutt [4] concluded that 50% of all decisions fail.
2. When reflecting about experiences, as Professor Kahneman notes, '*nothing in life is as important, as we may think it is, when we are thinking about it*'. This consideration would contribute to a lower level of stress and anxiety about perceived negative experiences.
   Intertwined with the decision-making activity, senior executives experience constantly enormous pressure. A great amount of politics stem from miscommunications or misperception of situations and dialogues in meetings and other offline interactions, impacting the subsequent personal ruminations in the executives' minds (i.e. the 'Remembering Self' in action). These ruminations create a huge nebula of disaffection among executives, negatively affecting their dynamics. Thus, similarly, a psychological coaching service to executives, as individuals, but as well sometimes as a collective, could remediate and mitigate many of these issues and impact positively their interactions. In terms of potential impact, according to a recent study by the American Management Association the estimated productivity loss because of stress-related factors is more than $100 bn in the USA [5].

9.2 Honesty

Let us move now to the 2nd dimension within THICOSIV: Honesty. Its goal in the framework is to help executives to lever the factors that increase honesty while to avoid the factors that increase dishonesty, and so ensuring to behave with integrity.

The science behind the identification of these factors is provided by Dan Ariely from his book 'The (Honest) Truth About Dishonesty' (2012; Harper Collins). The author analyses experimentally 14 forces shaping dishonesty and concludes 8 of them tend to increase it, 4 decrease it and 2 are neutral.

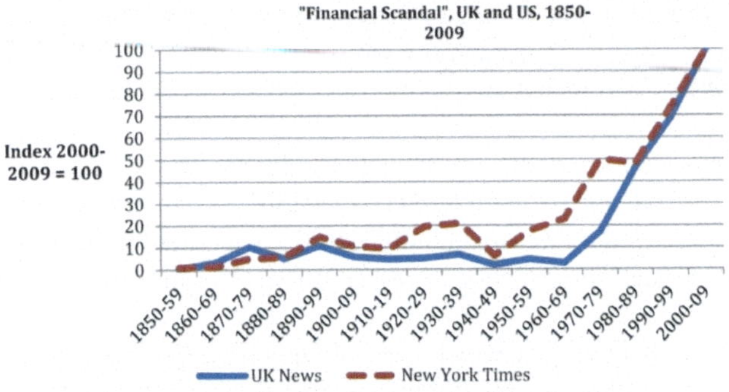

Source: UK news calculated from Gale Cengage online database of British newspapers. New York Times calculated from Historical New York Times online database hosted by Proquest.
Note: UK news popularity % = number of documents featuring 'financial scandal' divided by all relevant documents, where a relevant document is a news story published in the 'News', 'Business News' and 'Opinion and Editorial' section of a newspaper/periodical as defined by the Cengage database. New York Times = actual frequency of the term 'financial scandal'. For purposes of comparison, both series are indexed to = 100 for 2000–2009.

Sources: Toms, Steven. "Financial Scandals: A Historical Overview" (2019; Accounting and Business Research, 49:5, 477-499; DOI: 10.1080/00014788.2019.1610591)

Fig. 9.3 Financial scandals—UK and USA (1850–2009). Sources: [6]

Regarding the forces increasing dishonesty, I would differentiate them into two groups:

1. Forces you experience within yourself, such as *(1) ability to rationalize, (2) creativity, (3) 'one or first' immoral act, and (4) being depleted* (the latter references back to a failure of System 2 as per Kahneman).
2. Forces you experience with others, such as *(5) conflicts of interest, (6) others benefiting from our dishonesty, (7) watching others behave dishonestly, and (8) a culture that gives examples of dishonesty.*

A meta-study review of 300 years of past economic history (from the South Sea Bubble in 1720 to Bernie Maddoff in 2009) done by Professor Steven Toms [6] highlights that although financial fraud has been a constant, the opportunity for potential corporate fraudsters, their modus operandi and the factors enhancing or mitigating fraud risk have changed substantially over time. Since the mid-1970s, the imperative to produce shareholder value coupled with the increased complexity associated with financial innovation and deregulation has been associated with an upsurge in fraud and financial scandal, as illustrated in Fig. 9.3.

The study as well revealed a skew towards certain sectors, in particular banking and finance. After the 2008 Credit Crisis, authorities across the globe have imposed penalties in excess of $342 bn (figure as of Sep. 2017) to the banking industry, amount that is expected to reach $400 bn by end of 2020 [7]. The resulting focus on Conduct by regulators, like the FCA in the UK, is an attempt to curve these behaviours at both individual and collective level with the ultimate purpose to create personal accountability. Conduct regulation definitely touches every of these 8 forces driving dishonesty.

With regards to the 4 forces decreasing dishonesty, following Ariely, they are: *(1) pledges, (2) signatures, (3) moral reminders and (4) supervision.*

All four are easily recognizable in the practices many tax authorities have instituted across the world. The same goes for supervisory authorities of financial institutions, a clear example being the Senior Managers Regime (SMR) in the UK for senior executives of banks and other financial institutions. Under SMR, the onus of responsibility is now on the individual, and the 4 elements above are clearly encapsulated in the documentation senior managers must sign, as well as in the interviews and annual recertification process established to that effect.

Interestingly, and contrary to intuition, two forces do not have much effect on dishonesty: *(1) amount of money to be gained and (2) probability to be caught.* Pretty much pointing to Kahneman's hypothesis (referring to the Thinking component) that System 2 is not very much involved in whatever calculations happen (if any) when System 1 'authorizes' the executive's mind to go rogue.

Overall, and beyond the enormous regulatory effort to ensure executives' behaviour is honest, the responsibility for setting the tone of the culture in the organization resides with the CEO and his/her management team. I am of the opinion that nothing short of 100% integrity and honesty ought to be the minimum bar to be authorized to sit in that ExCo or OpCo, and any dent below that mark disqualifies the executive to continue with his/her responsibilities. Simply put, there is too much at risk for keeping a dishonest executive in that role, due to not only the direct consequences of that particular dishonesty, but also (as or more importantly) the cultural imprint and the associated array of impacts from potential future dishonest behaviour prompted to many other individuals across the organization.

Now, this opens a whole 'can of worms' regarding *how and who measures integrity and honesty in these situations? Whether the Board requires some specialized external counselling in these matters when cases do occasionally occur?* Questions that each institution needs to address and which I reckon they will in the context of the 'G' of the ESG principles being embraced across many Boards as I write.

Thus, to 'conclude the obvious' (or perhaps not so) from the first 2 dimensions of THICOSIV, the CEO and its top management must ensure sound Thinking and Honest behaviour to themselves and every executive in the organization. Individually and collectively, the mastery of Thinking conduces to overall executive effectiveness and sound collective decision making, while the mastery of Honesty ensures overall integrity across everyone. Twenty-first-century stakeholders do not expect of corporate executives anything less than the highest marks on both counts.

9.3 Influencing

The next 2 dimensions of the framework are as well part of the expected individual executive's endowment.

The goal of Influencing is to help the executive to master his/her behaviour in order to be able to lead effectively. 'How to win friends and influence people' by

Dale Carnegie (1936; Vermillion) is the classical book on this subject and has not lost any brilliance despite the decades past since first published.

This masterpiece is organized across key principles, for instance, 'how to win people to your way of thinking' or 'how to make people like you'. Among them, the 9 principles suggested for 'becoming a leader' I believe are on point for CEOs and C-level.

In the light of my sample of experience with executives leading teams in organizations, I would cluster these principles in 2 camps depending on how often they are present.

On the one camp, I see five principles in the 'frequent' group, where I would include:

- *P1—'Begin with praise and honest appreciation'*
- *P3—'Ask questions instead of giving direct orders'*
- *P7—'Give the other person a fine reputation to live up to'*
- *P8—'Use encouragement. Make the fault seem easy to correct'*
- *P9—'Make the other person happy about doing the thing you suggest'*

I believe a common theme underlies this group, which explains why executives use these principles frequently: positiveness. For human beings, it takes less effort and it feels more pleasant to deal with positive messages when interacting with others, either meaning it honestly or half-heartedly (effectively, executives sometimes need to 'fake it until they make it'). Therefore, providing praise or using encouragement, emphasizing the pros or inquiring people's views about the activity suggested, and lifting up reputations, have all positive connotations, sometimes resulting even more satisfying for the giver (i.e. increasing the leader's self-esteem) than the receiver.

On the other camp, the 'infrequent' group of principles, I would identify four:

- *P2—'Call attention to people's mistakes indirectly'*
- *P3—'Talk about your own mistakes before criticising the other person'*
- *P5—'Let the other person save face'*
- *P6—'Praise the slightest improvement and praise every improvement ("be hearty in your approbation and lavish in your praise")'*

In here I could point to a couple of motivations in action. For the first three principles, it is exactly the opposite rationale to the prior group, as we are talking about negative connotations. It is about mistakes and the natural human reaction is to stay away from them ('face saving'). Unlike these three, the last principle deals with positiveness, although what makes it less used by executives is the frequency of the praising. Though it is not difficult for leaders to praise, it is much more difficult to praise very often and for a large variety of deliveries, particularly minor ones. I think this tendency obeys to two potential causes, either the leader's very high standards allow for only a few high-quality instances to pass the 'praise triggering filter', or the leader's assumption that a majority of those minor achievements fall within the expected BAU of the person's job description.

Whatever the case, the fact is that leaders do not influence teams as well as they potentially could, and by a large margin. Employee satisfaction surveys point to how many of them leave organizations for feeling a lack of appreciation for their contribution and, quite shockingly, a not-small percentage of those considering leaving would desist from doing so if they received a mere 'thanks' from their line manager.

The organizational impact of executives' Influence skillset is very important, as highlighted by recent global study [8] over 25,000 employees across 20 industries:

- Only 1/3 of employees received recognition the last time they went the extra mile and only 25% felt highly valued at work.
- Only 9% of employees thought their average co-worker was very happy at work.
- 39% of managers considered their management was transparent in the organization, while only 22% of employees agreed.
- . . . as a result, 43% of employees would be willing to leave their companies for a 10% salary increase and 2/3 did not consider their organization had a strong culture.

9.4 Communication

Moving now to the Communications dimension, where the goal is to master this skillset to enable the executive to lead effectively, and for which 'The Language of Leaders' by Kevin Murray (2012; Kogan Page) provides one of the most complete frameworks out there. For this discussion I will lever just its core five elements, grouped in three bullets:

- *'Be Yourself, Better'*
- *'Mission & Values'/'Future Focus'*
- *'Outside In'/'Engage'*

Let us review, based on my observations across C-levels, the kudos and the failures that are common in the tricky exercise of leadership communication.

(A) *'Be Yourself, Better'*: the framework emphasizes the crucial role of authenticity in a leader; lacking which people would not commit because of mistrust and questions about the leader's integrity.

As professor Herminia Ibarra [9] highlights in her research, leaders today struggle with authenticity for 3 reasons: (a) more-frequent and more-radical changes in responsibilities that require a continuous 're-anchoring', not easy to accomplish; (b) global business involves working with people with different cultural norms and expectations; (c) social media demands a curated personal side of an executive, which can clash with his/her private sense of self.

Many executives mistake this point for 'permanent positivity'. These leaders make a conscious effort to show a smile and transmit positivity always under any circumstances. Yes, it is important as a leader to see the glass half full and encourage positively teams in tackling their day-to-day challenges. However, there are moments or even periods in the organization where everybody realizes that 'we are in trouble, we need to change things'... and still how many times executives can be seen smiling and transmitting positivity, even when is glaringly obvious that there is not much to celebrate at that very moment. Instances like these show when lack of authenticity clearly permeates the organization.

I remember a CEO with that constant smile, while at the same time was undertaking a ruthless restructuring that ended up halving the organization size in the span of 3 years. He kept smiling while everyone was looking at their right and left watching teammates to be made redundant and so wondering when their turn would come. A minimum dose of empathy would have helped to realize that smiling did not fit the situation. Unauthentic leadership is a killer of organizational morale.

The second key ingredient required is the ability to communicate with passion, in other words, to instil emotions in the audience. This one is more difficult depending on the type of person the leader is, either because of introversion or due to cultural traits. Instilling passion into the message delivered could be a bar too high for certain individuals. The fact is that audiences are by their very nature sensitive to emotions, like big antennas that can register any tone, body gesture and pitch and associate it with emotions, any kind of emotion. There is no communication without any emotion attached, even boredom is an emotion in itself.

Therefore, when the executive speaks there are always emotions of some type steered, the question for the leader is to consciously elicit the ones he intends, hopefully in an authentic way, so to generate the right impact on the audience. Embracing passion in the speech helps to generate positive emotions around your message to reinforce its authenticity and its retention in the audience's mind.

My record of C-levels is really mixed on this one. Perhaps, I have noticed a pattern among some executives that, probably induced by their communications training or habits, result in having a constant or similar style in every communication they do. I believe some variability in their style, purposely dialling up and down the passion instilled on them, would help to produce a richer spectrum of emotion in the audience.

(B) *'Mission & Values'/'Future Focus'*: the framework in this horizontal identifies the key elements of content for the executives' communication, distinguishing between the ones that appeal (1) the *'emotional level'* (Mission and Values, to which I would add as well Behaviours) vs (2) the *'thinking level'* (Vision and Goals, to which I would add as well Objectives), or as the book calls it the 'Future Focus'.

At (1) the 'emotional level', we start with Mission 'what important thing we are here to do' and follows with Values, 'how we do it', which becomes the principles that drive people's Behaviours, so 'how we are expected to behave within our team/role in accordance with the values'. By the way, at this point surely familiar for the readers, these elements are part of the Strategy Blueprint framework (ref. Chap. 2).

What I sometimes found are Missions that are not explicitly stated, because they are considered a waste of executive's time. I once had an experience where initially the CEO organized some meetings aiming to arrive at a Mission statement, and after several failed attempts to do so, both with and without methodology to facilitate the process, he decided that his organization could perfectly live without one!

Other times, I found the effort invested to distil a Mission was considered by the participants to be a 'ticking box exercise'. It usually made its way to the strategy materials only to be forgotten in any subsequent leadership communication.

On the other extreme, we all know of examples where Missions became a clear driving mantra for organizations, demonstrating there is a lot of value attached to a Mission provided the executives are conscious and able to leverage it.

When it comes to Values, however, it is rare for an organization that has not explicitly synthesized a list of these. Quite a different question is whether they reflect the real ones lived in the organization, as many times they are aspirational rather than actual. Also, it is key how actively executives demonstrate with their example how they actually 'live' these Values, so that effectively get reflected across the organization's Behaviours.

The *'tone at the top'* set in the Board and Executive Committee would embed and openly demonstrate the organization's Values. Consequently, their decisions should reflect these Values. Like, for instance, for a firm to brand 'Integrity' as a core value, expectation would be for immediately weeding out non-compliant executives caught in questionable behaviours. A famous example was a French bank that embraced the value of 'Frugality', which was illustrated by the rumour (or perhaps fact) that its CEO, having broken a leg, still decided to take a flight in economy class... *which executive would dare to demand a business class flight in that bank?*

Communication departments put a lot of effort to make Values visible, from compulsory 2nd page of every presentation pack to background in desktop screens or printed on the walls, even rendering them in 3D big letters at the firm's lobby.

This sounds fine but is certainly less compelling than when HR includes the Values in the 360 annual assessments of everyone in the organization, with dedicated objective and weighting in final rating, obviously linked to promotion and remuneration. It is at this point that most people really start to pay attention to what is being said in terms of expected Behaviours linked to Values.

For best practice, I witnessed departments having a session to reflect on how the organizational Values were demonstrated on the day-to-day Behaviours and actions in the context of that department and its interactions within and outside the organization. This was a way to distil the company's culture, a form of constructing a 'how to' way of doing things. That effort, multiplied by every department, times the HR Values-based evaluation process, equals real change in the way an organization behaves. Action then would exceed communication on this topic.

Turning now our attention to (2) the 'thinking level' that, as Mr. Murray explains in his framework, is more forward looking ('Future Focus' he calls it), and by nature becomes a little bit more tangible. This element of the communication framework is materialized by Vision and Goals, which are also part of the Strategy Blueprint framework (ref. Chap. 2).

Vision provides a qualitative description of 'what future success will look like'. As discussed in Chap. 2, quite often Vision gets confused with Mission, and many organizations either show statements with an eclectic mix of both, or get misidentified indifferently as one or the other. They are different but are related: while Mission is meant to be 'perennial' (the important thing we are here to do, at its core, yesterday, today and tomorrow), Vision could evolve naturally in time (the start-up will define future success perhaps over a 10 yr. horizon, once reached that point is now a middle-size company that will likely look at a different Vision over the next 10 years).

Goals, as seen in Chap. 2, refer to maximum 5–10 metrics of long-term targets, or target ranges, that the organization aims to deliver in order to track its progress towards its Vision. In contrast, Objectives are a next-level version of the Goals, max. 10 metrics, measured more into the short and medium term, as intermediate milestones towards the Goals.

Less is more with KPIs and quality is paramount in their selection, regardless of the time horizon.

Subsequently to having a strong dashboard of Goals/Objectives, it is imperative that there is a solid MIS and a focus of executives on communication and performance. I found another bank that had a stellar real-time MIS, but only for its top 10–15 executives at the Management Committee, which found very entertaining to see how their annual goal of Gross Lending was being filled on Monday mornings. Having said that, the rest of the organization, in particular the team of relationship managers accountable for delivering that goal, was on the blind side, without any visibility about how they were progressing against their Goals/Objectives. Hence, close to the year-end, to ensure teams were 'over the fence' to achieve their respective targets, we had to make print-screens of the top management dashboard and distribute them by email to all the team heads. This way, they could reckon the gap to target in aggregate so each of them in a collective effort tried to pull some more business before year-end, even without knowing individually if they were already on target; very pedestrian solution . . . and yes, fortunately, they made their year-end targets, to the relief of everyone.

(C) *'Outside In' / 'Engage'*: the framework in this vertical introduces the connexion with the external world (Clients and other Stakeholders) and the internal world (Employees). While outside stakeholders generate your Brand by giving their trust to the organization, the employees inside sustain your Brand by keeping the company's promise to the external stakeholders.

According to Mr. Murray, the company's promise is the kernel of *'Capabilities + Track-record + Integrity'* which clients and other stakeholders respectively test in terms of *'Competence + Judgement + Intention'*. Any distance between both sides becomes the Reputational Gap of the Brand. This gap needs to be brought 'outside in' so the organization understands it and reacts appropriately to close it.

In parallel, the company's promise is the result of another gap, the Engagement Gap between employees and the company. The company expects engagement from employees via *'Values/Behaviours + Efficiency + Innovation'* while the employees expect engagement from the company via *'Integrity + Empowerment + Motivation/ Vision'*.

Executives are in the middle managing both gaps simultaneously, where carefully crafted and timed communication is a key success factor to align actors towards closing the gaps on both counts externally and internally.

Across my C-level sample, it is interesting to find executives that have a natural inclination to focus their communication efforts towards either the external or the internal side. You can measure this bias by the time dedicated to external meetings with regulators, clients, banking peers, media, industry events... vs time dedicated to internal communications, townhalls, team visits, 121s, deep dives, etc... By default, executives, as individuals, have a natural incline from one or the other, normally driven by their professional upbringing (e.g. execs mostly cultivated in the front-line will not find their natural bias to fall towards internal communication once they reach C-levels).

The key success factor then is to find the right balance: first by having awareness of your natural inclination and purposely compensate it; second by reading well the current circumstances of the organization and its marketplace to readjust the mix internal/external dedication as required. Easy to discuss in theory but difficult to execute in practice given the time limitations of executives' diaries, so ruthless prioritization will be in order.

I leave the outer rim of the framework for you readers to explore in Mr. Murray's book, as it specifically tackles the techniques that best help executives to craft their communications on point for their purposes, such as audience-centricity, listening, point of view readiness, storytelling and signalling. Overall, a well-structured framework that is worth to master.

Thus, summarizing these 3rd and 4th dimensions of THICOSIV, the CEO, his/her top management and rest of the executives would gain enormously from improving their Influencing and Communications skillsets. The mastery of Influencing will ensure the teams are engaged in reducing attrition and generating a strong culture recognition. While the mastery of Communications will provide executives with the ability to connect internally and externally with authenticity, being able to instil passion when addressing critical strategy elements such as Mission, Vision, Values and Goals.

9.5 Organization

The first 4 dimensions (THIC) address the individual and his/her interactions with himself and others. The next 4 dimensions (OSIV) address the collective and its interactions with other internal collectives (i.e. Group, Divisions, Business Units, teams) and the external world (i.e. clients, competitors, investors, and other key stakeholders).

The first of these collective dimensions is Organization, where the goal is to learn to design and implement best-in-class organizational practice, for which the book of reference will be "Mobilizing Minds" by Lowell Bryan and Claudia Joyce (2007;

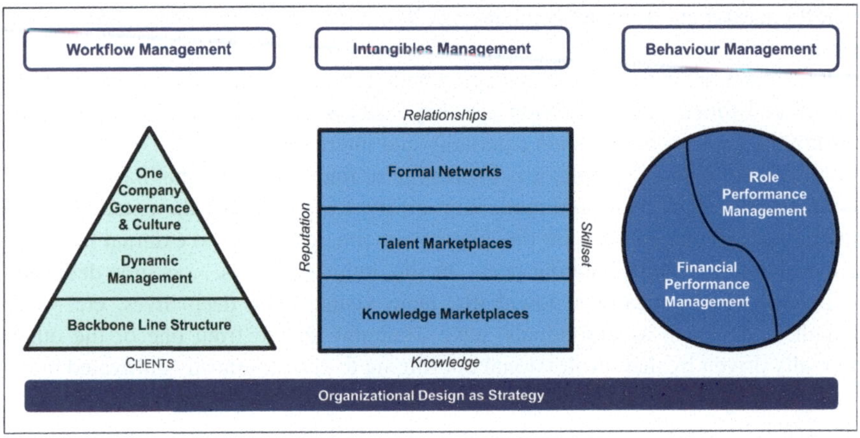

Fig. 9.4 Workflows + Intangibles + Behaviours Management framework. Note: the graphic depiction of this framework has been created for this book, so it is not original from the authors referred to in the source. Sources: 'Mobilizing Minds' (Lowell Bryan and Claudia Joyce; 2007; McGraw Hill)

McGraw Hill). Extremely well-researched work from these McKinsey partners that studies the complexity of the twentieth-century organization and explores what can become a best practice for the twenty-first century.

Complexity is the key concept. Like fat within arteries that ends up clogging the vascular system, complexity ends up constraining the growth and potential of large organizations by limiting both economies of scale and scope (provided via rents from intellectual capital, networks, branding and talent), making the firm unproductive.

Thus, the organizational challenge consists in how to eliminate unproductive internal complexity by redialling the knobs of Hierarchy (i.e. authority driven) vs Collaboration (i.e. self-interest driven). The authors propose 9 elements, grouped around the triad of *'Workflow Management + Intangibles Management + Behaviour Management'*, which I have taken the freedom 'to framework' in the picture in Fig. 9.4.

Starting with the bottom element, *'Organizational Design as Strategy'*: it embeds the need of an Organizational Diagnostic, which results in a Master Plan (target organizational model by year 3–5) plus a Game Plan (transition steps towards Master Plan) and a portfolio of Initiatives and Prototypes, properly surrounded by 'hearts, minds and behaviours' to buy-in into this change programme. Therefore, this would be the mechanism for making the organizational change ('how'). The remaining eight elements in the framework focus on the organizational levers per se to play with in order to design your twenty-first-century organization ('what').

Linking this back to the Business Model (Chap. 1), this framework for management of Workflows, Intangibles and Behaviours would support well the design efforts to evolve the 'Value Proposition Delivery' part from 'as-is' to 'should-be' (Sect. 1.4 in Chap. 1).

(A) *'Workflow Management'*: it is regulated by 3 elements...

'Backbone Line Structure', that for best-practice design would follow 3-layers of decision-making (Front, Senior and Top), centralized support functions, standardization of similar roles and clear chain of command. Ultimately, all oriented to serve clients (as the base of the pyramid in the illustration). Reading across vertically, Top-Senior-Front becomes a strong backbone hierarchy:

- The Front layer divided into 'Backbone Frontline Manager' for revenue-generating BAU line, 'Shared Utility Frontline Manager' for cost-centre BAU support, and 'Frontline Formal Project Manager' for cost-centre non-BAU projects (i.e. Strategy Development, Business Development and Implementation activity, as per Chap. 6).
- The Senior layer divided into 'Senior Backbone Leadership' which sets aspirations/accountability for the line, vs 'Senior Support Leadership' which sets functional compliance.
- The Top layer that focuses on long-term health of the enterprise.

'One Company Governance & Culture':

- 'One Governance' to ensure coordination across the firm and that for best-practice design would have two components: 'Powerful CEO', a leader that uses inspiration and aspiration to mobilize people, taking tough calls even if seniors disagree, and picks leaders meritocratically regardless of loyalties; 'Senior Top Partnership', among top 20–30 executives to ensure integrated leadership and cohesive management via 1 Parent Governance Committee and 10/12 Subcommittees.
- 'One Culture' as a common set of protocols, standards and values that define formally and informally how to conduct work, and so liberating talented people to seek opportunity and autonomy.

'Dynamic Management', to separate managing BAU from managing New Growth via three elements:

- 'Portfolio of Initiatives' to invest via a staged gated investment process and that levers familiarity advantages that the company enjoys versus competitors by mobilizing its intangibles.
- 'Integrated Process' to manage BAU earnings vs New Growth earnings making the necessary trade-offs for resource allocation to balance short-term versus long-term results.
- 'Strategy Committee' to monitor the Portfolio of Initiatives, meeting monthly and reviewing biannually with Parent Governance Committee.

In my experience across the banking industry, the Backbone Line Structure is the default organizational design; however, it is heavily encumbered and constrained by complexities such as matrix reporting, internal JVs, and lack of effective service level agreements between support functions vs frontline, which results in vertical, closed silos and inefficient, costly support. This reality is endemic across global or multiregional banks, and to my knowledge, no single one has been able yet to find a winning formula to scape this web of complexity.

I believe the reasons that preclude the simplification of the Backbone Line Structure reside precisely in the problems with the other two elements. Quite often, high level of politics and personalism plague the One Company Governance, with appointed CEOs being supported in weak sources of power, leading to endemic fragmentation and partisan grouping of top executives in different bands, which precludes at all the existence of a united Senior Top Partnership. In this context, organizational Culture is left to its own devices, which usually predicates from the example of these top executives, creating generally quite toxic environments that result in high employee turnover, burnout and mental health issues.

Regarding the management of BAU vs New Growth, there are banks that have achieved quite sound discipline over the years; however, there is a mainstream of institutions where it is still quite patchily managed. Though near all banks have a gated investment process, the way the new initiatives grow and find their way is often quite haphazard, not well integrated in the strategic planning process and far from a systematic analysis at portfolio level. On occasions, they find a side way to gain approval from decision-makers, outside the established conduit (to surprise and frustration of the project sponsors that followed the rules).

As a counterpoint example, the international division of a European bank was able to formulate a best-practice process to unite consistently the continuum from Strategy Development projects, towards Business Development phase through to Implementation programmes until arriving at BAU. The secret was the firm belief, shared between the Head of Change and Head of Strategy, that a new way of organizing the horizontal chain was possible. They jointly invested thinking time to redesign the process, including homogeneous nomenclature and clear criteria to move along the stages, always respecting that the solution worked for both functions. Then, they convinced the rest of the divisional ExCo of the benefits of moving to the new discipline. The feedback from the respective teams was resoundingly positive and the impact in terms of delivery was well appreciated by front-line units.

(B) *'Intangibles Management'*: it is also regulated by three elements...

'Formal Networks' are driven by self-interest in the value from knowledge and relationships, lowering the cost of collaboration and so generating most intangible value in organizations. They benefit from focus on topic areas, leaders that lever inspiration/persuasion, selected network members, some budget for infrastructure/training, incentives for membership, and working protocols.

'Talent Marketplaces' leverage market mechanisms to match self-interest of candidates with that of employers looking to fill roles with the best available talent,

especially in thinking intensive jobs. They benefit from One Company Governance & Culture, operating protocols, market-makers, set compensation ranges, set job descriptions, standard evaluation, and some intermediation for sr. roles.

'Knowledge Marketplaces' promote the exchange of insight among talented people by providing a fair reward to that person's time and effort so to make it exchangeable, and by organizing an internal Wikipedia (with brokers and incentives) so to make it affordable in terms of time and effort for the people seeking knowledge.

Most banks, in one way or another, have developed inroads along some or all of these elements. Nevertheless, in many cases their implementation has been far from best practice, having observed many of these initiatives to fall by their own weight when some of the key ingredients for success were not there. For instance, exemplifying Formal Networks, I have witnessed an Alliances & JV network being created in a bank, developed for 5–6 months only to decay as soon as the main sponsor changed roles in the organization. Also, several Talent Marketplaces launches becoming, after a few months, just web pages for posting internal roles. Regarding Knowledge Marketplaces, I have seen less examples, the closest being typical research management initiatives within departments, usually with the healthy intent to open up to other departments, but easily becoming either scantly nurtured share-point websites or overwhelmingly filled, disorganized share-drives.

The underlying illness of these well-intended coordination mechanisms is the 'problem of the commons'. Nobody has these activities in his/her job description, so their main fuel is self-interest. Therefore, the mechanism needs to be very well designed and greased so that enough participants attend the market regularly, otherwise very easily becomes too expensive for the effort and people give up. Careful best-practice design, as per principles indicated above, is the main recipe for success.

In this regard, I have witnessed a good example that started within a department, which eventually cross-fertilized to other departments. In a UK bank, to address the 'problem of the commons' for sustaining an array of activities such as knowledge database, internal website maintenance, internal trainings, best-practice repository and internal budget management, it was devised to divide these responsibilities among the team's junior members as a way to develop their leadership skillset; they were to take a rota ownership of 1 area for 6 months, building on the work previously done, and giving them the freedom to improve his/her area based on the rest of the team feedback and needs; they would be appraised by their 'community clients' and would have a measured impact in their evaluations, with a dedicated objective. The results went beyond expectations because of the positive spiral generated between the junior members' aim to show leadership by adding value on an area that served the rest of the team and the latter's feedback about needs and assessment of results.

(C) *'Behaviour Management'*: it is regulated by two elements...

'Financial Performance Management' where it is advocated a focus on the measurement of return on intangible capital (i.e. knowledge, relationships,

reputation and skillset) in complementarity to the traditional focus on return on capital. Thus, three metrics are suggested: profit per employee, number of employees and return on capital.

Within this approach, the Backbone Line Managers, as contributions centres, would be measured in revenues minus costs (including cost of capital), the latter based on volume; tracking should focus on performance targets, not on forecast. Shared Utility Managers, as cost centres, would be measured in marginal cost and fixed cost overhead, so they focus on cost-to-serve to frontline units.

'Role-specific Performance Management' where there are clear definitions by role of what constitutes superior/good/average/poor performance, aligning self-interest with collaboration, and evaluating performance vs expectations in relation to the peer group. Several best practices are highlighted such as a limited number of KPIs very tailored to the specific role, evaluation process by a committee of 6/7 managers plus chair and HR presence, ratings made from individual performance done by the line manager and mutual performance done by a 360 process, reward system closely following the evaluation outcome, and input from compliance process to test for alignment with values and behaviours (gathered via the 360 process).

Overall, there is a mixed bag of these practices among institutions. I have seen banks in the 90s where no evaluation was done, and reward was entirely the prerogative of the line manager. On the opposite extreme, I have seen as well a very detailed balanced scorecard process, supported by a very rigid IT system that involved lot of time to deal with, scoring +30 metrics at role level, and which report was bounced among 3 parties several times until arriving at its conclusion. Best-practice would surely be somewhere in between these two extremes.

In terms of financial performance, we see focus on return of capital (i.e. Return on Equity, Return on Invested Capital, Return on Tangible Common Equity, etc.), but much less so on profit per employee (except perhaps revenues over frontline employees used in some investment banks). This suggested new approach is valuable in situations like the one currently experienced in the banking industry where workforces are being constantly reduced with an eye set on efficiency ratios (i.e. cost-to-income); in this context, profit per employee becomes a salient KPI to watch for. With relation to the type of financial KPIs, the usual failure is to stop at the top-line, or perhaps revenues minus direct costs, on the basis of the lack of control over all the indirect costs and the lack of visibility of capital allocations; the solution comes down to having a proper and robust financial MIS bottom-up in the organization.

Regarding role performance, the practice of having clear definitions per role, and then several labels associated with the performance observed vis-à-vis the definitions, stems originally from management consulting, where usually it is performed with dedication and rigour. In banking, it started to be adopted in the functions and gradually has appeared in the front-line as well. In my experience is a very powerful practice that made the strategy & business development teams I led to really step up in performance, and it was also highly valued by them since it provided a ground of fairness (if executed properly). I had the experience to extend it to front-line teams as well, facing much more reluctance, in particular in places where the only focus had been on financial KPIs. This can become a problem, especially across front-line team leaders within the BU, because if they are supposed to deliver both financial targets and project development work, they will be inclined towards the former and will procrastinate on the latter.

As referred in Chap. 2, either for a separate or for a combined financial & role performance balanced scorecard, a critical success factor is the thoughtful cascading of KPIs across the hierarchy layers to arrive at each individual role. It demands to avoid the temptation of expanding to double-digit the number of KPIs at any echelon, as well as the adaptation of each KPI used to the roles specifically tackled at each level. In this way, the individual feels that he/she has the power to move the dial on his/her assigned KPIs, otherwise these will demoralize or frustrate employees.

In designing the 'should-be' Business Model, executives would benefit from considering the leverage of some of the best-practices above to reconfigure the pipes of how workflows, intangibles and behaviours complement each other in the process of delivering the Value Proposition to each client segment.

9.6 Strategy

For the Strategy dimension, the goal would be for the executive to learn to design and implement best-in-class strategy. Besides the book the reader has in his/her hands, the main book underpinning my best-practice selection for this topic is "Good Strategy, Bad Strategy" by Richard Rumelt (2011; Profile Books). As well, I would recommend two additional books already referenced in prior chapters (so they will not be discussed here): 'Blue Ocean Strategy' by W Chan Kim and Renee Mauborgne (2005; HBS Press), in Sect. 1.1 in Chap. 1, and 'The Strategy Execution' by Liz Mellon and Simon Carter (2014; McGrawHill), in Chap. 6.

It was for me a great satisfaction to read Professor Rumelt's book simple and clear definition of good strategy, because perfectly matched the structure of the Strategy Blueprint I had been using for many years (ref. Chap. 2). For Professor Rumelt, a good strategy requires a robust *'Diagnosis'*, followed by a *'Guiding Policy'* that specifies the approach to deal with the diagnosed problems/opportunities (what I referred to as Core Strategy), and a set of *'Coherent Actions'* designed to implement the policy co-ordinately.

Although at first sight following these three steps might seem simple, the practice of developing good strategy is not generalized, by any means. Chapter 11 will cover in more depth my take on the ailments that the function of strategy in many organizations suffers from. Banks that you might consider like-for-like in terms of business mix, size and geographical coverage, do follow remarkably diverse and inconsistent ways to develop strategy. In fact, within a given bank, different Divisions and BUs could perfectly be following heterogeneous and unconnected approaches about how they distil strategy. These differences are much larger than when you compare Finance of Risk practices in the same institutions.

As per Professor Rumelt, a good strategy has two sources of strength. First, it is unexpected because obliges leaders to say 'no' to a large variety of alternative policies and actions. Second, it discovers hidden power in situations by looking at things with a different, fresh perspective, reframing the competitive situation and highlighting new patterns to the players' SWOTs. Worth also to bear in mind the enemies of good strategy, which are social herding (i.e. popular insight sustained by group thinking) and inside views (i.e. ignoring lessons from other times).

The book compellingly uncovers for the reader a set of 10 sources of strategic power that is worth to briefly highlight and illustrate in the banking industry context.

1. *Strategic Leverage´* achieved by anticipating crucial pivot points that create an imbalance in a competitive situation and concentrating force on them to steer a larger payoff. For instance, like the focus post-2008 by the 3 largest US banks to expand their balance-sheets outside the US, anticipating the slow reaction of European banks given the weight of bad debts still not addressed from the crisis; this resulted for them in c.10% market share gain in 8 years and taking the top-3 leadership positions in the EMEA corporate & investment banking market.
2. *Proximate Objectives´* consists, within a situation of strong uncertainty, in concentrating to achieve a target that can reasonably be expected to hit, taking a strong position, and creating options around it. A good example was Lloyds after its acquisition of HBOS in the aftermath of 2008 crisis, where it inherited a franchise with a high level of impairments, the complexity of a large integration, while trying to survive the market liquidity crisis with government help. Lloyds management decided to refocus 100% on the UK retail & commercial banking market (the 'proximate') by fully restructuring, integrating and deleveraging the bank with the goal to ultimately paying back to the public shareholder. Therefore, any other objectives ('non-proximate') were deprioritized or exited (i.e. international presence, wholesale banking & markets, asset management, insurance, etc.). Lloyds arguably made a notable recovery, fully integrating 3 heritage retail franchises, cleaning up its balance-sheet, funding their expensive Payment Protection Insurance redress, to finally buying back the equity stake from the UK government in 2017.
3. *Chain-link Systems´* requires identifying what is the weakest unit in the chain that limits the performance of the system, so to fix or eliminate it to ensure the quality matching along the chain. Perhaps an example that illustrates this lever was the restructuring that UBS accomplished in its investment bank after the credit crisis. This bank, like many competitors, had a full suite offering along the Fixed Income and Equities space, with origination and sales & trading businesses both for flow and derivatives in a global basis. UBS in 2012 took the drastic decision to shed the weakest link of its verticals, Fixed Income, taking the

decision on the basis that Equities enjoyed a better competitive position and had a stronger synergy with the robust, high-growth Wealth Management division. Many other competitors took a much reluctant position to dispose so drastically of the full suite offering, which put UBS in the lead of the recovery among European players.

4. *Design´* defines how best to combine the various elements of the strategy (i.e. resources and actions) to mutually adjust and coordinate. The more challenging the situation the more coordination between resources and actions is required, either via more resources or/and more quality of those resources. As an example, Amazon has demonstrated how a careful design of the elements of its business model enables the organization to keep expanding across lateral businesses, to arrive at financial services. Starting from its core marketplace proposition and bringing together households and retail sellers of all type, it gradually opened up its internally developed capabilities to these companies: first with the logistic service, then with their cloud service (AWS) and more recently, leveraging their sales data, offering working capital financing to SMEs, reaching cumulative $5bn by 1Q 2019. At this moment, an SME can use Amazon not only to sell its wares online, but also to transport them to customers' homes, to record all the activity in its ERP based on Amazon's cloud, and to finance the sales cycle.
5. *Focus´* by attacking a segment of the market with business design supplying more value to that segment than other players. We have witnessed this power in action in the judo-economics strategy followed by many FinTechs and Challenger Banks, disrupting the traditional banks in specific client segments like SMEs or Millennials, or specific product segments like Payments or Lending, while offering a competitive advantage in terms of overall customer experience very difficult for the incumbent banks to replicate. As a result, FinTech leaders such as Revolut, Funding Circle or Wise in Europe, or Alipay or WeChat Pay in Asia have achieved extraordinary market penetration in terms of client acquisition and volume reflected in their valuations in subsequent equity financing/IPO rounds, validating their success (we will review these dynamics in more depth in Chap. 12).
6. *Growth´* is healthy as a source of power only if it is the outcome of growing demand for special or expanded capabilities fruit of enjoying a superior product or skill, which would manifest itself as both a gain in market share and superior profitability. Taking the FinTech examples above as organic growth cases, effectively they have demonstrated substantial market share grabs (e.g. WeChat Pay reached 40% of China mobile payments market in 2018), however many business models still do not show profitability (e.g. N26 or Revolut as of 2020). Taking incumbent banks as an example, many of the rapid internationalization expansions based on acquisitions that large universal banks pursued in the first half of the 2000s (e.g. HSBC, Citigroup) were aiming for growth; all of them delivered growth in size and numbers from aggregating acquired banks, but most of these expansions did not translate into more profitability and, in time, many of them had to be fully or partially exited (e.g. RBS, HSBC).

7. *Advantage´* is rooted in the differences among competitors, in their asymmetries. Competitive advantage stems from (a) producing at lower cost than competitors, or (b) delivering more perceived value than competitors, or (c) a mix of both. Low-cost advantage examples are large banks with retail deposits more than fully financing a conservative lending book (e.g. Wells Fargo) and so achieving low cost of funds and low cost of risk. An example of both advantages are FinTechs with state-of-the-art IT platforms and highly automated processes united to superb customer experience (e.g. Starling Bank or Monzo) and so achieving both low cost-to-income and high customer value. Examples of high perceived value advantage are red-carpet propositions for ultra-high net worth individuals like those of UBS and Credit Suisse, or the positioning of Goldman Sachs in the M&A advisory marketplace.

   Sustainability of a competitive advantage demands some sort of 'isolating mechanism' that precludes competitors to acquire it as well. You can feed the competitive advantage in 4 ways: widening the gap between buyer value and cost (i.e. deepening), bringing it to new markets (i.e. broadening), increasing the number of potential buyers or the volume per buyer (i.e. enlarging) and developing patent/copyright or constant business model change becoming a moving target for competitors (i.e. heightening). For instance, Revolut has followed 'deepening' by providing a fixed subscription fee with a gradually increased value offering (i.e. from the pre-paid card with no-fee cheap FX, to gradually offer free ATM access, travel insurance, airport lounges...), as well as 'broadening' by expanding its service from the UK to the EU, Australia, Singapore or the US in rapid succession. By contrast, Starling has followed 'enlarging' by opening its current account banking platform to a plethora of curated FinTechs to increase the volume of product/services cross sold to its customer base. Patent/copyright-based 'heightening' examples are much rarer in the financial services industry, where copycatting of offerings is very difficult to avoid.
8. *Dynamics´* consist of achieving advantage by exploiting external waves of change that upset existing competitive position status-quo, erasing old advantages and opening the space for new ones. The key to capture them is to understand the fundamental forces underlying the trend and develop a point of view about the associated second-order changes that have been set into motion. Any of five guideposts usually signal these dynamics:
   (a) Escalating fixed costs, as it happened with the investment banking industry post-2008 via the process of re-regulation and limiting variable compensation, which obliged banks to fix higher salaries to offset limitations on bonuses.
   (b) Deregulation, one of the key triggers of the FinTech revolution, especially driven in countries like the UK or China given the favourable regulatory disposition.
   (c) Predictable biases, such as plateau in S-curves, lack of room given an existing oligopoly or future winners will be the current ones; new entrants usually play to incumbents' biases of this type, like boutique M&A firms like Moelis or Houlihan Lokey that stealthily and progressively have been

winning market share during the 2000s out of large investment banks, when before they were dismissed as out of the game.

(d) Defence of skills and positions accumulated over time; typical incumbent response, which make them reluctant to change; we have seen it in the lukewarm reaction from quite a few large banks facing digital disruption, as they prefer to avoid revenue self-cannibalization at all costs, like the comparison between the more digitalized BBVA vs the more prudent approach to digital by Santander in the 2010 decade.

(e) Attractor states refers to the natural trend that industries show to evolve towards more efficient versions of themselves when facing changes in the structure of demand; demonstrated in the large switch of customers to FinTech providing payments solutions, having grabbed c.25% market share in Western markets, and so pushing incumbent banks to push digital transformation either within SWIFT rails (i.e. gpi, SWIFT's response to FinTech threat) or partnering with new FinTech standards like Ripple (i.e. payments via distributed ledger technology, so outside SWIFT rails).

9. *Inertia´*, defined like the organization's unwillingness or inability to adapt to change, which could stem from routine, culture or proxy (i.e. cannibalization avoidance). The examples mentioned above regarding FinTechs vs incumbent banks are on point, wherein the latter the element of inability becomes quite concerning. Examples in many large global banks like HSBC, Deutsche Bank or Citigroup, where many of their digitalization initiatives have not moved the dial or other more important imperatives took priority such as re-regulation, restructuring, managing low profitability or reducing an overextended multinational presence.

10. *Entropy´*, defined like the tendency of weakly managed organizations to become less organized and less focused. It goes back to the realization that many large organizations suffer from this illness (ref. Introduction chapter). The only solution comes from competent management that keeps constantly cleaning up and maintaining the organizational fitness, eliminating bad practices and behaviours. Like inertia, incumbent's entropy has been heavily exploited by FinTechs via their agile and nimble deployments. Equally, entropy is observable in banks inadvertently embracing complexity stemming from rapid inorganic growth like HSBC and Citigroup in the 1990–2000s; or more recently and at smaller scale, in Banco Sabadell acquisition of TSB from Lloyds Bank in the UK, finding it extremely difficult to spin off from Lloyds' IT systems that led to notorious outages affecting 1.9 million customers in 2018.

The key for best leveraging these 10 principles is to identify which ones are in action at a particular strategic setting. For instance, the irruption of FinTech start-ups innovating in the banking space, typically dominated by a few large and medium-size incumbents, touches several of them: focus, advantage (both in cost and perceived value) and dynamics (deregulation) from the attacker side, as well as inertia and entropy from the defendant side.

As a summary of the 5th and 6th dimensions of THICOSIV, all executives must master both Organization and Strategy. Mastery of Organization entails internalizing the different best practices for effective Workflow, Intangibles and Behaviour Management, which enable the executive to develop first-class organizational designs and informal networks to coordinate activity. Mastery of Strategy, the essence of this book, requires the executive to ensure strategy is based on solid Diagnosis, sound Guiding Policy and Coherent Action, and at its core demands to deeply understand the sources of strategic power of his/her company in its marketplace.

9.7 Investing

The goal would be to learn to take financial decisions with the 'investor hat'. It would not be a surprise for many readers to find that 'The Warren Buffett Way—Investment Strategy of The World's Greatest Investor' by Robert G. Hagstrom Jr. (1994; Wiley) is the book selected. As well worth to reference the original sources for investing inspiration by the Oracle of Omaha: 'The Intelligent Investor' by Benjamin Graham (1973; Harper Business) and 'Common Stocks and Uncommon Profits' by Philip Fisher (1958; Wiley), both cited quite exhaustively across Hagstrom's book.

In the book, Buffet acknowledges Graham and Fisher works as his bedrock for investing, in a respective mix of 85% vs 15%. Graham's methodology focuses on the essence of value investing, with its emphasis on thorough analysis, principal safety ('Margin of safety'), return focus ('Prospective RoE') and detachment from stock market's emotion ('Mr. Market's greed & fear'). Whereas Fisher's approach focuses on finding companies with above-average potential ('Company potential') and aligning the most capable executives ('Management capacity'). Contrary to Graham, Buffet puts less emphasis on portfolio diversification, preferring a reduced number of very well studied, bold investments and, once invested, focus on operational performance and reporting transparency ('Look-through earnings').

Buffet's business investment philosophy says, simply put, that you should invest as an owner, not as a stockholder, in his words, '*investing is most intelligent when it is most business like*'. Buffet's investing framework is structured via 4 tenets:

´Business tenets´:

- *Is the business simple and understandable?* focus on your 'circle of competence'.
- *Does the business have a consistent operating history?* avoid turnarounds and distressed situations.
- *Does the business have favourable long-term prospects?* avoid 'commodity businesses' and focus on 'franchises' (offerings with no close substitutes) with economic strength that can endure mistakes.

'Management tenets':

- *Is the management rational?* focus on their capital allocation decisions (mistakes: reinvest at low returns, grow via overpaid acquisitions).
- *Is the management candid with shareholders?* fully and genuine financial performance reporting that admits mistakes.
- *Does management resist the 'institutional imperative'?* avoid tendency of imitating other managers and reluctance to embrace fundamental change.

'Financial tenets': focus on...

- Return on equity: not on earnings per share.
- 'Owner earnings': cashflows minus capex and opex required for functioning.
- High profit margins: cost control.
- 'One dollar premise': for $1 retained, ensure there is $1 of market value creation.

'Market tenets':

- *What is the value of the business?* net present value of discounted future, over-the-cycle, operating cash flow (conservatively adjusted for risk) at long-term risk-free rate.
- *Can the business be purchased at a significant discount to its value?* ensure enough margin of safety for 15% yield (usual mistakes: price fully paid, low management quality or weak future economics).

Stepping back to reflect on the acquisitions directly witnessed across my career in banking, mostly during the growth period up to 2008, I find 2 counterpoints to apply the 4 tenets above in the moves made by Barclays in Spain in 2003 and South Africa in 2005 [disclaimer—for confidentiality reasons the analysis below is based exclusively on available public information].

The acquisition of Banco Zaragozano, with the intent to be integrated into the existing Barclays franchise, was a great example of value investment. Zaragozano was a medium-size bank in Spain, simply focused on retail and SME banking, that had a long-term successful history and a client franchise with growth potential that complemented well Barclays Spain. For instance, the latter's stronger retail banking in affluent segments would bring synergy to Zaragozano's retail, while its small commercial banking would be heavily reinforced by Zaragozano's more sizable SME business. The resulting management team would bring a selection of the best executives from both banks under the leadership of the chief of Barclays Spain, who had a great track record of organic growth to the date. The major focus of their integration was on the operating systems and branch network, generating solid cost synergies. In terms of financials, cost-to-income ratio control became the critical KPI for delivering the cost synergies of the integration. From a valuation perspective, in hindsight, Barclays effectively ended up delivering the integration plan 18 months earlier than anticipated, leaving the resulting franchise in 2006 with a profitable, growing c.500 branch network as the best positioned foreign bank in the country.

The acquisition of a c.55% majority stake in Absa Bank was a totally different investment experience. Absa was a successful #4 ranked bank in South Africa, with businesses across all the spectrum in retail, commercial, corporate and investment banking. Barclays South Africa subsidiary was very small per comparison, so the synergy case would have to come for exporting advanced expertise from the UK (e.g. Barclays Capital for corporate & investment banking) and eventually the integration of the 2 Sub-Sahara Africa (SSA) franchises (i.e. 9 countries from Barclays and 4 from Absa, eventually becoming Absa Africa). Therefore, this was not a simple acquisition, it was complex from many viewpoints. Management responsibility was left with the local Absa team, adding some executives from the acquirer in specific positions over time as the synergies were to be deployed. The dynamics between management and board were already complicated, post-Apartheid the country had established some rules to ensure better representation of the community in companies' boards, which made decision making, at least, tricky and politically charged. Like in previous acquisitions, the financials focus was on cost control in the integration efforts, but they were modest due to the small size of Barclays South Africa. Therefore, the bulk of the economics was predicated upon revenue synergies from more advanced offerings like Barclays Capital or Barclaycard, which unsurprisingly took much longer than expected to produce fruit. In addition, the difficult Absa Africa integration of 9+4 countries eventually took a decade to become fully effective.

It is in order to clarify that, in the decade post-2008 GFC, Barclays eventually exited both countries (Spain in 2014 and South Africa in 2018) as a way to reduce its Group geographical complexity and strategic refocus into the UK and USA transatlantic bridge to ultimately improve their single-digit return on equity. However, I would argue these exits do not need to have a bearing in the investment analysis of the pre-2008 acquisitions above, except perhaps for the negative effect that the Group's difficult situation might have played in delaying execution plans of Absa Africa during the post-2008 recovery period. In the case of Spain, I would argue the problems the bank experienced after 2009 real estate crisis have more to do with a strategy in 2007-08 for organic growth in mortgages and commercial real estate than anything related to the 2003 acquisition and subsequent integration.

In conclusion, Banco Zaragozano ticked strongly in the tenets of business (both local franchises were simple and complementary, their potential together high), management (wide pool of best leaders from both banks and reputed local CEO) and market (arguably, it can be inferred that value was created as highlighted by the 18-month ahead-of-schedule delivery of the integration business case). Whereas Absa presented a few red flags in terms of business (acquirer very small locally, had to bring business strength from its home country to add value), management (country-inherent difficult dynamics between Board and management) and financial tenets (value based on future revenue synergies, much less tangible and more elusive than cost synergies, as well as the very delayed integration of the SSA franchises).

9.8 Value

The goal here would be to learn to take business decisions that create value. The best practice selected book for this last dimension of the THICOSIV framework is 'Value—The Four Cornerstones of Corporate Finance' by McKinsey & Co partners Tim Koller, Richard Dobbs and Bill Huyett (2011; Wiley), extensively researched and full of exemplification. A book borne on the back of a widely acclaimed best-seller 'Valuation—Measuring and Managing The Value of Companies' also by McKinsey & Co partners Tim Koller, Tom Copeland and Jack Murrin (1990; Wiley), more focused on methodologies of value estimation.

The book starts with a review of the 4 cornerstones that drive Company Value:

'Core of Value': creation of value happens by investing capital to generate future cash flows at rates of return exceeding the cost of capital. Cash flow is driven by revenue growth and return on invested capital (ROIC), which compared to cost of capital (CoC) defines whether shareholder value is created (ROIC > CoC) or destroyed (ROIC < CoC).

'Conservation of Value': creation of value happens only when companies generate higher cash flows, not by rearranging investors' claims on those cash flows. Therefore, share repurchases, and financial reengineering do not create shareholder value, except if there is any tax saving associated; acquisitions only create value if the combined cashflows increase via growth, cost reduction or ROIC improvement.

'Expectations Treadmill': stock market performance is driven by changes in expectations, not just the company actual performance. It follows that a good company is not necessarily a good investment (as per Buffet's Way in the previous section), it depends on the expectations already priced in its stock value. Thus, it is important to understand the Total Return on Shareholders (TRS) and the performance expectations already embedded in the share price.

'Best Owner': value depends on who is managing the business and what strategy they pursue. Best ownership depends on the sources for adding value as an owner: a) unique links to other businesses in portfolio; b) distinctive skills; c) better insight/foresight; d) better governance; e) distinctive access to talent/capital/government/supplies/consumers. The best owner may depend on changes in the business life cycle and, for best practice, a regular portfolio review process resulting in targeted acquisition/divestitures is highly advisable in organizations, like the Portfolio Value Gap framework (ref. Chap. 7).

With these 4 principles in mind, the authors then review a framework for Managing Value Creation with a focus on the Value Drivers of growth vs ROIC in the short, medium and long-term horizons.

The overall intent is to strike the right balance between the short-term profits and ROIC while continuing to invest for the long term. Five key recommendations:

- *Organization*: management process should stem from the BU level where value is effectively created. Division level of aggregation hinders granularity.
- *Performance Measurement*: to reflect KPIs linked to the value drivers over the short, medium and long term.

- *Compensation*: to focus more on long-term value creation; the balanced scorecard should link strategy and long-term goals.
- *Strategic Planning & Budgeting*: to concentrate on long-term value drivers (not just financials) and be separate process at Group/Division level (aggregate top-down) vs BU level (bottom-up).
- *Board of Directors*: to deep dive as well on BU level performance and value creation.

This chapter is especially relevant for financial institutions worldwide in the decade post-2008, in particular within the US and Western Europe. Overall, the dramatic fall of bank valuations, with Price-to-Book ratios often below 1, has been driven by both anemic growth rates, mimicking the underlying subdued GDP growth of their respective economies, and for many a persistent single-digit Return on Equity (RoE) well below 10–12% cost of capital expectation range.

Underneath these low RoEs, factors such as asset restructuring, deleveraging, redressing/penalties, re-regulation and Central Banks' zero interest rate policy have been denting banking management teams' efforts to recover RoEs. In their quest to improve value, portfolio reviews have often led banks to exit many geographics, BUs or even entire divisions, generating large capacity reductions of personnel and risk-weighted assets. Some banks, mostly in the US, have succeeded in bringing RoE above CoE, some even quite sustainably, however many have been still struggling with it. Also, despite historic records of share buybacks and other financial reengineering of capital structures, investors have kept valuation multiples historically subdued reflecting poor performance expectations going forward.

C-suites need to enter a phase of much bolder decision-making about fundamental transformation of their legacy business models. The digital revolution provides both the threat and the opportunity to take bold action in investing for fundamental change towards the long term. Now, this is a marathon, not a sprint. Some banks have boldly embraced this path, like BBVA, ING or Goldman Sachs, and despite the tremendous progress in spearheading digital transformation still valuations do not see yet the positive expected result, it will take more time. A majority of large banks have preferred to play 'around the edges' on this opportunity. As we will discuss in Chap. 12, the threat here is whether FinTechs, BigTechs or digitally transformed incumbent banks will eventually take an insurmountable lead at the expense of the laggards' market shares, then it would probably be too late for any reaction.

Summarizing these last 2 dimensions of THICOSIV, every executive needs to master 'investor hat' decision-making, which is mastering the art of Investing and Value. Investing requires detaching oneself from the market passions and looking at core questions around the tenets of Business, Management, Financials and Market. Best-practice for Value requires applying the principles of Core Value, Conservation of Value, Expectations Treadmill and Best Owner.

* * *

This completes the THICOSIV framework for the design of a holistic executive mastery programme to achieve Leadership & Management Excellence across the organization... just reflecting for a moment, imagine that 80% of the executives across your organization commanded these eight skillsets even at 80% level, *what would the impact potentially be for your company?*

References

1. "Management" by Peter Drucker (1973; Collins).
2. "What Makes A Leader?" by Travis Bradberry and Kevin Kruse (Aug.2017; www.leaderonomics.com).
3. "That's Not How We Do It Here!" by John Kotter and Holger Rathgeber (2016; Portfolio/Penguin Random House).
4. "Why Decisions Fail: Avoid the Blunders and Traps That Lead to Debacles" by Paul C. Nutt (2002; Berrett-Koehler Publishers).
5. "The Organizational Cost of Office Politics" by Lawrence B. MacGregor Serven (Jan.19; American Management Association).
6. Steven Toms (2019) Financial scandals: a historical overview, Accounting and Business Research, 49:5, 477-499, DOI: https://doi.org/10.1080/00014788.2019.1610591.
7. "U.S., EU fines on banks' misconduct to top $400 billion by 2020: report" by Sumeet Chatterjee (27/09/17; Quinlan & Associates—Reuters).
8. "The 2019 Employee Engagement Report: The End of Employee Loyalty" (2019; TINYpulse).
9. "The Authenticity Paradox" by Herminia Ibarra (Jan-Feb.15; Harvard Business Review).

10 Company Excellence

Company Excellence sits, as it could not be otherwise, at the apex of the Holistic Management Strategy framework. Undoubtedly, the company's embracement of the relentless pursuit of excellence is an endeavour at the core of the CEO's role and necessarily a 'must' for the members of his/her Executive Committee.

Certainly, most would concur on the previous statement, the question is (by now a constant across the chapters of this book) . . . *how?*

Like in years-past efforts by stone masons erecting centuries-enduring majestic cathedrals, I believe that achieving Company Excellence is the result from a combination of 2 simultaneous crafts: Balanced Design (at the strategy phase, long-term) and Considered Decision-Making (at the execution phase, day-to-day).

Balanced Design comprises the key 'distinctive' elements that a company needs to build up in its architecture to achieve and sustain excellence in its performance. By their very nature, those elements are purposedly built upon a long time, following a well synchronized mechanism of checks and balances among its constituent parts. Somehow, it is the 'static', top-down, long-term ingredient of achieving excellence.

Considered Decision-Making speaks to the way decisions are made among the collectives of individuals at different levels across the organization on a day-to-day basis. Their cumulative effect over the years determines how the initial design manifests itself in the reality of the company which, by 'comparison' with the marketplace, determines whether excellence is being achieved or not. Somehow, it is the 'dynamic', bottom-up, short-term ingredient of achieving excellence.

It is important to reflect upon the features of distinctiveness/comparison and static/dynamic attributed to both crafts, respectively. To achieve excellence means necessarily a comparison among players and so a set of identifiable characteristics that make a distinction vs the rest. Also, achieving excellence in a given moment of time can be attributed to a specific, static combination of these characteristics; however, chances are that they will require change over time to keep the distinctiveness, and hence the need to adapt dynamically to the marketplace.

The first 3 sections of this chapter address the Balanced Design craft based upon the empirical findings by Jim Collins and Jerry I. Porras in their acclaimed book,

A. Gavieiro Besteiro, *Strategy in Action*, Management for Professionals,
https://doi.org/10.1007/978-3-030-94759-0_10

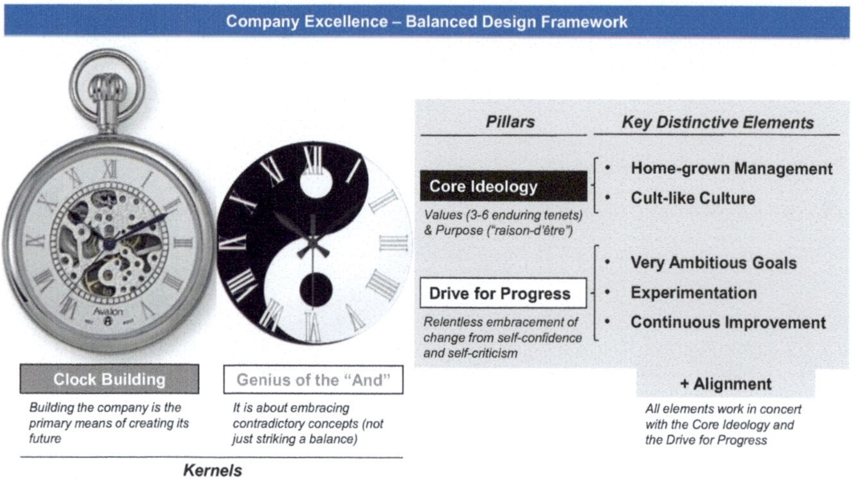

Fig. 10.1 Company Excellence—Balanced Design framework. Note: The graphic depiction of this framework has been created for this book, so it is not original from the authors referred to in the source. Sources: 'Build to Last' (Jim Collins and Jerry Porras; 1994; Harper Business)

'Build to Last' (1994; Harper Business). The last section of the chapter will delve into the Considered Decision-Making craft based upon my own observed practice across organizations in the financial services industry.

Collin and Porras' book is an attempt to distil the essence of excellence from a comprehensive sample of 18, as they called them, 'visionary' companies in relative comparison to a control group of 18 peers, next-to successful followers, in their respective industries. They draw from a long-term data sample starting in 1926 till 1990, both quantitative and qualitative, with the aim to identify the key drivers of that distinctive excellence. The framework below is my summary of the key distinctive components for Balanced Design (my terminology) found by Collins and Porras (Fig. 10.1).

Let us review these drivers in turn and place them into context by leveraging the case study of JP Morgan Chase & Co. (JPMC) over the last decade, which I will try to substantiate by extracting statements from its long-time CEO, Jamie Dimon, in his Letters to Shareholders and Annual Report presentations from 2010 (first year that the bank reached above the pre-Credit Crisis best year of performance, 2007) to 2019 closure.[1] Also, as a 'control' for comparison,[2] I selected Bank of America (BoA)

[1]The CEO Letter 2019 was published in April 2020, with the COVID-19 pandemic and economic crisis in full swing, so the letter purposedly switched its traditional strategic focus to address instead the impact and reaction of the bank to this crisis; therefore, the CEO Letter 2018 was taken instead as a main source.

[2]Given the more limited depth of material dedicated to this type of topic in Bank of America's CEO Letter to Shareholders and related material, the benchmarking with JP Morgan will be circumscribed to the next 2 sections of this chapter.

(with the added benefit for comparability of having the same CEO, Brian T. Moynihan, in role all along that period). Complementing the comparison between both, I also peppered in some specific examples from my own banking experience and from non-financial companies.

10.1 Balanced Designed: Two Kernels

I refer to these 2 components of Collins and Porras work as 'kernels' in the sense that each must be a fundamental business principle at the heart of the CEO and the conceptualization of his/her main role towards the company.

10.1.1 Clock Building

Principle: Building the organization is the primary means of creating its future.

This statement is a critical shift of perspective regarding the ultimate drivers of success of excellent companies, and postulates that they rely on the underlying processes and fundamental dynamics embedded in the organization. Following the metaphor, like the accuracy and reliability of a clock which depends on the skilful internal design, configuration, and assembly of its parts. Thus, the CEO would be the 'clockmaker'.

Therefore, this principle rules out alternative drivers often associated with excellence such as the 'great idea or vision' of the founder CEO or the 'charismatic leader' of the large multinational CEO.

Leaving aside his remarkable charisma, Steve Job's obsession with the internal 'machinery' of Apple, his focus on the design, multi-functionality and interconnexion of the Apple ecosystem of products, is a very well-known example of 'clockmaker' carefully adjusting the pieces of the organization towards a clear vision of excellence in its industry.

In the financial services industry, after 2008 Global Financial Crisis JPMC adopted a very purposeful Operating Model [1] that would deliver a franchise with 4 clear competitive advantages (using their own terminology):

- *"Complete"* (i.e. full product/service range)
- *"Global"* (i.e. all continents)
- *"Diversified"* (i.e. balanced mix of client segments, products and geographies)
- *"At Scale"* (i.e. large volume to lever competitive advantage from economies of scale)

Starting from a position described as "*head and shoulders above their peers*" [2] after May 2009 FED's first stress tests, JPMC's CEO embarked on a crusade about a decade long to strengthen the internal wiring of the bank, transforming its operating model along the above 4 dimensions. Mr. Dimon and his leadership team reviewed the bank bottom-up and top-down, carefully measuring progress and seizing the growth opportunities that the post-GFC world provided both at home and globally, so that the operating model was both realigning and growing at the intended scale.

In addition, JPMC's focus on building the organization is well illustrated in its CEO's belief [3] in focusing on the long-term (*"we much prefer to use our capital to grow than to buy stock… buybacks should not be done at the expense of investing appropriately in our company. Investing for the future should come first"*) and not being distracted by the short-term (*"earnings themselves in any one quarter are a function of decisions made over many, many years… the real damage to an organization comes from cumulative corrosiveness of trying to make its numbers"*).

As a point of comparison, right after his appointment in 2010, BoA CEO's Mr. Moynihan certainly made sure to articulate a vision ("*to be the world's finest financial services company*") [4] and strategy for the bank going forward (more detail on BoA's Operating Principles—discussed later on). Nevertheless, his Letters to Shareholders and Annual Reports (either 2010 or 2019) do not show a clear and determined focus on building the operating model (or equivalent concept) with a view to achieve specific competitive advantages in the marketplace; only by 2019, his Letter introduces a framework for Responsible Growth (discussed later) that may be considered a start in the direction of defining a winning operating model.

There are two traits a 'clock builder' CEO must have:

1. A solid vision and roadmap in their heads of how the different parts of the machinery need to align together to perform at excellence.
2. A keen ability to watch for the detail and understand how all fits together in the wider picture.

Mr. Dimon's articulation of the 4 competitive advantages sought after in its visualized Operating Model, his perennial focus on the long-term inoculating from the distractions of the short-term, along with his very vivid depiction about best-in-class management of business performance via continuous measurement and benchmarking (as we shall see later), are a constant year after year in his Letters to Shareholders.

Overall, while Mr. Dimon shows a solid focus on the Clock Building kernel, Mr. Moynihan, probably driven by the urgent need to address BoA's post-GFC problems when he took the helm in 2010, just simply skipped it till much later on. If we were to set a 'score' of alignment to the each trait underpinning Company Excellence's Balanced Design (4 traits across Kernels and Pillars), assigning 2 points for full, 1 point for partial and 0 points for nil alignment, then, the score would kick in for this trait with 2:1 for JPMC.

10.1.2 Genius of the 'And'

Principle: Excellence derives from simultaneously embracing seemingly contradictory concepts; both of them, not just striking a balance between them.

According to the authors, many companies when facing contradiction or alternatives (e.g. change vs stability, low-cost vs high quality and idealism vs pragmatism) tend to choose between them, or strike a balance, a mid-point in between ('the tyranny of the OR'). The authors discovered that success at excellent companies really emanates from embracing both dual contradictory concepts instead ('the genius of the AND').

Here Job's Apple example comes to mind again, by ensuring Apple's products embraced both top-end design with very powerful functionality within the same gadget. He was notorious for challenging teams to keep changing external designs and internal architectures until both high bars were met, never compromising with mid-points or, much less, sacrificing one in the benefit of the other (which was where most competitors in the computing industry sat in the 1980s and 1990s, usually design losing the battle) [5].

In the case of JPMC, the CEO's Letter to Shareholders 2009 [6] makes an in-depth discussion about developing leaders, and dedicates a section to '*the grey areas of leadership*' that illustrates several of the trade-offs that leaders at the bank are expected to embrace ('AND' not 'OR'): '*the rare combination of emotional skill, integrity and knowledge that makes a leader*'; '*leaders work to build something, nonetheless, compensation does matter*', '*big business needs entrepreneurs too*'; '*sometimes leaders should be supported and paid even when their unit does poorly*'. This conceptualization of management and leadership embracing apparently contradictory dualities perdures also in the 2019 Letter.

These concepts that may sound contradictory (under an 'OR' lenses), like '*why should we remunerate leaders when their units do not perform?*', become less so when adopting a different perspective (under an 'AND' lenses): over the long term, the bank is investing in these leaders to learn and become top-class executives, what necessarily passes for having them to experience underperformance and how to learn to revert back these tough situations.

If we look at BoA, although not clearly visible in the 2009 Letter, in his 2019 Letter the CEO equally embraces this concept even by making an explicit reference to 'Build to Last' book, applied to the bank's orientation to serve all stakeholders [7]: '*A concept we embrace—the "genius of the and"—applies to how we are delivering for customers, for teammates, for shareholders, AND for our communities and the society in which we operate*'; '*we believe we must continue to deliver great returns AND help drive progress on societal priorities*'.

Overall, both CEOs show a strong grasp of the Genius of the 'And' kernel, while Mr. Dimon illustrates the concept since 2009, Mr. Moynihan only starts to include it more recently in his 2019 Letter. Once again, full vs partial alignment in this trait respectively would make the cumulative score 4:2 for JPMC.

10.2 Balanced Designed: Two Pillars

I refer these 2 components of Collins and Porras work as 'pillars' because they reflect quintessential cultural traits of the organization, permeating horizontally, and vertically touching every corner of it.

10.2.1 Core Ideology

Defined as the core values and sense of purpose that guides and inspire people across the organization and remain fixed for a long time.

Core values are around 3–6 essential and enduring tenets, not to be compromised for gain or hurry. Purpose is a set of fundamental reasons for the company existence (as seen in Chap. 2).

Across the history of excellent companies, the authors identify Core Ideology as the primary driver, not necessarily shareholder value, adopting decisions often for pragmatic idealism.

The power of the Core Ideology does not stem as much from its content as from its perceived authenticity (i.e. the behavioural commitment-consistency effect from public acknowledgement of it) and its internal alignment (i.e. derived from training, succession management, performance evaluations and other reinforcing mechanisms).

It is difficult to find a financial institution that has not articulated its Core Ideology in the form of Vision, Mission and Values. What is more difficult is to ascertain to what extent people in these organizations really 'buy into' them and embed them as Core Ideology. My personal sample of experience in traditional banks shows that some banks had to change the statements of Values or Mission from time to time, in doing so acknowledging the previous versions were not fit-for-purpose, which make people wonder whether it is worth the effort to trust the new ones. In other banks, perhaps more determined in maintaining their Core Ideology over time, the issue was, in most cases, the high rotation of people, which makes difficult ideology adoption and stickiness; or worst case, the betrayal of Values and Mission by the unscrupulous behaviour from some parts of the organization, making as a consequence Core Ideology to look pretty much like trash paper.

As a contrast, for what I have observed within new FinTechs and neobanks, the elements of Core Ideology are often very strong, especially their Purpose or raison-d'être since many were born precisely as a counterpoint to traditional banks on a mission to disrupt the market and bring a fully new, fresh and friendly banking proposition to clients. What remains to be seen is, as some of these start-ups grow and become large organizations, how their Core Ideology endures the test of scale and time and whether they may feel obliged to adapt and change it to cope with their new scale and challenges.

At JPMC, its CEO identifies the Principles '*to manage the company consistently—and they have stood the test of time*'; these are addressed in depth across the 2019 Letter [8]:

1. *First and foremost, we look at our business from the point of view of the customer.*
2. *We endeavour to be the best at anything and everything we do.*
3. *We will maintain a fortress balance sheet—and fortress financial principles.*
4. *We lift up our communities.*
5. *We take care of our employees.*
6. *We always strive to learn more about management and leadership.*
7. *We do not worry about some issues.*

The last principle catches the eye as it identifies areas that would not be a focus for managing the business, as a counterpoint to established practices in other organizations (e.g. stock price, quarterly earnings, fluctuating markets, short-term economic reports, loan growth, missing budgets for good reason or charge-offs increase in a recession).

The remaining six principles correlate consistently (in brackets below) with the bank's 'Our Business Principles' document, which is organized under four headings[3]:

- *Exceptional Client Services* (customer)
- *Operational Excellence* (be the best / fortress balance sheet)
- *A Commitment to Integrity, Fairness and Responsibility* (community)
- *A Great Team and Winning Culture* (employee / management and leadership)

It is difficult to judge how consistent in time these principles have been within the bank (for instance, 2009 Letter does not address them as directly as the 2018 Letter does), and, more importantly, how visible they are in the behaviour of their +250,000 employees. What it is remarkable though is the fact that, unlike the CEO's letters from many other banks, Mr. Dimon goes to a long length and effort to explain his mind about the fundamental values that underpin JPMC and ensures its translation into a type of public document or charter.

If we look at BoA, Mr. Moynihan makes a purposeful effort as well to address the bank's Core Ideology, both in 2010 and in 2019. BoA's CEO 2010 Letter [9] shares as Vision: '*to be the world's finest financial services company*', followed by 6 Operating Principles:

1. *We are customer driven.*
2. *We are building and will maintain a fortress balance sheet.*
3. *We are pursuing operational excellence in both efficiency and risk management.*
4. *We will deliver on our shareholder return model.*
5. *We will continue to clean up our legacy issues.*
6. *We will be the best place for people to work.*

[3]JP Morgan Chase website.

By 2019,[4] these elements have evolved to become a Mission: '*to help make financial lives better, through the power of every connection*', followed by 4 Values:

- *Deliver together.*
- *Act responsibly.*
- *Realize the power of our people.*
- *Trust the team.*

The contrast between 2010 and 2019 is significant, calling into question how perennial the initial Principles really were (vs the current evolved version of Values) and, as importantly, whether the bank started by defining itself by a Vision to change tack subsequently by dropping this element to adopt instead a Mission element. I do not enter to judge whether this change has been for the better, but rather to point to the fact that it has not been a perennial feature as you would expect of Core Ideology.

Overall, I think both banks demonstrate the elements of the Core Ideology pillar but both with a mixed baggage, BoA showing a more inconsistent approach compared to the past and not addressing them in the 2019 Letter (only does so in their website), while JPMC dedicating an entire chapter of its 2018 Letter to this pillar but failing to explicitly address them in 2009s.

In this case, a 1:1 tie of partial scoring for both contenders in this section, which would make the cumulative score 5:3 for JPMC.

10.2.2 Drive for Progress

Defined as the relentless embracement of change, which stems from a deep human urge for improvement and must originate internally within the organization.

The authors identify 2 engines for this driver: self-confidence, which compels setting audacious goals, and self-criticism, which entices self-induced change in advance to hostile trends from the outside world.

Like the previous pillar, many financial institutions openly embrace Drive for Progress in their communications. However, instead of being genuinely originated within the organization, often it comes from either a 'me too' response to take the next surf wave of opportunity, like the banking globalization trend pre-2008, or an 'enforced' response as a consequence of threats imposed by the environment, like de-leveraging or re-regulation post-2008.

More importantly, very rarely you see self-confidence and self-criticism simultaneously in tandem. I believe this would be the trademark of genuine Drive for Progress because you can witness the 'Genius of the AND' at work: both self-confidence and self-criticism embraced so to pioneer (as opposed to react to) new opportunities and to prevent potential threats.

[4]Bank of America website.

In the case of JPMC, its CEO's 2018 Letter [10], when addressing the respective topics of fortress financial principles and management & leadership principles, makes crispy clear the bank's philosophy behind Drive for Progress:

- In terms of self-confidence: '*A fortress company starts with a fortress balance sheet. We have an incredibly well-capitalized bank with enormous liquidity. We believe that you also need to have strong, properly diversified earnings and margins . . ./. . . (both) provide the ability to withstand extreme stress*'.
- In terms of self-criticism: '*All companies are subject to inertia, insipid bureaucracy and other flaws, which must be eradicated. If a company isn't staying on edge, maintaining a fire in its belly and pushing forward, it will eventually fail*'. And he points why: '*We have an extraordinary number of strong competitors -we cannot be complacent. . ./. . . no matter what our current performance is, we cannot rest in our laurels*'.

In the case of BoA, its CEO's 2019 Letter [11] make use of a very thorough framework approach to define its commitment to Drive for Progress, referring to it as 'Responsible Growth', based on four straightforward tenets:

- *We have to grow—no excuses.*
- *We have to be client focused on our growth.*
- *We have to grow within our risk appetite.*
- *Our growth must be sustainable, which has three elements:*
  - *We have to drive operational excellence.*
  - *We have to be a great place to work.*
  - *We have to share our success with our communities.*

Overall, in my view both banks demonstrate a solid embracement of the Drive for Growth pillar, in both cases only well-articulated in the latter 2018/2019 materials, perhaps BoA showing a more advanced grasp by way of using this framework to structure its annual Letter. In fairness, another tie as both did not explicitly address this trait in their 2009/10 Letters.

This makes for another 1:1 tie in this section, which brings the final cumulative score to 6:4 for JPMC.

Finally, as sense check for this cumulative score of their respective alignment to the Company Excellence framework, *does it reflect in the comparative market performance of both banks?*

Figure 10.2[5] shows the daily stock market performance from 2nd January 2009 to 31st December 2019. Both stocks reflecting first their adjustment trend down from the Sept. 2008 credit crisis to reach simultaneous bottom in March 2009, then to initiate their recovery over the following 10 years, with bumps like in 2012 or mid-2016. Overall, 345% for JPMC vs 146% for BoA, near ×2.4 difference on a

[5] Barchart.com

Fig. 10.2 JP Morgan vs Bank of America—Stock Market Performance (2009–2019). Note: Daily closing price, from 2nd January 2009 to 31st December 2019. Sources: www.barchart.com

long-term horizon, which looks directionally aligned with the conclusions from the comparative analysis using the Company Excellence framework.

The next section will zero-in on the JPMC case to analyze the next level of drivers that underpin its 2 Pillars of Company Excellence.

10.3 Balanced Design: Five+One Key Distinctive Elements

Following Collin and Porras, these are the elements that make the pillars above. The first 2, Home-grown Management and Cult-like Culture, sustain Core Ideology; the next 3, Very Ambitious Goals, Experimentation and Continuous Improvement process sustain Drive for Progress. The '+One' element, Consistent Alignment, binds the other 5 elements all together. Once these elements are present in the organization, deepening the degree of this alignment makes all the difference in the pursuit of company excellence.

10.3.1 Home-grown Management

The continuity of Home-grown Management has had a significant impact in preserving the Core Ideology in excellent companies.

The authors identified 3 distinctive mechanisms in place when this happens:

1. Excellent continuous development and selection of managerial talent from inside.
2. Continuous strong pool of internal candidates for succession at each level of the organization.
3. Continuity in time of the leadership quality.

Once these mechanisms are in motion, they generate a mutually reinforcing effect, a positive spiral, which has a fundamental impact on employees, that is the belief in meritocracy and guarantee of high-quality leadership. This, in turn, impacts the organization facilitating a smooth succession at top management level, which ultimately helps to preserve the Core Ideology.

In the JPMC example, a glance at Jamie Dimon's management team back in 2010 and subsequently to 2020 allows to observe that a majority were home-grown leaders, in particular among lines of business, that successively were growing in responsibility till reaching the Operating Committee (top executive decision-making body at this bank underneath the Board of Directors). All chiefs of line of business, plus CRO and CFO have been 20+ years at JPMC, except for 1 that joined 13 years ago.

As important as the number of home-grown management is the quality of their leadership. In this regard, Jamie Dimon does not make concessions in its 2018s Letter [12]: '*Good leaders have the humility to know that they don't know everything. They foster an environment of openness and sharing. They earn trust and respect. They are not "friends of the boss"—everyone gets equal treatment. The door is universally open to everybody*'.

Now, many other banks have followed a similar pattern of Home-grown Management, *what other ingredients are needed to achieve and sustain excellence?*

10.3.2 Cult-like Culture

That culture reaches a 'cult-like' level is not common, but when achieved it is a very powerful element to preserve Core Ideology because enables people the autonomy to stimulate progress following a best-practice set of expected behaviours.

The authors identified 3 mechanisms to achieve Cult-like Culture:

1. Very high, demanding standards of performance and of belief in the Core Ideology.
2. Early test of cultural fit on employees (if they do not fit, they get expelled).
3. The mechanism is aligned to reinforcing signals (i.e. fervent belief, indoctrination, tightness of fit and elitism).

The expected people impact of Cult-like Culture is a high level of loyalty and ideology-aligned behaviour. The result at organizational level is empowerment and decentralization based on the ideological control that will bound the autonomous self-initiative of people.

In my professional experience, I lived this kind of culture in my time at McKinsey & Co., indisputably for many years the paramount of excellence in management consulting. The firm had developed an extremely well designed and greased operating model, merit of Marvin Bower,[6] which resulted in a very characteristic Cult-like Culture remarkably homogeneous across its offices worldwide. A manifestation of this cult-like feature is the 'priority order' enshrined in the principles of this consulting company: clients are before the firm, and the firm before the individual; partners make sure to indoctrinate new joiners and junior consultants with cult-like features like this one as they climb up the career ladder.

At JPMC, I believe the following excerpt from the 2018 Letter [13] where Mr. Dimon addresses his views about management and leadership, resonates quite powerfully to Cult-like Culture: '*For any large organization, great management is critical to its long-term success. Great management is disciplined and rigorous. Facts, analysis, detail...facts, analysis, detail... repeat. You can never do enough, and it does not end. Complex activity requires hard work and not guessing. .../... You need to have good decision-making process, with the right people in the room, the proper dissemination of information and the appropriate follow-up—all to get to the right decision. Force urgency and kill complacency.*'

It speaks eloquently about Cult-like Culture expected from management in this bank; even we can perfectly visualize this paragraph being shared in their internal management training courses to nurture young talent in their managerial path at the bank.

10.3.3 Very Ambitious Goals

Big hairy ambitious goals are a powerful element for stimulating progress in an organization.

The authors attribute the 'big hairy' adjective to goals that are:

1. Clear, compelling, no need of explanation.
2. More audacious to outsiders than to insiders.
3. Consistent with the Core Ideology.
4. The goal itself is the driver, not the leader.

Like war or an emergency, Very Ambitious Goals generate a high level of commitment and team spirit among people. At an aggregated level, it makes the organization develop the ability to repeatedly set bold goals, the chain of which becomes the driver for continuous improvement.

At JPMC, if we undertake some forensic work and try to distil the goals from the 2009 Letter [14], leaving aside the quantitative and focusing on the ambition embedded, the CEO was aiming at seizing great opportunities for growth across all lines of business; investing in both organic growth ('*into long-term profitable*

[6] 1903–2003, considered by HBS the 'father of management consulting'. He joined McKinsey in 1933, becoming Managing Director of the firm from 1950 to 1967 during which he developed what became to be known as the 'McKinsey Way', remaining in the firm till 1992.

businesses') and acquisitions ('*both small bolt-on and larger ones, provided are at the right price*'); he was visualizing doing so especially in the international space with the aim to provide a global reach for their global clients, accepting the fact that this globality would require large scale.

This ambition, written today, may look to some perhaps anodyne. However, written in 2010, barely 2 years after the GFC and concurrent to the Eurozone Crisis, when the bank had just barely reached back to its performance peak of 2007 and facing a tsunami of re-regulation, this ambition would look like effectively 'big and hairy' internally and definitely externally for many of its large competitors and regulators.

10.3.4 Experimentation

Many best moves in business do not come from strategic planning, but rather from trial and error, opportunism or accident.

The authors identified 3 watermarks underpinning Experimentation:

1. Ambiguity and small incremental steps.
2. Natural evolution drivers (i.e. variation and adaptation to the environment).
3. Purposeful respect of the Core Ideology.

A workplace characterized by these watermarks has a tremendous impact on individuals, making them feel a high level of autonomy for creativity. At organizational level, it leads to a built-in environment that fosters evolutionary progress.

Referring back to JPMC's 2018 Letter about management and leadership, I would highlight [13]: '*Test, test, test and learn, learn, learn. And accept failure as a "normal" recurring outcome*'.

One way the bank has shown in practice this embracement of Experimentation has been in the digital transformation challenge and opportunity. It has been one of the early movers among US incumbent banks, launching an array of POCs and partnerships across many fronts (e.g. SME lending partnership via OnDeck, AI applied to macro trading with Ravenpack and JPMC Coin as a blockchain-based stablecoin), accepting as well failures as they hit (e.g. closure of Finn in 2019 and Chase's online-only brand), and learning from failure to try it again (e.g. launch in 2021 of Chase online digital bank in the UK).

At the same time, the bank recognizes that still could do much more in technology Experimentation, as it reads in the Letter 2018 [15]: '*There are many capable financial technology (fintech) companies in the United States and around the world.. ./... We have acknowledged that companies like Square and PayPal have done things that we could have done but did not. They looked at clients' problems, improved straight through processing, added data and analytics to products, and moved quickly.*'

10.3.5 Continuous Improvement

Company excellence requires a never-ending cycle of self-stimulated improvement and investment for the future.

The authors find 4 traits associated with organizations enjoying this element:

1. They are terribly demanding of themselves.
2. They take continuous improvement as a way of life.
3. They build powerful mechanisms to create discomfort and stimulate change.
4. They build for the long term, while holding high standards for the short term too.

Continuous improvement provokes the individual to question how to do better tomorrow vs what he/she did today. At organizational level, it ensures a continuous drive for progress.

In Dimon's words back in his 2009 biography [2]: '*For any of our businesses you can get a reporting packet and it will tell you everything that's going on, including what's good and what's bad. What we aim for is continuous improvement. It's not like we think we get to a perfect place*'. If we look to test forward this trait 10 years later in the JPMC's Letter 2018 [13], in the section about management and leadership remarks: '*Facts, analysis, detail... facts, analysis, detail... repeat. You can never do enough, and it does not end*'.

There is an obsession about becoming best-in-class at what they do as an organization, which could be observed as well in the constant tracking of key performance indicators at all organizational levels (i.e. Group, Division and Business Unit) and drivers (i.e. market presence, financial and operating). Only by measuring and benchmarking against its peer group the bank can journey in a path of Continuous Improvement. Back to Letter 2018 [16]: '*On an ongoing basis, we analyse and compare ourselves with our competitors at a very detailed level. The analysis we do in more than 50 sub-lines of business and hundreds of products, incorporating not just financial data but also operational data, customer satisfaction and many other measures.*'

As importantly, JPMC does not only emphasize the importance of detailed measurement for sustaining Continuous Improvement, but also requires from its management the expectation to demand more of themselves by acting on the insights gained from that exhaustive analysis, as the Letter 2018 [16] points: '*Our management will always be very critical of its own performance: Acknowledging our shortcomings and mistakes and studying them intensely and learning from them make for a stronger company*'.

The numbers speak by themselves, by the start of 2020, JPMC proudly shows [17]: 2014–19 market share or share of wallet growth across all major businesses [18],[7] with revenue growth higher than industry average in every one of them.

10.3.6 Consistent Alignment

All the 5 elements above that underpin excellence in companies must work together both sustaining the Core Ideology and the Drive for Progress and managing the natural tension between these 2 pillars, since the former strives for continuity while the latter strives for change.

The authors emphasize that it is the whole system that matters, not just the individual elements. The system must be comprehensive and consistent, constantly displaying reinforcing signals around Core Ideology and Drive for Progress manifested in 4 subtle ways:

1. Little day-to-day details that guide employee behaviours.
2. Clustering of elements.
3. Continuous identification and correction of misaligned practices.
4. Continuous creation of new aligned practices.

At JPMC, Consistent Alignment can be traced to the description of its Operating Model [19] (in italics verbatim from the 'Firm Overview' investor report):

- Drive for Progress: Serving '*Exceptional Client Franchises*' with '*Competitive Advantages (Complete + Global + Diversified + At Scale)*'...
- Core Ideology: ... and leveraging '*Unwavering Principles + Long-term Shareholder Value + Sustainable Business Practices*' ...
- Company Excellence: ... equals to '*Resilient Outperformance*'

The Consistent Alignment of all these factors underpins JPMC's remarkable performance over the last decade.

As of 2020 start, JPMC has become undoubtedly the most successful multinational banking franchise, precisely in an industry where, since the Credit Crisis, many global players have shrunk and retrenched back to their local or regional markets. As the chart below illustrates, the bank multiplied by 3 its Earnings in the 2009–2019 period, reaching an unprecedented 19% Return on Tangible Common Equity while delivering historical record Diluted Earnings per Share (Fig. 10.3).

In relative terms to competitors, JPMC has proven its outperformance vs the banking industry over the long term [20]: '*#1 vs peers in the 2000–19 matrix of*

[7]Retail Banking (deposits, credit cards), Corporate and Investment Banking (markets revenues, investment banking fees), Commercial Banking (commercial real estate loans, commercial and industrial loans), Asset and Wealth Management (active long-term fund assets under management; global private banking assets).

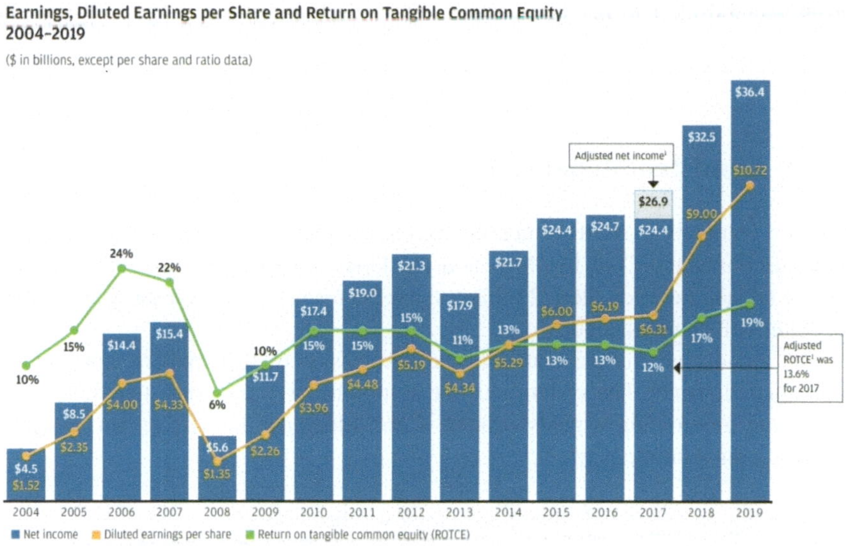

Fig. 10.3 JP Morgan Chase—Financial Performance. 1. Adjusted net income, a non-GAAP financial measure, excludes $2.4 billion from net income in 2017 as a result of the enactment of the Tax Cuts and Jobs Act. Sources: 'CEO Letter to Shareholders 2019' (JP Morgan; 06/04/20)

pre-tax income growth vs earnings volatility' (i.e. earnings growth adjusted by risk) (Fig. 10.4).

Equally, full trust in the sustainability of this Consistent Alignment makes JPMC confident to set ambitious targets again over the medium term [21]: '*(a) 17% Return on Tangible Common Equity; (b) <55% Overhead ratio; (c) 11.5–12% Common Equity Tier1 ratio*'. Before the COVID-19 Crisis, this would be an enviable scorecard that any CEO of a GSIB[8] would be glad to record as his/her successfully delivered medium-term performance.

* * *

Distilling the essence for Company Excellence's Balanced Design is like the philosopher's stone in alchemy, perhaps an art more than a science, where thanks to empirical research such as the one performed by Jim Collins and Jerry Porras allows to peek well below the surface. Perhaps within several decades of deeper advancements in psychology and sociology will enable us, like particle physics did for chemistry, to truly understand the conditions required to turn lead into gold in the practice of moving companies towards excellence.

Having said that, leveraging the framework these authors arrive at, applied within the context of the financial services industry in the past decade, allows us to at least point out a directional alignment between the Balanced Design that JPMC's CEO set

[8]Global Systematically Important Bank ('too big to fail' as per bank regulators' view).

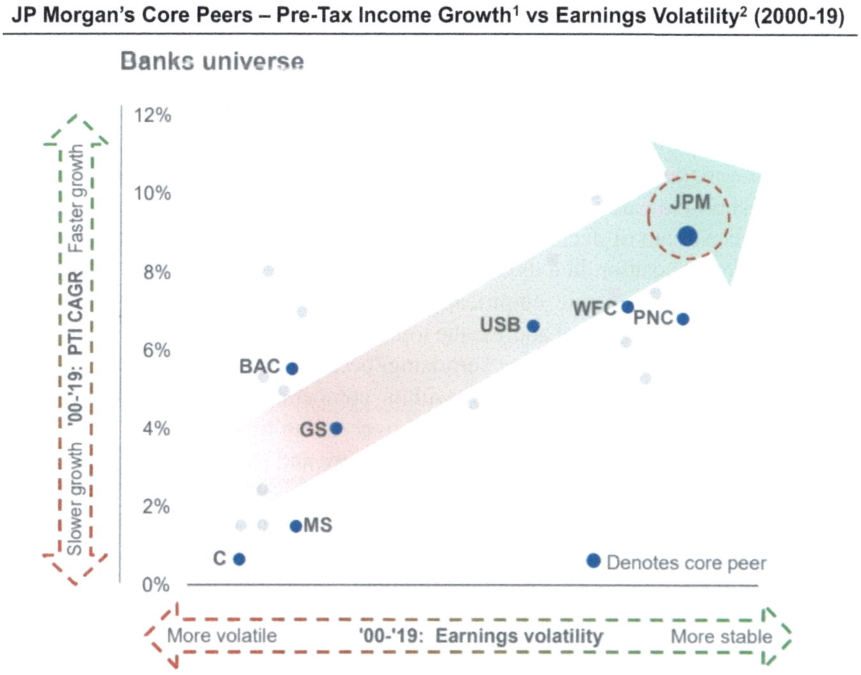

Fig. 10.4 JP Morgan Chase—Comparative Performance. 1. Compound annual growth rate ('CAGR') of pre-tax income ('PTI') between 2000 and 2019. For companies that have not yet reported full-year 2019 PTI, the 2019 data point has been replaced by the last-twelve month PTI as of 3Q19; source FactSet as of 4Q19. 2. Earnings volatility is defined as the r-squared of PTI growth through time. R-squared is a statistical measure that represents the proportion of the variance for a dependent variable that is explained by an independent variable or variables in a regression model. Perfectly equal PTI growth by year equals a score of 100, whereas a perfectly random path for PTI equals a score of 0. Sources: 'Firm Overview' (JP Morgan; Feb. 20)

out to accomplish for his organization and the outperformance it achieved in the marketplace over the long term.

10.4 Considered Decision-Making

The earlier referred statement by Jamie Dimon in his 2018 Letter of Shareholders, '*earnings themselves in any one quarter are a function of decisions made over many, many years*' [22], serves as a perfect preamble to the all-important craft of Considered Decision-Making for Company Excellence. The takeaway is crystal clear, a consistent stream of decisions is what builds performance, and I would argue that a slight competitive advantage on this front will cumulatively have a 'butterfly effect' in Company Excellence.

As mentioned at the start of this chapter, Considered Decision-Making complements Balanced Design to ensure excellence is achieved and sustained. Collins and Porras framework successfully distilled, from an empirical set of data upon a long period, a recipe of the distinctive elements of that Balanced Design. However, the external nature of their empirical effort did not allow them to address how decision-making, day over day, week over week, year over year, impacts the gradual execution towards that design or, once excellence is achieved in the marketplace, how the stream of decisions contributes to or detracts from the sustainability of that excellence position in a dynamic market.

I have not seen academic empirical studies on a cross-section of competing players within an industry that address the topic of how decision-making determines excellence among them. This is not surprising, because such a study would require witnessing internal decision-making within competing organizations simultaneously, at several organizational levels and over a long time, which is usually out of the question due to understandable confidentiality and practicality reasons.

Having said that, I believe professionals that, like myself, have had the privilege of working or consulting C-suites across many organizations over a long time, are in a position to offer, even if in an anecdotical fashion, a 'proxy answer' to this question by pulling from the cumulative observations about decision-making inside companies (obviously with due respect to confidentiality).

Based on this approach, I have put together a Decision-Making framework that identifies the four key elements that need to be tuned to the 'right wavelengths' to ensure decision-making bodies across an organization play 'towards' Company Excellence; these are: Definition, Taxonomy, Governance and Process (Fig. 10.5).

Definition of the decision to make is the starting point, precisely because it is not always evident how to define the decision, particularly when it belongs to a complex chain of decisions. Ideally, it would be structured as a 'go/no-go' decision, though in other cases it can only be reduced to several alternatives or options.

Taxonomy or classification of the decisions, because not all decisions are equal, there is the need to differentiate decisions so as to identify the right amount of information and analysis they may require, as well as the right place and time for making the decision.

Governance, because there must be rules of the game, clear and explicit, about how decisions are to be made and by whom across the organization's hierarchy.

Process, because 'garbage in, garbage out'. Decision-making is a practice that puts together quantitative/qualitative information with a variety of human minds, including their diverse rationality and emotions, in order to problem solve complex issues over potentially a broad array of alternatives, so to agree on a way forward. Therefore, process' quality and rigour will necessarily impact the excellence of the outcome, the decision.

Now, *how to determine that an element in the framework is playing 'towards' (vs 'against') excellence?* Logical question given the lack of systematic empirical evidence available to determine which Decision-Making practices are best for doing so. The way I suggest approaching this thorny topic is to look at the degree of potential bias/noise and politics that the configuration of that element could produce,

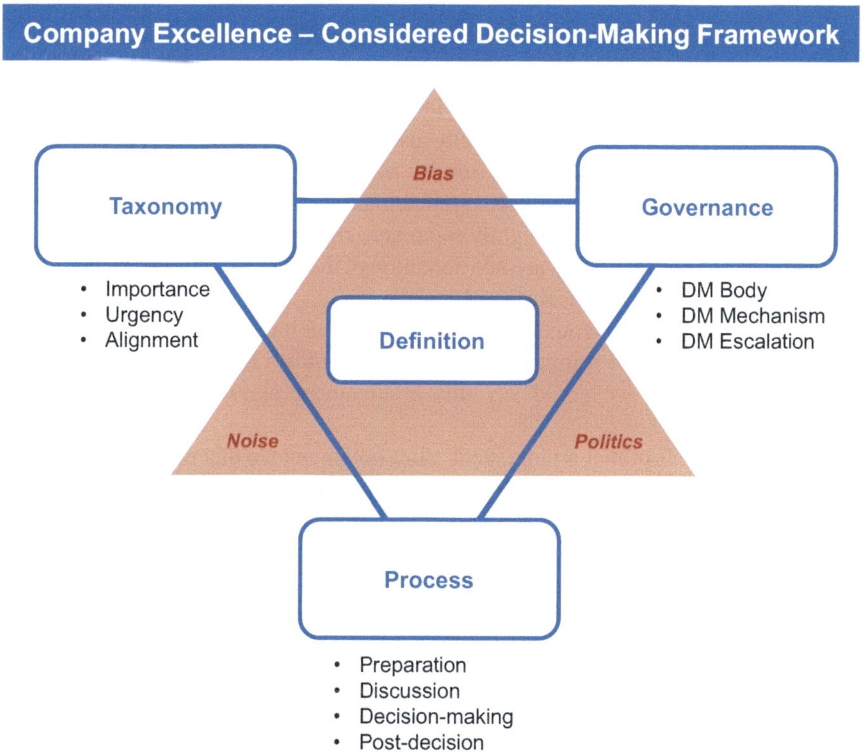

Fig. 10.5 **Company Excellence—Considered Decision-Making framework**. Sources: Sanitized example; AG Strategy & Partners (2021)

so that configurations that reduce (vs increase) bias/noise and politics would play 'towards' (vs 'against') excellence. To simplify terminology, I will refer to them across this section below as 'best practices'.

In this regard, I suggest to follow Professor Kahneman's work about biases (ref. Sect. 9.1 in Chap. 9) and his recent book (along with Professors Olivier Sibony and Cass Sunstein) about noise [23]. When referring to individuals or groups taking decisions, Kahneman et al define *bias* as a systematic error of judgment (e.g. a credit team where individuals systematically take a risk-adverse assessment in like-for-like cases vs average in the industry), and *noise* as the variability in the error of judgment (e.g. a credit team where individuals take widely diverse risk assessments for the same type of case). In statistical terms, they correspond to the average error and the standard deviation of error respectively.

In addition to bias/noise, I suggest adding a 3rd key driver of bad decisions to the mix: *politics*. This one also deserves a book in itself (I would recommend Professor Jeffrey Pfeffer's work [24]), and for obvious confidentiality reasons you will understand I refrain from exemplification in the next sections. It needs to be acknowledged that politics is not a fully independent variable to bias/noise, they overlap (e.g. a political move by an executive could trigger biases in the reaction of other executives, and vice versa); on the other hand, there could be decisions made, under a setting that purposely controls for bias/noise, where a political move on its own account may influence the decision for the worse (e.g. the year-end allocations from a bonus pool formula successfully used in the company over the years—assuming it is well-built then it is bias/noise free—suddenly altered by the political influence of an executive). I will keep referencing 'bias/noise' together like 2 sides of the same coin, while 'politics' slightly separately right after them, in order to signal that while the former generally are non-intentional, the latter is definitely intentional, so they involve separate ethical considerations.

Therefore, if the key elements of the Decision-Making framework in an organization are designed so to minimize bias/noise and politics from the individuals and groups taking them, we could say this arrangement plays 'towards' Company Excellence.

Notice that this 'optimal arrangement' does not guarantee that the decisions made are correct, which would be an impossible demand given that results from decisions are quite often determined by subsequent external factors, from the marketplace (i.e. clients and competitors) and/or stakeholders (e.g. government and society), not always predictable in any shape or form. The only feature that this 'optimal arrangement' ensures is the avoidance of bad decisions (or the minimization of the negative effect) originated because of bias/noise and politics. This in itself could be a source of a competitive advantage given the widespread negative impact these drivers have proven to have on organizations.

Figure 10.6 represents this idea.

A management team (decision body) takes numerous decisions (arrows) through a Decision-Making process, affected by bias/noise and politics, which then roll over into execution until the effect of the decision meets the external world, where both the marketplace and key stakeholders will react to (blue convex lens) and so determine the final outcome (performance target). The illustration purposely keeps the role of the execution 'neutral' to highlight the differences between A and B from a Decision-Making viewpoint only, however, it is obvious that issues of execution, very common, will have an impact as well on the resulting performance.

10.4.1 Definition

In many cases, the definition of the decision is straightforward (e.g. Do we become direct or indirect members of the Target2 payment scheme in the EU? Do we exit this loss-making business unit at this point or continue in it?), which easily results in a 'go' vs 'not-go' decision structure.

Quite often though, the decision forms part of an entangled chain of decisions, which requires careful structuring at inception. Here, timing and cause-consequence (i.e. dependencies) are key factors to consider to unentangle the chain. Ideally, you are looking for structuring the problem as a decision tree so as to identify the decision you are facing first.

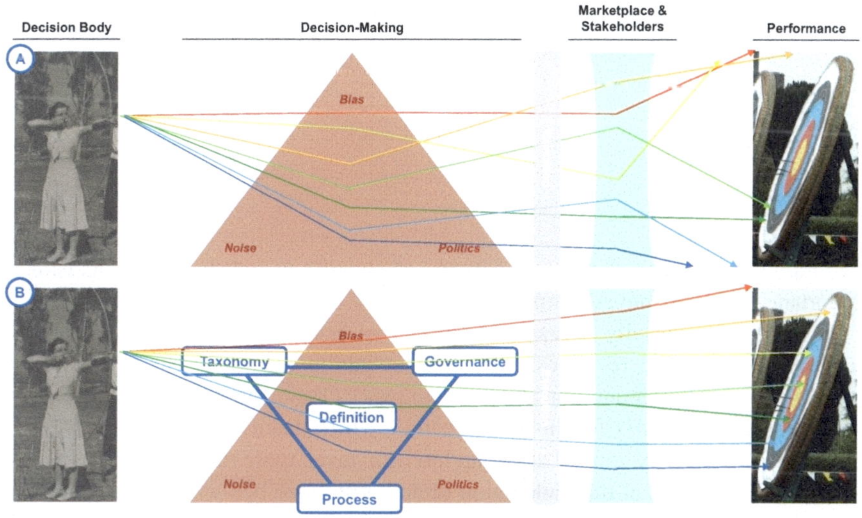

Fig. 10.6 Considered Decision-Making framework—Visualization. Images (edited versions): 'Students in archery class, Scripps College' by Claremont Colleges Digital Library is licensed under CC BY-NC 2.0; 'Adare archery' by Gatsby's List is licensed under CC BY-ND 2.0. Sources: AG Strategy & Partners (2021)

For instance, in a private equity acquisition of a European small payments bank, owned by an Asian group, there was the following situation: the target bank had a legacy IT system (i.e. let us call it V1) that was obsolete and about to be superseded by an upgraded version of it (i.e. V2) developed by the seller group; it was part of the deal to include V2 deployment (at an additional cost); however, the buyer had as well the plan to develop a new IT system for a new business line post-acquisition, and that IT system (V3) would be more state-of-the-art than V2, however, it would cover only 70% of all functionality from V1 or V2, and would take 18 months to be live. *What was the definition of the decision to make?*

The key was to realize that, in terms of timing, right now there was the option to include or not V2 in the deal (i.e. 1st nod of the decision tree):

- If the decision was 'yes' to include V2, then V1 would become V2, and subsequently, we could consider whether to supersede V2 with V3 or leave them in parallel (i.e. 2nd nod of the decision tree).
- If the decision was 'no' to include V2, then V1 would continue to be de facto system till V3 was ready (i.e. no 2nd nod here, as V1 was obsolete and V3 state-of-the-art).

In both cases, the gap between V1/V2 vs V3 needed to be analyzed and factored in.

Therefore, the decision definition was (1st nod of the decision tree): '*do we keep V2 in the deal (go), or do we drop it (not-go)?*' ... the subsequent decisions stem from that first one.

10.4.2 Taxonomy

I would highlight 3 key elements to consider in identifying and classifying decisions: Importance, Timing and Alignment.

Importance is usually measured in terms of potential impact, most often in quantitative terms (i.e. revenues, PBT or asset/liability size) but also sometimes in qualitative terms (i.e. reputation and brand impact). Organizations tend to have some high/medium/low matrix for this classification, which details the thresholds along a mix of metrics, usually applied at Group/Division level, more rarely at BU level; this matrix is usually part of the 'delegation of authority' (see below in Governance).

Best-practice that I have witnessed on this element has been in a UK bank that demanded at Group level that all high and medium importance decisions required a fact-based analysis performed by the business or function sponsoring the decision, analysis that had to be challenged independently by the Group Strategy & Planning team before submission to the ExCo for decision-making. Quite often the challenge review concluded a position opposite to the sponsoring unit, which made the discussion all the more interesting at ExCo!

Urgency captures the timing requirements of the decision. This element is less formally defined, but usually anything that must be decided within the scope of the next 2–4 weeks easily falls in the 'urgent' box.

A mistake that often happens in organizations, especially at BU level, where practices are much more heterogeneous, and sometimes also at Division level, because they easily become clogged by the escalation of unsolved decisions from BUs, is the accumulation of a backlog of urgent decisions which ends up consuming way too much time of the decision-making body's agenda, to the point that anything 'non-urgent' is skipped (i.e. the urgent prevails over the important).

A couple of practices to offset this issue: a) to set a minimum time slot for 'non-urgent important' items, so they can make gradual progress over time and avoid ultimately becoming 'urgent' and so adding to the bottleneck; b) to compulsory delegate all low-importance decisions (sometimes also medium ones) to the next level down (i.e. from Division to BU, from BU to Team Head).

The third element is to define the *Alignment* of the decision vs the Strategic & Financial Plan. Basically, we need to know ex ante to what part of our plan each decision, in particular high and medium importance ones, will have an impact. For a given decision, this can be made concrete by tabulating all the Strategic Priorities so to identify the 1 or 2 that this decision will impact the most; in terms of financials, by identifying the BUs and/or Functions whose P&L or balance-sheet the decision will potentially impact the most (quite often not just that of the sponsoring unit).

10.4.3 Governance

The 3 elements discussed here usually are already formally established in most organizations, definitely in the banking industry because of being a regulated sector (i.e. banking authority's compulsory requirement). In the UK for instance, the Corporate Governance Framework, along with the Corporate By-laws, define these elements.

The *Decision Body* refers to the hierarchy of Board, Board-delegated committees (such as the Audit Committee, Risk Committee and Remuneration Committee), Executive Committee (ExCo) and CEO or ExCo-delegated committees and subcommittees (such as Operating Committee, Risk Committee and Asset & Liability Committee). Each one will have its own charter or terms of reference that define member composition (chair, voting members, non-voting members), scope, delegation of authority, quorum and, quite crucially, decision and escalation mechanisms.

It is quite critical the pondered consideration of the size of the body. As a worst practice committees can reach 30–40 members (sometimes, cross-time zones to make it more challenging indeed in terms of communication!). Beyond smaller size (3–9 usually), best practice is to have a very clear definition of who does vote and who does not vote, ideally the latter members attending only the parts of the agenda within their scope (making the meeting less crowded—and less expensive).

Another best practice is to ensure the voting members represent a heterogenous mix of professional profiles, so it covers in terms of cumulative experience 80–90% of the topics expected within the scope of that Decision Body, avoiding unbalanced representation in favour of business or function. It seems obvious, but unbalanced committees are not uncommon. In this regard, regulators like the PRA/FCA[9] in the UK require banks under their supervision to produce a Board members' individual and collective skillset assessment.

The *Decision Mechanism* refers to rules of the game for taking the decision. For Boards, usually the By-laws will define them, for the rest of the bodies their charter would define it. Nevertheless, surprisingly often many charters do not show explicit rules for decision-making or are at best fuzzy. Without doubt, explicitness and clarity are best-practice here. For instance, for some committees it might be established that the Chair has the only and final say, which by default means that members are non-voting and expected to act more as a consultative body to support the Chair's deliberation; alternatively, it might be set that decisions will be reached by consensus or, in its defect, by majority voting, with the Chair (and sometimes also the Chief Risk Officer) having (or not) a veto to the voting result. This latter element, veto power, brings me to the 3rd element.

Decision Escalation refers to the procedure followed to untangle decision disputes or just 'un-decisions' within committees. The explicit acknowledgement of veto power to the Chair (and other members) could be associated with the automatic escalation of the issue object of veto to the next level up in the governance

[9] Prudential Regulation Authority and Financial Conduct Authority.

hierarchy. In any case, decisions that arrive at a committee for decision should be checked against the charter scope to trigger automatic escalation if it is beyond its delegation of authority.

What quite often happens in committees and subcommittees under ExCo level is that decisions that could be perfectly decided at lower levels get easily and promptly escalated towards ExCo simply because the dynamics among the lower body members are not conducive to take decisions (i.e. it is easier and less risky to bring it up—and less work, by the way). This results in the clogging of ExCos and Boards, and the waste of precious managerial time. Hence, the role of the Chair in avoiding unnecessary escalation is fundamental.

In addition, at this level the problem gets compounded with risk aversion, in particular at Board level, when individuals in these bodies do not have incentives to take risks (i.e. fear of blame for supporting decisions that could go wrong, and no or limited reward/upside in case the decision result is positive). This risk aversion is more noticeable in regulated sectors, like financial services. Boards and ExCos, after the re-regulatory wave post-2008, have become much more risk averse, which was the intent of the regulator in the first place; the question is whether risk aversion might have reached unreasonable levels. I would argue that the SMR regulation in the UK, where the onus of responsibility has been extended to the personal level for non-executives and senior executives, is nowadays making decision bodies sometimes just too afraid to take action, and definitely wary of taking even mild risks.

In terms of Governance, it is difficult to find 'optimal' configurations: a large multinational bank got the charters well-structured (after some Big-4 consultancy intervention) only to throw the baby with the wash water by allowing too many people to sit on the committees; a small bank managed to get the balance of members right across all committees, only to have many committees (for their small size) across the bank, so that near all the same members kept meeting again across each committee; an European bank took care of ensuring its Board and Group related committees worked to best-practice, only to leave the committees at Divisional level and below to develop widely heterogenous approaches to decision-making. There is value from and room for improvement in Governance out there.

10.4.4 Process

The Process of Decision-Making is where the rub touches the road, where information gets in contact with minds, individually and collectively, and where problem solving actually happens to arrive at a decision. If you reduce it to its essence, this is where the managerial function ultimately occurs, by making decisions, and where C-suites demonstrate whether they are worth their salt.

Out of the 4 key elements of the Decision-Making framework, the Process is the one that has the highest potential for improvement and impact in organizations, by a large margin. This links back to this book's Introduction, where we pondered why there is so much mayhem in organizations and hypothesized that the managerial part of the company was the key field where half of the battle in the marketplace was won or lost. This is so precisely because the myriad of cumulative decisions that managers, individually and collectively, must make day in and day out determine over time the company's performance and its excellence.

Within Process I distinguish Preparation, Discussion, Decision-Making and Post-Decision.

Preparation, as for near everything in life, is crucial. When it comes to decision-making you would expect a high level of effort dedicated to preparation, which is commonly the case as far as quantity (judging by the tonnes of PowerPoint presentations and spreadsheet models witnessed at every organization, at all levels), but much less so in terms of quality.

To understand the issue we need to visualize the situation first: preparation for a decision usually starts from a sponsoring unit, either business or function, that wants to get something approved (e.g. product investment, market expansion, disposal of business or staff restructuring), either prompted bottom-up or top-down. Usually, an internal team of that unit generates the proposal, with its rationale, analysis, impact modelling etc. sometimes aided by central function teams or even external consultants. The point is, in a Group with 4–6 divisions and 30–50 business units, chances are that the heterogeneity and mix of quality from these proposals is staggering, which comes down, among other things, to the lack of training on management strategy skillset and related supporting frameworks and techniques which have been covered in previous chapters.

To address this heterogenous quality, large organizations, in particular for Group/ Division level decisions, usually ask strategy teams to either (a) guide and support at inception the business/function to prepare their case according to some establish framework and practice, or (b) challenge at reception the proposal made by the business/function to prepare an independent view for the Decision Body.

Reducing the essence of quality Preparation for decision-making to a common denominator, normally is required:

1. To identify the key questions to answer, following a rigorous framework.
2. To unearth the right facts (analysis, insights) to address each question.
3. To challenge the questions and facts to test their soundness (the questions have to be independent, no overlaps; the facts have to be, ideally, baselined or triangulated with external benchmarks).

The teams can initially convey all of this information in whatever suitable media form, but its essence needs to be synthesized in a structured tool based on a sound framework (i.e. which considers both reward and risk) to support decision-making. In terms of frameworks, I suggest leveraging the ones provided by the HMS depending on the nature of the decision: at BU level, decision related to existing geography / business vs decision related to new geography / business; at Group/ Division level, decision related to the portfolio. In addition, to evaluate the risk side, I suggest following the Risk Management Framework of the institution (an example is provided in the last section). For some particular decisions, falling outside HMS, an ad hoc, MECE framework might be required.

For each piece of the framework, a succinct Overall Assessment would be synthesized from the questions/facts. Subsequently, the Decision Body will deliberate (as described in the paragraphs below) about the 2 final ingredients to add to each piece of the framework: Weight (*how important, high/medium/low, is this piece for the decision?*) and Incline (*is the synthesis for this piece pointing pro/neutral/against the decision?*). The next section illustrates this exercise in more detail supported by a Decision-Making Tool suggested as best-practice.

Discussion is the second element of Process. This is the most challenging one and usually the largest source of bias/noise and politics in the Decision-Making, being heavily influenced by the 3 Governance elements already analyzed.

Let us visualize again: 6–8 executives and a Chair to decide, for instance, the annual assessment ratings of the BU team members; first, *how well prepared are they coming to the meeting? Have they even read the materials?* You can decide for yourself as I am sure many of the readers have witnessed any or both extremes of this sample range: on the one hand, 1–1.5 h quick discussion, averaging 2 min per team member, where individual gut feeling and all type of System 1 biases/noises involved within a collective feeling of 'let me defend my team by subtly sending spanners to others' wheels', determined the decisions; on the other hand, 1 day structured discussion, where each team leader presented the case for their team members, all following the same structure and weight/rating methodology, where the team leaders provided input constructively to the case of each other, where 'borderline' cases were identified and discussed again to ensure fair comparison, and the overall shape of the result sense-checked in the next 48 h... well, that certainly determined a different set of ratings. *Which one would you prefer?... and in particular, if you were the subject of assessment?*

An important player in the Discussion phase is the Chair. Just a training intervention on best-practice to chair meetings would go a long way to improve the quality of Discussions. In an example of an Asian corporate bank, in the Credit Committee, the Chair was very quick at speaking his mind just after the business and risk teams had made their respective cases; the rest of the voting members, used to this habit, conveniently let the Chair lead and they prudently (and lazily) followed (usually supporting what the Chair said), a clear anchoring bias example. After being suggested to change the practice and to speak last, the Chair observed a welcome behavioural change among voting members: first, they started to prepare better for the meeting (i.e. reading the materials), each came with an individually formed view of the case, as a result the debate was enriched and the decisions more nuanced... I would like to think (not hard proof in this example) that the credit quality of the decisions of that bank was overall improved.

Given the criticality of the Discussion element, and the pervasive effect of bias/noise and politics here it goes a bold suggestion for Decision Bodies at Board, ExCo and even divisional ExCo level: hiring a professional psychologist or sociologist to act as a trainer addressing individuals, and as a 'referee' to coach collectively the Decision Body during the Discussion phase (e.g. illustrating live where biases/noise and politics emerge providing the opportunity to the members for course correction and 'returning the Discussion to signal'). Even if the impact in each individual decision is small, cumulatively certainly worth every penny

Decision-Making is the 3rd element of the Process and the summit of the entire framework.

Visualizing again: Thus, Preparation and Discussion for the decision has happened, and let us assume for a moment both were aligned to best-practice (with bias/noise and politics minimized); now time to take a call following the Decision Mechanism set forth in the charter of this committee. If it is a Chair-only decision, easy; if it is not, but there is wide consensus, easy, *but what if there is not consensus?* Horror, we need to vote.

Here the first choice the Chair has, if nothing is set in the charter in this respect, is to suggest whether to have an open vs a secret ballot. Research has mixed views on this choice. Secret ballot helps to avoid the effect of group thinking, follow the leader, clientelism among voting members... on the other hand, it does not encourage a rich Discussion, as some individuals might prefer to hide their preference to the rest or to avoid controversy, also it does not drive to openly evolve positions towards a majority or even a potential consensus, as nobody knows where everyone stands. Once again, a 'referee' could be of service to recommend open vs secret ballot for the voting depending on the specific circumstances of that decision.

A best practice devised to add rigour and reduce bias/noise and politics at the Decision-making point is to set 2 decision rounds, which is highly recommended for important decisions:

- *1st round*: At the light of the evidence and facts shared during the Discussion, the group would determine the Weights (high / medium / low) that each of the pieces of the framework will have towards this decision; after finishing the session, each member individually (without discussing with each other) would define, for each of the pieces of the framework, the Incline (pro / neutral / con) towards the decision; the resulting aggregation across members would become the 1st round vote for each piece of the framework.
- *2nd round*: The group shares the result from the 1st round (open or secret as per the 'referee' judgement), then get on discussing the positions and rationales by each member in particular for the pieces of the framework with more discrepancies; finally, a 2nd round of voting happens (again open or secret ballot as per the 'referee'), which allows an opportunity for each individual to change his/her mind.

At this point, it is worth to introduce recent advances in technology that could substantially improve the way groups vote and take decisions: Swarm Artificial Intelligence (or Swarm AI). Based on natural occurring group decision-making features such as the movements of schools of fish, flocks of birds or swarms of bees, Swarm AI enables human collectives to recreate similar systems moderated by AI algorithms supported via an online platform.[10]

Swarm AI has been shown to significantly increase group decision-making, of both large (20–100 people) and small (3–6 people) group sizes, from sporting events to forecasting financial markets [25]. For instance, in experiments of subjective judgment over 66 small groups, accuracy increased from 69% when members took the judgment individually, to 73% when the group took a plurality vote, and to 84% when the group used Swarm AI, the latter achieving 41% reduction of error rate (at high probability confidence); in addition, an aggregation of swarm decisions by several groups (as few as 3 groups) further increased accuracy to 91%.

How does it work in practice?[11] A question for decision is posed with several potential answers (2–6) shown in the corners of a hexagon in the screen; the individuals of the decision group independently move a visual icon on the screen with their mouse, with the purpose of collectively 'pulling' a graphical puck (i.e. reflecting the aggregated intent of the group) towards the corner that represents their preferred answer. The puck moves as a result of the collective action of all the individuals; each one adjusts real time the position and orientation of his/her icon with different intensity according to (1) his/her intent and (2) his/her reaction to the collective movement of the puck. That intensity is crucial because determines each participant's influence on the puck's move. It is like the popular tug of war game, only that made with many ropes (one by participant) connected at a centre point (i.e. the graphical puck); this centre point moves as people pull from their ropes with more or less strength.

The complex behavioural interactions among the collective are processed by Swarm AI algorithms, which have been previously trained based on natural swarming patterns, empowering the system to converge to an answer that optimizes the group's confidence and conviction.

Swarm AI could be introduced to support Decision-Making in a committee via a facilitator, driving some previous dry runs with the members, and then using the online platform to support the voting session (or the 2nd round voting if it is done under the 2 decision rounds approach). The way Swarm AI tool is constructed, where members move their icons on the screen individually, it would be equivalent to a secret ballot format. Notice that, under a 2-decision round approach, if the result of the 1st round is open and the 2nd done with support of Swarm AI, this would help to capture the benefits of both voting systems.

Post-Decision is the last element of the Process. Once a decision has been made, the real work starts, execution. However, to ensure a smooth and orderly transition from decision to execution is important to consider 2 components:

- What-if Scenarios and Risk Mitigating Actions: Given decisions are made in an uncertain environment, from the discussion should have become clear what are

[10] An example: www.unanimous.ai.

[11] For a live illustration, please check video at: https://unanimous.ai/what-is-si/.

the major drivers of that uncertainty (quite often external factors). The exercise for the group is to think worse/worst-case scenarios based on those drivers (e.g. GDP fall or competitors' reaction), translate them into underperformance (e.g. −20% revenues and +10% costs) and then select some thresholds (e.g. −10% revenues and +5% costs) that would trigger mitigation or remediation actions (e.g. price reductions or hiring freeze). This scenario planning would allow the Decision Body to be ready to react quickly in the case that those negative conditions materialize.
- Implementation Actions and Monitoring: Decisions would normally materialize in specific projects (with a senior sponsor—ideally from the Decision Body—project leader, team, workstreams, milestones, expected results etc., as reviewed in Chap. 6), they generate some dependencies on existing projects, and require communications to specific teams or internal/external stakeholders. These actions need to be captured and its delivery monitored, reporting back to the Decision Body.

All the Post-Decision activity above, along with the recording of the agenda/minutes of the discussions, is best centralized by a Project Management Office (PMO) or equivalent for the whole organization, in liaison with the Strategy team that would support the rest of the decision-making process.

Also, the Strategy team would use the next window (perhaps within a quarterly loop, as per Sect. 3.4 in Chap. 3) to update the Strategic & Financial Plan with the impact of those high/medium important decisions made, in particular from Group/Division level committees.

10.4.5 Tool

This final section suggests a tool that I have been able to roll out with success in a small UK bank, and parts of it are based in practices performed in some other larger organizations.

The Decision-Making Tool (DM Tool) comprises 5 steps that follow sequentially the Process above and include the rest of elements of the Decision-Making framework (note that for Step 2 below, regarding the framework choice, I have picked as an example a decision for an Existing Geography/Business at BU level, and so brought the relevant HMS framework):

- *Step 1*: To document the Decision Definition, Taxonomy (importance, urgency, alignment) and Governance (decision body, mechanism, escalation) applicable to this decision.
- *Step 2*: To succinctly gather and assess the questions/facts related to the decision's impact on the Strategy & Financial Plan as per the Business Model Framework. For each piece of the framework, synthesize an Overall Assessment and judge its Weight (high / medium / low) and its Incline (pro / neutral / con) towards the decision (go / not-go).

- *Step 3*: To succinctly gather and assess the questions/facts related to the decision's impact on the Principal Risks as per the Risk Appetite Framework.[12] For each piece of the framework, synthesize an Overall Assessment and judge its Weight (high / medium / low) and its Incline (pro / neutral / con) towards the decision (go / not-go).
- *Step 4*: To elicit any potential not-yet-captured Stakeholders' angle related to the decision. For the 'Go' vs 'Not-Go' options for the decision, tabulate the Overall Assessments from Steps 2 and 3 (only for the framework's pieces judged to be high and medium Weight). At the light of the tabulation, the members of the Decision Body take a final decision (pro / con) following the mechanism set in the Decision-Making element of the Process (refer to the previous section).
- *Step 5*: To document the post-Decision (what-if scenarios and risk mitigating actions / implementation actions and monitoring).

Figure 10.7 provides a snapshot of the tables used to support Steps 2, 3 and 4 of the DM-Tool.

A key success factor for the usage of the Tool is the ability of the team that develops it to synthesize, for Steps 2 and 3, the 'Overall Assessment' column from the bottom-up detail in the columns of 'Facts/Evidence' and 'Constraints/ Dependencies'. The careful wording and accuracy of this assessment is critical because it will anchor the judgment of the Decision Body. Equally important is the careful tabulation of the high/medium Weight's Overall Assessments into the table in Step 4, which will require to decide if an element is more a 'Pro' of Option 1 vs a 'Con' of Option 2 (and vice versa). Good quality Strategy teams are usually well equipped with this skillset, which makes them natural owners of the DM Tool to support the entire Decision-Making Process.

In the case of the small European payments bank, one particular decision was, in the context of being already a direct member of the SEPA payments scheme (i.e. for small ticket payments), whether ('pro') or not ('con') to join also the Target2 payments (i.e. large ticket payments) scheme as a direct member (instead of indirect member as they were)?

The management team started with the Strategic & Financial Impact Analysis (Step 2) by eliciting key questions following the Business Model Framework, which became nuanced and detailed as they progressed. For instance, in the Market Context piece, benchmarking which competitors were direct vs indirect members of the scheme, and why; in the Client Segments piece, determining what perceived advantages direct membership had, which ended up varying a lot across the segments; in the Value Proposition Definition piece, the pricing impact was of course very different in both options, with much larger net revenue margins per

[12]For a Financial Institution, the Risk Appetite Framework is established at Board level, and it defines the Principal Risks categories (they could vary from one institution to other depending on its business focus). For a given decision not all Principal Risks might have relevance, so some might be considered 'not applicable'.

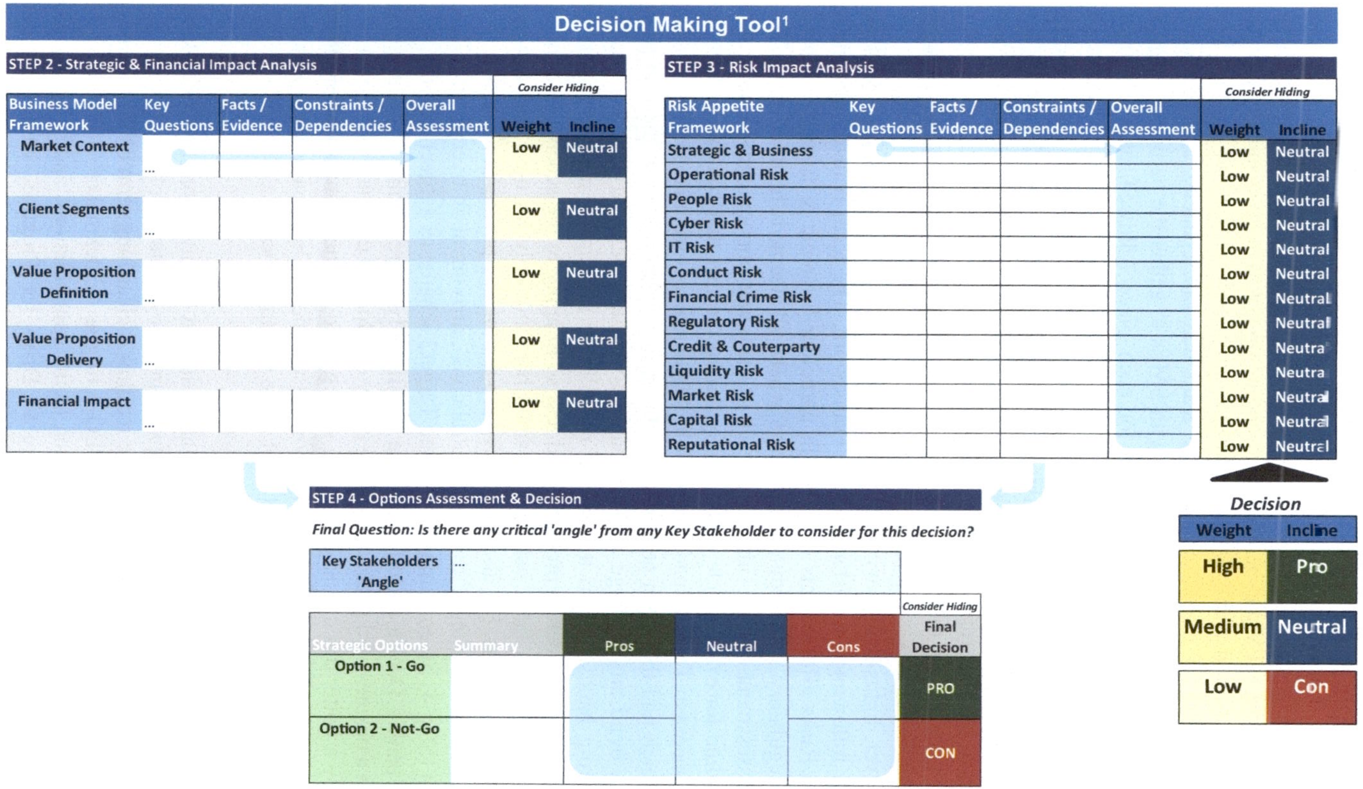

Fig. 10.7 Considered Decision-Making framework—Decision-Making Tool. 1. Steps 2–4 out of 5 steps. Sources: Sanitized example; AG Strategy & Partners (2021)

transaction by being a direct member; in the Value Proposition Delivery piece, the key consideration was the cost and time that would take the project to become a direct member, including the scheme validation; in the Financial Impact piece, all these nuances cascaded in terms of differential P&L business cases for both options, with the resulting NPV gap between both ending up not as large as initially thought because the expected volumes were modest.

In the course of the Discussion, the team had discrepancies and additional questions that required ad hoc sessions with SMEs to gather the pertinent insights. Then, a discussion about the Weights for each piece followed, and the Value Proposition Delivery was considered to be 'high' Weight, given its impact on resources very stretched by the delivery of other projects with higher stakes for the BUs. On the 1st round voting for this part of the framework (Step 2), the Incline resulted in a consensus of 3 pieces 'neutral' and 2 pieces 'con', the VP Delivery and the Market Context (apparently most of competitors were contented with being indirect members, as their focus was on retail clients for which Target2 was less relevant).

However, lights really switched on when undertaking the Risk Impact Analysis (Step 3), following the Risks Appetite Framework. The team realized that many Principal Risks affected this decision, in particular Strategic & Business, Operational, Regulatory and Reputational Risks where all deemed 'high' Weight. The overall assessment of the evidence for each of them was undoubtedly pointing to a 'pro' Incline for every single Risk, mostly due to the fact that continuing with an indirect access to Target2 made the bank highly dependent from its partner clearing bank (which had the direct access); in addition, it was witnessed in the European market a trend among large clearing banks to reduce these services for smaller non-clearing banks, due to the cost of compliance associated, usually providing not enough time to switch providers and less so to apply to the scheme as a direct member. This was a large risk for this small bank not only for their own internal intra-Group payments, but also in terms of reputation as a payments bank. Step 3's 'pros' overpowered Step 2's mixed 'neutral/cons', arriving at an overall 'pro' final Decision (Step 4) by unanimity to join the Target2 scheme as a direct member.

This bank's Decision Body, under a traditionally more intuitive conversation based on a business-led pack, could have easily overlooked the nuance of these risks driven by a hotter discussion centred on strategy and business, and so the decision could have fallen in the opposite direction. Discipline in Decision-Making Process supported by a rigorously managed Tool made the difference.

* * *

Company Excellence is undoubtedly an aspiration for any incoming CEO taking the helm of an organization. As reviewed in this chapter, Collins and Porras' research posits that achieving excellence requires a clear long-term commitment to develop a Balanced Design, with the CEO acting as 'Clockmaker' of that design, embracing the 'Genius of the 'And'' when facing contradictions, and balancing the five elements sustaining Core Ideology vs Drive for Progress, while ensuring alignment among them. Not a small feat.

In addition, excellence requires Considered Decision-Making that permeates across Board, ExCo and all committees across the company in their day-to-day activity. These Decision-Making best practices have a common denominator, the persistent attempt to minimize the bias/noise and politics that unavoidably permeate the dynamics of a group of human beings confronted with the need to agree on a course of action to address complex problems under high uncertainty. A Decision-Making framework is proposed that identifies the decision's Definition, Taxonomy, Governance and Process, the latter supported by a rigorous tool that considers both the Strategic & Financial Impact vs Risk Impact of the decision's options. The cumulative effect of all these decisions, ultimately will drive the company's performance.

Both, Balanced Designed and Considered Decision-Making, the long-term static dimension vs the short-term dynamic dimension, will converge upon time to determine whether or not the company achieves and sustains excellence in its marketplace.

References

1. "Firm Overview—Investor Day presentation" (JP Morgan; Feb.20).
2. "Last Man Standing" by Duff McDonald (2009; Simon & Schuster).
3. "CEO Letter to Shareholders 2018"—pgs. 17–18 (JP Morgan; Apr. 2019).
4. "CEO Letter to Shareholders 2010"—pg. 1 (Bank of America; Mar. 2011).
5. "Jobs" by Walter Isaacson (2011; Little, Brown).
6. "CEO Letter to Shareholders 2009"—pg. 23 (JP Morgan; Mar.2010).
7. "CEO Letter to Shareholders 2019"—pgs. 2, 9 (Bank of America; Mar.2020).
8. "CEO Letter to Shareholders 2019"—pgs. 8–25 (JP Morgan; Apr.20).
9. "CEO Letter to Shareholders 2010"—pgs. 1–2 (Bank of America; Mar.2011).
10. "CEO Letter to Shareholders 2018"—pgs. 16, 25 (JP Morgan; Apr.19).
11. "CEO Letter to Shareholders 2019"—pg. 3 (Bank of America; Mar.2020).
12. "CEO Letter to Shareholders 2018"—pg. 25 (JP Morgan; Apr.19).
13. "CEO Letter to Shareholders 2018"—pg. 24 (JP Morgan; Apr.19).
14. "CEO Letter to Shareholders 2009"—pgs. 4–5 (JP Morgan; Mar.2010).
15. "CEO Letter to Shareholders 2018"—pg. 16 (JP Morgan; Apr.19).
16. "CEO Letter to Shareholders 2018"—pg. 15 (JP Morgan; Apr.19).
17. "Firm Overview"—2020 Investors Day (25/02/20).
18. "Firm Overview"—2020 Investors Day (25/02/20)—pg. 9.
19. "Firm Overview"—2020 Investors Day (25/02/20)—pgs. 2, 13 and 24.
20. "Firm Overview"—2020 Investors Day (25/02/20)—pg. 14.
21. "Firm Overview"—2020 Investors Day (25/02/20)—pg. 24.
22. "CEO Letter to Shareholders 2018"—pgs. 17–18 (JP Morgan; Apr.19).
23. "Noise" by Daniel Kahneman, Olivier Sibony and Cass R. Sunstein (2021; William Collins).
24. "Managing with Power" by Jeffrey Pfeffer (1992; Harvard Business School Press).
25. "Artificial Swarming shown to Amplify Accuracy of Group Decisions in Subjective Judgement Tasks" by Gregg Wilcox, Louis Rosenberg, David Askay, Lynn Metcalf, Erick Harris and Colin Domnauer (2019; Unanimous AI, California Polytechnic State University, University of California Berkeley).

Part V

About 'The Future of Strategy'

The wind and the waves are always on the side of the ablest navigator (Edmund Gibbon).

Congratulations, as Chief Executive Officer of your company for quite a few years, this role has just been combined with the Chairman role. You have been successful at becoming the 'clockmaker' that, with vision and perseverance, has been able to fine-tune a superb body of executives across the organization sharing the best-practice principles of both Leadership & Management. Also, together with your executive team, you have been able to elicit excellence across the company, ensuring Balanced Design and Considered Decision-Making at its core. As a result, you run now the most admired company in your industry, the #1.

However, experienced as you are at this point of your career, your gut feeling is not resting. It is telling you that you must be alert, that the success your company is currently experiencing, justly earned after these many years of hard work, is not guaranteed in time.

Questions pop in your mind... *how do you prepare for the unknown unknowns ahead? Who could help you to understand in depth and time what are the potential systemic opportunities and threats that might be lurking your company and your industry?*

Well, then you think about these bunch of guys that usually put together the packs about the special or strategic topics, and that every year pop up with their strategic planning exercise. Not a large group, many joining from outside consulting firms (oh yeah, these bloody expensive firms full for brainy suits, which the Board ends up asking you to hire when the stakes are high to ensure we got a 'back up' paper). The Strategy team. Weird function, you reflect, always changing; you placed there several leaders in past years, who spent one, at most, 2 years before jumping to run some real business around. *Could they really help you to think deep about these unknowns?*

No sooner the 'unknown' word finishes the last question in your mind, another question thrashes the previous one, stemming from a recent lunch you had with some of your industry peers. Digital, *what the heck is all of that noise about? Is there any real signal you should be worrying from this myriad of start-ups playing techie games in the fringes of your turf?*

Your peers' conversation was a mixed baggage of all possible views, from 'this will destroy us if we let them', to 'let them grow and will buy them out', to 'no bother they will blow up like in the dot-com in the next market crisis'. Actually, you ended up more confused than anything else out of all these arguments.

Your gut again calls your attention, bringing up memories of what happened to those newspapers, music producers or movie rental chains, once these techie start-ups started playing in their space. Gulp! Probably you need to dedicate more time and conversations to clear this mental cloud around digital.

Unfortunately, for these matters there are not many books to fetch that may provide some bearings ... both topics still unchartered territories in terms of long experience, so let us open our imagination to the potential future.

One last time, let us turn to our maritime story…

* * *

The Napoleonic Wars were over a few years ago. In 1815, Waterloo marked the end of the French emperor on land, and, in 1805, Trafalgar at sea, where the British Navy won its most lauded victory in its near 400-year history. Now, Britain rules the waves… at least for this nineteenth century.

A few months into peacetime the Prime Minister, impressed by your organizational ability, asked you to take the more political job of First Lord of the Admiralty (*Executive Chairman*), an unusual step for a career navy officer. Not without some sadness you dutifully but effusively accepted the commission. Your job is now different, it is about looking ahead in time to anticipate what comes next, evaluate alternative policy responses and decide the most optimal way to reorganize fleets, garrisons and support lines to best serve the protection of the sea routes for the British commercial fleet around the world, of course within much tighter peacetime budgets.

Now, looking ahead is easier said than done. You learned from the war period about these few officers (*Strategy Team*) that informally gathered the best information possible about enemies' moves and distilled intelligence to our meetings at the Board of the Admiralty. That 'intel' sometimes made a big difference in your decisions. Since we moved to a peacetime situation the intel gatherings have been more random, less structured and several officers have passed through the post too quickly, so their experience has been somehow diluted.

Coincidentally, a few days ago you just bumped into Andrew Gardiner-Bonham, an old colleague from the Royal Naval College, now under the King's patronage. After a bit of mutual update on recent past careers, Andrew mentions his strong interest and dedication to develop best-practice in research and intelligence gathering to support decision-making across the military. He referred to some new ideas, probably advanced to their time, like creating an integrated department dedicated to this endeavour. We agreed to discuss the matter soon over a cup of tea at my headquarters. It looks like it was time for arranging this encounter.

Sunny, cold afternoon in late March. I rise to greet Andrew as he enters my office, visiting for our 5 PM tea. Some pleasantries and off we shoot into the subject matter. He asks me about what I had heard of the new steam engines for ships. I scratch my head, as trying to push my memory to produce some output, and I recall all started with some pilots attempted by a Scottish inventor or engineer, named William…, William Symington a couple of years after Trafalgar. It was an impressive effort, a stern paddled boat that served for a while towing on the Forth and Clyde Canal. Also, around 1812 in the Firth of Clyde, a man called Bell, Henry Bell, set up a service to Glasgow on a 25-ton steamboat, the *Comet*, which I believe it has been replicated for other routes around, like the *Margery* crossing the Channel and the *Thames* linking with Glasgow (*FinTech start-ups*).

'Well informed! that first one was the *Charlotte Dundas*', Andrew replies. 'If you look at other countries, for instance the US, perhaps you would like to hear about the *Clermont*'. I shake my head to show both ignorance and curiosity. He continued, 'around the same time William Symington and an American inventor by the name of Robert Fulton, financed by a rich politician, Robert Livingston, succeeded in steering a boat from New York City to Albany in the Hudson River at 5 mph all steam powered. This success kicked a myriad of ferry services around many rivers, lakes and the coast across the States. Thus, they are well ahead in the development and deployment of steamboats. Andrew finishes his point by recalling he heard that tons of investment, both private and public, were directed to it.

I nod, replying that perhaps in time steamboats could provide a fine service for passengers and cargo, but I could not visualize it crossing the oceans powering a ship-of-the-line for battle.

'Why not?' Andrew challenges me back with a smile. Guessing he had already the answer, I prudently reply that, as a starter, that exposed paddlewheel, either at the stern or midships, would be an easy sitting duck to be blown away with a single cannon shot, stopping the ship in her tracks immediately. Also, from what I gathered, these engines consumed a lot of coal, which would require the ship to be fully loaded with fuel for an Atlantic crossing, making it heavy and slow. Then there is the problem of refuelling, for which an overseas network would be essential, perhaps feasible to do in peacetime, but risky and challenging in wartime.

'Would these challenges be unsurmountable in time, you reckon?' Andrew asks continuing its Socratic inquiry. 'Well, not necessarily', I respond, 'I guess the winds of change are blowing everywhere, so perhaps some solution could be devised. For instance, you can ironclad around the propeller for protection, play with different fuels for efficiency, perhaps use larger size, stylized ships, like many clippers enjoy, to make the crossing more water drag efficient'.

Andrew then intimates that he had heard of some Swedish engineer playing with early ideas of how to 'hide' the propeller underwater, not so much for protection in wartime but for power efficiency and accurate steering in rough waters. Also, he heard about local engineers experimenting with iron cladding the ships' wooden exposed surface for protection.

'Very interesting insights Andrew', I reply. 'Well, I venture this would lead to an escalating spiral both in terms of speed and manoeuvrability of the ship by playing with the propeller designs; and in terms of protection/attack, new more powerful gunnery would be required to overturn the cladding protection, which probably would lead to stronger alloys and structures for the external cladding, which would demand in turn more gun and explosive engineering'. Basically, I could smell demanding and expensive investment dynamics at play.

'Bingo!', applauds Andrew. 'Exactly, these new technological innovations across steam power, propeller design, fuel quality, iron cladding, gunnery and explosive shells are creating a perfect storm to fundamentally alter navigation (*Digital Disruption*) as we know it, likely driving a closure to the age of sail, and giving birth to the age of steam' (*Digital Transformation*).

'Gulp! Andrew', I say, 'I think I will need you to bring your learned best practices in terms of military naval intelligence to the existing team and start a strategic programme to follow up all these intertwined innovation trends to help me and the Board of Admiralty to think through all this disruption ahead of us'.

'It would be my pleasure', responded Andrew.

* * *

This, my dear CEO & Chairman, is **Strategy in Action** looking at the ***Future of Strategy***.

Strategy Function 11

This first of the two closing chapters is a reflection upon the practice of in-house strategy development at Group, Division, and BU level, confined within the context of my 20+ years of experience serving different banking organizations, internally and externally.

Recent research [1] shows that among large-scale US companies, 57% expect the amount of time and effort they will spend on strategy will grow, versus only 2% think it will shrink. Undoubtedly, for this work many companies will recur to external major strategy consulting firms. 73% of these firms are rated by companies as being of 'high' or 'very high' quality, placing strategy consulting as #1 in the ranking of quality during 2017–2020 among consulting services of all types. Nevertheless, it is systematically confirmed during the last 4 years that there is still a wide gap when comparing perception of quality (in the 66–71% range) with perception of value (in the 37–42% range). Therefore, companies believe work done by strategy consulting firms is of great quality but question its value. Part of the explanation is surely due to the high cost associated with strategy consulting services, but probably another part may be due to the lack of ability within the organization to leverage the strategy work to its full potential.

By contrast, many other companies will entrust the strategy work to in-house strategy teams, usually led and nurtured by former strategy consultants transitioning to the industry. This becomes a more cost-efficient and sustainable way to internalize this work on what becomes a Strategy Function. Frequently, these teams are found at the Group level, and quite often as well at the Divisional or even Business Unit level in large organizations. Commonly they are formed by a majority of former management consultants, and there are connotations of both elitism and top talent associated with belonging to these in-house functions, reason why there are always many internal candidates, in particular with managerial career aspirations, willing to join the function.

Therefore, it looks like the Strategy Function and its output, developing and executing 'Good Strategy' (as per Prof. Rumelt), must be an important matter for organizations. Therefore, *how well is this function usually organized and*

A. Gavieiro Besteiro, *Strategy in Action*, Management for Professionals,
https://doi.org/10.1007/978-3-030-94759-0_11

performed? How can it be improved? What would be the expected company impact from fully leveraging high-quality strategy work?

11.1 Diagnosis

The Strategy Function is one of the less understood, the most ad-hoc organized and the most heterogeneously performed among all other functions in banking. Observing the Strategy Function and the strategy developed and executed during the 5–10 years of a typical cycle time-period for a CEO of Group or Division, you could typically identify up to five dysfunctions or 'malaises':

- *Confusing remit*, which usually overlaps with that of other existing functions such as Finance, Change, COO, Business Management, Chief of Staff or Corporate Development, without clear delimitations and, more importantly, coordination mechanisms in place. This confusion gets often compounded by the Strategy Function embracing orphan teams that do not find a natural 'owner' (e.g. client insight, client experience, internal consulting, cross-divisional synergies, etc.).
- *Ever-changing organizational structures*, which have a persistent tendency to keep being redefined in short time periods (i.e. they last steady 12–18 months at most), and not necessarily cover evenly the Divisions or Business Units, but rather in patches. In some cases, the function entirely disappears for a time, being reconstituted a couple of years later in the next reorganizational wave.
- *Heterogeneous content and practices*, constantly changing depending on the functional leadership change, very rarely building upon previously accumulated know-how but rather quickly dispensing of it, representing a huge, silent loss of intangible value in the organizations. The content issue reaches a climax at activity prioritization with the common confusion between what is important versus urgent, absorbing this team's capacity on the latter rather than the former, becoming a 'continuous firefighting swot team'.
- *Mixed and suffered talent pool*, usually with high drive and expectations of making a great impact, but subsequently experiencing high attrition, poor lifestyle and under-recognition; teams are usually composed of a hybrid mix of ex-consultants and internal people, with a wide variability in terms of possessing the intellectual capability to successfully develop this role; as a consequence, this pool often displays too much heterogeneity and too many gaps in the best practices of the trade.
- *Serendipitous reporting*, which is often the fruit of the power dynamics among C-levels, particularly at Divisions/BUs, where either the Divisional CEO wants the function subservient to his/her needs, or particular BU Heads want it for their own turf, or a Functional Head like Finance or Change ambition to have the 'strategy' title attached to their empire. Paradoxically, as it may sound given the very nature of this function, rarely it is organized as a direct reporting to the CEO because of its small size in terms of the number of people.

To the merit of most of the strategy teams I have known over the years, despite all the dysfunctionalities above referred, they have often managed to provide their stakeholders with a very good, in some cases even extraordinary, level and quality of service.

Nevertheless, given the critical importance that strategy has for organizations nowadays, especially under the ever-increasing level of uncertainty we are experiencing at the start of this twenty-first century and in particular in the banking industry, a paramount reflection raises: *How much more positive impact the Strategy Function could have for the whole organization if many of these drawbacks could be removed? Would this, by itself, become a differentiating competitive advantage for the institution that was able to achieve it?*

Let us think about it for a moment. I would argue that during the first 2 decades of this century the banking sector is facing the most daunting industry dynamics in its entire history. Four major transformational trends are converging:

1. *Continuous waves of financial markets dislocation*: the turmoil that started with the Credit Crisis in 2007–08 has continued underneath, resurfacing in different shapes like the Eurozone crisis of 2011–2012, the near Grexit of 2013, and the China and Oil crisis of 2015–2016. Just as I write the COVID-19 crisis, sparking in March 2020 an unprecedented fast crash of equity markets and oil worldwide, only offset by the main world Central Banks throwing the kitchen sink at it, but impacting global economies in a depth and length of still highly uncertain consequences. All along, the mitigation and revival sponsored by the continued global Central Banks' interventions, which has gone now to fully unchartered territory ($13 Tr cumulative QE pre-Covid plus expected $9 Tr post-Covid, zero interest rate policy, repo market recurrent auctioning, etc.), has helped but also added much more distortion to the natural price discovery function of markets. The general consensus agrees that these interventions have been heavily inflating prices across asset classes, at all lights demonstrated by the divergence of markets versus real economy post March 2020.
2. *Drastic structural shift of global and local financial intermediation vs desintermediation*: these market dislocations have driven the need for profound reregulation, deleveraging, recapitalization, business restructuring, and in-depth rethinking of economics and business models for banks. These trends have caused banks across many geographies, especially Europe, to struggle to make Return on Equity above Cost of Equity and, at the same time, sustain the funding for growth of the economies they serve. Hence, disintermediation has stepped up its capacity with an avalanche of private equity and debt funds taking an increasing role in financing the real economy in particular within private markets, as well as hedge funds and algorithm trading taking on liquidity and market making provision within public markets. Unlike banking, these 'shadow banking' balance sheets are far from regulatory scrutiny, and so they have developed their own growth generating their own dangers and imbalances from progressively lenient lending standards as we have advanced in the credit cycle, generating historical record highs of below-investment-grade corporate debt outstanding and of leveraged investment.

3. *Digital transformation from FinTech revolution, BigTechs and Neobanks*: benefiting from a great confluence of technological advancement, talent availability and excess of funding looking for venture, digital has been driving a full array of new business models to compete head-to-head with traditional financial services in practically all arenas. These trends have driven the surge of myriads of FinTech start-ups with +100 or so having recently reached 'unicorn' status (e.g. valuations > $1 B), new digital banks created in regulatory friendly jurisdictions (like the UK), and key moves by BigTechs (i.e. Microsoft, Apple, Google and Amazon) into financial services. Some incumbent banks (e.g. BBVA, ING and DBS) have spearheaded the reaction to this disruption, embarking on a bold and determined effort to digitalize their business models as a first-mover advantage to earn market share across client segments, product-lines and geographies; but the majority of incumbent banks have been slow to move and are starting to feel it in market share losses. More on this topic in Chap. 12.
4. *Shareholder-to-Stakeholder & ESG paradigm shift*: starting with the Business Roundtable statement about the purpose of the corporation in 2019 [2], signed by CEOs of many US large banks and corporations. It represents an intent for fundamental change, from delivering value to shareholders alone (as consecrated by Chicago Business School's thinking in the 1970s) to delivering value to all stakeholders, including customers, employees, suppliers and communities as well. This change needs to manifest in the way the organization sets goals and takes decisions from head to toe. In addition, the adoption in recent years of Environmental, Social and Government (ESG) principles in corporate conduct has become a de facto imperative globally. Thus, organizations have been striving to digest what does ESG mean for their business and activity. In particular, regarding Climate Change, the recent COP26 in November 2021 (just as I am sending this book to print) has made crystal clear that the largest investment and resource reallocation in history (in the order of $100–150 Tr. to 2050 [3]) is needed for the world to have a chance to keep global warming within the 1.5°C by the end of this century versus pre-industrial era, so to minimize climate catastrophe.

Therefore, within this highly volatile and uncertain context (to which we should probably add the geopolitical fragmentation and conflict derived from the rise of China as a superpower), it would be reasonable to suggest that, more than ever, banks need their Strategy Functions to deliver to the best of their abilities, so they could be able to lead and drive solutions to address the impact from and reaction to these transformational trends. However, instead, most of the banks are falling, as never before, to the lures of the plethora of management and implementation consulting firms all across the world (i.e. Big 4 firms are reporting record employees and profits, and have rebuilt in the last 8 years their strategy franchises from the post-Enron separation of duties period).

Not disregarding the importance that these professional service providers rightly possess as external sounding boards and insight feeders to C-levels, I think it is defensible to argue that organizations need to 'own' their strategy, as opposed to outsourcing it, and for that to happen the strength and effectiveness of its Strategy Function is of critical importance. However, the reality is that this function continues to suffer from the malaises above diagnosed.

11.2 Prescription

Therefore, based on having had the responsibility to create, nurture and lead several Strategy Function teams in several banks, and having worked or collaborated with many similar teams as an external management consultant or senior advisor across my career, this section addresses my suggestions to develop a best-in-class Strategy Function (summarized in Fig. 11.1).

11.2.1 Remit

The remit of the Strategy Function would ideally begin at Strategy Development (i.e. both strategy refresh for existing markets and 'blue-sky' strategy design for new business or geographical markets) all the way through Business Development (i.e. organic & inorganic growth strategy—which includes M&A and alliances/ partnerships) up to, but excluding, Implementation (ref. Sect. 6.2 in Chap. 6). For all of the above, the remit would include as well the Medium-Term Planning, in co-lead collaboration with the Finance function (ref. Chap. 3).

This remit finishes at the very moment where Implementation starts (i.e. where expense and investment effectively get executed), and so other functions take over leading the effort, either under an inorganic process (i.e. Corporate Development and Integration PMO functions) or an organic process (i.e. Change, IT, Operations, HR and Marketing functions).

Thus, it would be also a responsibility of the Strategy Function to engage these functions as necessary to ensure a smooth handover to the implementation stage. A clear framework for delimitation of responsibilities and coordination mechanism would ensure the appropriate alignment of all the above functions together.

On a punctual basis, there could be strategic ad-hoc projects outside the remit above that are allocated to this function. Here the key success factor is not to confuse, as above mentioned, the urgent with the important. Many urgent projects not necessarily are best suited for the Strategy function to lead; on the other hand, these ad-hoc projects must be important to justify this function capability's opportunity cost.

Finally, the remit would include the Group, Divisions and all BUs. In addition, the function would provide all the ad-hoc problem-solving capability required at the three levels, appropriately supported, only when required, by external professional services (i.e. serving as well as the right lead and coordination portal for these services across the non-implementation part of the chain).

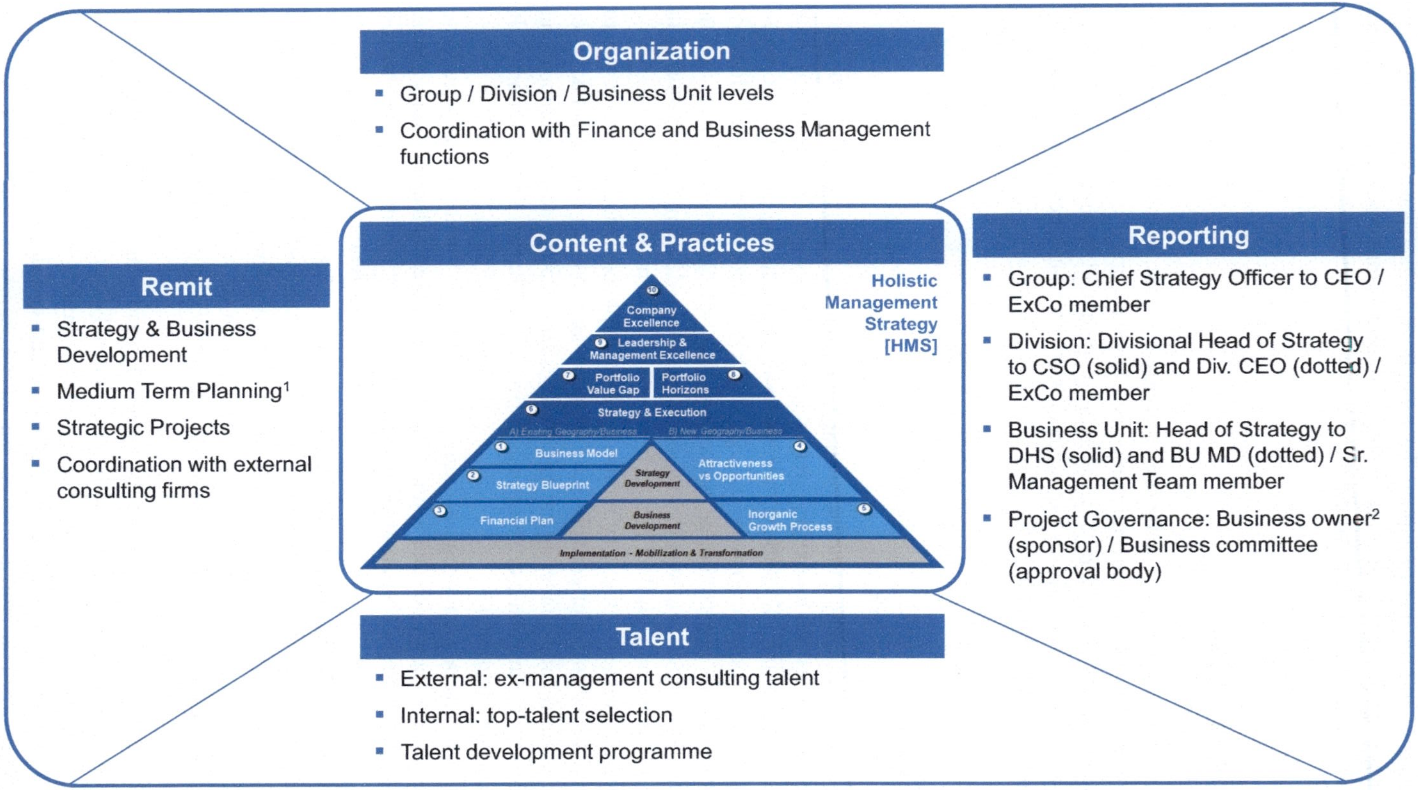

Fig. 11.1 Best-in-Class Strategy Function. 1. Co-responsible with the Finance Function; 2. Business owner: CEO, Divisional CEO, BU MD. Sources: AG Strategy & Partners (2021)

11.2.2 Organization

As a point of comparison, I would suggest looking at the Finance Function. It is often considered to be 'the other side of the coin' for the Strategy Function (i.e. strategy without numbers is like a submarine without sonar).

As a result of the market information imperative from public listing and regulatory supervision, in most banks, the Finance Function is normally very well organized and relatively healthy and steady with regard to each of the 5 'malaises' referred in the diagnosis. Its capillarity goes all the way from the Group, through Divisions, to each of the Business Units like blood vessels in a body, bringing up and down the bloodstream of numbers in the organization. *Why would not a Strategy Function benefit from a parallel organizational model?*

If we visualize it for a moment, this would be a Strategy Function that formulates and develops the strategy all the way to the point of implementation (as per the Remit above), from the Group & Divisional level (i.e. Portfolio Strategy—ref. Part Three-) to the Business Unit level (i.e. BU Strategy—ref. Part One and Two-). The involvement at the BU level is critical, because business strategy gets defined and executed only at this point in the form of the participation choices decided by each specific BU in its respective marketplace.

Given that this organization would parallel that of the Finance Function, it would complement the main Finance processes (i.e. Medium-Term Planning, Budgeting, Forecasting and Reporting), as they ideally should be based on a Strategy outcome and the later be backed by the numbers (ref. Chap. 3).

Importantly, the Strategy Function could coexist at each level with a Business Management Function (i.e. sometimes called Chief of Staff, COO or Executive Assistant function) that supports more the day-to-day job of the chief heading at each level.

Again, a clear framework for delimitation of responsibilities and coordination mechanism would ensure the appropriate alignment of all the above functions together.

11.2.3 Content and Practices

There is some key content to the Strategy Function that needs to be configured on an homogeneous basis for the whole institution, deployed thoughtfully along a proper time horizon and, once embedded, run with an appropriate frequency.

In an ideal situation (conscious that most institutions only practice a part of the list), this content would be five clusters of core frameworks, programmes and processes (from Group, through Division, to Business Unit) as described in the preceding 10 chapters of this book; as a summary that puts it all together from top to bottom (in reverse order to the chapters):

Company and Leadership Excellence:

- *Company Excellence*: a meta-framework that focuses on the combined value of a Balanced Designed, from 'Clock-building' the company and embracing the tension between Core Ideology vs Driving for Progress, with Considered Decision-Making best practice.
- *Leadership & Management Excellence*: a holistic programme to embed the eight THICOSIV dimensions of leadership and management excellence across executives: Thinking and Honesty/Influencing and Communication/Organization and Strategy/Investing and Value.

Portfolio Strategy:

- *Portfolio Value Gap*: to identify and correct any gap between the market value and the sum-of-the-parts valuation by acting on any of the three strategic levers: Business Performance Improvement, Business Organic/Inorganic Growth, Business Restructuring & Disposals.
- *Portfolio Horizons*: to identify the main strategic levers of focus for each BU in the portfolio upon three time horizons and deploying investment with resource reallocation discipline.

New Geography and/or Business Strategy:

- *Attractiveness & Opportunities*: to identify and prioritize a Portfolio View of geographies/businesses for expansion, and to generate a pipeline of Entry/Expansion Cases.
- *Inorganic Growth Process*: to deliver the entry/expansion execution through the four stages of Deal Origination, Valuation, Due Diligence and Deal Negotiation.

Existing Geography and Business Strategy:

- *Business Model*: starting from describing and anticipating, for each BU, Market Dynamics (i.e. clients & competitors), defining the Client Segmentation, Value Proposition Definition (i.e. products/services/pricing/positioning) and Value Proposition Delivery (i.e. front/middle/back, process/policies/procedures, IT, etc...), resulting in the Financial Impact (i.e. scenarios, P&L impact, balance-sheet impact, investment-divestment cases).
- *Strategy Blueprint*: process of development, for each BU, of its Purpose (mission/vision/values/goals), Diagnosis, Core Strategy (client, product and geographical strategy), and portfolio of Coherent Action (strategic priorities and action plans),
- *Financial Plan*: process of development of Financial Drivers' Analysis, Baseline Financial Modelling and Investment/Divestment Cases, which are aligned with the Strategy Blueprint refresh, becoming together the Medium-Term Plan.

Implementation—Mobilization and Transformation:

- *Mobilization*: includes the 5-step process to instil the feel of change of strategy across the organization (i.e. mobilize the village/gather the elders/power up feeling/energize people/build endurance).

- *Transformation*: includes the best-practices for each of the 6 elements of the general management framework (i.e. structure/segmentation/staff/systems/shared values/style).

The Strategy Function would ideally perform and behave across the whole organization as a single body that follows the same best practice both in terms of:

- *Content Development*: problem-solving, project management, stakeholder management, communication, thought leadership and banking knowledge.
- *Talent Development*: recruitment, training, coaching, evaluation, incentivization and promotion/exit.

Both content and practices ought to develop as a cumulative know-how, which is open for an upgrade from time to time, and once upgraded the new version gets adopted uniformly across the team and spread throughout the organization.

11.2.4 Talent

It is well-known that the most recognized management consulting firms such as McKinsey, BCG or Bain invest an inordinate amount of effort in recruitment. At the analyst and associate level, they target the top class of the best universities and MBA programmes worldwide, which themselves have been nurturing and harvesting *la crème-de-la-crème* of students.

All this effort is a cornerstone of their success. Undoubtedly, without this talent pipeline these professional services firms would not be at the level of performance they are in their marketplace. They are looking to harness the high horsepower of the talent pool, to train it with their cumulative best-practices from the consulting trade, and to create high-performing teams that can be able to tackle the most intractable business problems experienced by any of their clients in the multiple industries they serve.

I would argue, a large and complex banking organization should not aspire to have in their Strategy Function less quality of talent than that of any of these successful management consulting firms has. Compromising with less than that would be to jeopardize the effectiveness of the function since it is a key success factor upon which it predicates its existence. Otherwise, it would not be able to produce top-level output, and so unable to 'compete' with external professional services providers, and sooner or later the bank would become again fully dependent on them (i.e. strategy outsourcing). But, *how to capture this talent?*

The good news is that the high-pressure environment within these consulting firms generates a high level of natural attrition, so a constant outgoing stream of well-formed consultants arrives at the market every year. The Strategy Function can be nurtured from these sources with a high level of certainty.

Having said that, it is as well highly recommendable to include internal top talent within the Strategy Function. Several reasons:

1. Internal talent will know the bank and will know banking from its core (i.e. typically no external consultant can provide that level of banking experience).
2. It serves as a grooming ground on strategy for future leaders of the organization (i.e. it can even become an 'obliged' step so to be promoted to certain C-level positions in the future).
3. It accelerates the learning of the external recruited ex-consultants about the bank, its practices and culture.

Now, the internal talent needs to be selected through a rigorous mechanism. I would advocate not to be less stringent than what the consulting firms themselves use, so to ensure the Strategy Function harness the right level of horsepower in its talent pool.

As well, in order to have flexible capacity, there are in the market firms that provide access to vetted pools of ex-management consultants on a project basis (e.g. Eden McCallum, The Barton Partnership). These can complement the Strategy Function as needed so as to ensure a good balance between fixed and variable cost base of personnel, especially important for periods of peak workload for the function.

With that hybrid internal/external talent mix, then it is a question of homogenizing capabilities through the proper Talent Development best-practice of the Strategy Function. Some of the talent may decide to stay in the Function for a long career span; very likely, a majority will prefer to stay for a period (which needs to be set as a minimum of 2–3 years) and subsequently to move inside the bank to other businesses or functions. Thereby, the Strategy Function becomes a key entry and enhancement point of top talent for the organization.

Finally, the Strategy function size ideally must not be very large, definitely not like Finance (although, as referred earlier, it would mimic Finance's capillarity reach across all Divisions and BUs). Usually, a 'pod' of 2, Manager + Associate or Analyst, covering either 1 large BU or 2 medium/small BUs, reporting to a Head at Divisional level supported by 1 pod at the centre, can easily make a 10–15 member team per Division (with 4–8 BUs); plus another team at Group level, usually 15–20 strong max.; altogether, for a large bank with five Divisions (covering up to 40 BUs) would require 65–95 people at most.

11.2.5 Reporting

At the Group level, a Chief Strategy Officer (CSO) would head the function reporting directly to the CEO (or the Executive Chairman/President if the role is split and the responsibility formally attributed to him/her), and member of the Group ExCo. Also, it could be argued whether this role could have a reporting as well, perhaps dotted, into the Board as Executive Director, given the ultimate strategy ownership resides there.

Strategy would benefit from not being a function reporting under CFO or COO, unless his jobholder is deeply experienced on strategy development (not often the case). The main rationale behind sub-reporting has been the small size of the Strategy team, resulting often on a diminished influence capability and weight on the table because usually the CFO or COO lack the experience and formation to articulate strategy matters in a way that a well-formed CSO could do. Strategy and Finance should ideally be sister functions, able to look at each other 'eye to eye' and sit together in the Executive Committee.

In a parallel way, each CEO of division would count with his own Divisional Head of Strategy, reporting solid to the CSO and dotted to the Divisional CEO, being full member of his/her ExCo. The same would happen at the Business Unit level with a Managing Director and his/her Director of Strategy, again with solid reporting to Divisional Head of Strategy and dotted to Business Unit MD. At each level, a small supporting team would sit under each Strategy head person.

Solid reporting is essential to ensure the Strategy Function is a single body that follows the same practices both in terms of content development and talent development (as per above). More importantly, this would ensure the resulting strategy is 1 single edifice, as opposed to the amalgamation of often dissonant 30–40 BU/Divisional strategies.

The dotted reporting ensures the critical input from the ultimate business owner at each level (and, per extension, that of his/her management team) in both the recruitment and evaluation of the respective Strategy head and team.

Finally, it is important to emphasize at this point that the Strategy Function, like other sister functions, ultimately acts as a function that serves the businesses. As such the business owner, at Business Unit, Division or Group, is ultimately responsible for the strategy of his/her business (like it is for its financial or operational performance). Thus, all projects within the Strategy Function have their start with a business owner acting as sponsor, and their end with a business committee (at the right level) acting as the approval body.

11.3 Expected Outcome

A Strategy Function executed as per the prescription provided, I believe, would be a critical engine of value for the organization to the point that could become a distinctive competitive advantage for the institution that succeeds at achieving it.

The benefits:

- Eliminates all the confusion about who defines and how is developed the strategy in the organization, with clear periodic processes and practices, providing a second-to-none capability of ad-hoc, tailored problem-solving at all levels.
- Ensures consistency and coherence of strategy definition, development and execution along the vertical Board > Group > Division > Business Unit, and the horizontal Divisions/Geographies and Business Units within each Division.

- Provides for a smooth and homogeneous handover process from the strategy development stage, through business development stage, up to each functional owner of the implementation stage, both for organic and inorganic growth.
- Guarantees full and close coordination with the Finance function, so that there are not numbers without strategy and vice versa.
- Reduces considerably the dependency from management consulting houses, their expense, and ensures full coordination of the process and outputs from eventual engagements with these firms.
- Enables a continuous source of top talent, external and internal, for all parts of the organization.
- Minimizes conflicts of interest across the institution, establishing very clearly the business owner of the projects and the business committee for approval, eliminating grey areas and so ensuring governance accountability.

The cost, mostly in terms of personnel, of deploying the Strategy Function to full capillarity (i.e. reaching all Business Units) would be more than covered with the expense savings from the recurrent projects from many consulting firms. As a ballpark estimation for a Division with 5 Business Units, a team of 12 (1 head +5 directors +6 associates/analysts) costs c.£1 M per year (2010 estimates) and produces 40–50 projects per year. At McKinsey/BCG rates, this workload is equivalent to £15–18 M cost, roughly half of that for Big-4 providers. Extrapolating for a large bank with 5 Divisions, and including the Group level Strategy team, the budget would be in the £5.4–8 M range for the entire organization.

* * *

In summary, every CEO knows in his heart that a well-designed and embedded strategy along with a disciplined, coherent and consistent execution is the recipe for success. Now, delivering on this vision is often encumbered with many difficulties, which jeopardize the intended results.

In this chapter, I have shared my diagnosis, prescription and expected outcome for how a financial institution can change its Strategy Function from being currently very weakly defined to become a key driver of value-add in terms of content, best-practice and governance, spreading enormous positive impact across the organization.

Fortunately, this becomes an opportunity for the Board and CEO of a bank that decides to embrace it. I would advocate there is huge value at stake in doing this right and it can even constitute a source of competitive advantage… now, the question is back to you, Chief, *are you ready for seizing this opportunity?*

References

1. "Seven Skills For The Future of Strategy" (Feb.2020, The Barton Partnership—Global Research).
2. "Statement on the Purpose of a Corporation" (Business Roundtable; 19/Aug/2019).
3. "Climate Finance Markets and the Real Economy" (BCG, GFMA; Dec.2020).

Digital Strategy 12

This final chapter of the book looks at one of the topics that is at the forefront of many CEO minds across industries, Digital and the opportunity/threat that means for incumbent players. As usual across the book, my take on it will be from a financial services industry perspective; however, I think many lessons could be extrapolated elsewhere. Linking with the previous chapter, this topic would be one in the top list for CEOs to task to his/her Strategy Function.

The chapter starts the discussion with a review of the recent history of the co-evolution of technology and banking that can serve us as a canvas. Then, it introduces the disruptor, the FinTech start-up, explaining its root drivers and diverse focus across financial services. After that, a reflection is shared about the dynamics observed and anticipated between Incumbent Banks and FinTechs, adding the related movements as well by BigTechs.

In the last three sections of the chapter, we move to a meta-level analysis. First, it addresses what digital disruption means for the financial services industry and its immediate future, judging from what was experienced in other already digitalized industries. Second, applying some of the HMS strategy frameworks introduced in the book, I analyze how Incumbent Banks' strategy and execution can successfully deal with the imperative of Digital Transformation. Finally, I raise the head from the desk and set free our imagination to visualize where all of this could be heading over the long and very long term, anticipating the future of Digital Financial Services.

12.1 Historical Context of Digital and Banking

The six flashbacks below will help us to understand the main IT developments acting as underneath currents of social change and, as a result as well, of banking transformation.

First, in 1944 IBM built the Automatic Sequencing Controlled Calculator, the first general-purpose digital computer. In 1959 it evolved into the 1401 Data Processing System, the first mainframe computer dedicated to business applications,

A. Gavieiro Besteiro, *Strategy in Action*, Management for Professionals,
https://doi.org/10.1007/978-3-030-94759-0_12

which led to the 1964 famous IBM 360 series and subsequently the zSeries. Banks were early adopters of 'big irons' (as mainframes are usually referred to in the IT trade) to the point that currently '*92% of the top 100 global banks, nearly 100% of the global credit card transactions and 90% of Fortune 500 companies all depend on the IBM mainframe for computing services*' [1].

Second, back to 1974, Altair introduced the MITS Altair 8800 based on the Intel 8080 CPU, the first personal computer (PC). By mid-1975 Bill Gates and Paul Allen shipped the first BASIC operating system versions for the Altair computer, founding '*microprocessors and software*' (a.k.a. Micro-Soft) [2]. Shortly after, in 1976, Steve Jobs and Steve Wozniak designed the Apple I, followed by the Apple II in 1977, a keyboard computer with colour screen, expansion slots and floppy drive run on Mac OS (operating system). Though the big step up arrives on 12 August 1981, when the IBM PC is launched, with its Intel 8088 CPU, the 5.25″ floppy disk and PC-DOS (by Microsoft) [3], perfectly complemented on 20 November 1985 by Microsoft's launch of Windows, as its intuitive graphic user interface ('inspired' by Apple's). *As of 2019, it is estimated there are 2 billion PCs or equivalents in the world, approx. 75% run under Windows.*

Third, rewind to March 1989, Tim Berners-Lee working at CERN (European Organization for Nuclear Research) in Switzerland wrote a proposal for '*a large hypertext database with typed links*' that ended up implementing on a NeXT workstation, baptizing it as the '*World Wide Web*'. In the following months, Tim complemented his 'www' with the first web browser, html/http protocols and the first web pages. The 'www' was switched on outside CERN in January 1991, and the world stopped being the same ever since. *As of 2019, there are 1.9 bn websites worldwide, a daily circulation of 300 bn emails (btw, 50% spam) and 3.5 Tr. GB of daily traffic.*

Fourth, back to December 1980, where the first concept of 'online banking' is developed by the United American Bank (a Tennessee-based community bank) to allow customers to access their accounts from a TRS-80 computer linked via modem to the phone line in a paid subscription basis. Other major banks in the USA (i.e. Citibank, Chase, Chemical) followed up using a videotext service, also in the UK (Prestel) and France (Minitel). However, it is not until October 1994 that the three key technological developments above (mainframe + PC + internet) get together, when Stanford Federal Credit Union in the USA became the first institution to offer 'internet banking' (leveraging the new world wide web) to its customers. In 1996 NetBank was founded as the first internet-only bank [4]. Quickly during the mid-1990s, riding on the dot-com boom, a large number of internet banking offerings mushroomed around the world. *As of 2020, it is estimated there are 1.9 bn active online banking users worldwide.*[1]

Fifth, in 1994, the same year when internet banking became a reality, the concept of smartphone is born. IBM released the Simon Personal Communicator (SPC), including touch screen, email/fax service, calendar and address book. It is not until

[1] Statista.com

2001 though that the smartphone meets the internet via a 3G network by NTT DoCoMo in Japan, making videoconference possible. However, the true milestone arrives on 29 June 2007, when Apple launches its iPhone, the first smartphone that offered a full visual and easy access to the internet with a browsing experience similar to that of a PC. Soo after, in September 2008 an Android-based smartphone (T-Mobile G1 or HTC Dream by HTC) became Google's answer to iPhone, with many manufacturers joining this standard. Undoubtedly smartphones became a revolution and game-changer for the mobile phone industry as we knew it until then, but also for other lateral industries such as music, video and, in time, retail banking. *As of 2019, out of 9 bn mobile phones worldwide, 5 bn are smartphones.*

Sixth, the concept of 'mobile banking' starts with the SMS banking service via traditional mobile phones, linking for the first time to the web in 1999 (Fokus Bank, Norway). However, the introduction of the smartphone in 2007 and its 'Apps' makes mobile banking a widespread reality as soon as 2008 across many countries simultaneously. *As of 2018, out of the approx. 69%* [5] *of world population that has a bank account (c. 5.2 bn), 39% (c. 2 bn* [6]*) use online and/or mobile banking, growing 10% per year.*

After 50 years of IT evolution intertwined with remote banking access innovation, we find incumbent banks worldwide, still sitting on their closely held traditional mainframes, serving an important and growing part of their customer base remotely via internet-based access, who use either their desktops or laptops at home (online-banking) or their smartphones or tablets on the go (mobile-banking). At the same time, these banks maintain large networks of employee-intensive branches and call centres to provide approximately the same services only that to a dwindling user base. In other words, way too much capacity redundancy for the taste of any banking cost structure. Admittedly, the financial services industry at this point, willingly or not, is already in a fiercely competitive digital transformation.

It is at this specific historical juncture that a new actor enters the scene: the FinTech start-up.

12.2 Surge of FinTech

What is FinTech? The term is the combination of 'financial technology' and refers to new technologies that seek to improve and automate the delivery and use of financial services. At its core, FinTech is utilized to help companies, business owners and consumers better manage their financial operations, processes, and lives by utilizing specialized software and algorithms that are used on computers and, increasingly, smartphones.[2]

FinTech originally referred to computer technology applied to the back office of banks or trading firms. However, in recent years FinTech has grown explosively on the back of a broad variety of technological interventions into personal and

[2]Investopedia.com

commercial finance. From 2014 to 1H-2021, c. $0.8 Tr of cumulative investment has been directed to FinTech by Venture Capital, Private Equity and Corporate M&A via north of 22,300 deals. This 1H-2021 reached $98 Bn and 2456 deals, on its way to top the 2019s record of $215 Bn and c. 3800 deals [7].

Why? FinTech growth has been caused by the confluence of four key trends in a delicate time for the financial services industry, the aftermath of the 2008 Credit Crisis:

1. Alignment of smartphone's widespread adoption with the maturity and complementarity of several cutting-edge IT technologies: Application Programme Interfaces (API), Cloud, Big Data, Artificial Intelligence (AI) and the newly minted Blockchain (a new type of Distributed Ledger Technology (DLT)[3] underpinning Bitcoin, the first so-called cryptocurrency, launched in January 2009).
2. Change of consumer behaviour preferences, driven by the immediacy of delivery and customization enabled by the smartphone, allowing for high-quality customer service everywhere, anytime. This trait has been quickly picked up by retail goods and services industries and distributors, launching Apps that elevated the convenience and simplicity of digital interaction to paramount importance. This heightened experience has driven more enhanced and demanding customer expectations, which quickly expanded to other industries, like financial services.
3. Demand for alternatives in financial services post Credit Crisis. The latter made customers very disgruntled with incumbent banks, who heavily lost trust from society. People's financial lives across many countries suffered enormously, and they found banks often quite oblivious to their needs (i.e. mortgage foreclosures, credit tightening). Adding insult to injury, a large array of banking scandals popped up such as Payment Protection Insurance (PPI) mis-selling, small SME restructuring abuse, LIBOR manipulation, massive unauthorized account openings, etc..., resulting in a vivid image that fully justified customers' mistrust.
4. Regulatory barrier reduction driven by some governments to facilitate competition within the financial services industry, paving the way for many and diverse new entrants across products and segments. In the West, the UK and the US were some of the pioneers, but it was soon followed by many other jurisdictions. In the East, China, Hong Kong and Singapore also enjoyed a regulatory space already fertile for BigTech companies to expand their customer offerings into financial services, on the back of already high customer penetrations in smartphone-related communications like messaging, chats and social media at large.

Where? The four drivers described have concurred pretty much globally, and so a large array of start-ups have mushroomed in key cities around the world; albeit logically the concentration of talent and resources have made some of them to become 'FinTech Hubs' in terms of quantity, quality and investment volume.

[3] Important to distinguish the cryptocurrency from the DLT technology underpinning it; here I am referring to the later, which has a life on its own in terms of use cases well beyond the crypto space.

Among those hubs, we find some that would be the 'usual suspects' given their traditional pre-eminence in technology (San Francisco) or finance (London, New York or Singapore); but also, we find a number of less 'conventional' cities (Sao Paulo, Los Angeles, Berlin, Boston, Bangalore or Mumbai), as gathered by the Top 20 Global FinTech Hub ranking [8].

Overall, as of November 2021, there were near +26,300 FinTech start-ups worldwide, 41% in North America, 35% in EMEA and 24% in Asia-Pacific.[4]

In addition, it is important to add another location, the cyberspace, and within it, the cryptocurrency world. Here I include the ecosystem of DLT platforms (like Bitcoin, Ethereum, Solana or Cardano) and the respective cryptocurrencies that support their transactions, along with the myriad of Distributed Applications (Dapps) built upon them to serve a variety of user cases. Within those Dapps, a subset fully dedicated to financial services has come to conform to the Decentralized Finance (DeFi) space.

This world is purely internet-based, globalized and with its own generated governance, without any or light government regulatory framework depending on each jurisdiction (although this will start to change soon). It is linked to the fiat currency world via exchanges that produce the on/off-ramp service to convert fiat to crypto currencies and vice versa.

Overall, as of November 2021, there are +10,000 cryptocurrencies globally, with a total market capitalization equivalent to $2.5 Tr.[5]

How? FinTech and its underlying technologies enable the development of alternative business models for the provision of financial services to cover customers' needs [9]: pay, save, borrow, manage risks and get advice.

The traditional banking model has been satisfying these needs with a large array of products, respectively: cards/ATMs, deposits/funds, mortgages/consumer loans, insurance/derivatives, investment advisory. However, it does so with some gaps in terms of speed, cost, transparency, access and security. These gaps have provided the opportunity for creativity to step in to devise alternative FinTech solutions based on a combination of underlying technological innovations across multiple areas as referred to earlier.

For instance, successful FinTech start-ups like Revolut (UK-based, created in 2015), in just 5 years has been able to grow a 10 million customer base across the UK, EEA countries, Switzerland and Australia serving them only via their App, starting with a core proposition based on: 140-multicurrency pre-paid card usable across 150 countries, transfers at no-fee, banking FX exchange pricing, and draw cash in ATMs for free (up to a monthly limit). To that core, Revolut has been adding a variety of financial and non-financial services like travel insurance, trading, cryptocurrencies, concierge, airport lounges, vault deposits and wealth management. All of this has been achieved without a previously known brand or banking license

[4] Statista.com

[5] Tradingview.com

(only recently received one in Lithuania and it plans to apply for them also in the UK and Ireland).

FinTechs are effectively unbundling the banking business model. Start-ups pick up specific product lines, client segments and geographies where they develop deep inroads and then, as they grow, their business models evolve pivoting in different directions. Overall, there has not been near any area in financial services that they have not touched having, so far, a profound effect on retail and commercial payments (where estimates point to a 25% market share loss for incumbent banks), SME lending (in China, FinTechs gained 90% share in 2020 lending) and consumer finance (in the USA, FinTechs gained 70% share in 2020 lending) [10].

In addition, within the crypto world, based on blockchain platforms like Ethereum, DeFi solutions have been launched in recent years as an alternative to traditional financial services, leveraging the large money supply created by cryptocurrencies (e.g. Decentraland for digital asset/NFT trading, Terra for payments, Compound for lending/borrowing).

12.3 Dynamics of FinTechs Versus Incumbent Banks

During 2012–2014, the narrative of disruption threat associated with the FinTech revolution, positioned as a radical alternative to traditional banks, not surprisingly met a sceptic reaction by the industry. Being Vertical FinTechs comparatively such small-scale players focused on very niche product or segments, led to banks not to bother too much, with a few exceptions that were already 'digital believers' (i.e. BBVA, ING or DBS).

As we moved towards 2015–2016, prompted by the potential of some of the underlying technologies like blockchain, cloud and AI, a debate among financial institutions started to emerge, sparking curiosity among banking executives. As a result, they began to take on experimental moves aiming to understand the new innovations more in depth. Many Incumbent Banks opted to pursue one or several of these three routes [11]:

1. Joint-FinTech Programmes: several banks joining a collaborative effort around specific digital innovation themes, often along with non-bank participants such as governments, VCs, telecoms, FinTechs, BigTechs... where banks usually provide management mentorship, financial sponsorship and branding in exchange for exposure to and learning from the FinTech network. Examples: R3's Corda blockchain consortium, FinTech Innovation Lab and Linux Foundation's Hyperledger Fabric project.

2. Lead FinTech Programmes: individual banks leading a hackathon/incubator/accelerator of FinTech start-ups, in which each bank controls the programme scope, and sets exclusive partnership terms with a selection of FinTechs, exploiting first-mover advantage on those that result successful. Examples: Barclays Accelerator (with Techstars), UBS Labs (i.e. Innovation Lab in London, Wealth Innovation Lab and Y Think Tank in Zurich), Wells Fargo Start-up Accelerator or Mastercard Start Path.
3. Own VC Fund/FinTech Subsidiaries/In-house Innovation: individual banks establishing separate entities within their group with dedicated specialist teams to explore either:
   (a) Arms-length VC portfolio of investments in FinTech start-ups. Example: Santander Innoventures $200m corporate VC fund, with +27 investments (as of 2019) such as Kabbage, Ripple, Digital Asset Holdings, Tradeshift, Market Finance or Nivaura.
   (b) Direct portfolio of stakes in FinTech subsidiaries. Example: BBVA's array of direct investments like Simple and Madiva in 2014, Spring Studio and Atom Bank in 2015, Holvi in 2016, OpenPay in 2017, SolarisBank, Sinovation Ventures and Anthemis in 2018, and PrivacyCloud in 2019.
   (c) Dedicated Digital Innovation teams with monographic dedication to certain FinTech innovations. Example: HSBC establishing digital teams dedicated for each division (Retail & Wealth, Commercial Banking, Investment Banking) or BBVA client solutions teams per division reporting into a global head.

During 2017–2018, and possibly because of the closer interaction and mutual learning derived from the routes above, there was an evolution from competition to cooperation, where both sides started to genuinely explore the best avenues to form win-win partnerships. On the one hand, many Vertical FinTechs were successful at coming up with much more advanced solutions vs traditional offerings; on the other hand, Incumbent Banks enjoyed large customer franchises, brand and scale that FinTechs lacked. Hence, lot of room for partnerships, which ultimately derived as well into acquisitions.

While some FinTechs were designed from inception as fully digital banks with banking license and core digital IT stack, so-called New Digital Banks or Neobanks, like Fidor Bank[6] in Germany, Starling Bank or Monzo in the UK; other start-ups, as they grew, decided to apply for banking licenses mostly to benefit from the deposit insurance for their customers, like Revolut or Zopa in the UK.

From their side, as Incumbent Banks gradually realized that digital was not a noise but a strong signal, they started to confront tough decisions about strategy for digital transformation. Watching the lead from the 'digital believers' (for instance, BBVA began its digital transformation journey as early as 2009) and moving beyond the initial three routes above of FinTech exploration, the issue has become now how to internally reorganize the legacy bank towards a Digital Bank.

[6]Eventually acquired by French Groupe BPCE.

The reaction from incumbents to evolve their own Digital Banks mostly has focused on consumer payments and SMEs (business segments registering the bulk of market share losses to FinTechs) and has followed one of the first three models below (vis-a-vis Model D exemplified by a Neobank) depending on the degree of reliance on the existing proposition and infrastructure of the incumbent [12] (Fig. 12.1):

- OCBC in Singapore launched Frank (May 2011) as a digital brand where only the front-end of the proposition was genuinely digital, resting on the channels, back office and bank charter of the parent bank. This option usually concentrates on a narrow client segment (e.g. millennials), tailoring the value proposition accordingly.
- The next step in the ladder of digital bank models is to digitalize the channel as well, like is the case of Simple (launched in July 2012 as a checking account partnership with The BankCorp and subsequently acquired by BBVA in 2014). Including the channel in a holistic way (both mobile and online) provides a more complete digital CX for users but still limits the innovations in the proposition to the flexibility that the back-end of the legacy systems is able to provide.
- The next level is that of a digital bank subsidiary, like Hello Bank! by BNP Paribas (November 2013), where the entire front-middle-back end is digital from inception, relying only on the banking licence and capital from the parent bank. Here the new subsidiary is designed from scratch with digital best-practice in mind, with modular, cloud-based, API-based back-end systems, agile implementation and end-to-end CX. Quite often, the digital core offering levered by traditional financial services technology players like Finastra[7] or new FinTechs in this space like 10×, Thought Machine, Mambu or Leveris.

Realizing the complexity inherent to mixing digital and legacy, this last model has been followed more recently by many incumbents: Marcus by Goldman Sachs (for retail & commercial banking in 2016), Openbank by Santander group (for retail banking, 100% digital relaunched in June 2017, repositioning a 1995-founded online bank subsidiary), or Mettle by RBS group (for SME banking in October 2018).

Finally, to make things more fluid and exciting, regulators in the UK, EU and other jurisdictions have embraced the concept of Open Banking via two Payment Services Directives (PSD1 and PSD2). Their intent is to open access to Incumbent Banks' customer data by authorized third party players so to reduce banks' oligopolistic power, improve competition and empower back customers with regard to their data privacy and usage. PSD2 enables Payment Service Providers (PSPs) to act on behalf and with authorization of the bank's customers to either access his/her bank account information (Account Information Service Providers, AISPs) or to initiate payments from his/her bank account (Payment Initiation Service Providers, PISPs). In the UK, as of 2020, there were c.300 PSPs acting in one or both capacities, serving 2.5 million customers and businesses, producing c.60 bn of API calls annually.[8]

---

[7] Fruit of the 2017 merger of D+H and Mysis.

[8] Openbanking.org.uk

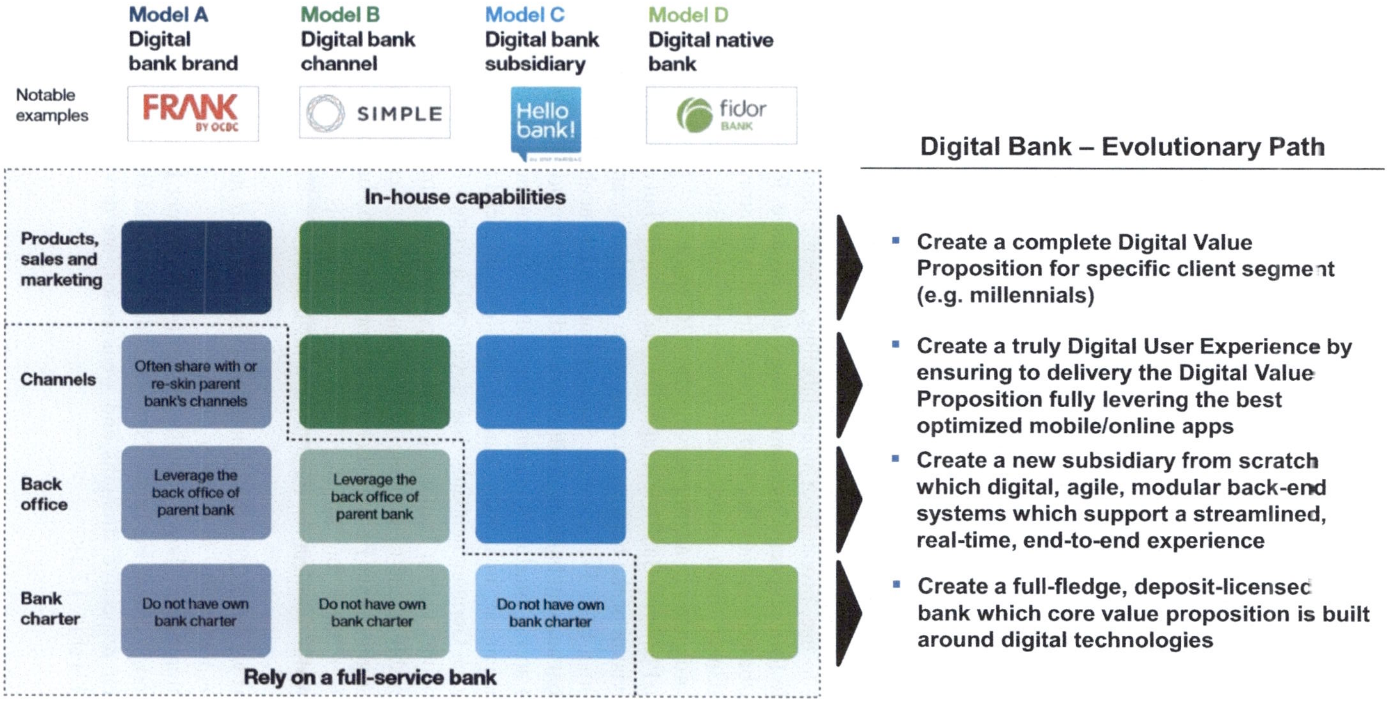

Fig. 12.1 Digital Banks. Note: Frank belongs to OCBC; Simple started on a checking account partnership with The BankCorp and now belongs to BBVA; Hello Bank belongs to BNP Paribas; Fidor Bank started VC owned and now belongs to BPCE Group. Sources: 'Designing a Sustainable Digital Bank' (IBM Sales & Distribution—White Paper; Jun.15; IBM). Reprint courtesy of IBM Corporation © 2015; "FinTech Food for Thought v.7" (Angel Gavieiro; Aug.17; AG Strategy & Partners)

Two key technologies have been essential to enable Open Banking:

- Open APIs: software developed by FinTechs or banks that enable a standardized interoperability among systems. In the context of PSD2, incumbent banks or new players need APIs to provide access to their systems in order to become compliant with open banking regulation, as well as to exploit the business opportunities that this new game provides acting as AISPs or PISPs.
- Cloud: BigTechs (i.e. Amazon via AWS, or Microsoft via MS-Azure) have stepped up to put together large IT investments in mainframe servers and internet connectivity required to allow the core IT stack of financial institutions (and that of many other industries) to live outside their walls (fully or hybrid), so to enable a 24/7 omnichannel, real-time, mobile access for both customers and employees.

This evolution has been embraced by FinTechs and banks with the development of entirely alternative value propositions, making Open Banking a reality:

- Banking as a Service (BaaS): Neobanks, small Incumbent Banks, or e-money licensed Vertical FinTechs, that develop API-based software solutions to enable third parties to use, privately or white-labelling, specific banking products and offer them to their respective customer bases. For instance, Railsbank, an international UK-based e-money licensed player, offers a wide array of APIs to enable banking products (from multicurrency accounts, domestic and cross-border payments, cards, etc.) to anyone serving the B2C space.
- Banking as a Platform (BaaP): leverages the BaaS concept but critically involving also the provision of the banking license, to serve either a captive or a mutually shared customer base. For instance, Starling Bank, a UK neobank, starting from its core current account banking product, opened its platform to a curated group of FinTechs to access Starling's customer base and offer multicurrency transfers, wealth management, insurance, lending, personal financial management, etc. SolarisBank, a German neobank, has developed a complete digital stack of banking products with a banking license to provide its infrastructure to third parties to enable them to become digital banks across Germany and, using passporting rights, other EU jurisdictions. By providing the banking license, the BaaP provider takes on the regulatory burden for its client's customers (e.g. KYC/AML[9] verification, local deposit insurance).

Therefore, as we finish 2021 the open question is: *how the dynamics among these different players will evolve in the near future?*

The illustration below shows how the moves by Incumbent Banks (both Large and Challengers), Vertical FinTechs, New Digital Banks and BaaS/BaaP players, enabled by their respective strengths and weaknesses, are driving four potential aggregations [13] (Fig. 12.2):

[9]Know Your Customer (KYC)/Anti Money Laundering (AML), both typical banking regulatory schemes.

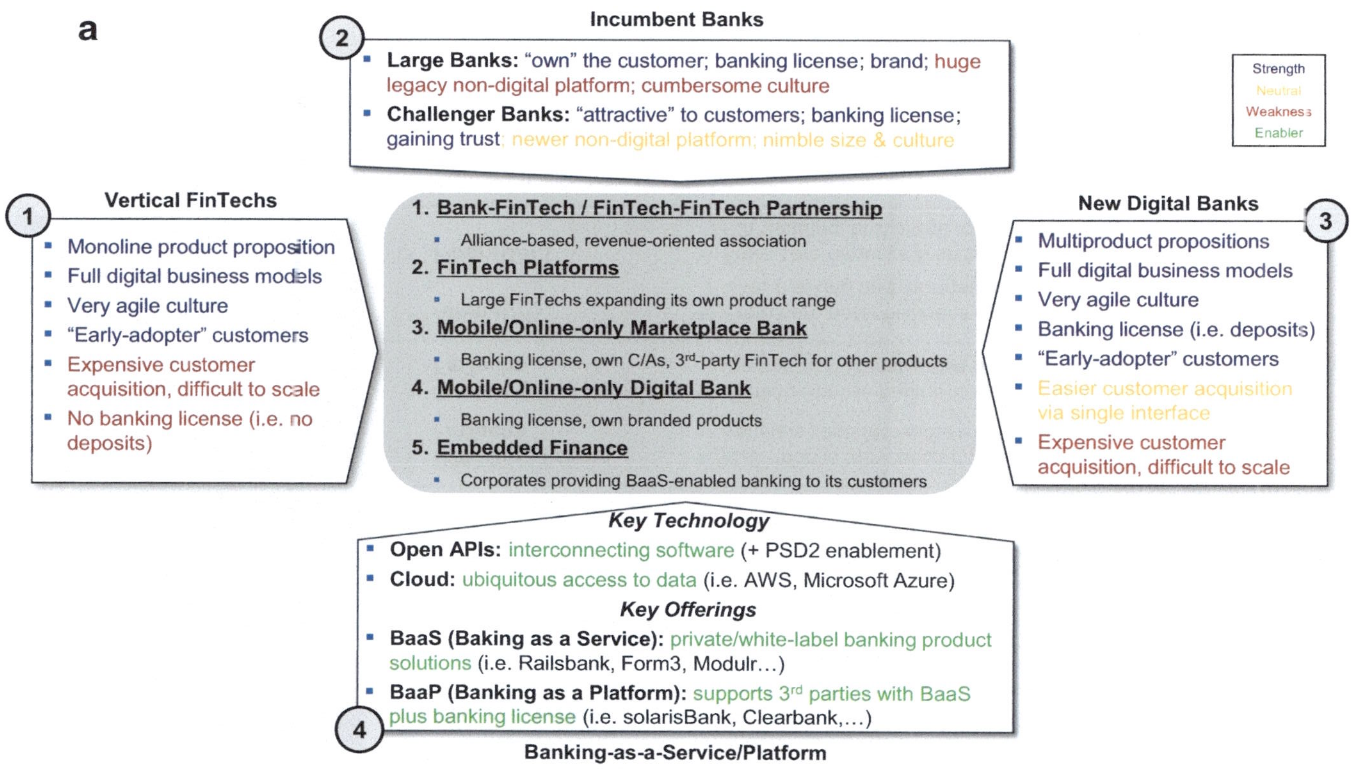

Fig. 12.2 (**a**, **b**) Fintech vs incumbent banks dynamics. Sources: 'The New FinTech Bank' (Chris Skinner; Apr.16; blog); 'FinTech Food for Thought v.7' (Angel Gavieiro; Aug.17; AG Strategy & Partners)

b

	Examples	Description
1 Bank-FinTech / FinTech-FinTech Partnership	**Metrobank / Zopa (UK)**	Metrobank to lend its funds via Zopa to consumers & microcompanies
	Moven / Payoff / CommonBond (US)	Moven (digital banking platform) aggregating Payoff (credit card debt advisory) and CommonBond (student loan refinancing) propositions
2 FinTech Platforms	**Square, SumUp, iZettle, Payleven**	From mPOS-acquiring… expanding to P2P SME lending, P2P payments, POS-MIS,…
	PayPal, AliPay, Paytm	From e-Wallets… expanding to P2P SME/consumer lending, online payments,…
3 Mobile/Online-only Marketplace Bank	**N26 (Ger.) / some FinTechs**	N26 (mobile bank accounts) offering Transferwise (P2P int'l transfers) and MoneyBeam (P2P payments)
	Starling (UK) / some FinTechs	Sterling (mobile bank accounts) offering Pay by Bank (payments), Transferwise (P2P transfers) and MoneyBox (ISAs)
4 Mobile/Online-only Digital Bank	**Atom (UK)**	From core personal loans & savings… extending to 3rd party SME banking and mortgages
	Fidor (Ger.)	From core deposits & social network… extending to 3rd party P2P lending, brokerage, crowdfinancing,...
5 Embedded Finance	**Shopify (Canada)**	From e-commerce online platform for SMEs… extending to offer business bank account
	Tesla (US)	From selling electric vehicles… extending to both offer & underwrite insurance

Fig. 12.2 (continued)

- Bank-FinTech/FinTech-FinTech Partnerships: in principle, a majority of FinTech-FinTech alliances would be revenue-oriented trying to complement products over a given customer franchise or sharing respective customer franchises. In the case of Banks, partnerships are as well equally relevant when they are cost/efficiency oriented, in particular with FinTechs focused on robotic process automation (RPA) or back-office optimization for instance.
- FinTech Platforms: in this case a successful Vertical FinTech, as it grows, starts to expand its product offering to the existing customer base, and/or to extend to serve adjacent customer bases, and/or moves into new geographies so to generate economies of scale. As shown earlier, Revolut has followed this path just up to the point to decide to apply also for a banking licence.
- Mobile/Online-only Marketplace Bank: follows the FinTech-FinTech partnership approach however based upon a pre-existing digital bank platform from one of the partners, by which the concept of BaaP enters into play. As referred above, Starling Bank is a very complete example.
- Mobile/Online-only Digital Bank: this is the path followed by many Neobanks when they decide to own the whole spectrum of product offerings provided to their customer base and includes also the digital bank subsidiaries (or partly digital versions) of Incumbent Banks. Good examples referred to earlier are Atom as neobank and Mettle in the case of RBS.
- Embedded Finance: this is the ultimate fruit of the BaaS and BaaP models, where following a B2B2C model, they enable corporates to offer banking products (from account-to-account payments, to checking and saving accounts, cards, insurance. . .) to their customer base. This combination has an enormous potential given it can revolutionize many B2C industries, and an obvious major threat to Incumbent Banks and card platforms (i.e. Visa, Mastercard).

On top of these five aggregations amongst players, it is reasonable also to expect consolidation via both corporate M&A moves by Incumbent Banks and FinTech unicorns (those with valuations +$1 bn), and of course exits or wind downs like any VC-driven investment boom would experience (e.g. dot-com boom and bust period in late 90s and early 00s).

While, as we have seen, the dynamics between Incumbent Banks and FinTechs have been very intertwined, the opposite has been the case between Incumbent Banks and the crypto space.

On the one hand, banks showed interest early on in Bitcoin's underpinning technology, blockchain, involving themselves in promising experimentation via consortia like R3's Corda or Linux Foundation's Hyperledger Fabric; though very few projects have reached production level, at most some DLT solutions have been adopted within confined bank's walls (like JP Morgan's Coin).

On the other hand, banks have been much more prudent in getting involved with cryptocurrencies themselves because of concerns about regulation and compliance (many of the platforms are permissionless[10] and anonymous, so very challenging to perform KYC/AML compliance on customers). Since 2018, some institutional investors, wealth managers and a few custodians have been playing with the adoption of crypto as an asset class, initiating small size investments via ETFs[11] on cryptos.

Nevertheless, the proliferation and wide adoption of cryptocurrencies, and within them the introduction of stablecoins like Tether or USDC (which generally try to mitigate the high volatility[12] of cryptos by being collateralized by one or a basket of fiat currencies), has prompted the reaction from Central Banks and monetary authorities across the world. *Why?* Because countries need to keep control of their money supply to ensure both effectiveness of monetary policy's transmission and financial stability. The fear is that proliferation of cryptos at a scale in a country would risk the fragmentation of its financial system, increasing the likelihood and frequency of financial crises (like the USA experienced between 1836 and 1913 when it did not have a central bank [15]). In this regard, let us watch the space of what will happen in El Salvador since the adoption of Bitcoin as a co-official currency in September 2021.

The official response has been the roll out of serious plans around the world to introduce Central Bank Digital Currencies (CBDC), under different scheme types (i.e. one-tier vs two-tier) and different target segments (i.e. retail-only vs both retail and wholesale). People's Bank of China has pioneered the efforts, in 2014 setting up a task force to study the case, in 2016 launching an institute for prototyping, in 2017 testing it with commercial banks, and in 2019 initiating pilots with its CBDC (e-CNY) in specific regions [16]. The EU, UK and USA, albeit more prudently, are following suit.

CBDC do matter to Incumbent Banks, in the first place because CBDCs under a one-tier scheme type would mean the Central Bank opening directly accounts with customers, bypassing the banks, which could jeopardize their deposit raising capability. Second, because it will require banks to adapt their systems and domestic rails, as well as to upgrade their customer offering related to CBDC's underlying DLT capabilities (i.e. smart contracts within a DLT platform allow for enormous creativity in terms of product development, as the DeFi boom is showing).

To finish this section, it is in order a reflection on BigTechs since they have not been addressed so far within these dynamics: BAT (Baidu, Alibaba and Tencent) in the East and GAFA (Google, Amazon, Facebook and Apple) in the West.

BAT have been a key engine of digital transformation in financial services starting in China and expanding across Far-East Asia, successfully leveraging their

[10] Anyone can join that DLT platform; as opposed to 'permissioned' platforms (like Corda and Hyperledger Fabric) where there are some requirements for joining and so the participants can be scrutinized for KYC/AML.

[11] Exchange Traded Funds (ETF).

[12] Jan.2019–Jun.2020, 1-month annualized volatility for Bitcoin 50–250% and Ethereum 25–200% vs S&P500 25–100% [14].

large consumer bases from social media and messaging to take on their financial services offering. Examples like Alipay (Alibaba) or WeChat Pay (Tencent) in payments or AntFinancial (Alibaba) in SME lending, have gained large market shares in China. This success has extended to launching the first Chinese digital banks like WeBank (Tencent) and MYbank (Alibaba). In addition, BAT have joined other large incumbent banks and/or TMT companies to develop digital ventures: Baidu and China Citic Bank forming aiBank (China), Ant Financial and Tencent joining Ping Ann to create ZhongAn Insurance (China) and the latter partnering with China Citic Bank to form HK Virtual Bank (HK) [17].

GAFA, per comparison, have been more prudent in their entry into financial services, surely cautious of the regulatory challenges associated with banking licenses, and so concentrating in areas non requiring the latter such as payments (Apple Pay, Google Pay, Amazon Pay), SME lending (Amazon Lending) or exploring the new territory of stablecoins (Facebook's Libra project, now rebranded as Diem). Many incumbent and new digital banks have established partnerships with some GAFA, particularly in payments but also with broader ambitions like the recent Goldman Sachs and BBVA partnerships with Amazon.

Beyond GAFA, a 'traditional BigTech' like Orange has made a very promising move launching the mobile-only Orange Bank [18] in France (2017) and Spain (2019), leveraging a wide partner ecosystem (Wirecard,[13] Backbase, inWebo, IBM's Watson, Salesforce, Franfinance and Moneythor), while Orange assuming a coordinator role.

I do not think it is far-fetched to anticipate within the next 5 years more ambitious movements by BigTechs into digital banking because of five key competitive advantages they enjoy:

- State-of-the-art command of technology and talent pools
- Sheer size of capitalization and investment resources
- Economics from cross-subsidization with own platforms' no-banking activity
- Large and highly engaged consumer base (i.e. #touch points, time spent in platform)
- (For Amazon and Alibaba) Large global network of B2C/B2B SME base

FinTechs, Neobanks, BaaS/BaaP players, crypto/DeFi, BigTechs... they either did not exist or were not looking at financial services barely a decade ago. At this point of the narrative, I think we can start to understand the current perfect storm for Incumbent Banks.

[13] Unfortunately for Orange Bank, Wirecard fell into disgraced bankruptcy in 2020, a good reminder of the risk side of partnerships.

12.4 Digital Disruption Impact on Financial Services

The question to answer in this section is: *what will be the expected impact on the financial services industry as a whole?*

In March 2017, McKinsey & Co. published the result of a cross-industry research to understand the effect of digital disruption across industries [19]. The analysis covered 10 industries along the spectrum of the digital penetration curve (as perceived by respondents), from as low as 31% (Consumer packaged goods) to as high as 62% (Media & Entertainment), being Financial Services (39%) slightly above the average (37%).

From an economic performance viewpoint, the researchers found that when industries go through a process of digital disruption a double pattern emerges:

1. Overall reduction of the revenue and profit pools in the industry, both becoming worse (on average c.6 percentage points) once the industry fully digitalizes
2. More skewed distribution of the pools, concentrating on fewer winners versus a long tail of underperformers (Fig. 12.3)

On the one hand, these patterns could be highly concerning for players, and especially CEOs of Incumbent Banks. On the other hand, CEOs intuitively know

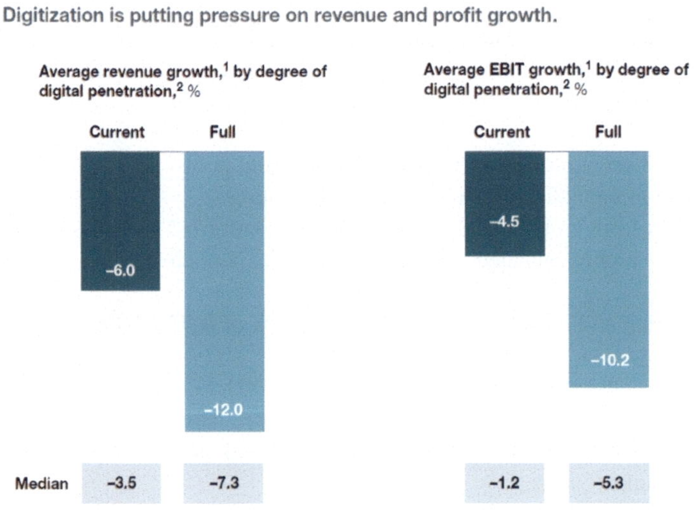

Fig. 12.3 Impact of Digitalization across Industries—Performance Evolution. (1) We based our model of average growth in revenues and earnings before interest and taxes (EBIT) at current and full digitization on survey respondents' perceptions of their companies' responses to digitization, postulating causal links, and calculating their magnitude through both linear- and probit-regression techniques. (2) Digital penetration estimated using survey responses; average digital penetration across industries currently = 37%. Sources: Exhibit from 'The case for digital reinvention', February 2017, McKinsey Quarterly, www.mckinsey.com. Copyright (c) 2021 McKinsey & Company. All rights reserved. Reprinted by permission

that the financial services industry counts with two quite large, though not unsurmountable, barriers of entry:

- Brand: the trust associated with a strong brand is #1 factor that customers across generations (Millennials, Gen.X and Baby Boomers in the UK and US [20]) look at a financial services organization. Trust goes together, not surprisingly, with high expectations by customers and regulators in terms of security, a non-negotiable must.
- Regulation: traditionally a high barrier of entry in terms of requirements about capital, funding, liquidity, compliance, conduct, operational reliability, security and management experience demanded by most regulators. However, as seen earlier in this chapter, regulators have been prudently relaxing these barriers in some jurisdictions to promote the entry of new competitors.

Proof of the power of brand as a barrier is illustrated by the comparison of deposit raising efforts among UK digital banks during 2018–2019: albeit all of them had to pay a substantial rate premium vs incumbent banks (i.e. c.50 bps[14]), the volume raised by 'new-branded' like Monzo (£390m in 12 months) or Starling Bank (£600m in 18 months) does not tally with the volume achieved by 'brand extensions' like 'Marcus by Goldman Sachs' (£6.5 bn in 8 months).

About the regulatory barrier, it is widely acknowledged by start-ups grown in FinTech-friendly jurisdictions (like the UK) that when they decide to internationalize, their market entry becomes quite tough in the US or some EU countries due to not only differences in regulatory frameworks, but also tougher expectations by some regulators.

These barriers can be overcome with time and resources (and so costs, requiring revenue scale to ensure profitable growth, in particular for FinTechs with shorter runways), but definitely serve to slow down the impact of digital disruption in the financial services industry. A recent cross-industry comparison by PwC [21] about market share loss to new digital entrants to a given industry shows that, after 10 years penetration, financial services has lost between 2 and 18% depending on the business line considered, while other industries recorded market share losses within the 35–70% range (Fig. 12.4).

A critical aspect that CEOs at Incumbent Banks would be interested to understand is: *what is the degree of potential disruption for each banking business line?*

The illustrations provide insights, at two moments of time during the last 10 years of FinTech disruption, about where the 'damage' has been concentrated in terms of client segment and product. The left-hand chart shows a snapshot of when the FinTech start-ups were midway in their disruption path (2015, McKinsey [22]), while the right-hand chart shows a snapshot of where digitalization is heading today (2020, PwC [21]); both charts provide a comparison of client segment target (or appetite) vs product line penetration (or maturity) (Fig. 12.5).

[14] Avg. deposit rates of Digital vs Incumbent banks (2018): (UK) 0.92% vs 0.44%; (US) 0.79% vs 0.27% [20].

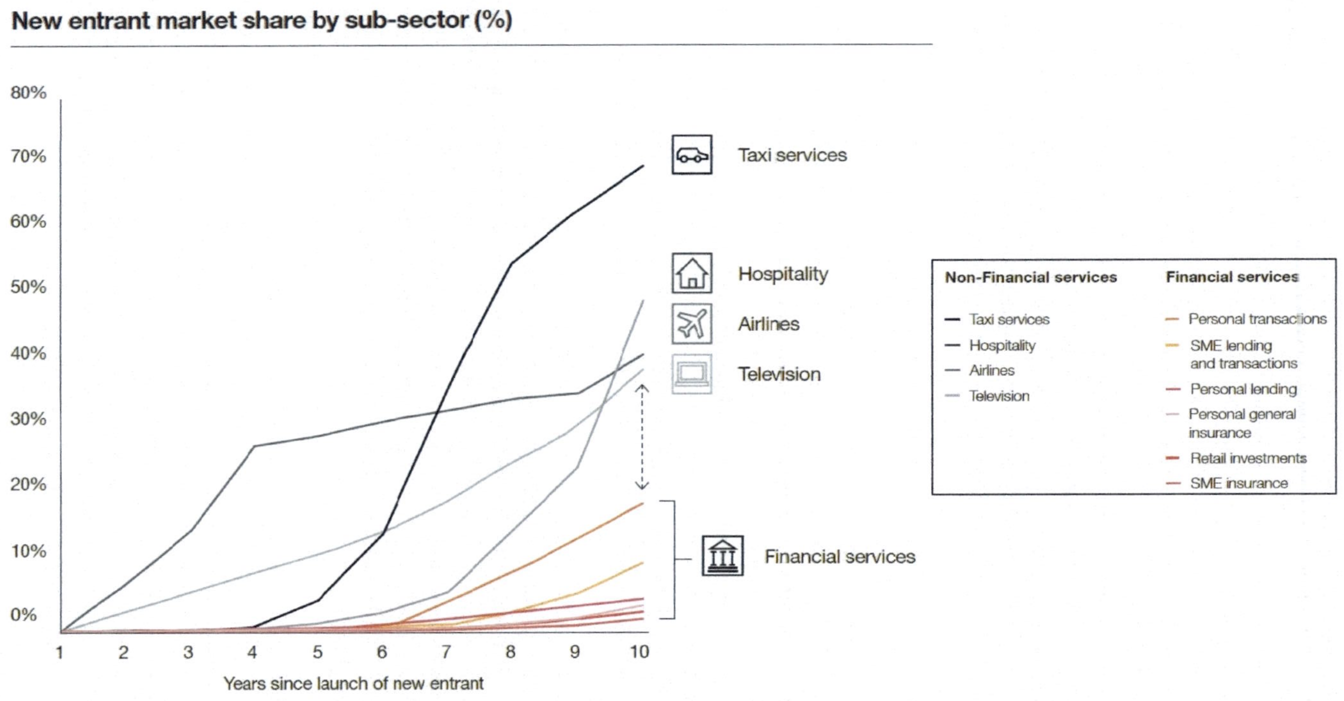

Fig. 12.4 Impact of Digitalization across Industries—Market Share Evolution. Sources: 'The Future of Financial Services in the UK: How to Harness Disruption' (Alan Gemes, James Cousins, George Doble, Arthur Hughes-Hallett, Isabella Yamamoto and Isabella Hadjisavvas; Feb.20; Strategy&-PwC). Reprinted with permission

Customer Segments vs Products (2015, % of total[1,2])

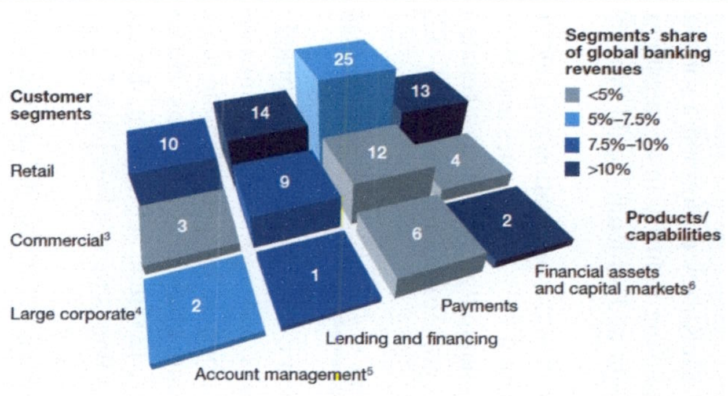

1.350+ commercially most well-known cases registered in the Panorama database; may not be fully representative
2.Figures may not sum to 100%, because of rounding
3.Includes small and medium-size enterprises
4.Includes large corporates, public entities, and non-banking financial institutions
5.Revenue share includes current/checking-account deposit revenue
6.Includes sales and trading, securities services, retail investment, noncurrent-account deposits, and asset management factory
Source: McKinsey Panorama (a McKinsey Solution) - 2015

Customer Appetite vs FinTech Maturity (2020)

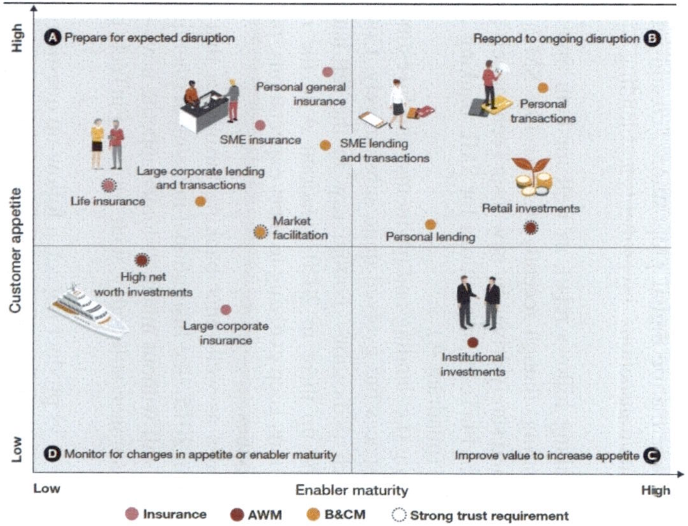

AWM = Asset & Wealth Management
B&CM = Banking & Capital Markets
Source: PwC – Strategy& (Feb.2020)

Fig. 12.5 Evolution of FinTech Focus on Financial Services. Sources: Left exhibit from 'Cutting through the noise around financial technology', February 2016, McKinsey & Company, www.mckinsey.com. Copyright (c) 2021 McKinsey & Company. All rights reserved. Reprinted by permission. Right exhibit from 'The Future of Financial Services in the UK: How to Harness Disruption' (Alan Gemes, James Cousins, George Doble, Arthur Hughes-Hallet, Isabella Yamamoto and Isabella Hadjisavvas; Feb.20; Strategy&-PwC). Reprinted with permission

Retail banking was in 2015 (62% of FinTech dedication—top row in the left-hand chart) and continues to be now in 2020, the underbelly of the incumbent banks with high customer appetite and very mature digital propositions, creating the perfect storm in particular for payments/transactions, investments and lending (quadrant B in the right-hand chart).

Commercial (or SME) banking follows retail, as well for both time horizons, focused on payments and lending; though recently it looks like SME insurance enjoys quite a prominent demand surely driven by new InsurTech models arriving at the market. Unlike retail tough, FinTech propositions for SME banking are still in evolution in terms of maturity (quadrant A).

Digital in Corporate Banking (i.e. lending and payments) and Investment Banking (i.e. markets facilitation) spaces has evolved quite substantively. Compared to 2015 (barely 11% of FinTech dedication—bottom row in the left-hand chart), customer appetite seems to be up there in 2020 (quadrant A in the right-hand chart), while FinTech propositions keep evolving to meet expectations, particularly high in market facilitation activities.

The right-hand chart includes as well other banking businesses that were not particularly of FinTech focus in 2015, like Institutional investment (then just part of the 2% in the left-hand chart, still without much customer appetite now—quadrant D), or Life and Corporate insurance still today with limited FinTech dedication (quadrants A and C).

Once understood the segment vs product impact, a follow-up question for CEOs would be: *how does digital disruption, as a result, financially impact both the top and bottom line?*

In the same research referred to above, McKinsey performed a solid analysis in this respect (numbers refer to the global banking industry in aggregate; albeit they are as of 2014, I reckon their relative weight and structure could probably be still representative as of today) (Fig. 12.6):

Most digital disruption efforts were targeting the origination and sales part of the banking value chain, which represented around 46% of revenues and 59% of profits after-tax at the time, being these activities naturally (given they exclude the costly balance-sheet provision) the main generators of return on equity (22%). Not good news.

Finally, a last reflection for incumbent's #CEOs: *how digital disruption is impacting RoE in the FS industry?*

Despite its slow market share penetration due to the industry's brand and regulatory barriers, as we have seen, FinTechs and new Digital Banks have made substantial progress in some banking areas, both in terms of eliciting high customer appetite and providing them with quite mature innovative solutions. However, there has been a growing consensus in the industry [23] that, at this point, the largest threat of digital disruption comes from Incumbent Banks themselves joined also, probably at bit later, by BigTechs.

Banks have the resources and the incentive to react: 'digital pioneers' embraced it from the very start, the rest explored it during the incubation period. Since then, many have built heterogeneous portfolios of FinTech investments, partnerships and

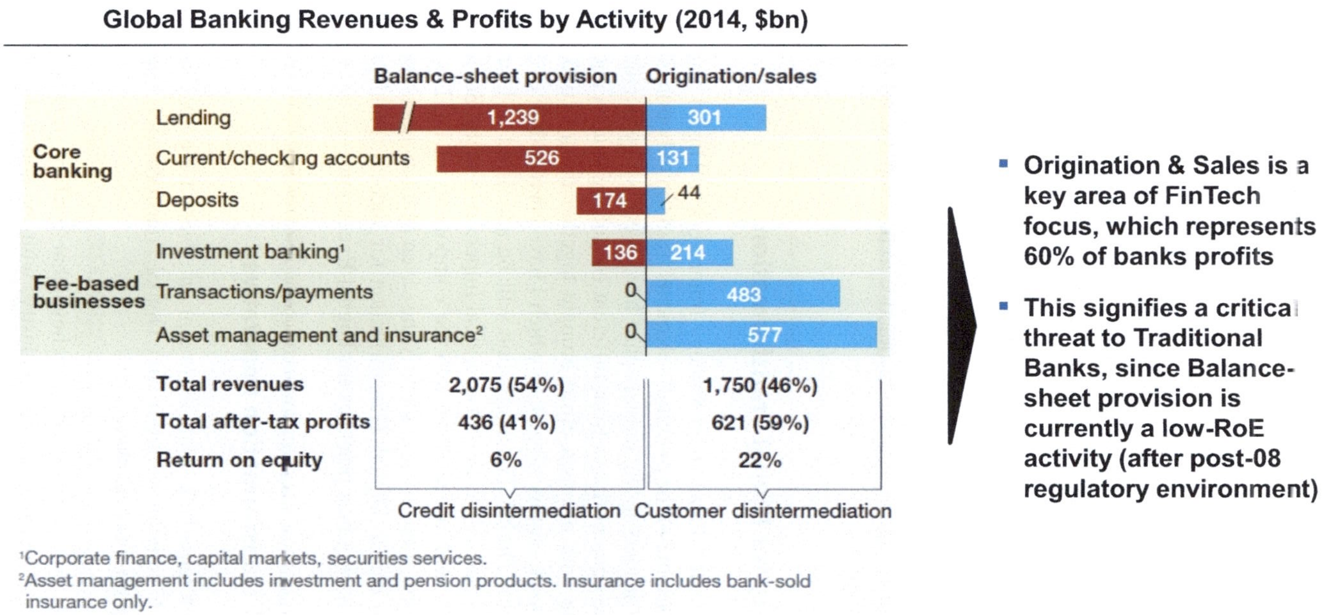

Fig. 12.6 Impact of Digitalization in Global Banking. Sources: Exhibit from 'Cutting through the noise around financial technology', February 2016, McKinsey & Company, www.mckinsey.com. Copyright (c) 2021 McKinsey & Company. All rights reserved. Reprinted by permission

digital subsidiaries, while kicking a rainbow of internal digital transformation initiatives to move from legacy to digital.

In this regard, Accenture [24] recently published research across 168 banks, clustered in terms of their reaction to Digital Transformation: spearheading digital ('digital focused', 12% of total), active ('digital active', 38%) and passive ('the rest', 50%), for the period 2011–2017:

- 'Digital focused' were the only winners in RoE (by 90 bps, from 9.9% to 10.8%) and are expected to keep winning towards 2021 (additional 150 bps in RoE).
- 'Digital active' had flattish RoE past performance (10.3%), but expected to pick it up towards 2021 (by 100 bps).
- 'The rest' were expected to keep RoE underperformance (below 9% levels).

Undoubtedly, out of these efforts, there will be winners and losers, which will depend on the strategy and execution they adopt for transitioning to digital. The next two sections of this chapter suggest best-practice to develop a winning strategy for Digital Transformation.

12.5 Strategy for Digital Transformation

Applying the Holistic Management Strategy framework to Digital Transformation, this section levers some of the pyramid's elements from top to bottom so to illustrate best-practice that leaders in the digital space have successfully pursued during the last 10 years. The content draws from different consulting studies and practitioner experiences along with my own effort brought together during 2016–2017 into a consistent framework on this subject, to which I have been adding ever since.

The Strategy for Digital Transformation will be addressed in four steps. First, starts from the acknowledgment of five critical Imperatives at the Board/CEO level. Then, it continues with a deep dive into the components of the Digital Business Model. At that point, steps back to identify the seven Meta-architectural Levers that need re-tuning to enable Digital Transformation for success. Finally, the analysis concludes by reviewing best practices for Digital Execution.

12.5.1 Digital Transformation Imperatives

As Albert Einstein remarked, '*once we accept our limits, we go beyond them*'. The Board, CEO and C-suite must 'buy-in' five Digital Transformation Imperatives [25] before embarking on this endeavour.

1. *'Only for Believers'*: they need to believe that FinTech represents a radical disruption of the financial services industry, with the added threat of potential new entrants from lateral industries like BigTech. Therefore, digital disruption is not a red herring.

2. *'Heaven Commandment'*: the Board must empower the CEO with a mandate to design and execute a strategy of Digital Transformation for the bank. They must accept that this will entail not only long term, patient organic and inorganic investment, but also impactful organizational realignment, revenue cannibalization across some business lines and an unprecedented aperture to partnerships with multiple third parties.
3. *'Broad Shoulders & Fast Legs'*: Hundred percent commitment by the C-Suite will be fundamental, each of them receiving an appropriate mandate and budget for the mission, along with the decision-making power to move fast when needed.
4. *'Beyond a Tech Job'*: everyone needs to acknowledge that this is not just a CIO or CTO priority, because it is not only (even fundamentally) about IT, but rather it is about radical business and cultural transformation.
5. *'Banker Insider Job'*: the C-Suite needs to anticipate, understanding how bankers think and operate, how to overcome their natural internal resistance to change, especially at levels 2–3 of the hierarchy.

Let us apply the HMS framework, starting with the top of the pyramid: Company and Leadership Excellence.

In terms of Company Excellence (ref. Chap. 10), the CEO, as a 'clockmaker', is the one that must take the leadership for what in all effect will be a radical metamorphosis of the organization. The enormous effort required, leveraging the metaphor, is like transforming an analogic clock into a digital one. Therefore, better he/she is a true 'believer' before embarking on this journey. This was the case in BBVA, with its long-time Executive Chairman, Francisco Gonzalez, a great supporter of technology and innovation, hired Carlos Torres as Head of Strategy & Corporate Development in 2008, a former McKinsey partner and head of its Business Technology Office in Spain. Both shared the same vision for digital transformation for the bank and gained the approval from their Board to start this journey in 2009 (eventually Mr. Torres became CEO in 2015 and Chairman in 2018, driving forward the digital banner during the last 11 years).

On the one hand, having a strong Core Ideology in the bank's legacy culture could be, at first sight, a blessing because it would make it easier to harness the troops towards the new digital mission; however, it could be a hindrance, since the organization's culture will need to evolve to embrace digital, which will be much more difficult in 'cult-like' cultures. As we will see below, ANZ stumbled on cultural issues in their radical organizational change towards agile in its retail bank, which made them take a pause for 2 years after the programme was relaunched.

On the other hand, Drive for Progress will play greatly towards the digital mission by leveraging very ambitious goals (e.g. becoming 'the Amazon of banking'), experimentation (e.g. incubators/accelerators, portfolio of FinTech investments or VC branch) and continuous improvement (e.g. leveraging the five core technological innovations from FinTech). All along, the 'Genius of the "And"' will be a powerful principle to have present in decision-making since effectively many contradictory concepts, both to be embraced, will emerge during the process (e.g. leveraging AI over existing customer databases while ensuring not to discriminate new customers from the biases embedded in this data).

Fundamentally, executives will need to carefully ensure the Alignment (or re-alignment) of culture from Core Ideology, to facilitate Drive for Progress to do its job for the digital mission.

In terms of Leadership & Management Excellence (ref. Chap. 9), digital transformation will be very demanding on each C-Suite executive across all the eight THICOSIV dimensions; however more exhaustively so for Honesty, Influencing, Organization and Investing.

Honesty: the process will inherently require the executive to acknowledge how much does not know, and so how much he/she will be dependent on others. Everything, from the basic understanding of technologies to the awareness of latest digital developments happening out there, to being able to let go past experience as applicable to think out-of-the-box to tackle new problems and, of course, to the humility of being able to learn from internal and external people from all generations. Only with a deep sense of honesty the executive will be able to successfully navigate these demands from digital transformation.

Influencing: the huge cultural challenge plus the change process' size and duration will drive teams and individuals towards very unexpected behaviours, which the executive will need to be able to handle successfully. Equipping themselves strongly in this skillset, both individually and collectively, sometimes with help from external coaches and psychologists would be very impactful for the teams involved. In particular, the challenge of the 'frozen middle' (i.e. middle management that has grown accustomed only to supervise, avoiding any direct task delivery), becomes imperative to handle, as it will be illustrated with the ANZ case in a subsection below.

Organization: digital will require new, innovative ways of working, of dividing and coordinating the tasks, like agile implementation, numerous JVs with FinTechs, informal subject matter expert forums, and tearing apart a lot of the silo mentality and complexity derived from traditional organizational matrixes and hierarchies. For instance, in 2017 ANZ in Australia started to reorganize the retail bank under the 'New Ways of Working' programme, moving employees from traditional hierarchy to agile teams of 10 people, called 'squads' grouped into 'tribes', organized around 6-week delivery 'sprints'. As of 2019, approx. 9000 employees, 50% of Australia's retail bank business, had moved to this new mode and productivity gains of up to 30% had been recorded; however, the programme took a pause to smooth out the cultural challenges and adapt the model in those areas where the agile method was proven not to be best practice.

Investing: the challenge here is for an incumbent bank to be able to stomach failure when it happens, and with digital transformation, it will occur from time to time; hence the importance of eliciting ex-ante the Board's appetite and boundaries. An associated aspect will be the potential earnings volatility, because of not only impairments and write-downs, but also revenue cannibalization. Overall, more likely than not it will be a rocky journey for shareholders, difficult in the first few years but hopefully happy at the end (ceteris paribus other market considerations). For instance, BBVA had to take in 2017 a $89.5m write-down on Simple investment, and as of December 2019 had invested 139m € in Atom Bank (2019: 90m € loss) out of which 56m € were impaired; on the other hand, in 2019 the bank reported +59% in digital sales of all products/services (×2 vs 2015), −31% in processing cost per transaction, +42% in US branch network productivity. Given the time gap to reap the rewards, the jury is still out with regard to the impact of digital on the bank's valuation but signs are promising.

Next step down the HMS framework pyramid: Portfolio Value Gap & Portfolio Horizons.

The Portfolio Value Gap (ref. Chap. 7) would foresee improvements in the share price coming from digital interventions via Business Performance Improvements, which usually would stem, in the short and medium term, from cost efficiency gains due to process automation and FTE redundancy. In the long term, share repricing would eventually come from Organic Business Growth once the digitalization effort enables the capture of excess market share vs competitors or even international market expansion.

The crux here is to understand that well-executed Digital Transformation will show in the top and bottom line of the organization gradually over time, and scale volume effects will probably take longer to manifest. Simultaneously, there would be risk of revenue cannibalization and the unavoidable transfer of part of the added value to customers (i.e. let us remember that industry revenue and profit pools shrink with digitalization). Therefore, it is not surprising that capital markets do not necessarily give credit for the digital effort immediately, and for some players perhaps ever.

The above-mentioned research by Accenture [24] provides operating, financial and valuation performance comparing the three groups of 'digital proficiency'. Effectively, within 2011–2017, the gains in terms of operating income over assets (from 1.17% to 1.29%) for 'digital focused' banks were driven by cost efficiency, while decreased for the other two groups. Clearly 'digital active' banks were progressing with reductions in cost on assets (from 1.65% to 1.44%), but still not offsetting the negative operating income trend (from 1.22% to 1.19%), probably because their digitalization efforts were still under development.

As a result, from 2011 to 2018, the market was able to re-rate Price-to-Book ratios only for the 'digital focused' banks, from ×1.05 to ×1.18; however, it barely did so for the 'digital active' banks (≈ ×0.98), though did not hesitate to penalize (from ×0.99 to ×0.83) the large cohort of digital laggards (i.e. 50% of the sample).

From a Portfolio Horizons perspective (ref. Chap. 8), reviewing what most institutions embarking on this journey have done we can typically generalize 3 Horizons for Digital Transformation (allowing for the license that, in a 'traditional bank's Portfolio Horizons', most of the initiatives below would belong to 'Horizon III', since they would not generate their result till the long term):

1. *Digital Experimentation*: which would cover the period of setting up incubators or accelerators, joining external consortia around specific technologies or

solutions (e.g. blockchain, trade finance, payments), trying some proofs of concept (POCs) and eventually pilots in specific businesses or functions.

2. *Digital Investment*: where there is a progressive approval of the budgets dedicated either to organic developments from pilot to implementation (even if limited in scope at first), or to inorganic moves via FinTech portfolio acquisitions, stakes or arms-length VCs. This horizon would include decisions to create separate digital banks from scratch.
3. *Digital Business Models*: where the banks start to move full BUs from a legacy business model to a digital business model, normally on the back of pilot implementations being rollout to full client segments, after a time in limited trial. The aim here is for a gradual digitalization of the portfolio of BUs across Divisions depending on the customer appetite and economics of the change of model. This would naturally provide a rainbow of end-states, all the way from drastic BU overhaul to specific process/channel digitization within an existing legacy model.

The dynamics of these 3 horizons for digital change would yield, at any point in time, a palette of Digital Transformation Portfolio along the lines below, considering the organizational remit of the change (i.e. Division vs BU) and the % of revenues impacted (within the respective remit) (Fig. 12.7).

Only a few programmes would end up being Complex Transformations, all mostly at intra- or cross-divisional level. The bulk of the digital efforts would be

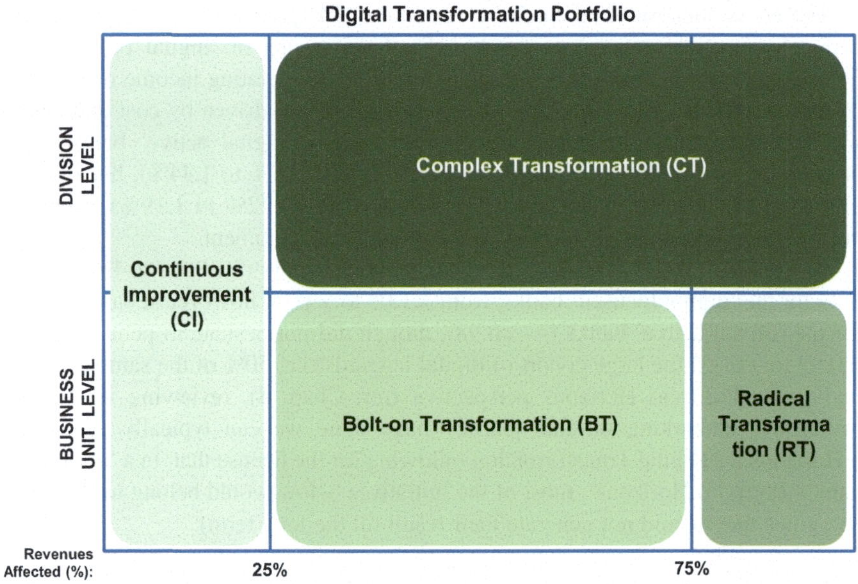

Fig. 12.7 Digital Transformation Portfolio. Sources: "FinTech Food for Thought v.7" (Angel Gavieiro; Aug.17; AG Strategy & Partners)

driven by many Bolt-on Transformations (usually at the BU level impacting a 25–75% range of revenues) and a few Radical Transformations (i.e. the full digital overhaul of a given business model). However, it is important to acknowledge the development of a quite wide array of digital initiatives that, being individually smaller in terms of impact, in effect contribute to the Continuous Improvement of processes and practices across the bank.

12.5.2 Digital Business Model

Let us bring the HMS framework to the bottom base of the pyramid: Strategy & Execution, at the BU level. This subsection will focus on the Strategy, leaving Execution for the following subsection.

I will show the application of the framework to the extreme case of radical transformation of a BU into digital and so illustrate the best practice for doing so leveraging a 'Digital' rendering (with HMS permission) of the Business Model framework (Fig. 12.8).

At the top a reminder of the 'north star' or ultimate Purpose of the Digital Bank: the interaction between client and bank has to be at the centre of the value proposition (all the rest follows from this premise).

I skip the discussion about the external parts outside of the Business Model (i.e. Market Dynamics and Financial Impact) since were covered earlier in the Sects. 12.2/12.3 and 12.4 respectively.

Turning then to the Business Model itself, starting with Client Segmentation. Like for any banking business model, we will identify the right client segments to serve, looking at their characterization and/or behavioural reality (ref. Sect. 1.2). What is different and crucial to understand when applying segmentation techniques to the digital banking world are the concepts of Customer Journey (CJ), Customer Experience (CX) and Digital Optimized Interaction (DOI).

The importance of CJ [26] in Digital Transformation stems from a basic question: *what would be the best possible experience a customer could have when interacting with our bank?*

To fully answer this question requires a dedicated effort to reimagine the entire journey of CX by leveraging user-experience designers and a cross-functional team (legal, compliance, operations, IT, etc.) with direct involvement of customers along the way. A journey redesign effort, for a given client segment, requires:

1. Scoping of the client engagement phasing, channels and products/services, usually keeping an eye on the value at stake and the cost involved
2. Zero-based design process to go beyond incremental improvement aiming at radical customer-centric experience shift

Once the CJ is redesigned, tested and refined then it starts a cycle of technology solution development, roll out and customer adoption, until the CX indicators feedback the targeted level of CX satisfaction uplift.

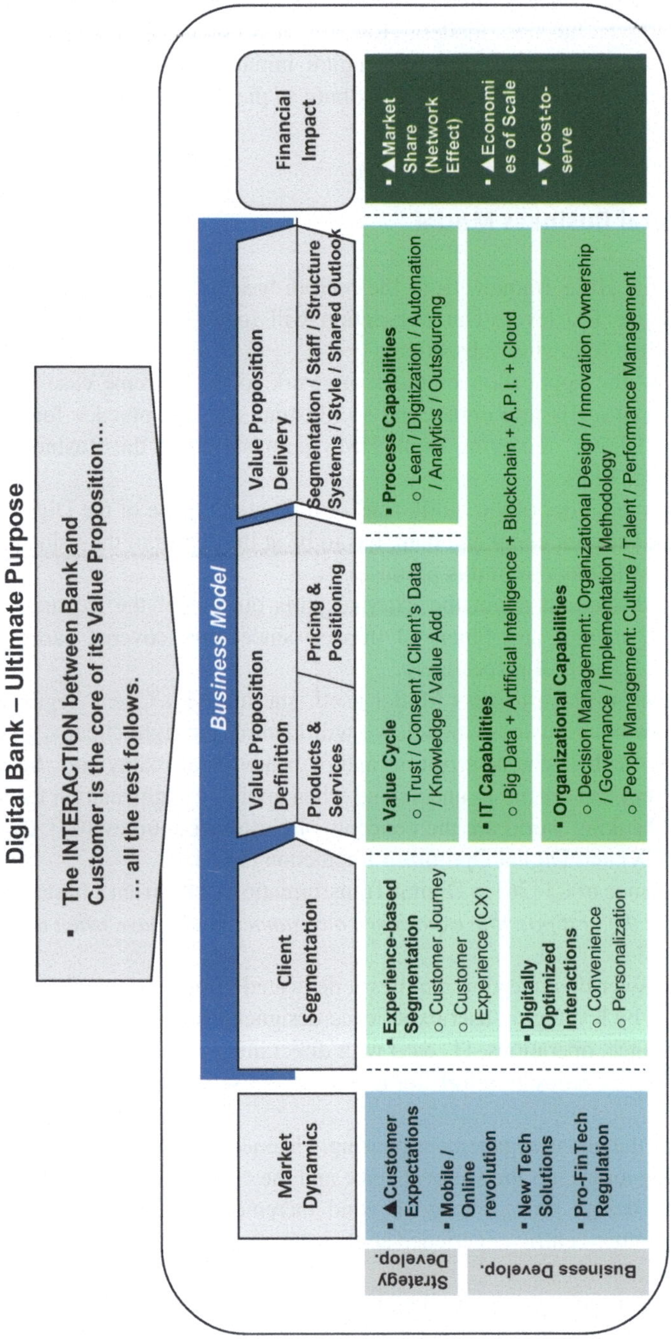

Fig. 12.8 Digital Business Model. Sources: 'FinTech Food for Thought v.7' (Angel Gavieiro; Aug.17; AG Strategy & Partners)

Therefore, by focusing on CJ what we are zero-in ultimately is CX, because the endgame is not the product or the service provided, but the experience which happens to the customer when interacting with the bank (at whatever channel and moment in time). Thus, a new Digital Banking Model will aspire at providing a substantially better interaction between client and bank, optimal compared to any comparable interaction provided by the legacy banking proposition (i.e. it needs to be explicitly benchmarked), hence the concept of DOI.

Therefore, DOI [12] refers to the ability to provide a tailored, fast and easy CX consistently throughout the CJ, in a context of constantly evolving customer financial needs of any type, any time, anyhow and anywhere. The key parameters to optimize for in these digital interactions are Convenience and Personalization.

The Business Model continues with the Value Proposition Definition (i.e. the 'what' we are bringing to our customers). I refer to Sect. 1.3 for considerations about product/service, pricing and positioning, of course as well applicable to digital banking; however, the distinctive crucial new element to address is the Value Cycle of data. While in a legacy banking model, most institutions manage tons of customer data, usually they do so in a passive manner for recording, storage, informational and regulatory purposes. In a Digital Business Model, we turn the concept of data on its head to become the centre of everything, the new oil of the twenty-first century.

DOIs are only feasible if the bank is able to make the most of the insights it can learn from the data available from its customers. This is when data earns its full power and value, as GAFA and BAT are very well learned in their respective original domains. Nevertheless, unlike GAFA and BAT (as Cambridge Analytica's notorious case illustrated), banks cannot afford to use that data in an irresponsible manner without facing the tough consequences of scrutiny and penalty by their regulators and, the tougher consequence of losing their customers' trust.

Here is where the concept of Value Cycle, first introduced by BBVA [27], becomes essential. It describes the reinforcing five steps that would enable financial institutions to responsibly leverage insights from their customers' data while honouring their trust and providing value to them (Fig. 12.9).

Starting with the Trust received from the customer dealing with us, we must gain his/her Consent so we can lever that Data to produce Knowledge that help us to enable personalized and convenient interactions via our Digital Business Model, and so Value Added for our customers, generating in turn additional customer Trust.

Let us move to the Value Proposition Delivery (the 'how' of delivering the 'what' to our customers), as described in Sect. 1.4. In this application to digital, we will address three critical Capabilities to successfully enable a digital model: Process, IT and Organization.

There are five Process Capabilities [28] that a bank must command to be able to sail Digital Transformation safely into port; it implies securing internally the right talent, both in depth and breadth, that will become an essential part of the agile teams deployed across the organization:

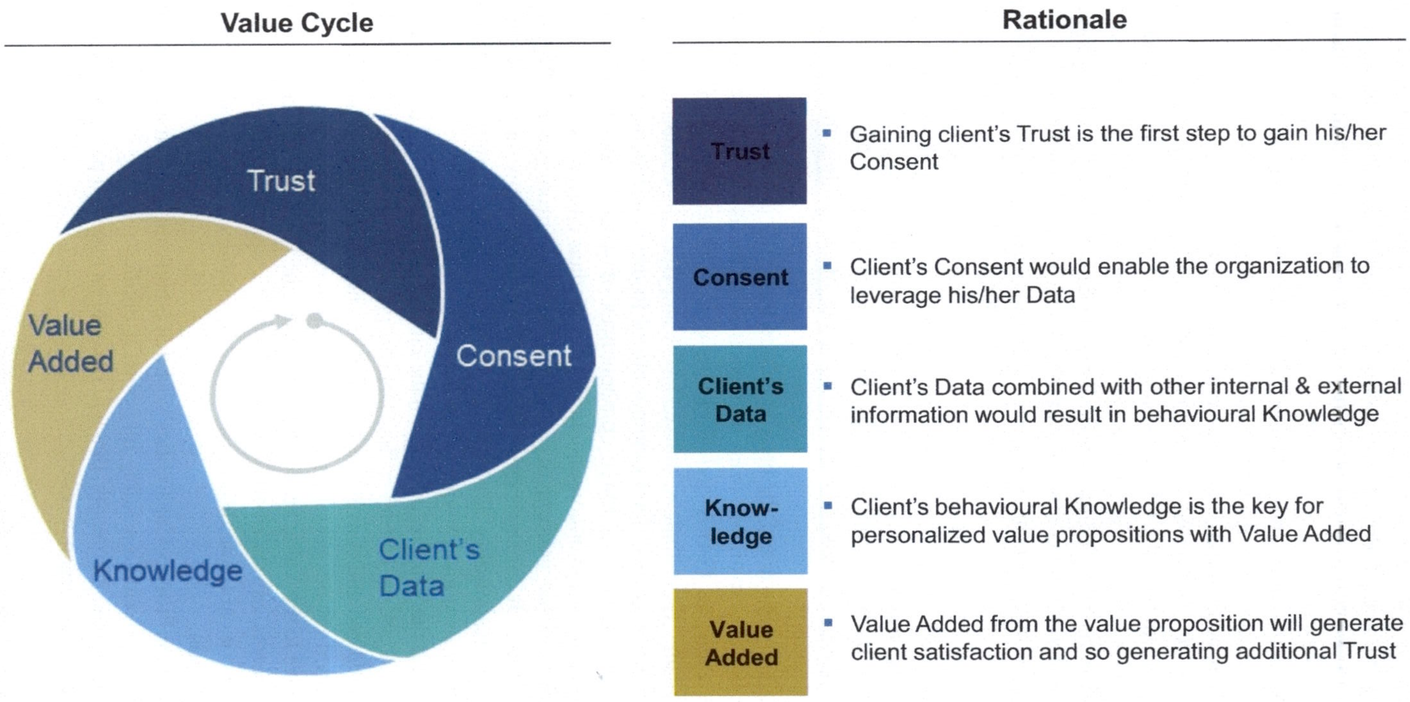

Fig. 12.9 Digital Business Model—Value Cycle. Sources: BBVA website (2017)

- *Lean* 'six-sigma' teams have been paramount in many industries, starting from the engineering world (e.g. black belts have been of absolute importance in GE since Jack Welch's times). Though also present in incumbent banks, they have fallen short of the prominence they deserve; digital disruption has only highlighted how much fat and complexity exists within banking processes, which will place Lean teams back in high value. My teams' experience in leveraging Lean with a BU in the Treasury Services space, resulted in 20% FTE savings, which we redeployed towards customer acquisition.
- *Digitization* refers to the effort of transforming paper and analogic data, still widely used across banks, into electronic form for digital processing. At the core, Machine Learning (ML) and Natural Language Processing (NLP) algorithms have gained enormous accuracy in digitizing written and oral communications. I still remember a project of credit risk process simplification performed by one of my teams in a Financial Institutions BU, where we concluded that was pertinent to add in the cover page of the pack with our recommendations a picture that spoke louder than 1000 words: a credit pack for the annual renewal of one of the main corporate clients, which paper stack exceeded 30 cm in height!
- *Automation* has been one of the most successful operations and IT functions within banking, enhanced recently also by AI algorithm deployments. Though most of their projects usually focus on taking parts of a process and reduce, ideally eliminate, their legacy manual interventions, instead of a full end-to-end process reengineering; this is so mostly because the entanglement of legacy processes would often make E2E automation attempts all but impossible. During the COVID-19 crisis, the demand for RPA solutions among banks skyrocketed since they needed to process record number of SME loan applications from the government's crisis support schemes.
- *Analytics* is another of the 'new functions', in particular when we talk about advanced analytics, although not all incumbent banks enjoy this capability beyond their credit and market risk modelling teams. Building this capability entails onboarding data scientists, software engineers and specialist data wranglers. First, they focus on cleaning up and re-arranging structured big data lakes from multiple unconnected legacy databases. Then, they lever these lakes to extract meaningful insights by applying different advanced analytics techniques (e.g. statistical clustering, regression analysis, Bayesian inference) including AI and its main varieties, ML for structured data or, its subset, Deep Learning (DL) for unstructured data. Amazon has revolutionized credit underwriting by providing credit facilities to its SME clients based on applying ML to their sales activity, departing from banks' traditional past-looking credit underwriting. OakNorth Bank, a UK neobank, has similarly developed its successful Acorn AI software for SME credit underwriting which it has licenced in the US market to local banks.
- *Outsourcing*, a traditional banking function particularly leveraged during the 1990s–2000s globalization boom. Traditionally, outsourcing's approach followed rules-based, volume concentration criteria with a view to optimize for cost within a minimum level of quality secured in their Service Level Agreements

(SLA). I recall a European bank project of Business Process Outsourcing (BPO) to India that aimed to move 15,000 roles from the retail bank setting up a JV with a local Indian bank for that purpose; 3 years later the bank had to call the effort off given the impossibility of being able to map the processes in origin for 'lift & drop & reengineer' to destination. In the new digital world outsourcing requirements differ a lot from the past, because it demands dealing with a large portfolio of FinTech start-ups of all sizes, in a fast and agile engagement, within an experimental framework of POCs, pilots and potential failures that have scarce fit within traditional outsourcing frameworks.

Moving to IT Capabilities, I thought the iceberg illustration in the picture below was a great visual to show the 'software scaffolding' that sustains DOIs. The five components are, in effect, the core innovations levered by the FinTech revolution, whose combinations make the essence of most of their disruptive business models (Fig. 12.10).

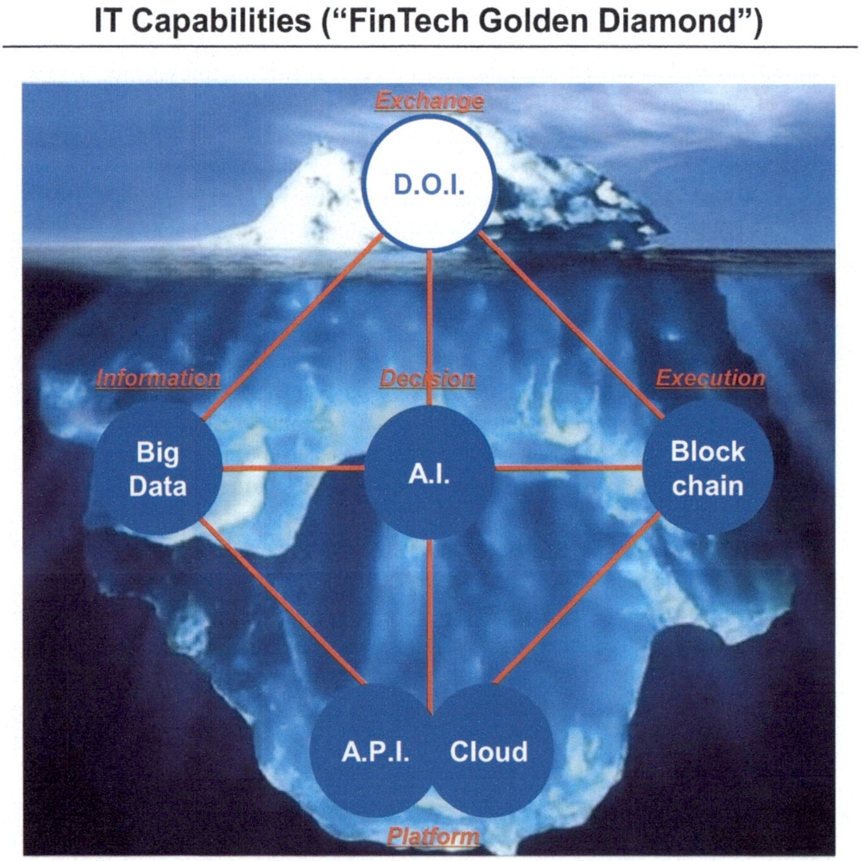

Fig. 12.10 Digital Business Model—IT Capabilities. Sources: 'FinTech Food for Thought v.7' (Angel Gavieiro; Aug.17; AG Strategy & Partners)

- *Big Data*: ability to capture and manage customer and transaction information, cleaned, unified, structured and scalable to cope with its exponential growth, in real-time and for any angle of insight generation.
- *Artificial Intelligence*: ability to extract insight, leveraging ML, DL or other statistical techniques based on self-learning algorithms out of the Big Data, ready for decision-making to spur action that tailors to both customer needs and bank's risk/reward appetite.
- *Blockchain*: ability to capture and register clients' transactions in distributed (instead of central) ledgers and, leveraging smart contracts, to ensure real-time, automated, straight-through-processing of its terms within highly tight cybersecurity.
- *Application Programme Interface*: ability to seamlessly develop applications that access the data of the bank's operating system, applications or databases, so to enable smooth two-way interoperable information sharing with third parties.
- *Cloud*: ability to provide 24/7, global, digital, omnichannel conduit to all internal and external activities of Exchange, Information, Decision and Execution of the bank.

The dynamics among the elements is what make Digital Business Models so powerful. Ultimately, the DOI is an 'exchange' between the customer and the bank (e.g. opening a current account, instructing a payment, seeking investment advice). These exchanges, along with the customers' data characterization, become 'information' which BigData has the role to securely store and have ready for potential insight generation (e.g. database of customer demographics, CRM database of customer behaviours, general ledger of current account movements). AI is the engine that makes the inquiries in order to generate insights to support 'decisions' (e.g. checking if a payment is legit or fraud, approve/deny application for credit line). Blockchain is an alternative to traditional centralized ledgers (and so, it could be argued that it is part of the realm of BigData, only with the difference of being decentralized among several parties), and the running of smart contracts on top enables then an automated 'execution' of the terms embedded in the transactions recorded (e.g. a fixed rate bond issued in a blockchain, over time would instruct automatically payment of coupons periodically and eventually pay back the nominal amount at maturity, while monitoring covenants and other legal terms in an ongoing basis, triggering actions automatically). These three technologies could be seen as a continuum of 'Information > Decision > Execution'. Underneath, acting as a joint 'platform' would sit the Cloud, with its externally based mainframes sustaining all the organization's core systems to ensure 24/7 omnichannel functioning, and the APIs as key communication software translators with the ecosystem of external parties a digital bank needs to connect to.

A further reflection about IT Capabilities is the fact that, during this subsection's analysis of the Digital Business Model, IT has not popped until so late in the discussion, which highlights the conclusion, as the '4th Digital Transformation Imperative' states, that it is not just an IT job.

The last of the three elements under the Value Proposition part of the Digital Business Model is Organizational Capabilities, which will be discussed in the following subsection in more depth and detail since it is where the bulk of complexity and molasses in Digital Transformation lies.

12.5.3 Meta-architectural Levers

At an organizational level, the effective execution of Digital Transformation requires addressing, as I call them, seven critical 'Meta-architectural Levers' that permeate across organizations determining the way change gets decided and executed. Because these Levers have been designed and developed in a way consistent with enabling execution for traditional legacy businesses, if they are left on their own devices they will certainly drive most digitalization efforts to failure.

In my conversations with C-level executives, I found a lack of holistic awareness about how these seven Meta-architectural Levers illustrated below impede many banks' digital efforts to yield success. These are part of the wider array of organizational capabilities in the organization; however, they are highlighted in the context of Digital Transformation because of the critical role they play in this effort in terms of Decision Management or People Management (Fig. 12.11).

Re-tuning these Levers depending on their starting situation and the digital ambition of each bank is, in my analysis, the 'philosopher's stone' in the alchemy of Digital Transformation.

We can visualize these Levers as dials, as per the next illustration. At a given point of time, each Incumbent Bank has each dial calibrated to a certain level, all of them fine-tuned for tackling the activity in the 'BAU way': BUs submit their investment cases under the annual strategic planning process, which after approval, get into the staged implementation gateway process, all of that taking several months until the first funding gets released.

Keeping these seven dials tuned at their traditional level, instead of becoming enablers of Digital Transformation they can become a hindrance. The dials need to be carefully re-tuned, in tandem and consistently, from their current status quo to a new position where they become effective enablers of digital change. The consistency and synchrony of the move is crucial, since any of them, standalone, could become the wall against which a given digital effort would crash onto (Fig. 12.12).

Let us review them in more depth. The first four Meta-architectural Levers are all about the Decision Management capabilities of the organization while the last three are about People Management capabilities.

1. *Organizational Design*: the current situation in many banks is that Operations & IT departments are centralized functions undertaking the monopoly of all technology developments, usually making use of the procurement gateway for external access or collaboration. The advent of digital in many banks has led to the creation of a third internal player, the Digital function, which necessarily must interlink with the 'incumbent' Ops & IT... easier to write it than to do it.

	Organizational Capabilities		From	To
Decision Management	Organizational Design	Digital & FinTech	Ops + IT (centralized, external access via procurement only)	Digital + Ops + IT (with open access to FinTech ecosystem)
	Innovation Ownership	Centralization vs Decentralization	Innovation centrally owned	Ownership at centre and BU-level (BAU + Innovation agenda for MD)
	Governance	Strategic	Annual MTP	Dynamic Strategic Planning with (bi)monthly Innovation Loops
		Operational	Quarterly OpCo (gated approvals)	Weekly OpCo (fast escalation)
	Implementation Methodology	Sequential vs Agile	Large, detailed planning, divided between Ops & IT	Agile multidisciplinary scums implementing solutions in frequent, short time runs (sprints)
People Management	Culture	Tradition vs Openness	Closed via central sourcing; traditional V&Bs	Open to FinTech collaboration embracing change, faithful V&Bs
		'Frozen middle'	Middle layer of non-crafting, non-learning managerial burocracy	Unfrozen middle, continuous learning, crafting leadership
	Talent	Internal	Digital focused on IT department	Digital training at different levels
		External	Traditional recruitment sourcing	Selective, creative recruitment of scarce digital capability gaps
	Performance Management	Innovation	Non-existing objective & metric	New objective, with tailored metric
		Change	Qualitative approach	Quantitative measure of change

Fig. 12.11 **Digital Business Model—Meta-architectural Levers**. Note: *MTP* medium-term planning, *BU* business unit, *BAU* business as usual, *V&Bs* values & behaviours. Sources: 'A CEO's Guide To Digital Transformation' (Martin Danoesastro, Grant Freeland and Thomas Reichert; BCG, May.17); 'ANZ digital chief: Tackle the "frozen middle" of your organisation or face irrelevancy" (Nadia Cameron; CMO; May.17; from interview with Maile Carnegie ANZ CDO at Adobe Symposium); 'FinTech Food for Thought v.7' (Angel Gavieiro; Aug.17; AG Strategy & Partners)

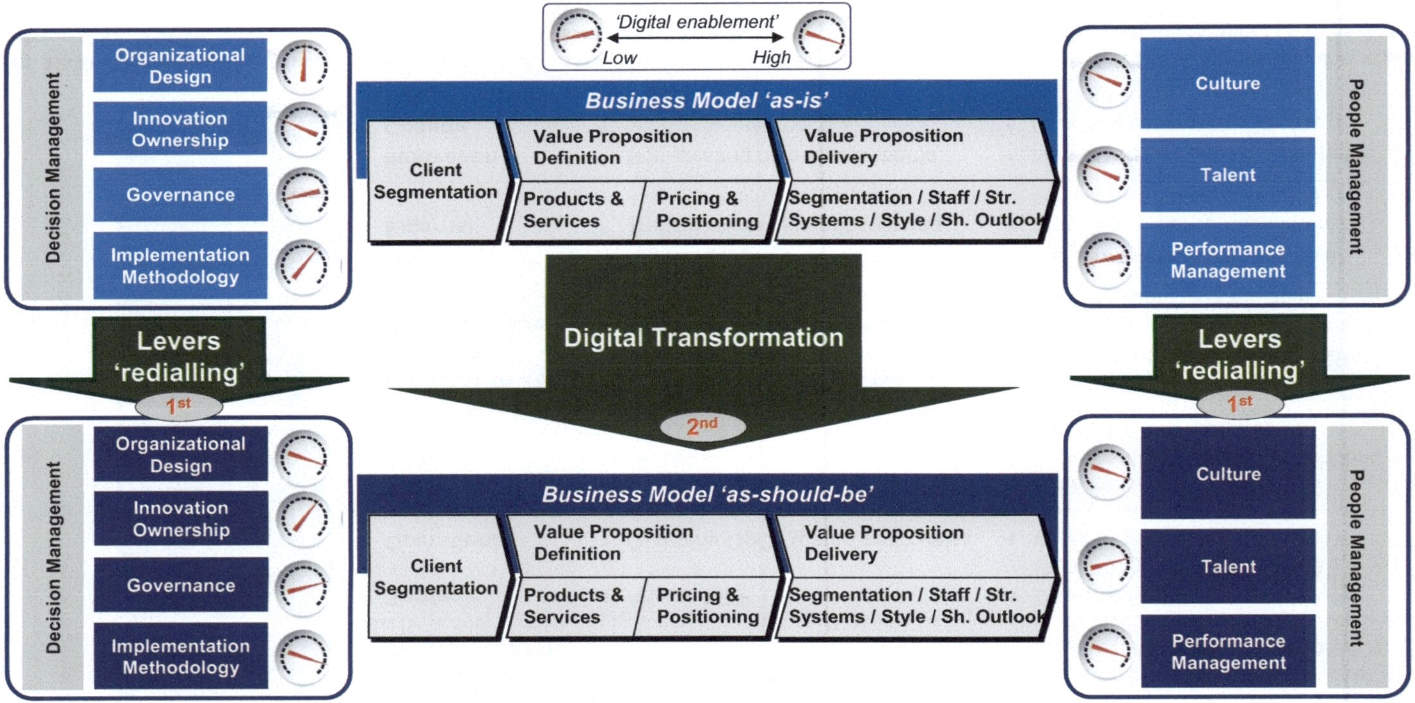

Fig. 12.12 Digital Business Model—Meta-architectural Levers: Redialling. Sources: 'FinTech & Digital Transformation—Food for Thought' (Angel Gavieiro; Aug. 17; AG Strategy & Partners)

In addition, there is the need to open the bank to interact with the FinTech ecosystem, the traditional procurement approach not being the ideal way to do so, as commented earlier. In this regard, rather than undertaking a drastic addition to the protocols of the procurement function, many banks found it more effective to assign, fully or partially in collaboration with procurement, the responsibility of engaging with the external FinTech ecosystem to the new Digital function, as pointed on the left part of the chart below.

One of the best practices for organizing this new function, as far as the FinTech liaison is concerned, is to differentiate the procurement of specialist capabilities on core FinTech related technologies (as identified earlier in this section) from the procurement of new FinTech solutions for specific financial services applications (e.g. SME lending, P2P payments). The rationale is that while the former might have potential use across different businesses and functions in the bank and will require a deep design collaboration with Ops & IT from the start, specialist solutions are normally of interest for one or a few BUs, which could be engaged first to test appetite before getting into design, POC and implementation (Fig. 12.13).

2. *Innovation Ownership*: a critical question with digital is to identify who owns innovation within the organization. Unlike other industries, not many Incumbent Banks have something akin to an R&D department. When they do, it is a centralized Innovation or Digital team that provides top-down direction, ensures multi-year investment priorities and usually owns cross-divisional digital initiatives. I believe Digital Transformation requires a dual ownership both at the centre, via the Innovation/Digital team and at each and every one of the BUs, where every MD would have a 'dual hat' of BAU and Innovation agenda, like shown in the right-hand part of the illustration above.

   Why in the BUs? Because at this level is where business strategy meets the marketplace, where actually the rubber meets the road. Thus, I would expect the MD of that BU (e.g. Mortgages) to be the best-positioned person in the organization to understand what his/her marketplace is doing in terms of innovation (e.g. new FinTech mortgage providers able to digitally load customer information, complement it with API-linked third-party oracles, run AI-based credit underwriting algorithms on it and so make approval decisions in 15 min). Also, the BU MD is best positioned to judge how these moves will impact his/her customer franchise and, accordingly, begin to engage with the Innovation/Digital team to joint problem solve the digital options (e.g. revamp CJ/CX, review E2E process with lean, automation and digitization functions, JV with a FinTech start-up offering a cutting-edge solution or launch an external digital mortgage bank). In addition, the business case for financing any of the options ultimately would have to be made and committed by the BU MD, so even better if it starts from him/her sponsorship in the first place. Under this new dual innovation ownership approach, it would be essential to separate the BAU vs Innovation operating agendas, portfolios and scorecard KPIs for the MD, still responsible for both but acknowledging both are very 'different animals'.

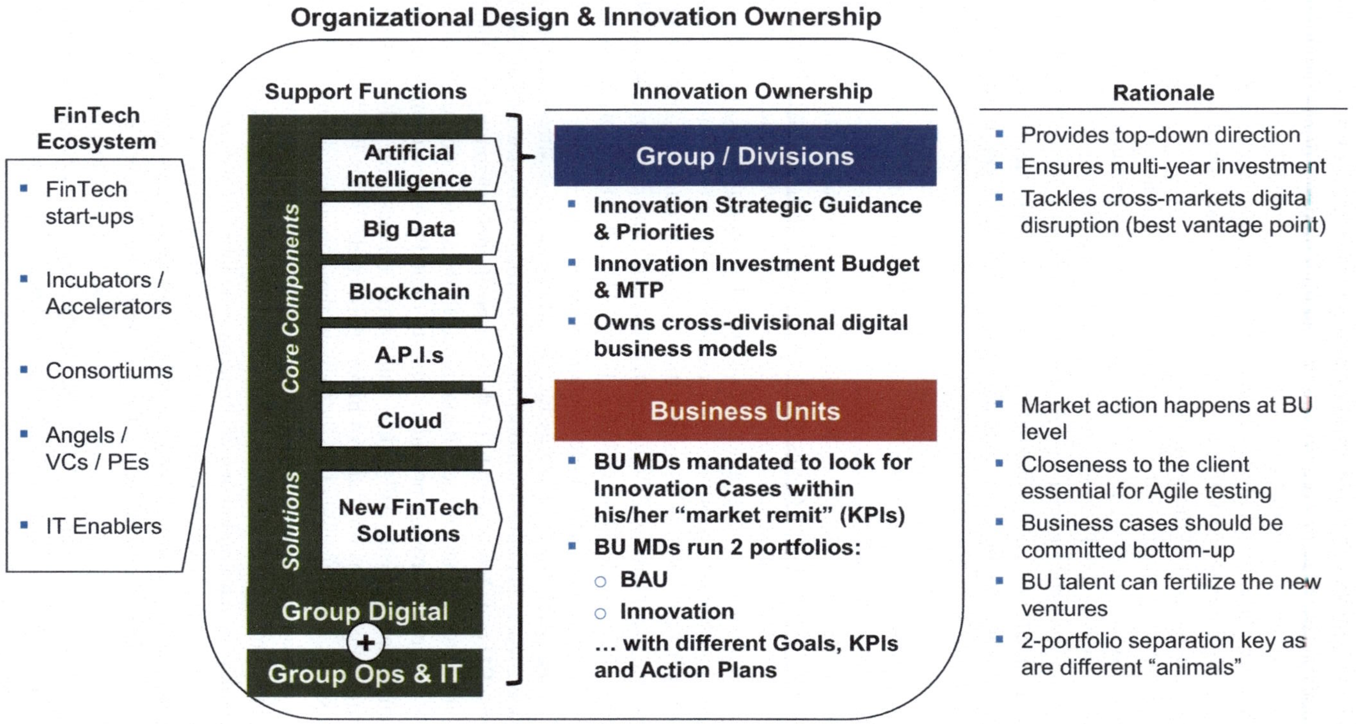

Fig. 12.13 Digital Business Model—Organizational Design & Innovation Ownership. Sources: 'FinTech Food for Thought v.7' (Angel Gavieiro; Aug.17; AG Strategy & Partners)

3. *Governance*: it is usual for banks to govern strategy via the annual strategic & financial MTP process (like described in Chaps. 2 and 3), and to govern operational execution via a periodic operating committee (OpCo) leveraging a gate approval process. Inconveniently for this process, the digital age brings the need for speedy decision-making and the necessary 'fail fast' experimental innovation. Therefore, new governance approaches are required in both camps.

   Dynamic strategic planning [29] would be a best practice solution that can be designed within the established MTP process. It would allow for frequent (monthly or bi-monthly) 'Innovation Strategy & Finance Loops' (as discussed in Sect. 3.4) that would work like windows for updating the Strategic & Financial Plan, where BUs could present any digital change proposal for their business model, detailed with three elements:
   (a) Strategic Analysis, of the client impact (CJ/CX) and specific value proposition modifications
   (b) Dynamic Planning, addressing the innovation scenario paths, real options or any negotiation knots[15]
   (c) Investment/Divestment Cases, with the incremental financial impact over the MTP

   From an Operational Governance perspective, it would be needed much more frequent OpCos (i.e. even on a weekly basis), with all relevant functions present, where investment delivery of the approved investment cases is decided, still gated but with faster escalation points. In addition, it would be best practice to delegate substantial authority to the agile teams to execute expenditure.
4. *Implementation Methodology*: not surprisingly, at the core of the FinTech revolution lies a fundamental shift in how software development, and the necessary operational process that it sustains, is performed. FinTech demonstrates that a move from the traditional sequential phased development to agile development and implementation has served these start-ups superbly well. However, for large financial institutions, it is not as easy as copy and paste, because their IT budgets are enormous (i.e. high risk) and the queue of software development and implementation oversize several times the existing capacity of any given bank.

   Still, there is plenty of room, as 'digital pioneer' banks like BBVA, ING or DBS have demonstrated, to combine the old and new world in smart ways, and so being able to lever the speed advantage from agile multidisciplinary scums sprinting to a minimum viable product (MVP) delivery. Well-defined Agile Teams leveraging Agile Methodology best practices [30] can make this a reality.

   First, Agile Teams, composed of multifunction, top-quality and attitude players, need an ordered roll-out plan, focus on CJ involving customers, and

[15] Points in time where outcomes are expected from negotiations among industry stakeholders involved in an innovation effort.

readiness for crisis management from organizational rejection (i.e. either of the seven Meta-architectural Levers throwing 'antibodies to the alien body').

Second, Agile Methodology requires both top-down and bottom-up coordination (i.e. consistent with the 'dual-hat' innovation ownership), an Agile Centre of Excellence that sets best practice and coordinates progress, and Agile Champions (i.e. unfreezing some of the 'frozen middle', as we will see below in the next Lever).

5. *Culture*: defines the proven, acceptable ways by which members of an organization address problems (as discussed in Sects. 2.1.1 and 6.4). Two aspects get combined in this critical, crucial, fundamental and essential lever. One is the gap between the 'traditional' values and behaviours of Incumbent Banks with the 'disruptive' values and behaviours of FinTechs, which when put together have proven to be often a large obstacle in terms of collaboration and even simple communication. The other has to do with the 'Frozen Middle' [31], basically a middle layer of non-crafting, non-learning managerial bureaucracy that is quite common among large banks, which will require mobilization and 'buy-in' for Digital Transformation to succeed.

   The illustration summarizes ANZ CDO's seven-element methodology for a Cultural Reengineering Programme, starting first with the core principle of accepting that culture can be reengineered (something that, I feel, not every C-suite executive would agree with). Then three elements that link very well with the Company Excellence framework (ref. Chap. 10): set aggressive uplift aspirations, evolve leadership to a delegated and distributed model, instil passionate purpose at all levels. The fourth element, to unfreeze the 'Frozen Middle' links with the '5th Digital Transformation Imperative' as discussed earlier in this chapter. Last but not least, a focus on transparency, being prepared for the new culture to openly transpire externally, a consequence of social media's power in this twenty-first century (Fig. 12.14).

6. *Talent* [32]: 61% of companies cite it as the #1 hurdle for Digital Transformation. It is a big challenge both internally and externally. Internally because in traditional banks the monopoly of digital knowledge sits in the IT department (i.e. however, IT-savvy seats in banking Boards are, nowadays, still below 5%!), but often it is antiquated. Thus, the questions would be: *how to upgrade this talent? How to spread digital know-how among the wider banking teams?* Externally because the young, top-edge, digital talent pool is limited, easily lured by BigTech packages and with little banking experience. Nevertheless, banks desperately need to recruit them, but reality says young talent shy away from traditional employee bank offering. Thus, there is the need to develop selective, creative recruitment propositions tailored to this talent pool, launch data scientist generation programmes (e.g. S2DS[16] by Pivigo in the UK), lever digital specialized recruiting firms, approve retention programmes and install mentoring/reverse-mentoring schemes.

[16] Science-to-Data-Science (www.s2ds.org).

Cultural Re-engineering Programme – Key Elements		ANZ Chief Digital Officer's Views
Core Principle	Accept that culture is 're-engineer-able'	"You can engineer culture…it's actually a scientific set of inputs and outputs… if you change these levers, it will change the culture."
Aspirations	Aggressively uplift aspirations	"Older companies have incremental aspirations….if you don't have what feels like an almost unachievable aspiration, you will fail."
Leadership	Evolve leadership to delegated & distributed model	"Companies set up to win in the 20th century, still haven't let go of command & control. With 21st companies, leadership models are all distributed... I'm going to delegate leadership down."
Unfreezing	Unfreeze the 'frozen middle'	"There are people who are no longer experts in a craft, who have graduated from doing to managing… will resist change like death. If they're not going to become craftsman and learn anymore, they need to move on."
Transparency	Prepare for your culture to openly transpire externally	"There is so much opportunity for your internal culture to leak out. If you want good customer experience, you have to have good employee experience."
Purpose	Instil passionate purpose all across, at all levels	"As a leader, if you don't have a high degree of personal passion for why you're trying to championing change, they will smell it. You need an organic, renewable energy source to keep going."

Fig. 12.14 Digital Business Model—Culture. Sources: 'ANZ digital chief: Tackle the "frozen middle" of your organisation or face irrelevancy' (Nadia Cameron; CMO; May.17; from interview with Maile Carnegie ANZ CDO at Adobe Symposium); 'FinTech Food for Thought v.7' (Angel Gavieiro; Aug.17; AG Strategy & Partners)

7. *Performance Management*: it is possible to find bank's balanced scorecards with change KPIs, but quite rare with innovation KPIs. Therefore, both need tackling, and not just with qualitative but also with quantitative measures. This would link to the earlier point of 'dual hat' at the MD of BU, so his/her scorecard recognizes in a different way the BAU vs innovation agendas. Also, Agile Teams need to embed end-to-end outcome ownership in the scorecards for all their members to ensure mutual accountability for success.

After this deep dive on the seven Meta-architectural Levers, let us elevate our lenses to gain perspective of how re-dialling the Levers potentially affects businesses and functions in an organization.

Professors Morten Hansen (Univ. California at Berkeley) and Jeffrey Pfeffer (Stanford Univ.) in their research on innovation found that the way individuals interact internally within organizations determine where these sit in a continuum between Best-Practice Focus, associated with a small, close-tie network, vis-a-vis Innovation Focus, showing instead a large, weak-tie network. The illustration below leverages this framework to map the main practices identified in the discussion about the seven Meta-architectural Levers and their expected evolution from current status quo to future state to enable Digital Transformation (Fig. 12.15).

The main takeaway is that Functions in the organization will have to drive the bulk of change of traditional organizational practices, with the biggest shifts required in Implementation Methodology (from sequential batches to agile teams), Operational Governance (from quarterly to weekly OpCos) and Organizational Design (from Ops & IT to add Digital and, within it, the digital centre of excellence). For Business Units the change in Innovation Ownership (from BAU KPIs to adding Innovation KPIs) is a crucial undertaking. On a separate dimension, the illustration shows the overall transition from a Traditional Culture to an Open Culture (blue ring) as a canvas over which all the re-tuning of Levers takes place affecting everyone across the organization, and that as we know needs to be led from the very top of the house.

12.5.4 Execution of Digital Transformation

This final subsection summarizes the highlights organized around a six-step execution framework for Digital Transformation compiled out of bank practitioners and management consultants[17] [28, 33], along with some of the key thoughts developed earlier.

All along Digital Transformation execution, there is the imperative to keep Customer Journey (CJ), Customer Experience (CX) and Digital Optimized Interaction (DOI) as the navigation tools that signal the north star.

[17] BBVA website (Apr.17).

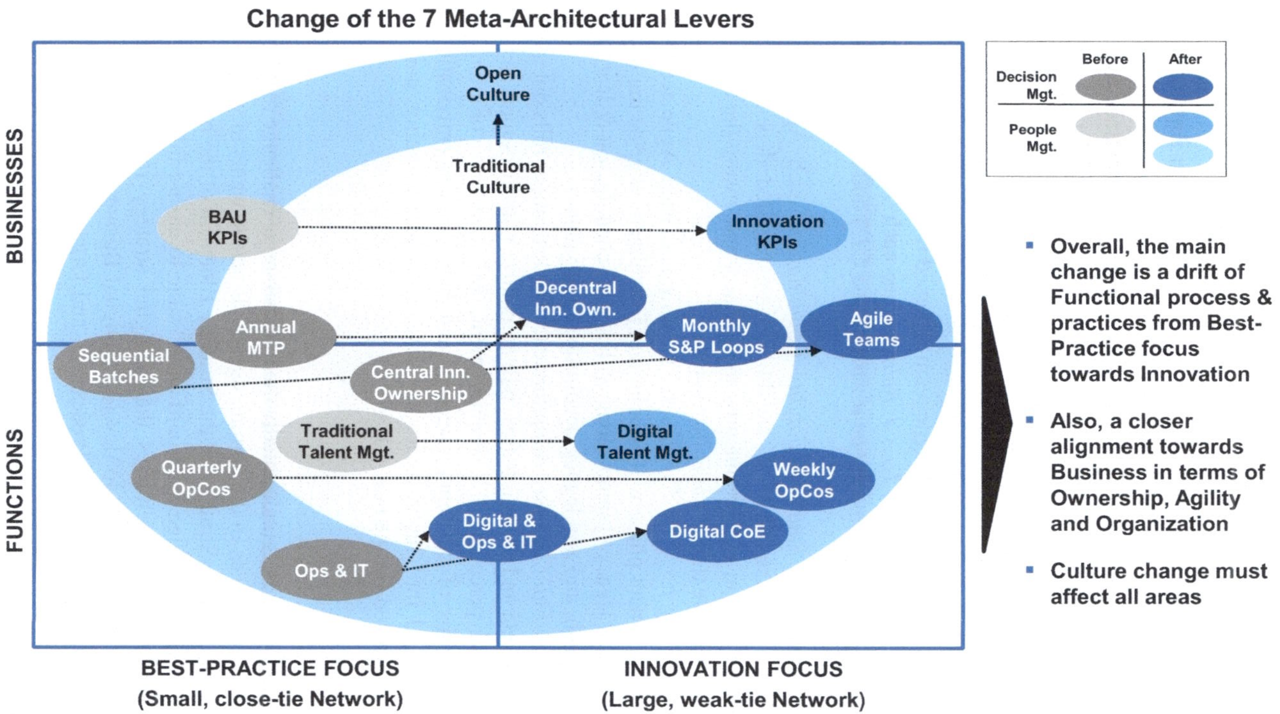

Fig. 12.15 Digital Business Model—Change of Meta-architectural Levers. Sources: Morten Hansen (U.C. Berkeley); Jeffrey Pfeffer (Stanford Univ.); 'FinTech Food for Thought v.7' (Angel Gavieiro; Aug.17; AG Strategy & Partners)

Six execution steps highlight the comparison between 'what used to be under legacy banking' (From) vs 'what would be under digital banking' (To). Underneath each step, a few key questions suggest the type of answers required before moving to the next one.

1. *From Separate Processes... To CJs*: BUs, with Digital team support, need to identify each CJ to understand both its Value Cycle data and the processes underneath; then, each BU needs to prioritize the value vs cost trade-offs for CJ changes. At Group/Divisional level, the top-15/20 CJs across the BU portfolio must be identified.
2. *From Siloes... To Integrated Programme*: the Digital team needs to define ownership of CJs between BUs vs Group/Division, governance in terms of decision-making, functions involved and Steer Committee members; plus the team culture required for the agile team assigned to each CJ.
3. *From Incremental Change... To CJ Reinvention*: each Agile team then will reimagine the CJ (i.e. *what would be a world-class CJ?*) and redesign it accordingly (i.e. *what is the CJ's edge?*).
4. *From Piecemeal... To Smart Capability Combination*: each Agile team will identify which processes and IT capabilities are required depending on the reimagined CJ design, execute intently and at pace, and ensure the team access to the right internal/external capability sources.
5. *From IT Long Cycles... To Continuous Deployment*: each Agile team in the software development phase will appoint an IT architect to decide the degree of connectivity with legacy systems along with sprint schedule, test & learn cycles, scale-up approach, and any legacy decommissioning plan.
6. *From Timid... To Full Customer Adoption*: each Agile team, as rolls out the MVP or subsequent beta and alpha releases, will empathize with customers to identify pain points and perceived CX improvement, will consider communications carefully in terms of customer targeting and behaviour incentivization, will align the new CJ introduction with any legacy decommissioning, and ensure policies are updated for the new CJ.

* * *

Digital Transformation is undoubtedly the main strategic challenge that any CEO of an incumbent bank faces in the coming decade. If he/she wants to win, the CEO must embed it in the Core Strategy of the Strategy Blueprint of the bank.

First, the CEO must engage the Board and C-suite to ensure full alignment and support around the five Imperatives that a digital strategy requires. Then, the organization needs to learn how to develop a Digital Business Model across each BU, ensuring to onboard the right Process, IT and Organizational capabilities to do so.

In parallel, it is crucial that top management gains awareness of the status quo of the seven Meta-Architectural Levers in the organization and what re-dialling is required for each one to effectively enable digital efforts. Finally, the entire bank needs to adopt best practices in digital execution to arrive at final business models that provide a Customer Journey and Customer Experience that ensure a competitor-beating Digital Optimized Interaction with clients.

12.6 Future of Digital Financial Services

After this review of the historical context of near three-quarters of a century of technology evolution in the financial services industry, the emergence of FinTech and its digital disruption dynamics with incumbent banks, and the deep dive on how to develop and execute a strategy for Digital Transformation, it seems appropriate to finish this chapter and the book by elevating the discussion to 10,000 ft height and look at the horizon: *what is the future of Digital Financial Services?*

First thing to notice in the question, like with a well-known Spanish aphorism from my native region of Galicia (‘*what is the colour of the white horse of St. James Apostle?*’), . . . Financial Services’ future will be Digital.

The exponential growth adoption of digitalization across society, at all levels, is unstoppable. The mutually reinforcing spiral of economic incentives, driven by economies of scale, scope and network, and behavioural incentives, driven by speed, convenience and personalization, becomes a perpetual motion machine powering Digital globally across most industries.

Second, proceeding with my speculative envisaging of scenarios, a key trend deriving from this spiral is gradually making financial services a feature of the background in real economy transactions, rather than a separate transaction itself. The idea is that people think about (and enjoy doing so) buying a house, a car, a holiday, a romantic dinner experience. . . not a mortgage, a car leasing, a consumer loan or a credit/debit card payment. In other words, *will digital financial services become invisible?*

This is an interesting one, because we are beginning to experience this phenomenon, starting in the world of small payments, for instance, in grocery stores. Amazon pioneered Amazon Go till-less stores in the USA in 2018 and in March 2021 opened a more advanced version in London [34], which allows customers, by identifying themselves on arrival with a barcode, to pick up all their shopping items and just leave the shop without passing by any till. Hundreds of cameras, depth sensors and DL take care of logging the list of products shopped and invoice the payment to the customer’s account at the Amazon Shopping app. Invisible pay!

I believe this example is the tip of the iceberg of the wider FinTech aggregation trend of Embedded Finance (discussed in Sect. 12.3). We are starting to see energy utilities (like Ovo Energy) pay interest rates to remunerate balances in their customer accounts; retailers (like Macy’s) providing buy-now-pay-later credit facilities to their customers at checkout; coffee shop chains (like Starbucks) enticing pay-now-buy later schemes offering a close loop of customers’ payment and balances; or taxi driver platforms (like Uber) providing a pre-booked ride to a customer who does not need to think about paying when dropping off and whose driver receives automatic payment on his account with the platform, plus a credit advance if he needs it for any sudden repair for his/her cab!

In the coming decades, we will see more and more corporates, and subsequently SMEs, that to improve the quality of interaction and value provided to their retail customers, they will embed invisibly financial (and non-financial) services within their offering.

Some estimates figure $7 Tr. for the value of the Embedded Finance market by 2030 [35]. I reckon the adoption might be slower than that, as it cannot be underestimated, as we have seen with banks throughout this chapter, how difficult digital transformation is for incumbents in any industry, and here we are talking about a vast variety of industries. But still, it will be a really large figure indeed.

Third, another important forward-looking reflection would be about the currency system in which Digital Financial Services will be based. *Will it be a fiat currency, CBDC and/or cryptocurrency system?*

The move towards digital currency is, as per the above arguments, I believe unstoppable. Having said that, I reckon that cash still will be around for a long time during this century. For a couple of reasons, the still large percentage of unbanked or underbanked population globally (31% of adults as of 2017 according to the World Bank) and the decades it will take for a full, global online/mobile banking coverage (around 53% of the global population as of Mar. 2021 statistics by DataProt[18]).

In terms of digital currency system, the move from fiat towards CBDCs I believe will happen given how much it is at play for Central Banks, albeit on a very gradual basis over the next decades as many of the Western authorities are following a prudent approach. Surely CBDCs around the world will co-exist with the fiat cousin within each country (as per the cash argument above), at least for a long while. Also, a win-win formula will be found to ensure commercial banks continue to operate without being fundamentally jeopardized by the introduction of CBDCs.

Within the degree of explicit or implicit regulatory 'leeway' that the Central Bank or monetary authority in each jurisdiction will decide to provide, cryptocurrencies will continue to develop because, like the internet in the 1990s, they have reached enough 'scape velocity' from users' adoption (i.e. the positive spiral of network economies has kicked in!), which will only keep attracting newcomers. This will be so despite occasionally facing financial crises, which are likely to be recurrent due to cryptos vast proliferation and large volatility.

Now, I visualize a clear segmentation between stablecoins vs non-stablecoins. While the former has the capacity for value storage over the long term, probably also under crisis,[19] because most are pegged to one or several fiat currencies (or other real world assets); the latter will not be able to store value in vast amounts on a permanent basis given their inherent volatility (like it happened in the crypto 2018 crisis, with

[18] www.dataprot.net

[19] Although, we know that at the peak of the 2008 credit crisis some money market funds 'broke the buck', and the fiat currency pools that collateralizes many stablecoins function like money market funds.

80% collapse of market value from peak to trough in 9 months). As a result, the growth of DeFi will certainly be more and more based on stablecoins since they provide a more solid bedrock upon which to build further DeFi financial products.

All in all, we will see the coexistence of cash/digital fiat, CBDC and cryptocurrencies for quite a few more decades.

Fourth and last, a more philosophical/PsyFi question: *what will the degree of human vs machine symbiosis (if any) be in the future of Digital Financial Services?*

In this regard, we can find the camp of those that believe that interaction among humans is essential for business, and so the generation of trust based on communication and emotional contact cannot be substituted by machines. Therefore, for critical services or transactions, being in finance or other industries, there will be always an element of personal interaction that must be there. Digital will complement, enable and enhance this interaction and, of course, take care of all the rest of non-critical services or transactions, but still, it will not be at the centre of humans' trust.

On the other extreme is the camp of some of the most tech visionaries, who could see a near future of Decentralized Autonomous Organizations (DAO), for financial services (and many other industries), where an organization made of rules of computer programme, controlled by a governance from its members and without government intervention, take care entirely of providing the service. This may sound like utopian but is currently being tried and tested at a small scale in the cyberworld of blockchain platforms as we have seen with the growth of DeFi Dapps, many of them being designed as DAOs.

If we look at this question from within a multi-decade horizon, I would be inclined to fall for the former argument, since there are many other key institutions of human society (i.e. law, government, business customs), gradually built over generations, that will take more generations to adapt and catch up with Digital before enabling a generalized move of finance to the DAO (assuming the solutions are mature enough to take on more complexity by then).

Having said that, and within the context of the cryptocurrency discussion earlier, I would anticipate DeFi market would skyrocket at first due to early adopters, mostly blockchain savvy users eager to put their crypto gains to work; to then gradually adjust, because for the rest of population adoption will depend on the degree of progress gaining trust and familiarity with the crypto environment; until Generations Z and Alpha reach maturity, definitely embodying an evolved sense of financial trust, as they would become DeFi's future cornerstone. Having said that, and unless a global financial meltdown happens (worth mentioning because in 2008 we were very close to one!), I do not foresee DeFi DAOs, and definitely less so generalized DAOs, would be able to replace the government-run, fiat/CBDC system-based, digital financial services at least during this century.

Now, let us introduce the PsyFi side of this speculative discussion. If we take a multi-century view (assuming that we manage to overcome the Climate Change threat!), I could visualize a DAO-driven world for many human needs (somehow like in the 29th-century plot of the animated movie '*Wall-e*', where humans lived 'pleasantly' in the Axiom starliner with all their needs automatically served—all settled within invisible finance I assume—. . . only that, if this is the case, I hope we do not accept the trade-off of the bodily degeneration price they paid!).

Looking at the human aspect of trust, I think that over long expanses of time (generations) the form and shape of how individuals and collectives trust each other could effectively evolve. As collectives, trust has in fact evolved throughout the history of human institutions, from feudalism, to monarchy, to nation-state, to parliamentary democracy. Similarly, as individuals, trust has evolved also in form and shape for commercial transactions, with the last 12 years of DLT platform's decentralized, anonymized trust experimentation christening the new concept of 'blockchain' into the roster of human institutions.

In addition, I think the confluence with other two key technologies, currently just at the embryo state, will at some point combine to take on the exponential speed velocity of the innovation S-curve to bring society entirely to a different level: Artificial General Intelligence (AGI) and Quantum Computing (QC).

AGI aims to create an intelligent agent that can understand or learn any intellectual task a human being can do. Companies like DeepMind, OpenAI or Google Brain are leading this race, with DeepMind recent achievements with reinforcement learning algorithms like AlphaFold 2 that has cracked the 50-year-old problem of predicting the 3D structure of proteins.[20] DeepMind foresees AGI could be reached, based on reinforcement learning technology, within the next 20 years.

QC leverages superposition and entanglement, physical properties of quantum particles, to construct devices with an order of magnitude of computation unreachable by traditional computers. Companies like IBM, Honeywell, D-Wave or Regetti are leading this race, with IBM having just launched Eagle in Nov. 2021, a top record 127-qbit QC.[21] IBM predicts to achieve quantum supremacy[22] with a 1121-qbit QC by 2023.

Once AGI & QC mature in a combined way, the reality of a DLT-based cyberworld where DAO companies can take over many of the functions currently provided by Digital Financial Services (and beyond) could become a reality, because of the same positive spiral of economic and behavioural incentives referred at the start of this thought experiment.

These scenarios, some playing over the next decades and some well beyond the end of the twenty-first-century horizon, involve digital technology that is being toyed with today. As such, dear CEOs, for some of you, I reckon related action plans could probably find their place within the three portfolio horizons of your Strategy.

---

[20] It would take longer than the age of the known universe to enumerate all the possible configurations of 3D folding for a typical protein by brute force calculation! [36].

[21] To simulate its computing capacity with classical bits you would need as many as the number of atoms in every human being in the planet! [37].

[22] When the QC can solve a problem that no classical computer can solve in any feasible amount of time.

References

1. "IBM celebrates 50 years of its landmark mainframe computer" by Ben Rosi (07/04/14; www.informationage.com)
2. "Idea Man" by Paul Allen (2011; Portfolio/Pinguin)
3. "Personal Computer History: 1975-1984" by Daniel Knight (26/04/14; www.lowendmac.com)
4. "History of Online Banking" by Ruth Sarreal (21/05/19; www.gobankingrates.com)
5. "2017 Global Findex Database" report (2018; www.centerforfinancialinclusion.org)
6. "Retail Banking: Digital Transformation & Disruptor Opportunities 2018-2022" (Juniper Research)
7. "The Pulse of FinTech – 2H 2019" (Feb.2020; KPMG) and "The Pulse of FinTech – 1H 2021" (Aug.2021; KPMG) by Ian Pollari and Anton Ruddenklau
8. "Global FinTech Index 2020" report (Dec. 2019; Findexable)
9. "FinTech: The Experience So Far" policy paper (Jun. 2019; IMF)
10. "FinTech Lending Industry to hit USD 390.5 billion by 2023" (Feb.20; The Paypers)
11. "FinTech: Are Banks Responding Appropriately?" by Jeremy Pizzala and Ian Webster (Apr.16; EY)
12. "Designing a Sustainable Digital Bank" (Jun.15; IBM)
13. "The New FinTech Bank" by Chris Skinner (Apr. 16; blog)
14. "BTC and Stock Volatility" by Thomas Chippas (16/07/2020; ErisX)
15. Pg. 52 in "Lords of Finance" by Liaquat Ahamed (2010; Windmill)
16. "Progress of Research & Development of e-CNY in China" (Jul. 2021; People's Bank of China)
17. "Bank-X: The New New Banks" by Ronit Ghose, Kaiwan Master, Rahul Bajaj, Charles Russell, Robert P. Kong, Yafei Tian and Judy Zhang (Mar.19; Citigroup)
18. "World FinTech Report 2020" (Apr.20; CapGemini - EFMA)
19. "The Case For Digital Reinvention" by Jacques Bughin, Laura LaBerge and Anette Mellbye (Feb.17; McKinsey & Co)
20. "Neo Banks – Performance and New Ideas" (Oct.18; Finnovate)
21. "The Future of Financial Services in the UK: How to Harness Disruption" by Alan Gemes, James Cousins, George Doble, Arthur Hughes-Hallett, Isabella Yamamoto and Isabella Hadjisavvas (Feb.20; Strategy&-PwC)
22. "Cutting Through the Noise Around Financial Technology" by Milos Dietz, Somesh Khanna, Tunde Olanrewaju and Kausik Rajgopal. (Feb.16; McKinsey & Co)
23. "Beyond FinTech: A Pragmatic Assessment Of Disruptive Potential In Financial Services" (Aug.17; World Economic Forum)
24. "Caterpillars, Butterflies and Unicorns - Does Digital In Banking Really Matter?" by Alan McIntyre, Julian Skan, Cecile Andre Leruste and Francesca Caminiti (Jun.19; Accenture)
25. "Digital Transformation in Banking: Is It a Mission Impossible?" by Sabrida del Prete (Oct.16; RBS)
26. "Digitizing Customer Journeys and Processes: Stores from the Frontlines" by Chandana Asif, Jiro Hiraoka, Tomas Jones and Prerak Vohra (Jun.17; McKinsey & Co)
27. "Value Cycle" (2017; BBVA)
28. "The Next Generation Operating Model for the Digital World" by Albert Bollard, Elixabete Larrea, Alex Singla and Rohit Sood (Apr.17; McKinsey & Co)
29. "Dynamic Strategic Planning for Technology Policy" by Richard de Neufville (2000; MIT)
30. "How To Go Agile Enterprise-wide" from interview with Scott Richardson, Fannie Mae CDO by Khushpreet Kaur (Aug.17; McKinsey & Co.)
31. "ANZ Digital Chief: Tackle the 'Frozen Middle' of your organization or face irrelevancy" from interview with Maile Carnegie by Nadia Cameron (May.17; CMO)
32. "A CEO's Guide To Digital Transformation" (Martin Danoesastro, Grant Freeland and Thomas Reichert; BCG, May.17)
33. "Digitizing Customer Journeys and Processes: Stories from the Front Lines" by Chandana Asif, Jiro Hiraoka, Tomas Jones and Prerak Vohra (May 17; McKinsey & Co.)

34. "Amazon Fresh till-less grocery store opens in London" by Leo Kelion (4/Mar/2021; BBC)
35. "Embedded Finance: a game-changing opportunity for incumbents" by Simon Torrance (Aug. 2020; www.simon-torrance.com)
36. "AlphaFold: a solution to a 50-year-old grand challenge in biology" by AlphaFold team (30/11/2020; DeepMind)
37. "IBM unveils breakthrough 127-qbit quantum processor" by IBM (16/Nov/21; PRNewswire)

Epilogue

They that go down to the ships, that do business in great waters, these see the works of the Lord and his wonders in the deep (The Bible, Psalms 107:23–24).

This book intent was to focus on just one critical dimension of management, strategy and the action of developing management strategy for business, as a plan, as a process and as a skill (the 'how').

The response suggested is the Holistic Management Strategy (HMS) framework, an inductive outcome from more than 20 years of professional strategy development in the financial services industry, leveraging real best-practice complemented by that of experienced industry practitioners, management consultants and academics.

HMS attempts to be a comprehensive system that can be used in a generalized way, applicable to large and small companies, single country or multinational, at Business Unit, Division and Group level. It is originally based on the financial services industry but hopefully also applicable across many other industries.

If anything, HMS at its core advocates that strategy would ideally be developed very differently at Business Unit level, which is the part of any organization that directly engages with the marketplace, versus at Divisional or Group level, where the game is about portfolio optimization.

In Business Unit strategy, HMS illustrates how differently to approach Existing vs New Markets (i.e. new geography or business). For Existing Markets (Part I), a cycle that starts from the Business Model 'as-is', defines its change over time via the 'Medium Term Planning' Strategy Blueprint & Financial Plan, including a Core Strategy (i.e. client/product/geography) as its guiding compass, in order to arrive at a Business Model 'as-should-be'. For New Markets (Part II), a vertical plus horizontal review of the respective market Attractiveness & Opportunities is complemented with a four-step Inorganic Growth Process. And for both, HMS offers the Mobilization & Transformation frameworks to transition from strategy to execution.

In Group/Divisional strategy (Part III), HMS establishes the discipline of Portfolio Value Gap, to identify the strategic focus in terms of Business Performance Improvement, Business Growth (organic/inorganic), Business Restructurings & Disposals (and Financial Restructuring) that can address the gap of the current share price 'as-is' versus 'as-should-be'. This discipline is complemented with the

A. Gavieiro Besteiro, *Strategy in Action*, Management for Professionals,
https://doi.org/10.1007/978-3-030-94759-0

Portfolio Horizons that identifies for each Business Unit in the Division (or Divisions within the Group) which of the above strategic focus drive the respective activities across the three-time horizons and the methodology of resource reallocation among them.

HMS addresses at the cusp of its pyramid (Part IV), at Group level, the key frameworks of Company Excellence and Leadership & Management Excellence. For the latter, looking at the leadership and managerial skillset of the CEO and C-Suite executives via the lenses of THICOSIV framework (Thinking & Honesty / Influence & Communications / Organization & Strategy / Investment & Value). For the former, looking at the unique role of the CEO, as a 'clockmaker', looking to carefully combine for the organization Balanced Design in the long term with Considered Decision-Making on the day-to-day, in order to achieve and sustain Company Excellence in the marketplace.

In last leg of the book (Part V), I do hope the articulation of the unexploited potential of the in-house Strategy Function entices CEOs and C-suites to seize the opportunity ahead, easily at hand just by implementing the suggested best-practices to put in value this high talented team. Also, the discussion about both 'known unknowns' and 'unknown unknowns' of Digital Transformation attempts to spark some thinking among readers, at least, to hopefully dissipate any doubts about digital's strength as a signal (vs noise) for the future of the financial services industry, at most, to provide a best-practice framework for a successful transition of your organization towards digital.

* * *

HMS is a framework and as such its value comes from its usage. At a deeper level, it provides the 'emptiness' for us to use, by filling it with content, the 'right content'; like the wheel's centre, the pot's clay or the house's wood in passage 11 of the 'Tao Te Ching'[1]:

Thirty spokes are joined together in a wheel,
but it is the centre hole
that allows the wheel to function.

We mould clay into a pot,
but it is the emptiness inside
that makes the vessel useful.

We fashion wood for a house,
but it is the emptiness inside
that makes it liveable.

We work with the substantial,
but the emptiness is what we use.

Like any model inductively derived from experience, HMS is necessarily incomplete. Certainly, it can be improved and surely will have some blind angles. I hope future authors can take it from where this book leaves it and build further insight and understanding of a craft, strategy, that like navigation is always an ever-evolving subject which benefits from further exploration and practice.

Finally, dear reader, I would like to thank you for the patience and interest shown in arriving at the end of this book. I hope it has provoked some food for thought and I wish any of the frameworks and ideas provided can help to evolve to the next level your business strategy.

Reference

1. "Tao Te Ching" by Lao Tzu, (IV-III century BC) -translated by John H. McDonald- (2019; Arcturus)

Dr Angel Gavieiro Besteiro
In London, November 26th 2021

Glossary

He who loves practice without theory is like the sailor who boards ship without a rudder and compass and never knows where he may cast (Leonardo da Vinci)

AGI:	Artificial General Intelligence
AI:	Artificial Intelligence
AISP:	Account Information Service Provider
AML:	Anti Money Laundering
API:	Application Programme Interfaces
BaaP:	Banking as a Platform
BaaS:	Banking as a Service
BAU:	Business As Usual
BD:	Business Development
BPO:	Business Process Outsourcing
BoA:	Bank of America
B/S:	Balance-Sheet
BU:	Business Unit
CA:	Confidentiality Agreement
Capex:	Capital Expenditure
CBDC:	Central Bank Digital Currency
CJ:	Customer Journey
CoC:	Cost of Capital
CPU:	Central Processing Unit
CRE:	Corporate Real Estate
CSO:	Chief Strategy Officer
CTO:	Chief Transformation Officer
CX:	Customer Experience
DAO:	Decentralized Autonomous Organization
Dapp:	Distributed Application
DCF:	Discounted Cash Flow (valuation)
DD:	Due Diligence
DDM:	Dividend Discount Model

A. Gavieiro Besteiro, *Strategy in Action*, Management for Professionals,
https://doi.org/10.1007/978-3-030-94759-0

DeFi:	Decentralized Finance
DL:	Deep Learning
DLT:	Distributed Ledger Technology
DM:	Decision-Making
DX:	Digital Transformation
E2E:	End-to-End
EVA:	Economic Value Added
ESG:	Environment, Society and Government
ETF:	Exchange Traded Fund
ExCo:	Executive Committee
GFC:	Global Financial Crisis
GSIB:	Global Systemically Important Bank
HMS:	Holistic Management Framework
IM:	Information Memorandum
JPM:	JP Morgan Chase
KPI:	Key Performance Indicator
KYC:	Know Your Customer
MECE:	Mutually Exclusive Comprehensively Exhaustive
ML:	Machine Learning
MTP:	Medium Term Plan
MoU:	Memorandum of Understanding
MVP:	Minimum Viable Product
NDA:	Non-Disclosure Agreement
NII:	Net Interest Income
NLP:	Natural Language Processing
NPL:	Non-Performing Loans
OOI:	Other Operating Income
OpCo:	Operating Committee
Opex:	Operating Expenditure
PAT:	Profit After Taxes
PBT:	Profit Before Taxes
PC:	Personal Computer
PISP:	Payment Initiation Service Provider
PMO:	Project Management Office
POC:	Proof of Concept
PPI:	Payment Protection Insurance
PSD:	Payment Services Directive
PSP:	Payment Service Provider
P&L:	Profit & Loss (financial statement)
QC:	Quantum Computing
R&D:	Research & Development
RBP:	Regulatory Business Plan
RM:	Relationship Manager
ROA:	Return on Assets
ROE:	Return on Equity

ROIC: Return on Invested Capital
RoRWA: Return on Risk Weighted Assets
RPA: Robotic Process Automation
RWA: Risk Weighted Assets
SD: Strategy Development
SLA: Service Level Agreement
SMR: Senior Managers Regime
SOTP: Sum-of-the-Parts (valuation)
SPA: Selling & Purchase Agreement
SSA: Sub-Sahara Africa
ToR: Terms of Reference
TRS: Total Return on Shareholders
ZBB: Zero-Based Budgeting

Bibliography

Books

1. Ahamed, Liaquat. "Lords of Finance" (2010; Windmill)
2. Allen, Paul. "Idea Man" (2011; Portfolio/Pinguin)
3. Ariely, Dan. "The (Honest) Truth About Dishonesty" (2012; Harper Collins)
4. Baghai, Mehrdad, Stephen Coley, and David White "The Alchemy of Growth" (1999; McKinsey & Co - Perseus Publishing)
5. Bakan, Joel. "The Corporation" (2004; Free Press)
6. Bryan, Lowell and Claudia Joyce. "Mobilizing Minds" (2007; McGraw Hill)
7. Carnegie, Dale. "How to win friends and influence people" (1936; Vermillion)
8. Collins, Jim. "Good to Great" (2001; Harper Business)
9. Collins, Jim Collins and Jerry Porras. "Build to Last" (1994; Harper Business)
10. Copeland, Tom, Tim Koller and Jack Murrin. "Valuation – Measuring and Managing the Value of Companies" (1990; McKinsey & Co - Wiley)
11. Dixit, Avinash and Barry Nalebuff. "Thinking Strategically" (1991; Norton)
12. Drucker, Peter. "Management" (1973, 2008 revised; Collins)
13. Dunn, Richard. "Navigational Instruments" (2016; National Maritime Museum)
14. Ghemawat, Pankaj. "Strategy and the Business Landscape" (2001; Prentice Hall)
15. Hagstrom Jr., Robert G. "The Warren Buffett Way – Investment Strategy of The World's Greatest Investor" (1994; Wiley)
16. Graham, Benjamin. "The Intelligent Investor" (1973; Harper Business)
17. Heath, Chip and Dan Heath. "Made To Stick" (2007; Penguin Random House)
18. Isaacson, Walter. "Jobs" (2011; Little, Brown)
19. Kahneman, Daniel. "Thinking, Fast and Slow" (2011; Allen Lane)
20. Kahneman, Daniel, Olivier Sibony and Cass R. Sunstein. "Noise" by (2021; William Collins)
21. Kim, W. Chan and Renee Mauborgne. "Blue Ocean Strategy" (2005; HBS Press)
22. Koller, Tim, Richard Dobbs and Bill Huyett. "Value – The Four Cornerstones of Corporate Finance" (2011; McKinsey & Co - Wiley)
23. Fisher, Philip "Common Stocks and Uncommon Profits" (1958; Wiley)
24. McDonald, Duff. "Last Man Standing" (2009; Simon & Schuster)
25. Mellon, Liz and Simon Carter. "The Strategy of Execution" (2013; McGraw Hill)
26. Multiple authors. "Mastering Strategy" (2000, FT – Prentice Hall)
27. Murray, Kevin. "The Language of Leaders" (2012; Kogan Page)
28. Nutt, Paul C. "Why Decisions Fail: Avoid the Blunders and Traps That Lead to Debacles" (2002; Berrett-Koehler Publishers)

A. Gavieiro Besteiro, *Strategy in Action*, Management for Professionals,
https://doi.org/10.1007/978-3-030-94759-0

29. Peters, Thomas and Robert Waterman Jr. "In Search of Excellence" (1982; Harper & Row)
30. Pfeffer Jeffrey. "Managing with Power" (1992; Harvard Business School Press)
31. Rumelt, Richard. "Good Strategy, Bad Strategy" (2011; Profile Books)
32. Sinek, Simon. "Start With Why – How Great Leaders Inspire Everyone To Take Action" (2009; Portfolio)

Articles

33. AlphaFold Team. "AlphaFold: a Solution to a 50-year-old Grand Challenge in Biology" (30/11/2020; DeepMind)
34. Asif, Chandana, Jiro Hiraoka, Tomas Jones and Prerak Vohra. "Digitizing Customer Journeys and Processes: Stories from the Front Lines" (May 17; McKinsey & Co)
35. Bird, Alan, Torsten Lichtenau and David Michels. "The What, Who and How of Delivering Results" (2016; Bain & Co)
36. Bollard, Albert, Elixabete Larrea, Alex Singla and Rohit Sood. "The Next Generation Operating Model for the Digital World" (Apr.17; McKinsey & Co)
37. Boston Consulting Group – Global Financial Markets Association. "Climate Finance Markets and the Real Economy" (BCG, GFMA; Dec.2020)
38. Bradberry, Travis and Kevin Kruse. "What Makes A Leader?" (Aug.2017; www.leaderonomics.com)
39. Bucy, Michael, Stephen Hall and Doug Yakola. "Transformation with Big T" (2016; McKinsey & Co)
40. Bughin, Jacques, Laura LaBerge and Anette Mellbye. "The Case For Digital Reinvention" (Feb.17; McKinsey & Co)
41. Business Roundtable. "Statement on the Purpose of a Corporation" (Business Roundtable; 19/Aug/2019)
42. Christensen, Clayton. "How Will You Measure Your Life?" (Jul-Aug.10; HBR)
43. Cameron, Nadia. "ANZ Digital Chief: Tackle the 'Frozen Middle' of your organization or face irrelevancy" from interview with Maile Carnegie (May.17; CMO)
44. CapGemini – EFMA. "World FinTech Report 2020" (Apr.20; CapGemini - EFMA)
45. Center for Financial Inclusion. "2017 Global Findex Database" report (2018; www.centerforfinancialinclusion.org)
46. Chatterjee, Sumeet. "U.S., EU fines on banks' misconduct to top $400 billion by 2020: report" (27/09/17; Quinlan & Associates - Reuters)
47. Chippas, Thomas. "BTC and Stock Volatility" (16/07/2020; ErisX)
48. Danoesastro, Martin, Grant Freeland and Thomas Reichert. "A CEO's Guide To Digital Transformation" (BCG, May.17)
49. De Neufville, Richard. "Dynamic Strategic Planning for Technology Policy" (2000; MIT)
50. Del Prete, Sabrida. "Digital Transformation in Banking: Is It a Mission Impossible?" (Oct.16; RBS)
51. Dietz, Milos, Somesh Khanna, Tunde Olanrewaju and Kausik Rajgopal. "Cutting Through the Noise Around Financial Technology" (Feb.16; McKinsey & Co)
52. Findexable Report. "Global FinTech Index 2020" (Dec. 2019; Findexable)
53. Finnovate Report. "Neo Banks – Performance and New Ideas" (Oct.18; Finnovate)
54. Gavieiro, Angel. "THICOSIV© framework" (2013)
55. Gavieiro, Angel. "Holistic Management Framework v.5" (Apr.17; AG Strategy & Partners)
56. Gavieiro, Angel. "FinTech Food for Thought v.7" (Aug.17; AG Strategy & Partners)
57. Gemes, Alan, James Cousins, George Doble, Arthur Hughes-Hallett, Isabella Yamamoto and Isabella Hadjisavvas. "The Future of Financial Services in the UK: How to Harness Disruption" (Feb.20; Strategy&-PwC)
58. Ghemawat, Pankaj. "Competition and Business Strategy" (2002, Harvard Business Review)

59. Ghose, Ronit, Kaiwan Master, Rahul Bajaj, Charles Russell, Robert P. Kong, Yafei Tian and Judy Zhang. "Bank-X: The New New Banks" (Mar.19; Citigroup)
60. Gluck, Frederick W., Stephen P. Kaufman, and A. Stephen Walleck. "Strategic Management for Competitive Advantage," (July/Aug. 1980; Harvard Business Review)
61. Heath, Chip and Greg Fisher. "General Management Framework" (2000; Duke University)
62. Ibarra, Herminia. "The Authenticity Paradox" (Jan-Feb.15; Harvard Business Review)
63. IBM Sales & Distribution - White Paper. "Designing a Sustainable Digital Bank" (Jun.15; IBM)
64. IMF Policy Paper. "FinTech: The Experience So Far" policy paper (Jun. 2019; IMF)
65. Juniper Research. "Retail Banking: Digital Transformation & Disruptor Opportunities 2018-2022" (Juniper Research)
66. Kaur, Khushpreet. "How To Go Agile Enterprise-wide" from interview with Scott Richardson, Fannie Mae CDO (Aug.17; McKinsey & Co)
67. Kelion, Leo. "Amazon Fresh till-less grocery store opens in London" (4/Mar/2021; BBC)
68. Knight, Daniel. "Personal Computer History: 1975-1984" (26/04/14; www.lowendmac.com)
69. Kotter, John and Holger Rathgeber. "That's Not How We Do It Here!" (2016; Portfolio/ Penguin Random House)
70. MacGregor Serven, Lawrence B. "The Organizational Cost of Office Politics" (Jan.19; American Management Association)
71. McIntyre, Alan, Julian Skan, Cecile Andre Leruste and Francesca Caminiti. "Caterpillars, Butterflies and Unicorns - Does Digital In Banking Really Matter?" (Jun.19; Accenture)
72. People's Bank of China. "Progress of Research & Development of e-CNY in China" (Jul.2021; People's Bank of China)
73. Pizzala, Jeremy and Ian Webster. "FinTech: Are Banks Responding Appropriately?" (Apr.16; EY)
74. Pollari, Ian and Anton Ruddenklau. "The Pulse of FinTech – 2H 2019" (Feb.2020; KPMG)
75. Pollari, Ian and Anton Ruddenklau. "The Pulse of FinTech – 1H 2021" (Aug.2021; KPMG)
76. Porter, Michael. "How Competitive Forces Shape Strategy" (1979; Harvard Business Review)
77. PRNewswire. "IBM Unveils Breakthrough 127-Qbit Quantum Processor" (16/Nov/21; PRNewswire)
78. Rosi, Ben. "IBM celebrates 50 years of its landmark mainframe computer" (07/04/14; www.informationage.com)
79. Sarreal, Ruth. "History of Online Banking" (21/05/19; www.gobankingrates.com)
80. Sadun, Rafaella, Nicholas Bloom and John Van Reenen. "Why Do We Undervalue Competent Management?" (Sept.17; HBR)
81. Skinner, Chris. "The New FinTech Bank" (Apr. 16; blog)
82. The Barton Partnership - Global Research. "Seven Skills For The Future of Strategy" (Feb.2020, The Barton Partnership - Global Research)
83. The Paypers. "FinTech Lending Industry to hit USD 390.5 billion by 2023" (Feb.20; The Paypers)
84. Toms, Steven. "Financial Scandals: A Historical Overview" (2019; Accounting and Business Research, 49:5, 477-499; DOI: https://doi.org/10.1080/00014788.2019.1610591)
85. Torrance, Simon. "Embedded Finance: a game-changing opportunity for incumbents" (Aug. 2020; www.simon-torrance.com)
86. TINYpulse. "The 2019 Employee Engagement Report: The End of Employee Loyalty" (2019; TINYpulse)
87. Visalli, Frederick W., Stephen P. Kaufman, and A. Stephen Walleck. "Thinking Strategically" (2000; McKinsey Quarterly; McKinsey & Co)

88. Visalli, Stephano, Charles Roxburgh, Toos Daruvala, Miklos Dietz, Susan Lund and Anna Marrs. "The State of Global Banking – In Search of a Sustainable Model" (Sep.11; McKinsey & Co)
89. Wilcox, Gregg, Louis Rosenberg, David Askay, Lynn Metcalf, Erick Harris and Colin Domnauer. "Artificial Swarming shown to Amplify Accuracy of Group Decisions in Subjective Judgement Tasks" (2019; Unanimous AI, California Polytechnic State University, University of California Berkeley)
90. World Economic Forum. "Beyond FinTech: A Pragmatic Assessment Of Disruptive Potential In Financial Services" (Aug.17; World Economic Forum)
91. Zak, Paul J. "The Neuroscience of Trust" (Jan.-Feb. 2017; Harvard Business Review)

Webpages

92. Bank of America. "Letter to Shareholders 2010" (Bank of America; Mar. 2011; www.bankofamerica.com)
93. Bank of America. "Letter to Shareholders 2019" (Bank of America; Mar. 2020; www.bankofamerica.com)
94. BBVA. "Value Cycle" (BBVA; 2017; www.bbva.com)
95. JP Morgan. "Firm Overview – 2020 Investor Day presentation" (JP Morgan; Feb. 2020; www.jpmorgan.com)
96. JP Morgan. "Letter to Shareholders 2009" (JP Morgan; Mar. 2010; www.jpmorgan.com)
97. JP Morgan. "Letter to Shareholders 2018" (JP Morgan; Apr. 2019; www.jpmorgan.com)
98. JP Morgan. "Letter to Shareholders 2019" (JP Morgan; Apr. 2020; www.jpmorgan.com)
99. McKinsey & Co. Coley, Steve. "Enduring Ideas: The Three Horizons of Growth" (Dec. 09; McKinsey Quarterly; www.mckinsey.com)
100. www.barchart.com
101. www.dataprot.net
102. www.insights.com
103. www.investopedia.com
104. www.openbanking.org.uk
105. www.statista.com
106. www.s2ds.org
107. www.unanimous.ai

The manufacturer's authorised representative in the EU is Springer Nature Customer Service Centre GmbH, Europaplatz 3, 69115 Heidelberg, Germany. If you have any concerns regarding our products, please contact ProductSafety@springernature.com

Printed and bound by CPI Group (UK) Ltd, Croydon, CR0 4YY
30/09/2026
02225493-0009